DYLAN THOMAS:

The Complete Screenplays

For Aeronwy Thomas

Dylan Marlais Thomas was born in Swansea on October 27, 1914. After leaving school he worked briefly as a junior reporter on the *South Wales Evening Post* before embarking on a literary career in London. Here he rapidly established himself as one of the finest poets of his generation. *Eighteen Poems* appeared in 1934, *Twenty-five Poems* in 1936, and *Deaths and Entrances* in 1946; his *Collected Poems* were published in 1952. Throughout his life Thomas wrote short stories, his most famous collection being *Portrait of the Artist as a Young Dog*. He also wrote filmscripts, broadcast stories and talks, lectured in America, and wrote the radio play *Under Milk Wood*. On November 9, 1953, shortly after his thirty-ninth birthday, he collapsed and died in New York. His body is buried in Laugharne, Wales, his home for many years.

DYLAN THOMAS:

The Complete Screenplays

edited by John Ackerman

APPLAUSE
BOOKS
211 WEST 71 STREET • NEW YORK NY • 10023

DYLAN THOMAS: THE COMPLETE SCREENPLAYS
edited by John Ackerman

First American edition published by Applause in 1995

Introduction and other critical material © John Ackerman 1995

The Films, Betty London, The Shadowless Man © The Trustees of the Dylan Thomas Estate, c/o David Higham Associates; *This is Colour* © ICI; *New Towns for Old, Balloon Site 568, Wales - Green Mountain, Black Mountain, These Are the Men, Our Country, Young Farmers* © COI; *CEMA*© CEMA; *The Doctor and the Devils, Twenty Years A-Growing* © Mrs Rust and The Trustees of the Dylan Thomas Estate, c/o David Higham Associates; *The Three Weird Sisters, No Room at the Inn* © Pathé; *The Beach of Falesá* © Stein & Day; *Me and My Bike, Rebecca's Daughters* © Triton: *Poetry and the Film* © Gotham Book Mart & Gallery.

Published by arrangement with J. M. Dent

Library of Congress Cataloging-in-Publication Data

Card number 95-80737

ISBN: 1-55783-226-9 (cloth)   ISBN: 1-55783-239-0 1997 (paperback)

APPLAUSE BOOKS
211 West 71st Street
New York, NY 10023
Phone: (212)595-4735   Fax: (212)721-2856

Contents

Introduction

Dylan Thomas had a passion for the cinema. At fifteen his essay on film as an art form, titled 'The Films' and published in the Swansea Grammar School Magazine, heralds his life-long involvement with the medium of film. His last but one public appearance was at a symposium in New York, with the American poet Robert Lowell, on 'Poetry and the Film'. In what he called 'his stories towards a Provincial Autobiography . . . about Swansea life . . . adolescence in the suburban nights',[1] written six years later, Thomas evokes in 'Old Garbo' the 'young dog's' fantasies when visiting the local cinema having left school at seventeen to work as a junior reporter on the *South Wales Daily* (later *Evening*) *Post*. It shows his gift for comedy, parody and self-parody.

> I went to the Plaza. 'Press,' I said to the girl with the Tyrolean hat and skirt.
> 'There's been two reporters this week.'
> 'Special notice.'

> She showed me to a seat. During the educational film, with the rude seeds hugging and sprouting in front of my eyes and plants like arms and legs, I thought of the bob women and the pansy sailors in the dives. . . . The sinuous plants danced on the screen. If only Tawe were a larger sea-town, there would be curtained rooms underground with blue films. The potato's life came to an end. Then I entered an American college and danced with the president's daughter. The hero, called Lincoln, tall and dark with good teeth, I displaced quickly, and the girl spoke my name as she held his shadow, the singing college chorus in sailors' hats and bathing dresses called me big boy and king, Jack Oakie, and I sped up the field, and on the shoulders of the crowd the president's daughter and I brought across the shifting-coloured curtain with a kiss that left me giddy and bright-eyed as I walked out of the cinema into the strong lamplight and the new rain.

Dylan's film-going had started as a schoolboy in the 'Uplands Cinema' near his home, remembered in 'Return Journey' as 'the flea-pit picture-house where he whooped for the scalping Indians . . . and banged for the rustlers' guns'.

Mervyn Levy has recalled how he and Dylan, when living almost penniless in Chelsea in the early 1930s, would go to the then fashionable News theatres in the late morning and stay till closing time, fortified with crisps and lemonade! Dylan's Chelsea friend during the war years, Theodora FitzGibbon, remembers they regularly went to the Classic Cinema in the King's Road 'to see any old film which took our fancy. Once we were asked to leave as we sobbed so loudly.'[2] Always fascinated by the world of film, while staying in Hollywood with Christopher Isherwood on his first American tour Thomas said the person he most wanted to meet was Charles Chaplin. Invited for the evening to Chaplin's home Dylan lamented that nobody in Laugharne would believe it, whereupon Chaplin expressly cabled Caitlin! Dylan's professional's delight in Chaplin's 'commedia dell'arte' parody of the perfect host, butler and maid reminds us Thomas was probably the finest actor among the great poets in English. There was early recognition of his talent as a young amateur actor – he once considered becoming a professional actor – and later for his gift of mimicry and parody, as both writer and performer. Certainly his comments on film performance are sharply amusing.

Writing to Pamela Hansford Johnson in January 1934 Dylan lists *Film Pictorial* among his daily casual reading, and more importantly later that month he sent her a letter in the form of a comic play, 'Spasma and Salnady', anagrams of their names, where Salnady (Dylan) names the films he particularly enjoyed.

> The Cabinet of Dr Caligari, Atalanta, Student of Prague, Edge of the World, Vaudeville, Waxworks, the Street, M, and Blue Angel (all German); Sur Les Toits de Paris; Potemkin (Russian); The Gold Rush, the Three Little Pigs, and the Marx Brothers comedies (American). The 'Bill of Divorcement' was not a film at all, but a screened play very badly and very theatrically acted, with the exception of the girl; the plot was disastrously altered, and the introduction of that wretched 'unfinished sonata' reached the depths of pathos.[3]

Earlier 'Salnady' exuberantly dismisses the film star John Barrymore as 'that Mountebank of an actor . . . a bunch of mannerisms and a profile', and Thomas was later to write filmscripts himself from both novels and stage plays, but what is notable in this listing is the nineteen-year-old's informed, sophisticated taste – even allowing for his desire to show off to his first serious, and highly intellectual, girlfriend. Importantly, the

German films with their expressionism and comment on inner emotional darkness, their links with culture and the avant-garde in their surrealistic images and their concern with dreams and madness and the then fashionable Freudian psychology, specially thrilled the young poet. At this time, too, he defended the cinematic imagery – 'Those words and images were essential'[4] of 'Our Eunuch Dreams', his poem on appearance and reality and dream.

> In this our age the gunman and his moll,
> Two one-dimensioned ghosts, love on a reel,
> Strange to our solid eye,
> And speak their midnight nothings as they swell:
> When cameras shut they hurry to their hole
> Down in the yard of day.[5]

Almost certainly it was the opening dream image of a human eye being dissected by a razor-blade in Luis Buñuel's and Salvador Dalí's film *Un Chien Andalou* (1928) that inspired 'Death instrumental/splitting the long eye open' in 'I, in my intricate image'.[6] The horror films with their grotesqueries, their echoes of Poe and the decadents were also close to the adolescent morbidity of the early poetry and stories of this inveterate film-goer.

But a few years later it was war-time. To his relief Dylan was unlikely to be called up after being listed grade III in his army medical, but feared being directed to uncongenial war work. He was also desperately short of money due to the shrinking of the literary market, particularly the small magazines. He now knew he had to find regular employment that would both provide an income and safeguard his freedom. Astutely the film-struck Dylan decided to seek work as a writer of filmscripts.

2

In search of work in films Dylan Thomas arrived in London on Saturday 7 September 1940. It was an oddly propitious time. That evening the blitz on London began and was to last for many months. But British propaganda, aimed now particularly at those living in an increasingly bombed, devastated and war-torn country, and with the aims of keeping up morale and the fighting spirit at home, turned increasingly to the visual, immediate and dramatic impact of film. The war-time documentaries that Dylan Thomas wrote and contributed to were to prove his most serious and enduring film work.

'That warm afternoon in early September', recalls Theodora

FitzGibbon, she first met Dylan, who had come to London for an appointment with Donald Taylor, the director of Strand Films; and he stayed with her and Peter Pulham, the painter, in King's Mansions, Chelsea. This led to discussions between Theodora and Dylan on their shared delight in the cinema — 'we both knew quite a lot about it — particularly the early silent cinema, where as small children we had been entranced in the wonderful world of imagery, in which anything could happen: *Dr Golen, Dr Mabuse, The Cat and the Canary, The Cabinet of Dr Caligari*, and in the thirties, James Whale's *The Old Dark House*. The latter we knew almost by heart . . . re-enacting large parts of it, squabbling for the best bits, which Dylan insisted on doing.'[7] But the subject matter of Dylan's documentaries, such as his most successful *Our Country*, was more immediate. On that first evening they went for a drink to the nearby Embankment pub, the King's Head and Eight Bells, which was to prove his Chelsea favourite during the years he worked on documentaries and lived in Chelsea. Theodora FitzGibbon sets the scene as they looked up the Thames Embankment to the city.

> As we turned the corner there was in the sky a monstrous tower, looking like a giant puffball of smoke, away to the east. . . . When darkness came, the smoke had turned to a red bank of flames . . . the 'all clear' sounded, and by then the sky was the colour of a blood orange, a seething flaming mass . . . a little before nine o'clock the siren went again, and using the fires as beacons, the Luftwaffe sent wave after wave of bombers into the holocaust, until three o'clock next morning . . . places were bombed until they resembled desolate heaps of rubble, and at least a thousand people had been killed, many others trapped, wounded and made homeless. The planes flew up the Thames, which was lit up like a horrifying pantomime, past London Bridge, Victoria, Chelsea, dropping their deadly cargo indiscriminately . . . the winter of the bombs, or the Blitz had begun.[8]

It was a baptism of fire for which Dylan Thomas had arrived just in time, but it inspired such poems as 'A Refusal to Mourn the Death, by Fire, of a Child in London', 'Ceremony After a Fire Raid' and 'Deaths and Entrances', the work of our first, and first great civilian war poet. This war-time experience, continued when he lived in Chelsea and also when he walked through blitzed Swansea in February 1942, was the background and inspiration also of his documentary filmscripts, which sometimes share and echo the language of his civilian war poems. But as we shall see, it shaped not only the response to Britain at war but the vision of a post-war Britain such sacrifice implied.

Donald Taylor, whose Strand Films offices were then in 5a Upper St

Martin's Lane, met Dylan Thomas a couple of days later in a pub in St Martin's Lane, probably the Salisbury, which was popular with writers and actors and enjoyed a bohemian atmosphere, though that evening it was almost empty due to the bombing. Donald Taylor immediately took to Dylan, and later recalled in 1963 that they formed an instantaneous friendship that never broke down.[9] Taylor had already read *Twenty-five Poems* and he was keen to employ good writers, even without previous film-making experience, and his script writers included Graham Greene, and later Philip Lindsay, the prolific novelist who became a close friend of Dylan, and Julian Maclaren-Ross who worked with Thomas in the Strand Films offices in 1943, by then in 1 Golden Square, Soho. Returning to Wales after the meeting and getting away from the continual bombing, he wrote to his Swansea friend Vernon Watkins that 'I get nightmares like invasions',[10] a reminder that at that time the threat of invasion also loomed.

It is likely that it was a year later, in the autumn of 1941, that Dylan Thomas was employed as a script writer for Strand Films, being paid £8 and later £10, and eventually ending up on £20 a week plus expenses. In the intervening year he was desperately hard up and still seeking a reserved occupation – preferably in films. Staying with his parents in January 1941 he laments his 'homelessness and pennilessness' when applying for a literary grant; in April he writes 'that unless I'm careful and lucky the boys of the Government will get me making munitions. I wish I could get a real job and avoid that.'[11] His poverty forced him in the summer of 1941 to sell his 'Notebooks' of early poems and prose for £25. But he wrote to Vernon Watkins from London on 28 August that 'I am still looking for a film job, and have been offered several scripts to do in the near future'.[12]

Donald Taylor's company Strand Films was the largest documentary film-making organisation, under contract with the Ministry of Information and producing seventy-five films a year in 1942. Dylan Thomas's varied scripts that year included *This is Colour, New Towns for Old, Battle for Freedom, Balloon Site 568, CEMA* and *Young Farmers*. Taylor has confirmed that Thomas was immediately and successfully put to work on a series of films, writing and fixing scripts under his direction. His work in films was totally professional, working with a team as usual in film production, variously contributing as director, compiler, producer, deviser, and voice-over narrator in the commentary. Clearly he soon acquired wide and practical knowledge of film techniques. Caitlin often complained to Taylor that Dylan was wasting his talent but she has confirmed that Dylan 'never took the job lightly; he was keenly interested in the new techniques that he was learning, and he was hoping to move on to other forms of film writing when . . . the film industry revived after the war. . . . Dylan was as conscientious about his writing for Donald Taylor and later for Sidney Box at Gainsborough Films as he was in his other literary work.'[13]

But Dylan liked the sociable lifestyle of the film makers, was fascinated by the 'translation of words to screen',[14] and enjoyed experiencing on location the daily lives of people at work and in their war-time settings. He was himself a fire-watcher on the rooftop of the Strand offices in Golden Square. Asked whether he had smuggled a girl into his sleeping bag one fire-watching night on the roof, he quipped, 'Then she must have been a very *little* girl.'[15] During his work in films from 1941 to 1948 he also uniquely enjoyed a regular income; and his employment being indirectly linked to the Ministry of Information it was the 'reserved occupation' he had sought during the first year of war.

'My war work' was how Dylan Thomas touchingly and humorously referred to his propaganda documentary films. Such scripts as *Our Country* provide a vivid and moving picture of war-time Britain, London in the Blitz, northern towns and rural areas, Wales and Scotland. There is the wider picture of a world at war in *Battle for Freedom*, while *These Are The Men* savagely mocks the Nazi leadership for their crimes in 'setting man against man', evoking in contrast 'the makers, the workers' throughout the world at their fruitful daily tasks. *Balloon Site 568* shows how Thomas was at his best in writing dialogue as he shows the war-time recruitment of women for the WAAF (Women's Auxiliary Air Force) and their life and leisure on a barrage balloon site, and similarly in *Conquest of a Germ* the dialogue between doctors, patients, nurses and medical research staff leads on to the celebration of the discovery of penicillin and its alleviation of suffering in war and the years of peace to come. It is the snatches of dialogue that enliven the *CEMA* (Council for the Encouragement of Music and Art) documentary's aim of 'bringing the best to our people – to cheer them on to better times'. Aiming to raise public morale in a Britain suffering heavy bombing and civilian as well as battlefront casualties, these documentaries also promote a vision of a better future, a post-war society of social welfare and full employment worth fighting for as in *A City Re-Born*. Thomas's scripts often have a sharp political edge that reflects his political, social and cultural views.

The documentaries also make a point of including people from all parts of Britain, with strong regional accents identifying their lives and background. This reflected the greater social mixing in war-time and the desire for a more equal society, and certainly the variety of accent, the directness of dialogue and social vision contrast with the middle-class tones of the commerical war-time cinema with its stiff-upper-lip platitudes.

Thus Dylan Thomas's dialogue in *New Towns for Old*, with the strong Yorkshire accent of the city councillor, has punch and vigour. His genially outspoken comment on the plans for post-war rebuilding in place of the slums and pollution of the industrial city streets of Smokedale, where children play in the grime and squalor of nearby factories and pits, is very persuasive. The (Labour) city father explains that the plans for rebuilding Smokedale apply to other similar towns, so that the finale almost comes across as post-war election propaganda, especially in the final shot of Councillor Jack Clem facing and pointing to the viewers and declaring 'You're the only folk that can make these plans come true. Not only plans for this town. But for every town. For *your* town. Remember! It's *your* town!'

Even more strongly and historically political is *Wales – Green Mountain, Black Mountain*, which Dylan Thomas both scripted and produced. Recording Wales's contribution to the war effort, and particularly celebrating the vital work of the dockers and coal and steel workers in South Wales, Thomas deliberately recalls the unemployment and depression of the 1930s, the poverty and despair of the 'old-young men' in evocative verse whose rhythms and pictures stay in the mind.

> Remember the procession of the old-young men
> From dole queue to corner and back again,
> From the pinched, packed streets to the peak of slag
> In the bite of the winters with shovel and bag,
> With a drooping fag and a turned up collar,
> Stamping for the cold at the ill lit corner
> Dragging through the squalor with their hearts like lead
> Staring at the hunger and the shut pit-head
> Nothing in their pockets, nothing home to eat.
> Lagging from the slag heap to the pinched, packed street.
> Remember the procession of the old-young men.
> It shall never happen again.

These verses of the 'old-young men' is an echoing litany as their procession rises in a visual crescendo with a shot of a large factory gate being closed. 'The words were unforgettable and therefore the visual image which was associated with it became so.'[16] It was a shot shown in film after film. The shot of those grubbing for coal went back to 1936 – a visual slogan of the documentary movement. Some of the material was used from a film Donald Taylor made in 1936 for the National Council of

Social Services, *Today We Live*, including the queue of men outside the Labour Exchange, the side view of men rummaging on a slag-heap with the wind blowing about them, and the man closing colliery gates.

These films often had a set pattern, beginning with 'some war-time documentary actuality'[17] like the establishment of Pit Production Committees in the mines – the subject of Dylan Thomas's script *Fuel for Battle* or life in war-time in various parts of Britain as in *Wales – Green Mountain, Black Mountain* or the bomb-devastated Coventry in Thomas's *A City Re-Born*. Then came 'an emotive recapitulation of the "dreadful conditions" of the pre-war years'[18] with evocation of their unemployment and despair, *Wales – Green Mountain, Black Mountain* stylistically the most compelling. Contrastingly, in the war-time struggle the government organised and mobilised financial and human resources, leading to full employment and social improvement, not leaving matters to inefficient private industry and private profit – points strongly made in *A City Re-Born*. In this script again following the argument that a more just post-war society can be similarly financed and organised, Thomas's 'Commentary' declares: 'In war we work together to destroy a common evil – in peace we must work with no less vigour for the common good.'

The script *Fuel for Battle* (August 1944) celebrates the miners' vital contribution to the war effort, showing how pit production increased when the miners themselves advised management on the newly formed Pit Production Committees, ending pre-war conflict between management and workers. *A City Re-Born* (1945) combines dramatically factual evocation of Coventry's destruction by bombing with informed yet easily accessible, humorous and casual conversation between its citizens on their enthusiastic planning for the city's better post-war life. While both these later films demonstrate Dylan Thomas's mastery of dialogue, in the earlier *Wales – Green Mountain, Black Mountain* the narrative reaches its impassioned climax with declamatory verse, both crusading and political in its protest against unemployment and poverty. Dylan Thomas remembered not only his script but the shots of the film in this section in his broadcast (*Welsh Poetry*) three years later, when he wrote of poets writing in

> passionate anger against social conditions. They wrote of the lies and ugliness of the unnatural system of society under which they worked – or, more often during the nineteen-twenties and thirties, under which they were not allowed to work . . . the coal-tips, the dole-queues, the stubborn bankrupt villages, the children scrutting for coal on the slag heaps . . . the still pit-wheels, the gaunt tin roofed chapels in the soot, the hewers

squatting in the cut . . . . sag-roof factory and plumeless stack, stone-grey street . . . . . the capped and mufflered knots of men outside the grim Employment Exchange.

Certainly these images closely follow scenes in the film, while the opening strictures on the pre-war situation is one often taken up in the documentaries.

In *Fuel for Battle* and *A City Re-Born*, as in *Wales – Green Mountain, Black Mountain* social unity is the sub-text of the documentaries, the instinct to unify rather than divide; and this is also so in the nationwide scenes of *Our Country*, whether the hop fields of Kent, the mines of the Rhondda Valley, Sheffield industries, the West Country, Scottish fisheries, Dover Cliffs or London's bombed but busy city streets, albeit everywhere the signs and threat of war, whether planes overhead, the carnage of air raids, army tanks, soldiers, sailors at sea and convoys, ack-ack guns. It is worth remembering, too, that these non-commerical films were shown in factory canteens, church halls, social centres, adult education classes and working-men's institutes – their aims to inspire war-time patriotism and solidarity, to inform and to provoke discussion – very much as in the discussion groups featured in *A City Re-Born*. Film was the most potent medium for political propaganda, for its popularity and immediate impact and especially for its power to visually and emotionally dramatise issues and policies ('Going to the pictures!' we called our war-time visits to the cinema in South Wales).

Donald Taylor had worked in the 1930s for John Grierson, who sought to use films as an educational and sociological instrument, and when he founded Strand Films he was joined by Paul Rotha. The shot of three workers standing heroically against the sky in *Wales* is a 'socialist–realist type image'[19] in the 1930s documentary style. There must be no return to poverty and unemployment is the ringing message of *Wales – Green Mountain, Black Mountain* (1943). The 'stylistically most arresting example of the "never again" part of the argument though entirely typical in comment may be found in *Wales*'.[20] Sometimes, as here and in *A City Re-Born*, the recapitulation of pre-war conditions was allied to a vision of a more generous post-war society in housing, employment, a national health service, and the abolition of homelessness and poverty. People of all classes had shared the Blitz, blackout, rationing, so all classes should share the better future.

Thus Dylan Thomas's *New Towns for Old* was directly electoral in its appeal, bringing to mind Lord Boothby's famous quip: 'The MOI did not win the war, but it certainly won the election for Labour.'[21] Dylan Thomas was reported in *Strand* magazine to have said in March 1947, when the Labour Government was in trouble during the winter freeze-up: 'One should tolerate the Labour Government because running down Labour eventually brings you alongside the Conservatives, which is the last place you want to be.' Instinctively on the left, he was one of the few poets of the 1930s who remained steadfast in his political allegiance throughout his life.

As a youthful revolutionary Thomas declared in *New Verse* in October 1934: 'I take my stand with any revolutionary body that asserts it to be the right of all men to share, equally and impartially, every production of man from man and from the sources of production at men's disposal'. While in 1946, soon after his work on the documentary films, he replied in the September number of *Horizon* to the question 'Do you think the State or any other institution should do more for writers?': – 'The State should do no more for writers than it should do for any other person who lives in it. The State should give shelter, food, warmth.' 'He was actually far more censorious of the *status quo* than any of the other British poets'[22] was Brinnin's claim. Certainly Dylan Thomas was comfortably at home with the political ethos of those working on the documentary propaganda films. The morale-raising vision of a more just post-war society, emotively projected in many documentaries, was part of the atmosphere of reform in which the Beveridge Report was so popularly received in 1942, though 'Churchill's initial response was to try to stop the report's publication'[23] as he had discussion of post-war planning and peace aims. Interestingly, in later years Dylan Thomas vividly recalls the war-time days of rationing and disrupted lives in his 1948 filmscript *No Room at the Inn*, and the sometimes desperate plight of evacuee children.

In his documentary *These Are The Men*, Thomas characteristically stresses the solidarity of common tasks and fruitful labour that 'the makers, the workers' shared worldwide until the Nazi leaders, savagely mocked in this film at their Nuremberg rally, 'set man against man'. 'Here is "Resistance"' wrote Dylan Thomas to Donald Taylor in September 1944, enclosing his script for a documentary titled *The Unconquerable People*, and it was fascinating to come upon this manuscript of what he called 'the Resistance story'. Written for four voices, the film begins by describing 'free peoples' going about their daily tasks 'in the thundering workshops of the earth . . . working in the fields'. Their countries invaded and occupied, 'the unconquerable common people' begin their fight back, and Thomas makes a point of including not only workers in all trades and professions but the women too.

we were among them *we* carried guns
the wives the sweethearts the daughters the mothers . . .

and the heroic resisters are named and celebrated country by country:

Poles and Slavs and Russians and Czechs and Frenchmen
guerilla fighters partisans and men of the Maquis
we were all comrades . . .

Eloquently written in the tone and style of fiery reporting, and exhilarating in its drive and vigour, it takes in dramatic incident ('Resistance began clumsily, hastily, with a knife in the dark'), and concludes with the flourish 'We were the People's Army: and we won!' It vividly conveys one of the faces of a time of war.

In *Our Country*, the poet's most celebrated documentary which opened at the Empire Cinema in Leicester Square, we are taken on a tour of Britain to meet factory, agricultural, industrial workers and fishermen. It is a panoramic view of war-time Britain, poetic in the evocation of such settings as London's bombed streets, the orchards and hop fields of Kent, the Welsh mining valleys, but above all in its lyrical, impressionistic vision of the inwardness of ordinary, everyday, distinctive lives. Some of the lines on the blitzed London streets are close to the images and language of the war-time elegies, particularly 'Ceremony After a Fire-Raid' which Thomas was writing at the same time. *Our Country* was spoken of as 'the sole and successful experimental film of the war period. It says important things in a new way . . . this new way involves poetry, impressionism, and in general a lyrical approach . . . "Our Country" says a great deal about Britain, and says it with deep emotion.'[24] His last documentary was *A Soldier Comes Home*, released in November 1945.

'Writers should keep their opinions for their prose'[25] declared Thomas and his work on these documentary films encouraged him to articulate his political and social views, as well as to depict realistically and with economy people, place and incident. Similarly he extended his gift for dialogue and the swift delineation of place and person beyond the mostly autobiographical Welsh settings of his earlier stories. The writing in the documentaries has a clarity and directness, a narrative drive that contributed to his later dramatic development. Nor did he forget his role as jester, but alas his film documentary *Is Your Ernie Really Necessary?*, whose title is a parody of the war-time slogan and admonition 'Is Your Journey Really Necessary?' (which I remember seeing uneasily as a child on holiday train journeys from South Wales to London), was suppressed. Dylan Thomas made this in collaboration with a well-known comedy director, Oswald Mitchell. The actor Hay Petrie played all the parts, and in one scene as a signalman in his box played 'The Bells of St Mary's' on his signal levers. In another he was dressed like a chorus girl, and repeated by optical process twelve times he looked like a chorus line. When they saw the film (which had cost £4,598) the Ministry of War Transport were horrified and abandoned it. Complaining in a letter to Caitlin of 'doing three months' film work in a week' he added, 'I do not care a bugger about the Problems of Wartime Transport'[26] – probably referring to this lost documentary film!

3

Dylan Thomas began full-time work in films when he was twenty-seven. It was Donald Taylor's view that the great thing to remember about Dylan was that he was a complete chameleon and could adapt himself to any company and play any role, and certainly relaxing for the evening in the neighbouring Soho pubs after his day in the Strand Films offices he enjoyed the sociability of the bohemian literary, film and theatre world. In the exchange of gossip and anecdote he both listened and performed, relishing a racy phrase or snatches of dialogue and tall stories, scribbling a note on his cigarette packet. Despatched by Caitlin to find Dylan as he failed to visit her in hospital following the birth of their daughter Aeronwy in an air raid, her sister Nicolette Devas recalls how she found him in the Anglesea, near their Chelsea flat in Manresa Road. She joined in the round of celebratory drinks but 'Dylan was in one of his brilliant talking moods', so that she forgot her purpose and they didn't leave till the pub shut! Such incidents point to the chameleon and actorly side of his personality, the voice that later brought him fame as broadcaster, reader and lecturer. Certainly he became famous among the bars of Chelsea, Soho and Fitzrovia in war-torn London.

Jack Lindsay, whose brother Philip worked with Dylan in Strand Films and became a close friend during his Chelsea years, tells how 'the half drunk Dylan, charming and over-flowing with bonhomie and his particular kind of wit and humour . . . was the boon companion, who at his best wove round himself delightful flights of fancy and liked to reveal his remarkable powers as a mime, a parodist, a pricker of all pomposities and falsities'.[27] Clearly he was now the raconteur whose gifts of comedy and imagination led to the comic inventions of his later work in films, radio, stories and of course *Under Milk Wood*. Though Dylan was the most frightened during the air raids, Theodora FitzGibbon remembers how he kept them all laughing and took their minds off the danger with his humour and play-acting. Thus writing to Vernon Watkins of the imminent threat of the German rockets, the V1s, he refers to London 'which will be shelled terribly by things that scream up into the stratosphere . . . and then pour down on to Manresa Road,'[28] where of course he lived. Later riding down Regent Street in a taxi with Vernon when a V2 cut out overhead but landed some distance away, a trembling Dylan quipped 'Wasn't it funny? I was sure we were going to be killed, and all I could think of was that I hoped I'd be blown to bits, because I couldn't bear the thought of my body being found with a copy of *Reveille* open at the pin-ups page.' 'I should have been all right,' Vernon answered seriously, 'because I always carry Kirkegaard in my pocket.'[29]

They may well have been travelling to Chelsea from the back bar of the Café Royal, where Dylan often went at lunch-time as it was near the Strand offices. Julian Maclaren-Ross has provided a vivid picture of their daily working life on filmscripts, beginning with his first sight of Dylan in 1943 in the lift, neither knowing who the other was.

> Dylan wore a green pork pie hat pulled down level with his slightly bulging eyes: like the agate marbles we used as Alley Taws . . . but a darker brown. His full lips were set low in a round face, a fag-end stuck to the lower one. His nose was bulbous and shiny . . . divested of hat and raincoat . . . Dylan was revealed to have on a very respectable dark blue suit and a white shirt with a bow tie and celluloid collar . . . . He was stockily built and robust looking rather than fat. His hair, light brown in colour and not dull gold as the romantics would like it . . . covered his round skull in tight woolly curls. His full cheeks were carefully shaven.

That first meeting Dylan Thomas noted that Maclaren-Ross, though from Scotland, had no accent, and of his own accent said, laughing, 'Cut-glass, they'd call it down in Wales', adding, 'I don't speak Welsh either.'[30]

Ross immediately joined Dylan on 'The Home Guard' script, never completed and long lost, and as neither had been in the Home Guard, 'what we concocted was a lively comedy-thriller set in a village "somewhere in England", stuffed full of eccentrics and containing also a fifth column group, a delayed action bomb, and a German parachutist who'd been in civvy street a music hall Master of Disguise'.[31] Ross's account reads like an early version of *Dad's Army* and obviously Dylan would have delighted in such a mixture of a comic, parodic thriller, like his later feature film *The Three Weird Sisters*. By autumn 1943 the subject was out of date and a documentary titled *Home Guard* had been made in 1941, with no reference to Dylan Thomas!

Even at this stage they both wanted to script features, planning a mystery film in collaboration entitled *The Whispering Gallery* or *The Distorting Mirror*, a throwback to *Caligari* and *The Cat and the Canary*; and having a penchant for such pictures Ross relates that they tracked down vintage examples all over London. Dylan provided the basic idea of the film. Various people are being shown around the whispering gallery of a stately home open to the public and suddenly a voice says out loud, 'I'll have this place.' No one can tell who spoke, the camera pans various faces as the film begins. The heir irons out methodically all those in his way, recruiting his murderous accomplices in a deserted amusement park, and is to be seen unrecognisably reflected in the Hall of Mirrors – hence the alternative title. Dylan favoured a super-villain, male and female, whose sex was changed by an operation half-way through![32] Clearly Dylan delighted in fantasy and thrillers whose plotting helped pass enjoyably both office and pub hours. Not that he needed to come in every day, since Donald Taylor took the urbane view that scripts should be delivered, not necessarily written there. But Dylan enjoyed this Soho film and bohemian pub world, and was no doubt glad to have his day away from the one-room flat. Nevertheless Thomas allowed himself only a pint of bitter at lunch-time and was shocked when Maclaren-Ross suggested they keep a bottle of whisky in the office. It was in the evening Dylan took to the pubs.

Caitlin, with their baby daughter Aeronwy, often went to stay in Wales to avoid the bombing, particularly when the V1 rockets made their glass-roofed studio in Manresa Road far too dangerous a home, and Dylan often joined them for weekends and longer spells in the safe countryside of Blaen Cwm, across the estuary from Laugharne, and Talsarn in Cardiganshire. For a time in 1944 they retreated to Bosham in Sussex, when the bombing on London resumed, called 'the little blitz', and they also stayed with Donald Taylor in Hedgerley Dean in Buckinghamshire in the summer of 1944.

Importantly, and pointing towards Thomas's later scripts for feature films, not to say *Under Milk Wood*'s techniques of presentation, Ross records that:

> We also shared another ambition, which was to write a film script, *not* a Treatment as the story-form is called, but a complete scenario ready for shooting which would give the ordinary reader an absolute visual impression of the film in words and could be published as a new form of literature. Carl Meyer, the co-author of *Caligari* and creator of many of the great early German silents, who invented the mobile camera or rather

caused it to be moved about, is said to have written such scripts, but neither Dylan nor I could get hold of a script by Meyer, and the only ones we knew which almost succeeded in doing what we had in mind were those printed in *The Film Sense* by Sergei Eisenstein.

The rules we laid down ourselves were that the script had to be an original specially written in this form and not any kind of adaptation, and that actual film production must be possible. Our main obstacle consisted in the camera directions, which if given were apt to look too technical, and if omitted would lose the dramatic impact of, for instance, a sudden large close-up, which Dylan however hoped could be conveyed by one's actual choice of words. In fact we were attempting the well nigh impossible, as anyone who has read the printed versions of *Marienbad* or *L'Immortelle* by Robbe Grillet will realise, and perhaps Dylan himself in *The Doctor and the Devils* came as close to it as any writer ever will. [33]

'An absolute visual impression in words' and 'the mobile camera' are apt comment on the aim and technique in that 'play for voices', *Under Milk Wood*. Significantly, too, Ross's view here that 'an absolute visual impression of the film in words could be published as a new form of literature' was echoed in Bonamy Dobrée's review of *The Doctor and the Devils* when it was published in 1953 – the first screenplay to be published as a book before its film production (over thirty years later).

His adventure in a new form, that of the published film-script before handling . . . is extraordinarily powerful, actual as only a poet can make it; and this new form makes us wonder whether this may not be a pointer towards the way novels may be written in future. . . . It is written, of course, in film language; we 'dissolve to', the camera 'tracks back', we see someone 'in close up'; but we soon get used to all this, and adapt our imaginations to the whole movement, or the series of disjointed movements which make up the whole. The question arises: Do we need to see it on the film? Perhaps the answer is: We shall not need to see it only when the script is written so well as this one. That will be a rare occurrence, but a master in the art of the novel might well become a master in this new form. [34]

In this instance it was a master in the art of poetry and the short story who was devising a new literary form. Donald Taylor, introducing the publication of *The Doctor and the Devils* as the first screenplay published before production, emphasised it was 'no doubt due to the literary quality, unusual in this medium'. [35]

It was Taylor who commissioned Dylan Thomas to do *The Doctor and the Devils* script, based on his own researched story of the Edinburgh body-snatchers that had long fascinated him. Taylor had wanted to move into features. After his taste of documentary film writing Dylan Thomas was also keen to widen his script writing, which he had come to enjoy as well, of course, as liking this way of earning a fairly regular income. When Donald Taylor closed Strand Films at the end of 1943 and set up Gryphon, Dylan Thomas continued with him, so that he was continually in employment. While at Gryphon Films he wrote *The Unconquerable People* and *Our Country*, but turned particularly to feature-filmscripts like *Twenty Years A-Growing*, *The Doctor and the Devils*, *Suffer Little Children*, and the plotted outline of a now lost Robert Burns script, based on Catherine Carswell's biography, and some work on a *Crippen* script not yet traced. Donald Taylor was also interested in making a film of Thomas's *Adventures in the Skin Trade*, and Dylan Thomas planned the last shot. It was to be of the young man, Samuel Bennet, standing naked in Paddington Station, having shed all his skins but with an empty beer bottle slipping off his finger and shattering on the platform. But nothing came of it.

Enjoying each other's company and play-acting, Donald Taylor and Dylan would decide during the day what role they would play going later to the pub. Dylan's favourites were a Welsh country gentleman, a BBC actor and reader of verse, or a drunken Welsh poet. It is likely Thomas was writing *The Doctor and the Devils* during the two months he stayed with Donald Taylor, who worked with him on this project. When Dylan was staying with Caitlin in Wales or elsewhere he was able to work on his scripts, calling at the office in London on a Friday, pay day. While in Talsarn he wrote to a London friend that 'I have been here for over a week with Caitlin, with milk and mild and cheese and eggs, and I feel fit as a fiddle only bigger. I watch the sun from a cool room and know that there are trees being trees outside and that I do not have to admire them; the country's the one place you haven't got to go out in, thank Pan.'[36] In remote Cardiganshire he was safe from the bombing, there was plenty of farm produce to enjoy, and he delighted in the Pan quip as he writes in his quiet room.

In September 1944 the family settled in their sea-facing bungalow, 'Majoda', in New Quay, Cardiganshire, perched just above the sea and enjoying a fine view of that beautiful Welsh coastline. It is the 'cliff-perched town at the far end of Wales' in his descriptive essay on the place, 'Quite Early One Morning', not only the initial inspiration of *Under Milk Wood* in its setting but also where he wrote *Twenty Years A-Growing*, based on Maurice O'Sullivan's book about the Blasket Islands, the English translation by Moya Llewelyn Davies and G. Thomson published in 1933.

Like *The Doctor and the Devils*, in this script, albeit unfinished, undoubtedly it is its literary quality that makes it so enjoyable to read, above all the poetic evocation of the natural life of these wild, remote islands off the coast of the south-west of Ireland. In this script Dylan Thomas's favourite poetic themes emerge: the seasons, both in their immediate beauty, colour and movement but also in their mythical, legendary past, and always the haunting presence of a childhood spent close to nature. This was near the time he was writing his now famous poem of re-created childhood, 'Fern Hill'. Birds and animals, dawn in the countryside, the continual sound and movement of seascapes and changing light are expressed in Thomas's exact, visual style. If a film were made it would be one of rare visual beauty. Thomas here expresses the twin themes of change and renewal, the debate between traditional peasant man and urban community with its technology. Thomas did in fact spend a day on the Great Blasket in August 1946, while on holiday in Kerry. But there was the daily scene and impact of the seascapes of Thomas's New Quay home, including the long cliffside walks into New Quay and his favourite pub, the Black Lion. Always facing Majoda were the wide maritime horizons of the Irish Sea. Notable in the script were the camera directions, also anticipating the involving visual techniques of *Under Milk Wood*, such as the use of 'The Voice' to recall childhood scenes. Such terms as 'cut to', 'dissolve to' occur, as in *The Doctor and the Devils* script. As in nearly all his scripts, there are, too, moments of comedy. It was here also that he completed the documentaries *The Unconquerable People* and *Our Country*.

By this time Dylan Thomas was more interested in scripting full-length feature films than shorts, and in a letter to Donald Taylor in February 1945 he apologises that he was keen to get on with *Suffer Little Children* and didn't want to do a 'short' film.

> Please take no notice of what I said about 'Labour': I'm proud to be asked to try to do the script: my only fear is that I shall not do a very good job of it: I am not, as you know, politically very acute, and will have to rely, as usual, upon emotionalism. But I will send off the opening sequences in a few days, and you will tell from them whether I should go on alone with the scripting or whether I should work at it closely with you and, alone, do only the dialogue – and the descriptive-visual writing.[37]

As Dylan Thomas notes here it is dialogue, descriptive-visual writing, and the emotional impact he is best at in script writing. We know, too, that he had as little interest in political theory as he had in literary theory, which he made fun of in his American tours, or indeed film theory – as we shall see in his often mocking contributions to *Poetry and the Film*. I wonder whether the direct political title anticipates a summer 1945 General Election, but there is no other reference to the film, either as script or its making.

It was in March 1945 that Taylor sent down John Eldridge, one of his main directors, and his assistant Fanya Fisher, to help Dylan with a script he was late with, possibly 'Labour', probably *Twenty Years A-Growing*, when the famous shooting incident occurred after a row in the Black Lion with a Commando Captain who had taken part in sabotage attacks behind the enemy lines. It seems the row was provoked by what Fisher, a Russian-born Jew and a Communist, thought was an anti-Semitic remark by the Commando. After a scuffle the Commando went to another pub on his own but returned to the bungalow later than night.[38] Dylan was fond of Fisher who helped him at Gryphon, an assistant on *Fuel for Battle, A City Re-Born* and *A Soldier Comes Home*. He relates events then, with some drama, in a letter to Vernon Watkins of his being 'caught, however innocently . . . in a Case of Attempted Murder, Caitlin, I, and three others . . . the Commando Captain started a fight in the local hotel, in which I took a small part, lost, returned home to the bungalow next to mine, and, when I also had returned home and was talking to Caitlin and three others, fired many rounds from his Sten gun through our paper-thin walls, missing us by inches and Aeronwy by feet. It's all very nasty, and I'm as frightened as though I had used the Sten gun myself. He also had a hand grenade . . . now Caitlin and I go to bed under the bed.' He jokes in another letter that day: 'I am caught in a police court case, someone fired a Sten gun at us; I hope he missed.'[39]

The case came up at Lampeter Assizes, and the jury found the Commando not guilty, the judge finding lack of evidence. But of course the drama of the event and the impending trial hardly assisted Thomas's concentration on his work, though he told delightfully dramatic versions of the story for years afterwards. Recently visiting Majoda I saw that the bullet-hole marks were still visible near the top of the sitting-room wall!

4

In the summer, no doubt unsettled by this incident, and with the war ending and change in the air, Dylan Thomas left New Quay. Gryphon Films, too, came to an end in the autumn, though Donald Taylor and

Bunny Keene, who also worked for Taylor, later arranged for Thomas to work for J. Arthur Rank's Gainsborough Films. The British feature-film industry flourished just after the war, and Thomas worked on two scripts for British National. One was *The Three Weird Sisters* (1948), a thriller-type melodrama set in a Welsh mining valley and of particular interest as it vividly highlights political and cultural conflicts and the very personal cross-currents of the poet's Welshness.

In *No Room at the Inn* (1948), with its evocation of war-time England, Thomas's dialogue is again very successful, particularly in the scenes describing the children's play and exploits, in such Dickensian characters as Mrs Waters, and Mrs Voray's flirtations and encounters. It is a memorable period picture of class differences in a country town having to cope with evacuees and war-time's divided lives and daily struggles. Thomas was now living in Oxfordshire, first in Hollywell Ford, in a summerhouse in the grounds of A.J.P. and Margaret Taylor's home, bordering the River Cherwell. But Margaret Taylor found for Dylan the Manor House, South Leigh, near Witney in 1947. His steadfast patron, she also provided a caravan for him to write in, moving it on to South Leigh. He wrote his script for a film, *The Shadowless Man*, at this time, and Margaret Taylor probably encouraged him on this. One of his closest friends here was Harry Locke, an actor who took part in the film *No Room at the Inn*.

This meant that during his years as a regular broadcaster and writer of feature-filmscripts, Dylan commuted several days a week between Oxford and London. It was a time when he constantly asks in his letters for more time to complete his scripts. It is reported, reliably it seems, by the production manager of *The Three Weird Sisters*, that Thomas spent three weeks virtually locked up on the top floor of the Royal Court Hotel in Sloane Square, Chelsea, writing this script, food and drink (limited) supplied.[40]

Sidney Box contracted Thomas to write three scripts in 1948, one of which, *The Beach of Falesá*, was based on Robert Louis Stevenson's story, a writer whose work he knew well and admired. Jungle devilry, murder and romance in an exotic South Seas setting is the basic plot, but it is Thomas's evocation of tropical nature, sensuous and with its own mystery, that distinguishes the script, and again he brings in familiar Welsh colour and background to his characterisation of the missionary, who becomes a vivid nonconformist preacher in Dylan's transformation. Thomas also completed the first part of *Me and My Bike*, a film operetta on a man who rides a succession of bicycles through his life, finally pedalling to heaven. Dylan wrote to Ralph Keene, then a film director with Gainsborough, that 'I feel very enthusiastic about it. Sidney's [Box] carte blanche as to freedom of fancy, non-naturalist dialogue, song, music, etc is enormously encouraging.'[41] Certainly its mingling of song, rhyming and poetic fancy makes it very different from his other filmscripts. As usual with such unfinished scripts he provided a synopsis of its later development. Many years later it was the basis of a television film made for BBC Wales.

Dylan's third and last filmscript very much returned to a Welsh setting and was a historical political drama. *Rebecca's Daughters* portrays conflict and riots in rural West Wales in the 1840s with verve and comic incident. It concerns the tollgate taxes and the protest against them, including their burning, led by Rebecca and his fellow rioters, dressed as women. Dylan Thomas's evocation of the night-time clandestine gatherings, the darkly thrilling atmosphere, is particularly effective. The wit and comedy, particularly in the portrayal of the grasping but decadently effete local aristocracy, especially the vivid Sir Henry usually accompanied by his similarly drunken cat 'Rover' about his shoulders, contributes to the script's flair. In Karl Francis's recent film of *Rebecca's Daughters* he is splendidly played by Peter O'Toole, and violent political protests, the romance of Rebecca (the dashing aristocratic Anthony Raine in disguise) and Rhiannon whose sympathy is also with the downtrodden peasant farmers, and the amusing ball in Sir Henry's mansion that ends the film, keep much of the political edge and the comedy of the script. Occasionally the wit in the dialogue has a Wildean touch. In his letters to Sidney Box and Ralph Keene Dylan Thomas mentions a filmscript *The Forgotten Story* he wanted to work on, but there is no further reference to it.

Because Thomas was being pursued by what he called 'the Income Tax Dracula',[42] for tax due on previous earnings as well as those in film work, life was becoming difficult. But he attended script conferences at the West London Studios, though always keen to adjourn to the Shepherd's Bush Hotel, and once he got started on a script he wrote quickly. Sadly he did not follow through an offer from Clifford Evans, the actor, to write the script of a film story that turned out to be *A Run for Your Money*, in which Hugh Griffith, who had recently taken the part of the miner agitator Mabli Hughes in Dylan Thomas's *The Three Weird Sisters*, splendidly played a wily harpist begging on the London streets. Thomas wrote to Evans: 'I had agreed that I should work on this film for Ealing only if Ealing paid me what Sidney Box was prepared to pay me: ie £1000 for a shooting script. Also I said that I *would* be agreeable to a treatment only if I was given more time and, consequently, more money.'[43] Ealing would offer only £250 and a time limit.

In July 1949 Dylan Thomas wrote: 'I am just beginning the first treatment for Gainsborough of a technicolour film of "Vanity Fair" (with, dear God, Maggie Lockwood)',[44] and it seems he did some work though no script has been traced. In September 1950 he joked he had tried 'to sell myself to Metro-Korda-Odeon as a Celtic Noël Coward, a Welsh J.B. Priestley, a Swansea Rattigan, a Laugharne cockle'.[45] His last film project was in January 1951, when he went to Persia with Ralph Keene to write a documentary filmscript for the Anglo-Iranian Oil Company, humorously commenting later that they 'sent me out to write a film script to show how beautiful Persia is and how little as a mouse and gentle is the influence there of that Company: my job was to pour water on troubled oil'.[46] But soon after his return the oil company was nationalised. Thomas later did do a broadcast talk, 'Persian Oil'. There was, too, a recession in the film industry. Additionally it was to America, with readings and lecture tours, that Thomas now turned his attention. Brinnin organised these American tours, and his review of *The Doctor and the Devils* two months after Dylan Thomas's death tellingly concludes: 'The technical brilliance of *The Doctor and the Devils* reminds us, as we are so often reminded now, of the silence death has imposed on a voice that could speak so eloquently in so many forms.'[47]

This collection includes twenty-three filmscripts, and two commentaries on film by Dylan Thomas. It was exciting research to discover fourteen documentaries, particularly the luck and literary detection that led later to three filmscripts not previously referred to, including the notable *Fuel for Battle* and *A City Re-Born*. In the absence of scripts, I have made transcripts from the films *This is Colour, New Towns for Old, The Three Weird Sisters* and *No Room at the Inn*. Regarding the eight feature-films, I have provided edited, shortened versions of *Twenty Years A-Growing, The Beach of Falesá, Me and My Bike* and *Rebecca's Daughters* (all previously published), to make possible the inclusion of all the scripts.

Where the original scripts carried gross typographical errors and inconsistencies silent corrections have been made.

THE SCREENPLAYS

The Films

This essay was published in Swansea Grammar School Magazine in July 1930, when Dylan Thomas was fifteen. It suggests he had already read Paul Rotha's recently published *The Film Till Now*; certainly he was already a keen film-goer. His comments on acting bring to mind that his delight in acting had already started at school, for he acted in Drinkwater's *Abraham Lincoln* in 1929 and he had recently played the lead in *Oliver Cromwell*.

THE FILMS

The evolution of the motion-picture from the crude experimentalism of pre-war years to the polished artistry of today has taken place during a very short period. It was not until the beginning of the twentieth century that it was possible to present natural things in natural motion on a screen. Today, less than thirty years later, every shade of physical emotion, however slight or subtle, can be shown among natural and often naturally coloured surroundings.

The first picture that could be taken seriously was produced by D.W. Griffith in 1907. He brought a greater sense of balance and artistic understanding to that film than had hitherto been thought of, and introduced the now familiar tricks of the 'close-up' the 'fade out' and the 'cut back'. He realised the importance of motion-pictures, not as freak exhibitions, but as works of art produced through an entirely new medium. The first film that was taken seriously was Adolph Zukor's 'Queen Elizabeth', produced in 1912. Zukor had been for a long time contemplating the introduction of famous stage-stars on to the screen, and he made his first attempt at this by casting Sarah Bernhardt as Elizabeth. The film met with instant appreciation, but, with a few notable exceptions, stage-stars have not been successful on the screen, partly from the more exacting demands of silent presentation and partly because good stage technique does not necessarily mean a good screen technique.

In 1914 D.W. Griffith produced 'The Birth of a Nation'. This was quite easily superior to every other pre-war film. It was devastating in its racial results, causing rioting and some bloodshed, but it proved more than ever to him that motion-pictures were world-wide influences.

During the war, the few English studios that had been trying to compete with the many more American ones, were entirely suspended. When English producers turned back to their trade in 1919 they found that America had got complete hold over the world, and dominated every market. It was not until two or three years ago that England woke up to the fact that English producers were bringing forth many very fine films. Up to then the public had been so used to seeing thousands of American pictures and occasional and almost invariably bad English ones, that they did not get to know that there were some really intelligent producers at work in England. Now, the pictures produced in this country are quite as good and nearly as many as those produced in America.

The stories of the early films were simple and obvious, but as time went on and the public became more sophisticated, it was necessary to think of plots that did not always deal with the human triangle, or the hero, the heroine and the villain in a breathless intrigue with an inevitable ending. Consequently the hero became more humanised, and even the heroine had her faults, while the villain was not branded by a cloak and a series of sinister gestures, but was allowed more ordinary dress and movements. Then, as plots wore thinner and thinner, the classics were taken from their shelves, dusted, abridged, renovated by superior intellects, and finally, were represented on the screen with more taste and understanding, until today many of the best films are those based upon, or woven round, famous novels and plays.

Film-acting requires distinct subtlety of action. Spoken words are, as often as possible, eliminated, and visual symbols used instead. That is, nearly the whole effect of a film depends upon the comprehensibility of features, facial expressions, and movements of the body. The early actors, dependent so much upon speech, found themselves at a loss to adapt themselves to the screen. Consequently, their acting was exaggerated and absurd. They magnified every emotion and overstressed every facial expression. They indulged almost invariably in orgies of grief, hysteria, and inarticulate anger. Henry B. Walthall, in 1914, showed that such exaggeration was unnecessary, by giving a new and delicate film performance in 'The Birth of a Nation'. He employed the slightest gestures and the most illuminating innuendoes. His acting was a landmark in the progress of the motion-picture. From his time has come a long line of actors and actresses who have made themselves universally admired for their brilliance and charm.

In the few points I have dealt with, I have made no mention of sound. The coming of the talkies has widened many fields and narrowed many others. There is no way of treating the motion-picture with sound and without sound: they are far too differentiated. Sound-technique is in the same state now as silent technique was when D.W. Griffith evolved his own methods of pictorial representation, adding inestimably to its progress. Whether there will be a Griffith for sound-films is a matter that is best left to time.

Synchronised films up to 1930 have been distinctly disappointing. Crudity was expected, but both American and English producers have taken sound for granted, and have been over-confident of themselves. The older and established producers, especially, have merely added it to their screen-properties, without realising that it is something new which cannot be tackled by any old methods but which requires a special way of approach. Even film-pioneers must start at the beginning of sound-film production, and learn what there is to be learnt.

This is Colour

Made by Strand Films for Imperial Chemical Industries the subject is the history, production and use of British dyes. Its didactic seriousness and detail certainly educate and inform, and the introductory section on the meaning of colour and how we observe the colour of a rose, and closing section showing links with the visual world of colour in our daily lives, such as traffic lights, have particular interest. The film was made in technicolour, and there was a remake in 1945. A reviewer (*Documentary News Letter*, May 1942)[48] commented interestingly on its appeal for its time.

> The film is a sight for sore eyes. In a world which war is making drabber every day, with its camouflage, its khaki and its rationing of paint and wrapping, *This is Colour* gives us seventeen minutes of pure visual pleasure. The treatment fortunately is academic, thus coordinating what might have easily turned out to be colour riot. It first discusses colour in general terms . . . of prisms, of sunlight and of a red rose in the moonlight. The discovery of new dyeing methods leads us on to experiments with dyes and then to their manufacture. In a superbly mysterious sequence, with the camera moving slowly across the dark paraphernalia of the dye factory with its flamboyant splashes of colour, we see the dyes being prepared and applied. The rollers turn, placing colour upon pattern and colour upon colour, reeling out yards of gaiety.

I have made this transcript from the film.

THIS IS COLOUR

Every morning as the sun rises it brings back to the world colour which was lost in the darkness. And the light of everything we look at depends more than most of us realise on colour. Why is a rose red in sunlight, and why in moonlight does it lose almost all its colour? To answer these questions, we must ask another. What is colour? In the first place the colour of anything depends on the light that is shining on it, for colour is light and light is colour. All colours come from the light of the sun. In the rainbow you are seeing rays of sunlight falling on a screen of raindrops. The raindrops split up the sunlight into the seven colours of the spectrum. We observe the spectrum artificially by using a spectroscope. The white light takes the place of the sun. As it passes through the prism, this is the part of the raindrop it splits up into its coloured parts, the colours of the rainbow. Doing it the other way round we can collect the colours together and they become white once again. We can do this another way by means of this wheel. It's made up of the colours of the spectrum and as it turns, faster and faster, the colours combine and the result is – white! The surface of anything you look at is absorbing some colour rays and is affecting the rest, and its effect strikes the eye, and that's how we get our impression of colour. When an object is absorbing all the colour rays and reflecting none of them we call it black. If it is absorbing none and affecting them all we call it white. A red rose in sunlight is absorbing all the colours except the red, which is protected.

When a man paints a picture he treats the canvas in such a way that it reflects certain colours. But when he prints or dyes a material he's doing the same sort of thing. For thousands of years man has been painting and dyeing things without a real scientific knowledge of colour. He made his colours from grasses and flowers, mosses and seaweed and ferns and barks and roots and berries and other natural substances. Even today the people of the Hebrides still use this method in making Harris tweeds. But though some of these natural dyes are first class they are limited in their range, and it's often a long and difficult job to make them. We obtained all our dyes from natural sources until the 19th century. In this period British science discovered a source of colour in the most unlikely of all materials, coal. Coal is all that's left of the vast forests which covered the earth in pre-historic times. In fact coal is the vegetable substances of those forests that owed their luxuriant growth to the light and heat of the sun. It was from coal power, then the useless residue of the gas industry, that an eighteen-year-old English chemist called Perkins discovered in 1856 a rich mauve dye. From his discovery came a great new industry, the manufacture of synthetic colours or dyes. Direct successors to Perkins are the skilled scientists working in modern laboratories, and still today as they continue their explorations into the unknown, their basic materials come from coal.

Like most scientific work the discovery of a new dye is by no means easy going. Take green, the most common colour in nature. The scientists, unlike nature, find it a most difficult problem to make good green dye by artificial means. As early as 1912 a brilliant green dye was evolved. This was a sort of dye known as vat dye. Vat dye is currently used for colouring materials directly because they won't dissolve in water and won't take directly on the fibre of the material. So they have to be treated with chemicals that change them into a form which can be easily dyed on to the cellulose material like cotton. But in 1912 when this was tried with the new green dye it was found that the green wasn't fast, that is the colour wasn't reliable. A drop of dilute sulphuric acid which illustrated the effect even of the ordinary acid of the air, turned it blue. Eight years later a team of British chemists at Carlisle solved the problem by a simple chemical process. They methylated the dye itself on 11 September 1920 and when the same tests were made with sulphuric acid the colours stayed fast. The result was the best green dye yet made.

This chemist is preparing a simple orange dye. He's firmly checking up on the quality of the ingredients, but this sort of test is an important part of normal routine. This particular colour will be what's known as an azo dye. Azo dyes are made by combining together two chemical compounds. Neither of these is a dye but they both contain chemical groupings which when the chemist combines them like this will produce a definite colour. Now he throws in some ordinary salt. This precipitates the dye, so that it can be dried off ready for use.

This porcelain dish is filled with thermodynitride which the chemist is beating with a copper fork. The smoke results from an important chemical reaction, a reaction which represents a major discovery in this field of British chemistry. From this discovery comes the only perfect blue pigment. Pigments are used for making paints and also for colouring things like rubber, plastics, and linoleum in a way that is impossible with dye stuff. The liquid isn't the finished product but it contains the pigment which is filtered off as a powder. The first blue pigment ever made.

But the discovery of new dyes and pigments isn't the whole story. Dyestuff chemists are continually experimenting in the methods of applying dyes to all sorts of material. This hank of cotton surprisingly enough is being dyed yellow. Like the dye's green this dye has to be converted to a viable form before the cotton can take the colour. Once the blue solution has thoroughly dyed the cotton all that remains to be done is to re-form the original yellow dye.

All dyes won't dye all materials. This man is dyeing three separate hanks made up of natural silk, viscous rayon and acetate rayon, all widely used in everyday life. He uses only one bath, which contains three distinct dyes, and each hank comes out a different colour. This is because each dye only 'takes' on the material for which it has its own special affinity.

For nearly a century now scientists have been secretly experimenting into the nature and mystery of colour, creating around us this new age, to build an age of colour. In the factories technical chemists take over from the laboratory worker. Here the cubic centimetre of the test tube gives way to the yellow measure of the production vat. Here new discoveries come into production, side by side with dyes that have been in constant manufacture for many years . . .

Without colour the new blocks of flats over our cities may all look alike, but with colour they become the separate places of people who can never be standardised. And colour is essential to the organisation of the community too. Colour helps to conduct the traffic. The bus conductors would find their work twice as hard if their tickets weren't coloured. Safety on railways depends on colour. And so does much of the efficiency of the great modern offices. Colour control indicates the various departments, it speeds up distribution, it co-ordinates the filing system, it saves time and trouble in the building of radio sets by making the wiring and components easy to identify. It's the means by which staff in the first office can tell at a glance that letters and parcels have been properly stacked. Young or old you live in a world of colour. There's everyday colour and living colour. When work's over colour is a holiday by itself. You take it away, so much beauty and gaiety are taken too. Colour box and bricks, egg boxes and jigsaw kits make children happy while they learn. Bright toys teach their hands and their minds. In them and many other ways colour brings to the work-a-day world a kaleidoscope of dazzling beauty.

New Towns for Old

This script on the re-planning of British towns after the war was one of Thomas's most successful, and is so because of the lively and persuasive dialogue edged with both imagination and a genial tone. A 'Homefront' film, its call for post-war 'new schools, new hospitals, new roads, new life' was an electoral appeal, concluding 'You're the only folk that can make these plans come true.' The reviewer in *Documentary News Letter* (June 1942)[49] observed that 'it . . . details the essential problems which must be solved in the period of reconstruction after the war. . . . The style adopted is very pleasant. It consists of a dialogue between two men as they walk through the various streets of "Smokedale" and discuss the things they see. One of the men takes the lead and is virtually the commentator. . . . "Propaganda value": Very good for the Home Front, particularly since the film makes it clear that plans for the future are bound up with the war effort which we are engaged in here and now.' This is a transcript I have made from the film.

NEW TOWNS FOR OLD

The film shows the town of Smokedale, its heavy industry including mining and steel production alongside the streets and homes of its inhabitants and workers, and desolate lots where children play happily. A Smokedale City Councillor/Father is showing the places to a visitor from the South of England, some at a distance, sometimes the noisy sounds of industry in close-up. Sheffield seems to be the location of some of the scenes; Councillor and visitor look down on 'Smokedale', spread below them.

CITY COUNCILLOR: Now this is Smokedale. Half a million people live there − down at 'Deep. (*noises of heavy industry*) Let's take another look. Let's see how folk live there. Don't forget there's folk still living like this in most other big towns. (*sounds of children playing, Councillor pointing towards them*) There! Look at that! That's wrong!

VISITOR: What's wrong? The houses are fit to live in, aren't they? They are not condemned, are they? The kids look happy enough.

CITY COUNCILLOR: Ay, but they shouldn't be! . . .

VISITOR: Well, you can't say they're unhappy. (*sounds of children playing happily*)

CITY COUNCILLOR (*sternly*): But they shouldn't be 'ere! Lads shouldn't have to play in a place like this. Kids shouldn't have to grow up in soot and muck. It isn't right! What can they hope for? What can they look for'ard to?

VISITOR: But you've only shown the worse parts. All cities have their slums. (*Scene now moves to newly built, modern blocks of flats.*) Ah! Now this is much better.

CITY COUNCILLOR: Ay, these flats are better than houses that were 'ere. But look at them works right on top o' them. One or t'other should be 'ere. They can't live together. One or t'other should go.

VISITOR: But you can't move a town about like that.

CITY COUNCILLOR: Can't we? Look down there!

VISITOR: Hm! Bomb damage?

CITY COUNCILLOR: No! We pulled it down ourselves. These were slums worse than ones you've just come from. Now see, we can re-plan a town if we want to. And we have planned it an' all! I'll tell you about it. (*waves his pipe towards the scene of new flats and environment with satisfaction*) It all started about twenty years ago. We got a new council in. Just scraped in, but they decided to clean up town. Up to this war we'd 26,000 slum 'ouses condemned and 14,000 we'd already got rid of, and 'itler knocked us a few more down . . . But you can't knock down 'ouses without building new ones. And we built 30,000 on 'em, 30,000 new houses, right away from works, right away from soot and muck.

CHILDREN'S VOICES (*shouting at play*):   Don't stop! Come on, run! Come on! Come on! Run! Run! (*noise of running and excitement grows*)

VISITOR: Yes, that's all very well, what you going to do with the places you've cleared, you've still got factories left in them – and look there's one there, and *there's* a row of houses. Now, what're you going to do?

CITY COUNCILLOR: Ha! We got that taped! Council brought in a chap specially for the job, to make proper plans for all this.

NEW VOICE: The city engineer wants to see the plans.

CITY PLANNER: Now gentlemen, these are the plans we propose. There's the new elevation of electric show rooms, the new Assize Courts, the low rent flats, and social centres.

CITY COUNCILLOR: We've begun to build a new Smokedale. New flats, new 'omes away from smoke, away where they should be! Ay, but we haven't built just anywhere. We've kept green belt. We can get right away t' country an' moors! Ay, and new schools, new hospitals, new roads, new life. (*rousing music*) But war's put a stop to all this. Just for a time. When this war's won we've got to re-build all our big towns. All our big towns, like this. (*noise of building*)

VISITOR: Yes, we've got plans for *your* town alright. But who's going to be the bid and say, Jack Clem? Who's going to make them come true?

COUNCILLOR (*Jack Clem*):   They are! You are! (*pointing to viewers*) You're the only folk that can make these plans come true. Not only plans for this town. But for every town. For *your* town. Remember! It's *your* town! (*Facing viewers, and speaking in tone of confiding appeal, his comment that the realisation of these ideas for post-war improvement in housing rests in the viewers' hands has particular force and punch.*)

Balloon Site 568

This eight-minute documentary, in which Dylan Thomas's script is almost entirely in dialogue appropriate to each scene, shows the recruitment of women for the Women's Auxiliary Air Force (WAAF) and their learning to look after a barrage balloon site, an important war-time job we see them do, and enjoying their new life. Dylan Thomas himself contributes as narrator, reading 'Commentary' and 'Commentator'. The film was reviewed in the July 1942 *Documentary News Letter.*[50]

A dress shop assistant (blonde sex-appeal), a domestic servant (practical-Scottish), and an office secretary (feminine-efficient) . . . apply to join the Balloon Service. A pleasant interviewer [but with the starchy middle class voice of authority] warns them the job is tough; but they accept it, wanting to do something more productive than they found in their civilian jobs. After some weeks of training . . . the girls go to 'a place in the country', recognisable to those who saw *Squadron 992*. They get familiar with their floppy elephantine charges. The weird flock of balloons going in to bed makes a striking picture. . . . The girls get along happily with new friends and new jobs. The cheery domestic servant takes to driving a winch; our blonde shop assistant, at a canteen dance, turns down a date – the group is going off to its balloon site next day. It's not an inviting place, in an industrial town, with winter slush underfoot. But they know they are doing important work. . . . The story flows naturally, usually by a dialogue reference to the next stage. This snappy exposition and the good technical quality keep interest alert right through. There is a pleasant sound opening of the girls singing one of their choruses.

Propaganda Value: A job, which the film admits must at times be hard . . . is shown to be an inviting one. . . . The film should bring recruits to the Service.

There is an important wider issue. Women are ready to don uniform and get down to a job which can be tough. We have moved a little since *Squadron 992* so pleasantly mirrored our then conception of total war.

Dylan Thomas accompanied Ivan Moffat, a friend who had introduced him to Donald Taylor and was director of this film, on location. This was at Cardington, a Women's Auxiliary Air Force base, where the film was made. He recalls that 'the lady commandant, a senior WAAF officer, was on a raised platform reviewing perhaps two hundred uniformed WAAFs as they marched past. Dylan and I were both on the platform with her, improbable as that may seem now, and seemed then. Dylan turned to her in the course of this and said, "You have the most superb body, ma'am" and as she cast a look of reproof at him, added, "of women".'[51]

DIALOGUE FOR BALLOON SITE 568

Song over titles: 'At six o'clock in the morning, they made me greet the day, and after cleaning up the huts to the cook-house I made way. When the breakfast it was passed to me it made me rue the way that I became, a patriot to help to win the day.'

(MUSIC)

COMMENTARY: Jean Selby, Shop Assistant.

(TRAFFIC)

Ruth MacDonald, Housemaid.

(CLOCK CHIME)

Pat Baker, Secretary.

(TRAFFIC)

Myvanwy Thomas, Barmaid.

(CONVERSATION IN BACKGROUND)

RECRUITER: Good morning, will you sit down.

BARMAID: Thank you. I want to join the WAAF as a balloon operator.

RECRUITER: Good. What is your age and occupation?

TYPIST: Twenty-two. I'm a stenographer.

RECRUITER: You want to be a balloon operator do you?

HOUSEMAID: Yes. I wanted to do something much more worth while than being a housemaid.

RECRUITER: It's hard work, you know. Out of doors in all weathers and needs physical strength. Think you could stand it?

SHOP GIRL: Yes, it's that sort of work I want.

RECRUITER: Fine, and we want girls like you to man the balloons and to release as many men as possible for other work. If you pass your Medical, you will go to learn how to handle and repair balloons at a Training Station in the country.

(SINGING ON ARRIVAL)

CORPORAL: You lot together?

Yes, Corporal.

Right. B hut on the left. Oi, you've got the rest of the day to get fixed up in there, you start your basic training tomorrow.

LECTURER: Right, is that clear?

CLASS: Yes.

LECTURER: So don't run away with the idea that your balloon is intended to bring down a Nazi bomber every night of the week. What it will do is to make bombing inaccurate by keeping the 'planes high, and more important still, cut out low level attacks and dive bombing altogether. Any general questions?

HOUSEMAID: Yes. What decides whether a balloon stays up or down?

LECTURER: Partly the weather, but generally it is decided between Balloon Command and Fighter Command.

NEW LECTURER: Do you think you could repair a balloon yet?

GIRL: No, not yet.

ANOTHER GIRL: When do we use these emergency repairs anyway?

LECTURER: Should your fabric get torn, when you have had orders to raise your balloon you will carry out an emergency repair. You have got to know how to repair your balloon on the spot. Is that understood?

CLASS: Yes, sir.

ROPE LECTURER: This knot's known as the sheep's bend. Have you got it?

BARMAID: Yes, is that right?

LECTURER: That's correct. Now show me where it's used on the balloon.

BARMAID: I think it's used there.

LECTURER: That's correct, right.

TYPIST: I find it cuts a bit.

WIRE INSTRUCTOR: Yes, well of course you will at first, but you've got to be able to learn how to splice wire, otherwise you will be in a bit of a fix if anything goes wrong when you get on your warsite.

WINCH INSTRUCTOR: When you are on your warsite you will have to maintain your winch.

HOUSEMAID: Can we see it work?

INSTRUCTOR: Yes, just a minute. When we have been round this model, we will go outside and see the actual winch in operation. Start up winch!

(WINCH NOISE)

HOUSEMAID: Start up winch.

GIRL'S VOICE: Port side ready.

INSTRUCTOR: Stop winch.

GIRL: Stop winch. Balloon flying thirty feet, tension four hundredweight, no slack on drum. Start up winch. Haul in winch third gear.

INSTRUCTOR: Stop winch. Hard on that tail guy. OK, come on, take her to bed.

(VOICES SHOUTING IN HANGAR)

SHOP ASSISTANT: Are you going to the dance tonight, Pat?

PAT: Yes, are you taking anyone?

SHOP ASSISTANT: Well, you know Jack the Corporal who took the wire class, I asked him to come along at 7 o'clock.

(JAZZ MUSIC)

CORPORAL: How about coming along to the camp cinema tomorrow night?

GIRL: No good, sorry. We will be on duty for three weeks at our practice warsite.

OFFICER: Well, now you have arrived on your practice warsite. As you can see for yourselves, conditions are not likely to be particularly comfortable. You will have to turn out at all hours of the day and night and in all sorts of weather conditions. You will be half frozen, you will be ankle deep in mud, you will bed your balloon in a gale. If you get through this alright, as I know you will, you will be ready for the worst site in the whole country. You may be in a town among people, I hope you will be, or by yourselves in the country, but either way, the job is the same and it is a vital one.

(TRAIN AND FACTORY SOUNDS)

COMMENTATOR: Warsite 568.

VOICE: Port side ready, tension handling guys, slips and bags.

HOUSEMAID: This is too much like work before dinner.

BARMAID: That's right. Here comes the ration van.

HOUSEMAID: Thank heaven for that.

WOMAN OFFICER: How's everything?

TYPIST: Very well, thank you ma'am.

OFFICER: Right, the rations are just coming up.

TYPIST: Thank you. Hello, what have you got?

RATION GIRL: I've got your dry rations.

TYPIST: Thank you.

SERGEANT: Where's Selby?

TYPIST: She's up having tea with the people who are looking after her, Mrs Jarvis.

SHOP ASSISTANT: Well, thanks very much Mrs Jarvis. I've enjoyed myself a lot.

MRS JARVIS: That's right my dear, come back tomorrow and I'll have a nice hot bath ready for you.

BARMAID (*singing*):   They fitted me in uniform and put me on parade, when a great, fat hefty Sergeant . . .

SERGEANT: Quiet everybody, I said quiet. Operational orders, balloon skyward 2,000. Come on everybody, crew out.

Grumbling and muttering.

(WINCH SOUNDS. MUSIC)

BARMAID: Start winch, off handling guys slips and bags.

CEMA

In a 1942 letter to the actress Ruth Wynn Owen, whom Thomas met in Bradford that year when she was with a touring company and he was making a film documentary about the theatre in war-time, Dylan Thomas writes, 'Your letter came just after seeing you on the films, you with your wand, showing a ladderless leg in the wings.'[52]

Dylan Thomas was probably on location for the filming of the rehearsal of *The Merry Wives of Windsor* by the Old Vic Company which was touring provincial theatres, and this reference to 'wand' suggests the fairies in the play's final Windsor Park scenes. Bolton was the chosen location as they 'wanted to film a rehearsal with smoking chimneys in the background'.[53]

Other locations include an industrial town's first exhibition of paintings by living artists, and the Jacques Symphony Orchestra playing the first movement of Tchaikovsky's Piano Concerto in a factory canteen. The closing comment by the Soldier concerns a harp trio playing Vaughan Williams's arrangement of 'Greensleeves' in a village church. Following the documentary style a variety of settings in different parts of the country is chosen to show a united Britain enjoying the arts in war-time.

Later in the same letter lamenting a grey London, and wishing 'I were on the Halifax moor talking to you', Dylan complains of the Strand Films office where he is writing it, providing a vivid picture in his annoyance but ending with his usual wit and sense of comedy.

I write to you in a ringing, clanging office with repressed women all around pushing typewriters, and queers in striped suits talking about 'cinema' and, just at this very moment, a man with a bloodhound's voice and his cheeks, I'm sure, full of Mars Bars, rehearsing out loud a radio talk on 'India and the Documentary Movement'.

CEMA (COUNCIL FOR THE ENCOURAGEMENT OF MUSIC AND ART) 1942

(Strand Film. Directors: John Banting, Dylan Thomas, Charles de Lautour, Alan Osbiston, Peter Scott, Desmond Dickenson.)

Film introduced by R.A. Butler, President of the Board of Education, outlines the purposes of the Council. The film is rich in picture and sound, taking us to a rehearsal of the 'Merry Wives of Windsor', a Factory Concert, and includes Tchaikovsky and a Philharmonic trio sequence, seeking to give the impression that the workers of Britain are getting entertainment of a high standard, and so too members of the forces on leave. It is very much in the spirit of 'Beveridge' with its social idealism, harmony and cultural aspiration. It also shows the use made of available buildings like churches and canteens in the war-time sense of community. These items of dialogue bring a humour and lightness of touch to the earnest endeavour of the film that is 'Bringing the best to as many of our people as possible to cheer them on to better times!'

(Scene at art show, as people casually look at the exhibition of paintings.)

1ST GIRL: Oh, that's a nice one. I bet it's in Devon. I've an aunt lives there – you know the religious one.

1ST MAN: What is this, the Chamber of Horrors?

2ND GIRL: I like paintings of everyday life.

2ND MAN: 'S'all right, but I like battle-scenes.

NEWTON: What do you think of this one?

3RD MAN: 'S'not too bad, but what's the point of it all these 'ere art? Pretty pictures don't win anything. Not now anyway.

NEWTON: We all know what we're fighting against, but don't you think we sometimes forget what we're fighting for?

3RD MAN: Not pretty pictures!

NEWTON: Yes, but they're part of it. We've got to fight because if we didn't we wouldn't be free. Free to work, to play, to listen, to look at what we want to.

3RD GIRL: I like that (*looking at painting*), but I don't know why.

NEWTON: Well, I'll tell you why *I* like it. Look how the artist has taken your eye up to those steps and then along past these two little figures right out to sea to the end of the breakwater. It sort of takes you on a journey and it's a picture that makes you feel you're going somewhere!

4TH GIRL: I can't draw for toffee.

NEWTON: Yes, but you don't know till you try. You see, it's like using another language. We can all say what we think, but why not try to paint and draw as well. You've got plenty of things to draw; look at that picture for instance. That one was done by a stretcher-bearer in his spare time. That's why CEMA has got the exhibition together, and lots of other exhibitions like it . . . just to let you and me have a chance of seeing what kind of pictures are being painted in England today at war!

(*The 'Merry Wives of Windsor' rehearsal and Factory Concert follows, and soldier going into a church for a concert makes the concluding comment.*)

SOLDIER: When I said to Charles I was going to a harp recital, he said 'What!'

Young Farmers

This script urges that every boy and girl should grow up with love and knowledge of the land, and the film deals first with a school's young farmers' club and shows how its activities may be combined in the school lessons, its accounts worked out in the arithmetic lesson while in the geography lesson the children learn about the nearby country village of Teesdale. We then visit its Young Farmers' Club. The propaganda aim is that children, especially town children, should be helped to 'realise, as this war has already shown, what a great and worthy future lies in the land. We must help them to learn to care for, value, and respect it.' The film was shot in Eggleston, County Durham.

YOUNG FARMERS DIALOGUE

Reel 1

FOREWORD: In town and country young people are learning the importance of agriculture and the land.

TEACHER: As I told you yesterday we are going to spend this morning's arithmetic lesson drawing up the accounts of our school's Young Farmers Club. We enter our expenditure on one side and our income on the other; now, Johnson, you have charge of the rabbits, have you the accounts ready?

JOHNSON: Yes, sir. At the beginning of the term we had four rabbits which cost us two pounds, now we have twenty-two. Our feeding stuffs cost eight and sixpence. The wood for the hutches were made at school, which cost us two and sixpence, because we got it second hand. We have just sold sixteen rabbits, and we have three pounds four.

TEACHER: Good! Now for gardening. That is for you, Mary.

MARY: Our seeds and fertilisers cost us four pounds, fourteen and a penny. The total saved came to twenty-two pounds four and eightpence, leaving a profit of seventeen pounds ten and a penny.

BOY: In July we had a lot of eggs, three dozen, and very nice they were too, sir. They also provided two dozen chickens for the school kitchen, and the girls cooked them themselves.

TEACHER: Good! That means we have produced quite a lot of valuable food. Now that's how we work out our accounts. You see, sums and accounts aren't just things we learn from school books. We couldn't run our club without them, and now we'll go on to the geography lesson. No! No! You won't need those atlases and text books today. Your arithmetic lesson today has been all about our Young Farmers Club, and now our geography lesson is going to be concerned with a Young Farmers Club too, but not ours. I believe that every pupil who comes to this school, whether he is going to be a miner, a policeman, a nurse, an architect, or an engine driver should learn to love the country, to know about the land, and all it produces, learn about plants and animals, and how to care for them, and above all the country crafts and customs. Now here is a country village, it's in the Dales, not very far from this school. Unlike us, everyone in this village has been born and bred on the land. Now let's look carefully. This is the River Tees, quite close to the village.

It enters the valley at high force, and flows on through the Dale to the village of Teesdale. Teesdale has a village green, with the Blacksmith's shop just here. Close by we find the village pump. 'The inn', the church, and the hall where all the village meetings are held, from the Mothers' Sewing Party to the Young Farmers Club.

Young Farmers Club

CLUB LEADER: The Young Farmers Club has been going in our village since 1931, since then I have watched this Club grow, increasing its membership and its activity. Now, as you all know I am not only your Club leader but also a farmer.

Our people have been farming in the Dales as far back as we can trace. We've had the same farm in our family for nearly two hundred years. Most of you Young Farmers have learned to rear your own cattle, and I know that you've made a good job of it. You can keep your animals of your fathers' farm now, and so can you, Tom. What about Dick here, he hadn't got much room on his father's holding, but he brought up a couple of little pigs proper. We are all of us Young Farmers in the Club whether we keep bees, livestock, or just have a potato patch in the back garden. Yes, we're all Young Farmers whether we train dogs like John Anderson, who had a couple of the best in the country, or whether we're just learning sheep shearing or stone walling, but this war, I doubt, has made a bigger difference to us all – to begin with, we have lost a number of our older members, but those who are left know that we farmers are more important to the country now than ever. What's more, the Club has turned to more vital work, such as making silage, so's we can feed cattle in winter, and do without imported food for them. Then, too, there's all the other jobs you've tackled such as hoeing the turnips, planting and growing potatoes so as to meet the increased demand and so on.

Classroom

TEACHER: So you see, their Club is different from ours. But learning to understand life in the country is also one of the most important parts of our education. So that is why I have used your geography lesson to describe this village to you, but there is another reason also, the young farmers of the Teesdale club have asked us to spend a day with them in the country next week.

CLUB LEADER: Now then, you youngsters, I am not going to keep you any longer. Off you go, anywhere you want to. I suppose you will be wanting to see all the things our young farmers are doing. Well, you will find them everywhere doing all sorts of jobs – most every kind of job there is to be done on a farm. Later on you'll be seeing how some of us have learned to judge stock, and know what are the good points and the bad points to look for. After that we are going to see if living in country air makes us better at games than you young farmers from town.

Reel 2

MILKMAN: Would one of you like to try your hand at milking?

BOY: Yes!

MILKMAN: Come along then, you. Let's see your hands. Tenderness is most important in milking. Come along and have a try.

Games (children shouting)

FARMBOY: Well, now that you in the town Club have seen a bit of what we in the country Clubs are doing. Of course we have not had nearly enough time to show you all we do, but we hope that when they get back to town they won't forget us, or what they have seen today.

COMMENTATOR: We believe that everyone, wherever they are, whatever they are, should learn to love the land. The children, boys and girls of today, our future citizens and farmers. We can help them realise, as this war has already shown, what a great and worthy future lies in the land. We must help them to learn to care for, value, and respect it. The land must never become spoiled, neglected, or forgotten again.

Wales – Green Mountain, Black Mountain

This film was part of the 'Pattern of Britain' series, and the synopsis reads:

> Wales is a country of great contrast. On the green hills are the farms; in the valleys the black mining villages. Before the war, in many parts of Wales, young men waited in vain for work; now all who can work are working hard digging coal out of the rich mountains, rearing sheep on mountain slopes which new-sown grasses have made good pasture again – In town and village, in the mines, foundries and shipyards and on the farms, life throbs with work for all. Never again must there be young men with no work in derelict towns.

The synopsis of the film shots describes it as an impressionistic survey of Wales at war.

> Continuity is provided by film of the Welsh countryside, which underlines the imagery of 'mountains' in which the whole film is couched: the balance of the film, which exists principally to illustrate the soundtrack, shows the castles left by the old war (against England), as an introduction to the new war – steelworkers – dockers – pithead scenes from the Rhondda mines – agriculture – sheep farming – agricultural research at Aberystwyth – quarrying – Welsh chapels – children – women (sewing and at the whist drive) – Druids. Film concludes with a reminder of recent Welsh history – the social and economic changes that industry brought to the valleys, and the hardships of the depression, from which only the arrival of new industry with the war brought.[54]

The wide and knowledgeable picture of Wales reminds us that Dylan Thomas, as producer with Taylor as well as script writer, was involved with selection of location shots also. But what is particularly significant is his concern, through the scenes of mountains, sea and agricultural landscapes – a feature of South as well as North and West Wales – to evoke the unity and harmony of Wales at war: a necessary part of its wartime role and contribution. The opening references to Wales's old wars against the English helps establish this historic unity. Certainly it is Dylan Thomas's most many-faceted and comprehensive picture of Wales and Welsh life. In the roots and precision of its poetic power, in its political passion – and the verses on 'the old-young men' are among the most authoritative in English twentieth-century political poetry – it is perhaps the finest of his documentary scripts. I think of such images as how in 'the splintered darkness of the mines. . . . They go down like ghosts in black'; how steel workers 'fight to the rhythm of iron forests thrusting between flames'; in the northern hills 'dogs bark the sheep home'; 'the voices of children playing . . . in the cattle-voiced meadows'; 'churchyards where the stone angels stand cold in front of the sun'; and, aptly for the thirties, 'the power and wealth of the world were rocking, rocking'; while 'the rocks of St David's echo and stand like cathedrals in the spray'. In its many exactly and hauntingly detailed mountain and valley scenes, chapel and industry settings, it is a realistic, often bleak Wales of poverty and struggle, but the ever-present mountain, metaphor of unity, strengthens. The single reference to 'Britain at war' draws attention to how it has called on the 'once-denied, helpless and hopeless men for all their strength and skill at the coalseam and the dockside, the foundry and the factory', adding 'the world shall never deny them again'. It is a resonant moment in the film, as is an early shot when an elderly woman places flowers on a grave with a high memorial cross, seemingly a First World War remembrance of past killing as the commentary runs 'men who would murder man'.

Dylan Thomas's script met some obstacles. It was rejected by the British Council as being unsuitable for overseas audiences because of the unemployment commentary. The Ministry of Information took over, but the film had to go to the MOI's Welsh office in Cardiff, who also thought the script 'unsuitable' – 'Dylan Thomas was not a "real" Welshman – he lived in London – so perhaps a certain Welsh professor might be approached to write a new script?'[55] Fortunately, not to say sensibly, this suggestion was rejected in London and the Strand Film was released without alteration to the script. Fortunately too, though unusually, a Welsh-language version was made.

Such criticisms regarding Welshness he mocked in his BBC Wales broadcast *Swansea and the Arts* (October 1949): 'Many of the artists stay in Wales too long, giants in the dark behind the parish pump, pygmies in the nationless sun, enviously sniping at the artists of other countries rather than attempting to raise the standard of art of their own country by working fervently at their own words, paint, or music.' In his earlier (1946) broadcast *Welsh Poetry* he comments on Welsh writers in English: 'There is a number of young Welshmen writing poems in English who, insisting passionately that they are Welshmen, should, by rights, be writing in Welsh, but who, unable to write in Welsh or reluctant to do so because of the uncommercial nature of the language, often give the impression that their writing in English is only a condescension to the influence and ubiquity of a tyrannous foreign tongue. I do not belong to that number. . . . It's the poetry, written in the language which is most natural to the poet, that counts, not his continent, country, island, race, class, or political persuasion' (*Dylan Thomas: The Broadcasts* pp. 220 and 31–2). It is of course *The Three Weird Sisters* which highlights the political and cultural cross-currents of Dylan Thomas's own Welshness, and certainly the filmscripts, like the broadcasts, demonstrate his (poet's) view 'Writers should keep their opinions for their prose.'[56]

WALES — GREEN MOUNTAIN, BLACK MOUNTAIN

Morning mist glides over Snowdon, over the mountains where men of Wales for centuries fought their enemy, the English, over the castles, over Harlech and Conway and Carnarvon garrisoned by the English kings in the long and far-away wild wars . . . Morning mist over the vale of Llangollen and over the oldest rocks in the world – the ageless, world-backed, morning-waking mountains . . .

And the mist moves too, but yellower and greyer now, over cold, bare hillbacks and violent, grassland peaks, from green to black mountain, from green to grey Wales . . .

Morning is breaking over Wales at war. Not the long and faraway wild war of the mountain Welshmen and English kings, but the terrible near war of England and Wales and her brothers and sisters all over the earth, against the men who would murder man.

In the furnaces of Llanelly, in the roaring cauldrons of the Swansea Valley, in the stamp and clatter and glare of the black and red works where the fires never go out they fight with blinding, blasting rods and pistons, rams, they fight to the rhythm of iron forests thrusting between flames, they fight with the white hot muscles and arms of steel.

In the docks of the South they fight with ropes and crane and hoists, they load the ships to slide into the mined and death-sprung waters, and all the quays are alive, loud with war.

In the Rhondda Valley they fight with pick and shovel and drill, they fight the cruel obstinate dark rock middles of the mountains for minerals and metals. They go down into the splintered darkness of the mines, into the blind propped under-world with horses and canaries. They go down like ghosts in black, only their smiles are white.

Wales is a mountain of strength.

And in the north the farmer drives his sheep over the wind-blown heights. This greener Wales is a strong mountain too. The shepherds whistle to their collies, and the dogs bark the sheep home. A bleating world of wool moves high above the sea and river, over the valleys puffed and threaded with trains that rumble into towns, trains that take the mountain fleece into the distant mills.

It is not only the miner and the farmer, the steel-worker and the shepherd, who fight for peace among their mountains. In Aberystwyth, at the University Department of Agriculture, Professor Stapledon has succeeded in breeding new and more luscious kinds of grass. Out of years of experiment new plants have come to being. New life has grown out of science and from the laboratories, and the research stations' green fresh meadows stretch into the unpredictable distance.

Many of the hillsides of Wales have been sown with these grasses now, and more sheep can live on every acre. High up the sheep graze on miraculous grasses. A new strength has been given the mountains.

But below in Llanberis at the foot of Snowdon, men still work the stones for richness, scaling and hacking those steep hillsides, those high hewn walls that have known for hundreds of old years the rope ladder and the nailed boot, the pick and the grappling iron of the Welsh slate quarrymen. Now on the roofs of buildings in London and Paris and New York, the slates of Llanberis quarries lay under strange skies.

The new grass and the old stone in the mountains of contrast.

The new war, the old singing in the mountain villages, in the squat grey chapel at the grey butt-end of the street, Bethesda, Smyrna, Capel Horeb, Capel Seion, with a hand blown organ or an old harmonium with a wheeze and a cough or in the tall, stern chapel built in the seventies or the eighties as a rock of respectability in the strange new industrial life that went on at the foot of the mountain, the tall stern father and mother of a mountain, grey and bare over the blackened chapel roof.

But the singing in the chapel is never grim or grey. The voices of quarrymen or shepherds, colliers or small farmers, tradesmen from the scorched valleys, or ploughmen from the long fields, the voices of children brought up to play Indians on the slagheaps, or pirates in the cattle-voiced meadows, are sweet and powerful, wild and gentle, as the weather over the mountains or the windlike movements of light and shadow through the high, chill streets.

Here in the chapels of Wales, Bethesda, Smyrna, Horeb, and Seion, the young and the old come to sing and worship. To listen to the poetry and oratory of the preacher, they will come down miles of mountain, or climb up from the sooted valley towns, they come to talk at the chapel doors when the service is over, or in the churchyards where the stone angels stand cold in front of sun and factory smoke, they come to talk among the poorer gravestones with their gifts of valley-soured flowers or their remembrance of wild flowers from high in the unspoiled fields.

On week-days the women meet in the chapel hall, the mothers and the grandmothers, the whist drive and the jumble sale committee; there are concerts and Eisteddfods, the young people dance, and the old, remembering, watch them. Here the bards and minstrels meet, as they met in the Middle Ages, though the lovely valleys of the south where they played on harps and sang are barnacled with smoking chimneys, and clustered with bad streets.

The findings of coal, copper, iron ore and anthracite brought power and wealth to the valleys that had needed nothing but the peace of their fields and the honour of the labour of their own hands. The valleys grew rich, houses spread over the hills, smoke and dust blew over the unrecognisable meadow. The field of brick and steel. The valleys grew rich but all the time the power and wealth of the world were rocking, rocking.

Then the days when the pits stopped, the factories closed their gates, the furnaces died out, and the great sheet of smoke that floated over industrial Wales came down like blinds over the blind windows of the mean streets, came draping down over the houses without hope, over the locked shop and the leaking roof. At the corners lolled the old-young men, or they walked their thin whippets over the dirty grass, or they scrabbled on the tips for fishfrails of coal.

Remember the procession of the old-young men
From dole queue to corner and back again,
From the pinched, packed streets to the peak of slag
In the bite of the winters with shovel and bag,
With a drooping fag and a turned up collar,
Stamping for the cold at the ill lit corner
Dragging through the squalor with their hearts like lead
Staring at the hunger and the shut pit-head
Nothing in their pockets, nothing home to eat.
Lagging from the slag heap to the pinched, packed street.
Remember the procession of the old-young men.
It shall never happen again.

It must not happen again. Already new industries are on their way to Wales, to the Rhondda Valley. The Treforest industrial estate is one shape of Wales to come, but out of the sickening, deadening idleness must come the pride of Labour again: out of the huddle of slum and alley must come the clean broad road and the cool, white house. Britain at war has asked these once-denied, helpless and hopeless men for all their strength and skill at the coalseam and the dockside, the foundry and the factory. The world shall know their answer, and the world shall never deny them again.

For as long as the salt wind blows over Cardigan Bay,
And the Pembroke coast, whitewashed with gulls meets the mountain day,
And the rocks of St David's echo and stand like cathedrals in the spray,
The voice of Wales is the voice of all free men.
We will work to win. War shall never happen again.

Battle for Freedom

This film shows the world in the third year of war, and it stresses the global nature of the war. The new nations of the British Commonwealth fight alongside Britain, Russia, America and China to win freedom for all men.

The film reviews the strategic situation in the Atlantic, Russia, the Middle East, the Pacific and the Far East, showing the particular part played on each of these war fronts. Following the script we see the wide theatre of war. The opening film sequence shows enemy leaders and troops, followed by shots of Commonwealth agriculture (as enemy goals). Film of the war in Abyssinia is contrasted with Commonwealth schemes of education and eventual self-government. The tour of Commonwealth fronts shows troops training, agriculture and industry in South Africa, Australia, Canada, India. The Jamaican Spitfire fund and the neutrality of Eire are mentioned, and such leaders as Field Marshal Smuts are shown, and de Valera making a speech. Shots of the enemy include a Nazi parade with banners and view of Hitler, and Japanese forces advancing. We see Abyssinians attending their injured; there are also pastoral shots such as one of a plough and harvester; a shot of a Red Cross camp with a bomb burst among hospital tents. On the Far East front we see Indian, Chinese, and Australian troops. There are also scenes of shipyard workers, troopships and soldiers waving, and contrastingly a man walking along a road leading a bullock cart; and an aerial view of city lights at night. Later there is an aerial shot of bombs falling and a view of Blenheim, Hurricanes and Sunderland planes taking off. The film features various battle areas including the Russian front, RAF bombing and the defence of the Atlantic trade routes.[57]

In this documentary Dylan Thomas's script narrates and highlights the drama of the battle being shown, though interestingly it advocates both caution ('Today our world faces its greatest danger') in 1942 and determination ('Preparing . . . for the attack which must come'), always emphasising the present freedom and hope for greater freedom in all nations post-war. Dylan Thomas allows himself a vivid poetic image when he speaks of the British coastal patrol planes spying for U-boats as 'the flying sentinels'.

BATTLE FOR FREEDOM (Commentary)

The third year of the Second World War. And loud and savage from their victories, the Axis Powers are now grimly confident that world domination lies within their clutch. For Germany has conquered Europe; Germany has cut off the Mediterranean Basin as a supply route to the United Nations; Italy obeys, stabs and betrays; Japan has torn away the island of the Far East: and Malaya, Singapore and Burma. Already they see, ripe for their picking, the whole wealth of raw materials of the British Empire.

Canada's wealth of wheat, and her vast mineral resources.

Dairy produce from the farms of New Zealand.

The wool, the coal, the pig iron of great Australia.

Tea from the plantations of Ceylon.

Gold of South Africa.

To *their* colonies and protectorates, as well as to their own drugged or chained people, the Axis Powers bring all the advantages of a new civilisation. 'Remember Hongkong!' but remember, too, Abyssinia, Guernica, Rotterdam. These men and women have been protected. Forever. And these people of the British Colonies, without the civilising influence of bayonet and gas-bomb, have been brought new weapons of science to fight against disease and suffering, and have been taught to use them. They have been given new knowledge, new skill, new careers and professions, hospitals, maternity centres, schools and laboratories, a new sense of social responsibility, and a system of training by which, in the days that must come, in the days that are coming, they may achieve full independence and self-government.

They shall achieve that freedom and independence already known by the great peoples of the Dominions, those New Nations made of men and women from all over the world: people from Britain that is still free; people, who may keep their own language and religion vigorous and alive here, from France, that shall be free again; people from Holland, Austria, Spain, and Portugal; people from great fighting Russia; people even from Germany, Germans who have never known Hitler's tyranny.

In these Dominions, their children are brought up in freedom and for freedom, a generation taught to value the best of the old world, taught to become proud citizens of the New Nations, and to ensure that their world is not dragged down into the folly and crime of war.

But today our world faces its greatest danger. Almost at the eleventh hour the Commonwealth of New Nations fight side by side with Russia, China and the United States, with one gigantic determination to triumph over disaster.

The Empire straddles across the whole earth, there can only be one answer to the tremendous dangers menacing it upon every side: fullest collaboration of all its militant effects.

As the storm centres of conflict spread everyday brings fresh evidence of the vital importance to the United Nations of the chain of Empire countries, linking their effort right round the globe.

Out of Jamaica, which has known so many troubles of its own, came the original idea that caused ten thousand troubles to our enemies: the idea of the Spitfire Fund.

Out of South Africa, from the men of different races, colours, ways of thinking, came the will to fight, under the leadership of Field Marshal Smuts, against the enemies of freedom: to fight in the Army, the Air Forces, the factories and the mines. To pour out tanks, and planes and the weapons for the Libyan campaign.

Out of Australia, threatened by the enormous success of Japanese aggression, threatened more dangerously each moment of the dark, dangerous day that is war, comes, the huge determination of its democratically-elected Government to turn out from her factories all the war materials for the invasion that may come at any minute. More and more shells, rifles, guns, tanks and aeroplanes, these are the answers to the great test of strength that Australia must undergo.

Japan strikes! And as the black-out comes down over her unafraid cities, Australia is ready to strike back.

Canada is further away from the immediate threat of war on her own soil, but all the varied life of the vast Dominion is devoted to the struggle. From the richness of her soil comes an unending food supply and a vast wealth of minerals to manufacture the munitions of war. All the free peoples of the world hear Canada's fighting voice!

And from Australia and New Zealand and South Africa, men come to Canada to learn to fight in the air. Imperial strategy dictated that Canada – not Australia – must be chosen as the centre of the greatest air-training scheme in the world. Canada, her only frontier with America, a line drawn on a map: Canada with all the resources of the USA within her reach; Canada, bound to Britain by the Atlantic lifeline; Canada, that has bound herself to fight in the cause of freedom all over the earth.

All over the earth the Axis Powers strike, threaten, and crouch to strike again.

Despite their refusal of the Cripps proposals, the people of India are, more than ever before, determined to withstand and throw back Japanese aggression. For well they know that a successful Japanese invasion would mean slavery – would mean that the certainty of the British promise of India's independence would vanish like smoke. A country which has only recently started to produce from her own raw materials the precision weapons of war, India stands, United and ready, ready to give bomb for bomb, bullet for bullet, in the invasion which she expects at any minute, and which she does not fear.

Meantime, nearby Eire preserves her uncontested neutrality. 'The belligerent nearest to us, Great Britain,' says Mr de Valera, 'has not behaved unworthily.' Nor will the behaviour of Great Britain alter.

In Western Europe, Britain has stood at bay for two years. Now, as the campaign in Russia continues with unparalleled ferocity, so the Empire Allies begin their series of commando expeditions on to the coasts of Europe: a series of small-scale raids that fill the Nazi conquerors with the fear of an imminent invasion of the occupied continent.

And while these raids grow in intensity Russia, still the chief hope of subjugated nations, is desperately counter-attacking, striking again and again to delay the long-heralded Nazi offensive against the Caucasus.

Russia fights for her blood and for ours! And for the Russian, the British, the Dutch, the Americans and the Chinese, Britain's RAF still hammer at the industrial areas of Germany and German-occupied Europe. Each fuel-tank which goes up in smoke, adds to the Nazis' problem of supplying fuel for their offensives.

The Mediterranean, long the storm-centre of world wars! The Mediterranean Basin, where with the Libyan conflict still undecided – the battle roars and spreads.

Allied troops on the deserts of North Africa must be kept supplied with all the materials of war. And every effort must be made to intercept Rommel's war supplies. The British Navy is on the offensive, pledged to sink every Axis supply ship it can find – pledged too, to bombard and blast Rommel's North African ports.

The Atlantic, major source of supply of the United Nations! The Atlantic, where the Axis Powers are concentrating all their efforts, their submarines and surface raiders, to disrupt the supply lines from the New World to the old.

These supply lines that must be kept open, at any cost or sacrifice, by the ships of the Royal Navy guarding the homeward convoys. By the Coastal Patrol 'planes, manned by Empire airmen operating from England, the flying sentinels spying for U-boats all day and night, contacting the Allied destroyers and corvettes to destroy our enemies under the water.

The Pacific, storm-centre of the Far-Eastern war. Here, and in the East Indies, Axis-partner Japan has achieved the most sensational successes of modern destruction. Allied strategy in this zone is to prevent Japan's thrust farther westward, and to keep open the supply roads from America to Australia already cut off from the rest of the Empire.

Sunbathers and surf-riders of Australia's Bondi Beach are manning the guns now all around the threatened coasts. The Allied forces of America and Australia under General MacArthur, will not only defend the Commonwealth – bomb for bomb, bullet for bullet, bayonet for bayonet – but will attack the enemy in his newly gained bases and take aggression back to where it came from.

While China, who has resisted Japan for 4½ bad years, repaying treachery with historic courage, is violently impeding her enemy's westward expansion, through Burma towards the Indian Ocean. Across the Indian Ocean Allied supply routes from the Cape run up into the Red Sea to feed the armies of the Middle East and to link India with Britain herself. Japan's calculated attack upon India, and her threat to the Seychelles and Madagascar aims at control of the Indian Ocean, thus cutting our lines and communications.

But, along the Indian Ocean coasts, from the Burmese frontier right down to the Cape, guns are brought into position to face the enemy, troops are hurried there to meet and beat back the Japs.

And in England now, there are the large Empire forces growing in numbers every week as the convoys bring them over. Side by side with the soldiers of England, learning to beat the Germans at their own blitzkrieg game, rehearsing the tactics, of aggression, not of defence, as the new mechanised weapons pour out from British factories, from the immense plants in Canada and the USA.

The new Nations of the commonwealth side by side at last with Russia and the USA making a New Nations of the world united in a war to the death against the living death of slavery under Fascism; in a total war against totalitarian oppression; in the bitterest struggle of the history of mankind. Liberty against butchery, against the German locust and the mechanised plague of Japanese annihilation.

In England now, the free men of the Empire are preparing to attack; preparing with all their will and skill and strength for the attack which must come.

These Are The Men

'A powerful denunciation of the Nazi leadership for their crimes in "setting man against man", visually based mainly on imaginative re-use of Nazi propaganda, especially "Triumph of the Will" ' – reads the 1943 synopsis, and a more recent comment read 'Brilliant – especially by comparison with much other propaganda. The combination of denunciation and ridicule with broad aspirations, all voiced in Thomas's words, is very powerful and effective; it is very well realised.'[58] The reviewer in *Documentary News Letter* March 1943 declared that 'Dylan Thomas's verse frequently cuts like a knife into the pompously bestial affectations of this race of supermen.'[59]

These Are The Men uses a shortened version of Leni Reifenstahl's 'Triumph Des Willens', a record of the 1934 Reich Party Congress at Nuremberg, produced by order of the Führer. Dylan Thomas's script 'superimposes upon the Nuremberg speeches of the Nazi leaders a set of orations in English in which Hitler, Goebbels, Goering, Streicher and Hess report their sins and mistakes as frankly as if they were victims of one of those notorious "confession drugs" '. The reviewer comments regarding the propaganda value that, 'In its insistence on the essential anti-Semitic and anti-Socialist character of German leadership, the film strikes a blow for clear thinking about the true nature of the war – and strikes a blow, therefore, for clear thinking about what must be the nature of our war aims, if the sacrifice of blood is to be worthwhile.' Edgar Anstey, who was involved with seventy-six documentaries linked with the MOI, similarly highly praises the power of condemnation in the film, though he is finally sharply critical of delay in such denunciation, the Government late in catching up with popular feeling.

It combines political passion and technical ingenuity in the most pitiless condemnation of individual Nazi leaders that has yet appeared in the cinema. Special verse by Dylan Thomas has been superimposed upon Leni Reifenstahl's official Nazi film record of a pre-war Nuremberg festival, and when Hitler, Goering, Goebbels, Streicher and Hess speak we hear, instead of their original words, the ranting of homicidal maniacs confessing the crimes which have bathed the world in blood. The sickening avowals of drug-taking, murder, hatred of Socialists and Jew, are punctuated by frenzied roars of 'Sieg Heil' from the massed storm-troopers. The film shows the ordinary decent, peace-loving men who have been ruined by Nazism . . . the verse often cuts deep, but the film comes too late. Before the war was the time when propagandists needed freedom to expose the Nazi leaders. It is little consolation to hear that the Government is now in agreement with the man-in-the-street.[60]

The film opens with ordinary men going about their day-to-day work, and we see these peaceful men plunged into the horrors of war worldwide, including 'never-lost Stalingrad' and 'the tank-churned black slime of Tunisia'. It is poetically charged, eloquent commentary, a script with strong rhythm, drive and impact.

THESE ARE THE MEN

A Strand production. Devised and compiled by Alan Osbiston and Dylan Thomas from an idea by Robert Neumann. Produced by Donald Taylor. Spoken by James McKechnie and Brian Herbert.

Commentary written by Dylan Thomas

A MINISTRY OF INFORMATION FILM

A German Eagle. A Swastika. The sweep of an arena lined with men. The titles are superimposed: THESE ARE THE MEN.
(The mood of the opening sequence of the film is quiet and slow. From a height we look down on to men baking bread, men going about their work quietly and efficiently, men of no particular nationality, just working men. We see them in the bakery, in the fields at harvest time, on the dock side, on a trawler, in an iron foundry.)
A bakery. Bakers at work. A bread oven in the distance.

A VOICE: *'Who are we?* We are the makers the workers the bakers
  Making and baking bread all over the earth in every town and village,
  In country quiet, in the ruins and wounds of a bombed street
  With the wounded crying outside for the mercy of death in the city,

Through war and pestilence and earthquake
Baking the bread to feed the hunger of history.

(The bakery gives way to workers – workers on the land and on ships;
workers in factories . . . . .)

We are the makers the workers the farmers the sailors
The tailors the carpenters the colliers the fishermen,
We dig the soil and the rock, *we* plough the land and the sea,
So that all men may eat and be warm under the common sun.

(Now we see behind the workers, behind the work they are doing, the
shadow of war. The men are still doing their jobs, jobs that are done all
over the world, pottery, carpentry, sleeper-laying, steel-making. This
is their peace-time work, but we see too what they or their brothers all
over the world are doing now – fighting on every front.)

(Scenes of workers – scenes of war)

We are the makers the workers the wounded the dying the dead
The blind the frostbitten the burned the legless the mad
Sons of the earth who are fighting and hating and killing now
In snow and sand and heat and mud,
In the streets of never-lost Stalingrad
In the spine-freezing cold of the Caucasus
In the jungles of Papua
In the tank-churned black slime of Tunisia.
We are the makers the workers the starving the slaves
In Greece and China and Poland, digging our own graves.
Who sent us to kill, to be killed, to lose what we love?
Widowed our women, unfathered our sons, broke the hearts of our
    homes?
Who dragged us out, out of our beds and houses and workshops
Into a battle-yard of spilt blood and split bones?
Who set us at the throats of our comrades?
Who is to blame?
What men set man against man?
Shout, shout, shout out their name!'

(The bakery. The oven flames fill the screen. They become a Heil of
hands raised in the Nazi salute. We hear the frenzied 'Sieg Heil' of
masses of men and women who crane their necks and push their
fellows, for this is the Nuremberg Festival. From a great height we
look down on to a mighty crowd packed round the arena of a stadium.

In the arena stand two vast phalanxes of Storm Troopers and the Reichwehr. Between the mass robot ranks, three tiny figures walk towards a rostrum at the end of the stadium. A roll of drums raises steadily to a crescendo as the three figures mount the platform to join their fellow criminals. On the platform we see Hitler, Hess, Goering, Goebbels and their satellites.)

THE VOICE: 'These are the men – these are to blame.'

(Hitler begins to speak, to shout in German. Over the German we hear an English voice, a would-be translator.)

HITLER: 'I was born of poor parents.
I grew into a discontented and neurotic child.
My lungs were bad, my mother spoilt me and secured my exemption from military service.
Consider my triumphant path to power:
(The crowd roars)
I took up art.
I gave up art because I was incompetent.
I became a bricklayer's labourer,
A housepainter,
A paperhanger,
A peddler of pictures,
A lance-corporal,
A spy on socialists and communists,
A hater of Jews and Trade Unions,
A political prisoner,
But my work was known.
Patriotic industrial magnates financed me.
Röhm and others supported me.
Later I betrayed and murdered Röhm and the others.
They had fulfilled their purpose.

(The crowd roars) Heil! Heil!

I am a normal man.
I do not like meat, drink or women.

(The crowd roars) Heil! Heil!

Neurosis, charlatanism, bombast, anti-socialism,
Hate of the Jews, treachery, murder, race-insanity.
I am the Leader of the German People.'

(The crowds stamp and cheer with joy.)

GOEBBELS: 'My father was the son of a peasant, my mother a blacksmith's daughter,
But I was cleverer.
After Heidelberg University, I became a writer of plays,
a poet, a journalist. None of my work was accepted.
And this was because the editors and publishers were *Jews*.
Unemployed, Jew-hating, crippled, frustrated and bitter,
I joined the Nazi Party.
Streicher and I founded a newspaper to propagate obscene
lies against Jews and Socialists, and said that the
Liberty of the Press was one of the greatest abuses of
Democracy.
Consequently I was appointed Propaganda leader to the whole of
Germany.'

(The crowd roars)

GOERING: 'I began well.
I was the son of a Colonial Governor.
I was rich.
I became an officer and an air-ace of Germany.
After the war I took to drugs
And twice was confined in a lunatic asylum as a drug-addict.
Then I joined the Nazi movement.
Helped to organise the Storm-troopers, the Gestapo, and the Secret
Police,
And established contact between
The Nazi Party and Mussolini's Fascists.
I am a normal man:
Twice married, twice mad.
Gangsterism, brute force, wealth for the few, cocaine and murder.'

(The crowd roars) Heil! Heil!

STREICHER: 'I am Streicher, a lover of animals, a torturer and murderer of Jews.'

(Still they cheer)

HESS: 'I was one of the first members of the Nazi Party:,
a reactionary, anti-Jewish ex-officer, restless, discontented, a believer in Blood and Iron. As early as
1920 I knew that Hitler was the Saviour.'

HESS: (In German)
'Heil Hitler! Sieg Heil! Sieg Heil! Sieg Heil!'

HESS: 'I became the Deputy Führer of Germany.
In 1941 I flew to England, hoping to arrange a dis-
honourable peace between Germany and the pro-German
elements I imagined I would find in England.'

HESS: (In German)
'Sieg Heil! Sieg Heil! Sieg Heil!'

HESS: 'I was wrong I am a prisoner.'

(Heil! Heil! The crowd roars. We see the massed Gestapo, marching,
led by Himmler, and the crowd of youths who watch the ghastly
parade.)

THE VOICE: 'And these are the men, the young men, the callow boys
Who have been taught the knuckle-duster and the rubber hose.
You are young only once: you could have learned to love:
You have learned to maim the weak and to spit on the Jews.
You have been taught to betray your country and your people,
Your own flesh and blood, your comrades all over the earth;
Young men like you have hacked and blasted
The lands and the homes of strangers who did you no harm,
Burned men and women alive
And left a slug-trail behind you of terror and death.
You obeyed your leader's word.
You must suffer his reward.'

(From the marching Gestapo we go to German prisoners being
marched in Africa and Russia.)

'And the betrayers are betrayed, and the promises of victory
Turn stale and sour under African sun and Russian snow.'

(Dead Germans – frozen corpses in the snow.)

'Where is your triumph now in the purgatories of Stalingrad?
How many of you will never return to the towns and villages you
know?

(We fade out on masses of crosses over the graves of German soldiers.
Back in Germany – the faces of youths and young boys.)

'Some of the young men, not utterly scarred and poisoned,
Who have grown into manhood out of a school of horror,

May yet be our comrades and brothers, workers and makers,
After the agony of the world at war is over.'

(The leaders who have betrayed them, who have poisoned their minds, and who want to spread their filthy doctrine all over the world, stand together on a raised platform.)

'But for those who taught them the business of death,
Who crippled their hearts with cruelty, never, never, never
Shall there be pardon or pity: no hope of a new birth.
They shall be put down: Forever.'

HITLER: He screams:—
'We are the men – Sieg Heil! Sieg Heil! Sieg Heil!'

(The film fades out to a bar of the Horst Wessel song.)

Conquest of a Germ

Sending a message to Caitlin that he'll be late home from the Golden Square offices of Strand Films in 1943, Dylan explains that: 'I'm tangled with doctors and M and B; one doctor is facing me as I write. . . . I am going, as you know, to meet another doctor – someone called Peter Gorer – at the Gargoyle at 7 o'clock tonight. I won't be finished until 6.'[61] A month later he writes from Manresa Road, Chelsea, to Donald Taylor that: 'I was going to hold up M & B anyway, in spite of Elton's demands.'[62] Sir Arthur Elton was supervisor of films at the Ministry of Information and Thomas was then working on his script *Conquest of a Germ*, dealing with the discovery of antibiotic drugs, then commonly known as M and B. As script writer Thomas evidently had to seek the technical information he required, and his comments show the busy and varied activities such research demanded. In his script, too, Thomas makes a point of referring to the searchlights visible from the hospital windows and the many battlefronts where the drugs played their part.

In his 1944 *Spectator* review Edgar Anstey writes that it:

represents a brave and imaginative attempt to tell the story of the sulphonamide drugs in terms both scientifically accurate and warmly human. The film traces the achievement from its beginning with the German-invented Prontosil up to the final discovery of M and B 693, setting the scene within the framework of a single doctor's experience in utilising the discoveries to save lives, at first in hospital and finally on the battlefield . . . this is an honest film which attempts to establish a valid relationship between science and the community.[63]

The film title is followed by the words: 'This picture is dedicated to the Research Workers and Doctors who discovered the sulphonamide drugs. In a short time these drugs have revolutionised the treatment of many diseases. Today they are preventing suffering and saving life on this battlefield.' We then see nurses walking along the corridor, a doctor walking towards the camera and an operating trolley being wheeled by, a doctor examining a patient, preparing a syringe, and a sister injecting the patient. There are also military hospital scenes.

CONQUEST OF A GERM

YOUNG DOCTOR'S VOICE: Yes, this is St Joseph's Hospital. Main corridor. Nearly ten o'clock in the morning. My first morning as Resident Medical Officer, Doctor Thompson, RMO.

Good morning, Nurse . . .

Hope that didn't sound *too* dignified – *too* important. Don't want to make a bad impression straight away, put everybody's back up. Still I *am* important. Responsible for three hundred beds. Three hundred lives.

Wonder what he's got?

Good luck.

Oh, yes, I remember. That case of Harvey's – tumour. Wish I could see it.

On you go. Better get used to the place straight away, don't want to get lost . . .

Good morning, Sister.

Anything doing?

Oh yes, of course. There's a case just been brought in. Motor bike smash. Compound fracture. Brought in late. Why has he been left so long?

Looks like septicaemia. Blood poisoning.

Should have been simple if it hadn't got infected.

Pretty late now.

You might be losing your leg, old man. Only don't tell him that.

There should be *some* way of preventing infection: some way of keeping the wounds fresh until they can be dealt with. Save a thousand arms and legs . . .

Is it going to hurt, Doctor?

Take it easy sonny.

You won't feel a thing.

Sonny. A few years older myself!

Remember how Sister used to frighten you when you were a Casualty Dresser straight down from Oxford? Remember! She was the starchiest, severest, most utterly competent . . . face like a Derby winner too . . .

Thank you, Sister.

Don't think I've got over it yet . . . The way they look at you.

Now you mustn't upset yourself. Only a little fever.

Yes, Sister. Don't like it at all. It's childbirth fever all right. Puerperal fever.

She'll have to be isolated *at once*. The rest of the women are in danger.

Her husband would like to see you, Doctor.

What can I tell him? When a baby's born it leaves a raw area within its mother's womb, which is really a kind of wound – which is what happened to your wife.

But where do the germs come from?

They're everywhere, in the earth, in the dust, in our clothes, on our skin, in our mouths – our throats, and if germs get into the wound they grow and multiply and produce poisons which delay healing. Then they cause blood poisoning.

We take tremendous precautions when a baby is born. The labour is conducted in a specially clean room or Theatre . . .

The patient's skin is cleaned to remove germs . . . clean clothes – specially sterilised gowns and gloves . . . *masks* so that the germs won't escape from the doctors' and nurses' mouths – all the instruments boiled . . .

But we fail sometimes even then.

Perhaps the germ might have come out of her own throat . . . What must it be like to know that your wife is dying . . . Nobody's ever been as near to me as that woman upstairs is to that man now . . .

But can't you kill the germs with an antiseptic, Doctor?

Yes, sometimes, we can use antiseptics, to prevent wound infection, especially in the case of small superficial cuts, but . . .

– But they've got to be used at once or the germs multiply and get under the wound; antiseptics can't reach them there; they can't be injected round the wound; you can't take them by the mouth; you can't drink a disinfectant to cure a festering cut. Perhaps I should have told him that.

Better call on Gregory; been reading about Colebrook's experiments again. Testing the German claims for their new dye: Prontosil.

GREGORY: Prontosil! I wonder what there really is in it. Seems by all accounts to kill germs in mice when it's injected, just like antiseptic, only it doesn't harm them.

Not many experiments with people yet – I wonder, I wonder . . . you never can tell with germs. Medical ideas come to nothing sometimes. And then every now and then – You were up with Stephenson, weren't you, Thompson? He's working with Colebrook at Queen Charlotte's now, on this stuff. Why not take a couple of days off and go and see him. You might learn something interesting.

THOMPSON: Thanks – I will.

I will all right . . . That'll be next week . . . next week in London.

THOMPSON'S VOICE: There are the ones that had only germs – 'm all dead!

Dead as that woman's going to be back in my ward at St Joseph's –

Now for the ones that had Prontosil as well – Okay! Okay! No, there's two dead ones!

Just what the reports said.

Good to see it for yourself. Good to experiment for yourself.

STEPHENSON: Why don't you have a shot at it yourself, Thompson? Our people tell me they're getting astonishing results. Kenny told me about the woman who had a temperature of 104 dropped to normal in fifteen hours. But you can't be sure yet.

You've got to go on and on experimenting.

We can let you have some Prontosil to take back to St Joseph's, then
you can try it yourself.

THOMPSON'S VOICE: I could try it on that woman in my ward!

The woman dying –

What's Colebrook's dose again? Into the vein every four hours day
and night.

WOMAN'S VOICE: O God thy kingdom come make me a good girl
. . . Oh, God!

All over the country there are women dying and crying in this fever.

Babies being born out of agony, leaving their mothers mad and dead.

Surely there must be some way of saving all that death and agony,
surely – surely –

. . . every four hours day and night . . . inject every four hours day and
night . . .

. . . day and night . . .

. . . day and night . . .

– It's working! It's working! It works! *Prontosil works!*

God, to see it with my own eyes.

She's coming out of the fever, she's coming out of death. Now we must
go on experimenting. This is only the beginning.

WOMAN'S VOICE: I've been dreaming, Doctor, have I been asleep?

THOMPSON'S VOICE: Oh yes, it works – Sulphanilamide now . . .

. . . Doctors aren't magicians, pulling universal cures out of their hats.
They've got to work, experiment, research and work together all
over the world.

Prontosil was a German discovery. Then the French thought that it
might be digested in the body into two simple substances, only one
of which was active against germs.

Dr Fuller in *this* country *proved* that this was so, showed that
Sulphanilamide was the active substance.

Sulphanilamide could be produced on a large scale widely used . . .

saving innumerable lives from blood poisoning . . . some germs escaped its action . . . chemists began making other compounds of similar chemical structure to Sulphanilamide . . .

. . . the effect of each was tried on experimental infection in mice . . . a few of these new compounds were found to be even better than Sulphanilamide – *Sulphonamides*!

These drugs will change the whole future of medicine.

How's the pneumonia case, Sister?

Good, let's have a look at him.

Pneumonia's on the way to being over. Sulphonamides can really cure two things now: childbirth-fever and pneumonia. The Sulphonamides aren't any universal panacea, but God, they can cure those two hellish things.

How's your other young patient, the . . . Meningitis?

Remember her two days ago, Sister?

See any difference? Less than ten per cent die now.

Convalescent now!

How many tablets? Twenty-six tablets of M and B – Sulphapyradine.

Good night, Sister.

Good night –

Good morning, Nurse. Pretty little thing, wonder what her name is. Ask Jackson. Irish, do you think? She's nervous. She wouldn't believe that I was nervous too, coming up this corridor. Nearly five years ago.

Nearly five years ago –

Now the hospital is my whole life, isn't it? Or is it?

What's the name of the new nurse, Jackson? The one with red hair. Irish isn't she?

1ST DOCTOR: Heard the latest in the Sulphonamide story? Colebrook's a Colonel now. He's going over to see Legroux at the Pasteur Institute . . .

2ND DOCTOR: Been testing the effects of blowing Sulphonamide powder into wounds on animals.

THOMPSON'S VOICE: I see. If only it works. What a difference it would make to war wounds!

Something *new* must come. Medicine can't stop. In places all over the world there are doctors and chemists working on – what?

They're trying new things now over there on the battlefronts, over there in another world.

And here I'm looking out at the night, and the search-lights, looking at the night lights on the sleeping wards where some people never sleep, looking at the faces of 'my patients'. My world, or is it still?

Time is passing, the leaves of the calendar falling – the war is moving on.

They're bringing up a new batch straight away, sir. It'll be pretty heavy after last night, sir.

The guns are quieter now. Can hear myself think. If I can bear to think. A new batch coming up; stretcherfuls of dead and dying, bombed, burned, blind –

The one way to avert dangerous blood poisoning is by immediate operation; to remove all the damaged and infected tissues right up the front line; but so many casualties are picked up late and don't reach the surgeon soon enough.

We're using *Sulphonamides* as an antiseptic for surface wounds, but for deeper wounds something better has got to be found. Now we *have* got another drug and that's thanks to Fleming and Florey – *Penicillin*!

It looks as though it'll help enormously in the local treatment of wounds.

There'll be lives we can save in war, now, just as wonderfully as we can save lives by Sulphonamides; as we can really cure child-birth fever and pneumonia. Nothing can stop the progress of the cure of suffering.

There'll be poor bloody wounded legs that'll be able to walk again. And hands that can work again.

Dust and dress – shall return to dust and . . .

. . . must be getting tired . . .

Didn't think one man's world could change so much.

A new batch coming – on my way now –

The Unconquerable People

Sending Donald Taylor the script of *The Unconquerable People* in early September 1944, Thomas explains that:

Writing it was made more difficult by my not knowing for what countries the film is intended, nor whether it will be shown before the war is over or after. I have worked on the assumption that it *will* be after – or, anyway, after all the chief countries of resistance have been freed; and so the Resistance story must be told in the past tense: 'we were free; we were occupied; we were maltreated; we made sporadic attempts at revenge; for these we suffered; we learnt that Resistance must be organised; we became a movement; we became an Army; we fought and won. Now we are free again.' Following that rough line, I have, as you'll see, stopped short at 'we won'. I wanted to hear from you before writing the short section of 'now we are free again': to hear whether the treatment is in accordance with the plan we roughed out together. I haven't put in any visual indications at the side of the commentary. You know all the material there is at hand, and I, of course don't. When the 4th Voice begins there is, I remember, a Russian resistance-meeting sequence which would go well. I don't know if you agree, but I haven't *mentioned* underground press telephone-exchanges etc. but have indicated, perhaps sufficiently, in the commentary towards the end where the press etc shd be seen.

Do let me know if it's at all satisfactory: and what to write at the end. Just the 'now we are free again' stuff?

Anyway I do hope it is something to work on. It is in a sufficiently loose form for me to be able to change it around drastically at a moment's notice.

I have quoted the letter at some length since it shows how closely Thomas worked with Taylor on these documentaries, and it is the fullest account of how he went about this work, considering visual material and what such material is at hand, and where in the script it is appropriate. Light is thrown on his working methods also in his reference to the loose, easily changeable form, also in his postscript note that 'On reading through, I see a couple of rather too-literary phrases which I shall cut out in next (and final) version. "Steely sea", for instance. Out!'

But 'steely sea' remained, for in a letter two weeks later it seems a confused response had been received and Dylan Thomas replies, 'I've read through Resistance many times and added a valediction. I can't do more until I know more of your, & MOI, reactions . . . you hoped the MOI would consider making a more ambitious film than they'd intended. This commentary can be expanded, contracted, re-written or thrown away and started again at a moment's notice.' No film was made, nor is there another reference to the script, though there is an interesting reference to the progress of the war in Dylan's last paragraph: 'Do tell me: has V2 really arrived? Here [New Quay] there are rumours.' It was in September the German V2 rockets began to bomb London. There is, too, a postscript regarding the opening of what Dylan Thomas still calls 'Resistance': 'You'll notice I've suggested that we cut out the opening lines "We were free." Surely, "we" weren't?'[64] In October Thomas sent Taylor *Our Country* – clearly a busy time for the poet.

Probably Thomas's earliest use of numbered voices, this is particularly apt for this kind of documentary film. It is a dramatically structured play of Voices as the story unfolds, opening lyrically, then darkening when the Germans invaded and 'the butchered cities bled like animals' and 'the death of children ran like a river'. The 2nd voice tells of collaborators and betrayers, familiar faces, and the drama and rhythmic drive picks up again as Resistance begins, when the enemy took hostages 'And the whole earth/Was our weeping wall.' Dylan Thomas sustains the power of metaphor as individual heroic acts of defiance become the partisan groups of the 'Unconquerable Common People' in the occupied countries – 'An Army that grew up in the dark.' Carefully and deliberately Dylan Thomas names the main countries of resistance, names the many trades and professions of the workers involved, and stresses that all members of a family risked their lives in a 'People's army'. It is lucid, dramatic verse, providing a narrative and celebration of an important arena of war.

THE UNCONQUERABLE PEOPLE

1ST VOICE: We were free.
We were people at peace in our own country.
We were proud

of the land we sowed and the fields we ploughed.
Peace was there
in the harvesthomes of the earth and the simple air
and the voice
of the will of the people awoke and rejoiced
among trees and flowers
to the rhythm of The Riches of the Earth Shall Be Ours.
We were men
who lived and worked and loved in the country then
and the young
corn growing was dear to us as our mother tongue
and the fruit
laden trees would seem to grow from the root
of our hearts.
We were people at peace in the country parts.

2ND VOICE: We were free.
We were people at peace in our own city.
We were proud
of the streets we walked and the loud seasurge of the crowds
and the vast
and single heart of the people beating fast
and faster
to the rhythm of The Will of the People Shall Be Master.
Peace was there
in the thundering workshops of the earth and the hammer-pulsed air.
We were men
who lived and worked and loved in the cities then.

1ST VOICE: Labourers
in another land we were your neighbours.

2ND VOICE: We were friends
of the unconquerable common people from here to the earth's ends.

1ST VOICE: On a day when the birds were singing
and the corn stood ripe in the sun
and the old people busied in their bits of gardens
and children were playing after school was done
and we were working in the fields
near to our home
finding the world and the weather good,
the Germans came

in a black murdering endless unbelievable flood
of iron and steel and flame.
On a day when the corn stood ripe in the sun.
On the Day of Blood.
And our blood ran over the corn.

2ND VOICE: And our blood streamed in the streets.
The butchered cities bled like animals.
Blood poured from the ripped buildings' throats
and the arteries of the hospitals.
The death of children ran like a river
and a generation lay drowned.
Like a disease on fire
the Germans spread over the land.

1ST VOICE: They occupied our villages.
We were numbed
with horror.

2ND VOICE: They occupied our cities.
We were dumb
with grief.

1ST VOICE: We who were free
were prisoners then in our own country
branded and bound in a cage of misery
manacled in a sullen house of hate.
All we could do, we thought, was

2ND VOICE: Wait.
Wait.
Wait.

1ST VOICE: Wait, watching the sun go down and the moon come up
over the earth
the burned and broken earth that had changed, for us, in the birth and
death
of a single day, from a great garden good to live in
to a bloody desert of blindness and a wilderness of madmen.
We wished that we had died
with the others.
We were 'occupied'!
We wished that we had died
with our sons our daughters our wives our lovers.

We were 'occupied'!
We thought the word
burned in our brains like a word in hell.
There was another word.
We found there was another kind of man upon the earth.

2ND VOICE: Collaborator.
Betrayer.
Judas-man.
The scum
and slime
of the damned.

1ST VOICE: They were men we had known all our lives.
We shall remember them every second of our death:
The slimy spite-eyed lickspittle the toadying fawner
the spy of the gutter the cringing informer sly at the street corner:
Yes, we knew them:
They came into their own.
And the one who always sided with the strongest
and the one who always bore false witness
and the scorned genius whose failure had turned sour in him
and who found that his only genius was for treachery
and the opportunist
who took the opportunity to sell his people for profit
and the businessman
who conducted business with the enemy of his people
whining that 'A man must live' while a thousand died
spitting upon his memory . . .
They came into their own.
And we

2ND VOICE: We stood in the ruins of our freedom
not knowing which way to turn,
numbed and dumb in the burning dark
that had swallowed the sun,
infamy on all sides in the shapes of men,
rape and murder in the shape of the German . . .
Impotent in our anger
we thought that the only escape could come
from the firing squad or the gas chamber.
We waited, waited, in that prison of hate
they had barbed around us –

1ST VOICE: But not for long.
Men cannot chain
forever the fury of Man
against their evil
though they break his bones.
Resistance began.
Resistance began
clumsily, hastily, with a knife in the dark
and a stone
whirled on a rope
round the sentry's neck.
The birth of Resistance spurted out
in a few stray shots
in an alleyway at night,
momentary mutiny,
an isolated act of sabotage,
a suddenly improvised ambush
in the cobbled passages
of the locked villages
and then:
there was another word from hell:
Hostages.

3RD VOICE (*a woman's*):   They came to our houses
and took away our lives:
We saw our lovers
dig their own graves:
we saw our husbands and sons
standing against a wall:
we heard the machine guns
and saw our lives fall.
And the whole earth
was our weeping wall.

2ND VOICE: They chained us more tightly then,
and hate beat behind every window like a heart.
And every German soldier, striding down the street,
his rifle cocked ready,
had a companion by his side:
Fear like a skeleton walking.
Fear of the innocent:
Fear of the unarmed:

Fear of the women's eyes:
Fear of silence . . .
There could be no waiting for us now.
It was the enemy who was waiting
waiting for the darkness and the silence itself
to pounce and strike
waiting for the shot in the dark
the thrown knife
the noosed rope from the alley doorway.
But nothing happened.
We had learned our mistake.

1ST VOICE:　We met, then, in the deep woods outside the villages,
in the gulleys of the bare mountains,
by lamplight in the caves we had known as boys.
We met in the cellars under smashed houses
in the unused pit-tunnels
in the sewers of the towns . . .
We made our headquarters in a shepherd's hut
on the height of the hills,
under a broken viaduct,
in a forgotten clearing of the ageless forest . . .
We chose our leaders . . .

4TH VOICE:　Individual acts of resistance, however heroic, are
useless.
The unarmed patriot who pits himself against the armed and
heavily fortified enemy is blind and purposeless.
To commit single, irresponsible acts of sabotage is to bring yet
more reprisals down upon us.
Resistance must be made into a movement of all the
people against their oppressors.
Everywhere in every town and village groups of patriots such
as ourselves have come together secretly and dangerously to
plan the destruction of the common enemy.
It is our first duty to make contact with all other
centres of resistance in the country . . .

2ND VOICE:　To send out messengers
Silent and secret
past the fortress villages
through the minelaid forests

along the trappers' paths
down the gunspiked valley
in the teeth of the enemy
to send the silent
riders out
ghosts on horseback
through the barbwired night
to send the runners
through the dynamite darkness
carrying the plans
of one group of partisans
to the camp
of the next group . . .

1ST VOICE: We are ready
the message would run
with a couple of rifles
and a hundred men
hatchets and stones
clubs and sticks
scythes and billhooks
and bricks and rocks
waiting for the signal
ready to attack
the lorryfuls of guns
at twelve o'clock . . .

2ND VOICE: More guns more guns
more guns to fight.
A convoy goes by tonight.

1ST VOICE: Rip the guns from the hands of the dead Huns.
Slaughter the invaders with their own weapons.

4TH VOICE: Tap the wires
Learn the movements
of the troops
Loot the stores
Fire
the camps
Dislocate the lines
Intercept the despatches
Lay mines

Blow up the bridges
Wreck the trains
Ambush the reconnaissance parties
Kill Germans
These are your duties.

2ND VOICE: Who were the resisters the ones
who did their duty
who slew the sentries
and seized the guns
who swept down ruthless
like a steely sea
on village after village
and set them free
who were no longer
a haphazard company
armed with anger
but a united force
fighting to strategy?
Who were the resisters
the ambushers the wreckers
the underground fighters
the saboteurs the strikers?

1ST VOICE: We were small farmers and country labourers
timbermen trappers who had never seen the towns
townsmen mechanics clerks and tradesmen
drivers of cattle and lorries and cranes
painters of canvasses painters of houses
cobblers teachers thinkers men from the dockyards
and shipyards factories ships and trains
fishermen poets miners carpenters
the men who worked with their hands and their brains . . .

3RD VOICE: Who were the resisters? They were our sons
our husbands our lovers our brothers:
we were among them *we* carried guns
the wives the sweethearts the daughters the mothers . . .
and the old, proud women
we too were soldiers
driving out the Germans . . .

2ND VOICE: In every invaded country our cause was the same –
And the Unconquerable Common People was our name.

1ST VOICE: Poles and Slavs and Russians and Czechs and Frenchmen
guerilla fighters partisans and men of the Maquis
we were all comrades fighting the same enemy . . .
we were the same army fighting in many countries.

4TH VOICE: We were an *Army*, equipped and trained,
who had been fugitive men
an unarmed brotherhood underground
a band of anger in the lanternlit caverns . . .
an *Army* that grew up in the dark
in cellars and slaughter rooms
holes in the ground
sewers and catacombs
in secret places
in mud and blood
out of the living spirit
out of the soul of the dead . . .
We were an *Army* who were once a rabble
of fighters who had only faith
faith in the masterless will of the people
to drive our enemy off the earth –
out of the light of the sun.
We were the People's Army: and we won!

Our Country

Our Country was Dylan Thomas's most celebrated documentary and Edgar Anstey, who belonged to the Documentary Film Movement, provided a particularly informed, not to say combative review in the *Spectator* in June 1945.

All that has been said and written about the deadening effect which official sponsorship might have upon the arts is challenged by *Our Country*. Here is a film made to the order of the Ministry of Information which is much too boldly experimental to have been sponsored by an exponent of private screen enterprise. . . . Commercial speculators of the film industry venture only upon the more familiar and well-trodden corners of the documentary field, but *Our Country* breaks free from the bonds of narrative continuity and surface-skimming clichés of normal commentary and plunges into visual impression and poetry. The film was designed as a portrait of fighting Britain for foreign consumption. It [the film] consists of a series of episodes bound together by the journey of a merchant-seaman on leave who wanders observantly over bombed London, the hopfields of Kent, the revelries of a country harvest, the forestry camps of Scotland, the urban intensities of the industrial North. In Wales a class of schoolchildren wish him good morning in their native tongue . . . in Kent a buxom woman darns his socks, he helps with the harvest and hears a Welsh choir; he watches fishermen argue . . . from a girl in a blitzed city he hears and sees conjured up an account of the passing terrors of the local blitz.

Our country represents the most exciting and provocative film . . . for many a long day.[65]

The film certainly fulfils what Donald Taylor had in 1941 highlighted as the aims of these documentaries – both to enable people in this country 'to see on the screen the fine part their native land is playing in helping to win the war' and to 'make people all over the world . . . appreciate for what we are fighting'.[66] *Our Country* was originally made for distribution in the

USSR. The first commentary by Stanley Holloway was rejected, and the request to write the final commentary went to Dylan Thomas.

The originality of Thomas's script and the new and fresh view of Britain projected in the documentary may have prompted the use of an 'Introduction' spoken by an American serviceman based here (and written by Sam Spewack). He emphasises it is the response of somebody new to the British scene – as of course would be the case of audiences abroad.

> The picture you're going to see . . . is a picture about Britain – about its country and its people . . . it is . . . a privilege to see Britain in war-time. . . . For the things in this picture are real – that is the people are real and the scenes are real . . . their [the cameraman and director] job was to record things as they happened, not to make them up . . . there is a sailor in this picture. . . . You see his ship, you meet his friends. You follow him through farms, through factories . . . this man's journey was necessary – how else could he show you Britain in celluloid?

John Eldridge was director, Donald Taylor the producer, both friends of Thomas and well acquainted with his work, and this film particularly illustrates the creative relationship between script writer and film technicians – as in this case the fusion of a poetic, impressionist script and the cinematic realism of the visual narrative, particularly in its direct relationship with Britain at war. Thomas was very aware of this, as we shall see in comments in a letter on this script. Thus the casting of a sailor who travels the country, and through whose eyes we see it, was an interesting one. He was a merchant seaman who had already been torpedoed three times and was on sick leave after his last torpedoing when asked to play the part. More than once he was lost at sea in an open boat, and he returned to active service after making this film. The Sheffield girl was released from her war work for this film, Eldridge spotting her there while she was talking in the street to a friend.[67] In the documentary tradition, too, the people we see, whether at work or relaxing, are the real face of Britain at war. Opening and closing shots of the sea evoke it as a defence, while Blitz shots of ack-ack guns, the interior of an iron foundry, the making and polishing of guns, Rhondda coalfields with Welsh choral singing, dark skies lit by searchlights and planes demonstrate the presence of war through the land – as does Dylan Thomas's script, for 'he overflowed with illustrative or interpretative ideas'.[68]

One of Dylan Thomas's most fascinating letters was written to Donald Taylor on his *Our Country* script, particularly the cuts 'in the verse-commentary' which Thomas accepts from the film production needs, but notes that it 'did affect the continuity of the verse'.

I'm sending you the words of *Our Country*. I took away a typed copy but, as most of the corrections to be made were only of punctuation, I made such a mess of the typesheets I decided to write out the whole thing afresh. Going through it, as I did, carefully, it's my opinion that it may be a mistake to have the words printed in the premiere programme. For two reasons. First: the cuts you made in the verse-commentary, which, from the point of the film, were essential, did destroy some of the continuity of the verse *as verse*. The words were written to be spoken & heard, & not to be read, but all the same there was in the original version – before your most necessary cuts – a literary thread, or, at least, a sense-thread, which is now broken. And, second: I think that, to many people, a reading of these words before the film will suggest an artiness that is not, I think, in the film. If, for instance, Alf Burlinson, who is loud in his praise of the film and of the verse (inseparable we hope), had first of all seen the words written or printed down his reactions to the film would, I think, have been different. Written down, the verse looks a little chaotic – as it's bound to be. And, to Alf and others, 'modern'. Heard spoken to a beautiful picture, the words gain a sense & authority which the printed word denies them.[69]

The opening presumably refers to the film's premiere, but importantly it shows Thomas's awareness of learning and benefiting from film work. His emphasis that his words are to be spoken and heard is so close to his view of the importance of reading his poetry aloud – as when sending to Vernon Watkins a couple of months earlier his recently completed 'Poem in October': '[I] wd like very much to read it aloud to you. Will you read it aloud too? It's got, I think, a lovely slow lyrical movement.'[70] It was of course direct experience of the destruction and suffering of war, particularly the bombing – not only in London but in cities like Swansea, and Coventry and Sheffield (film locations) – that prompted his need to re-create the joys of childhood and innocence in Welsh land and seascapes, our 'Edenie hearts' at peace.

Language and feeling in Thomas's *Our Country* script are echoed in poems on those killed in the air raids such as 'Among Those Killed in the Dawn Raid was a Man Aged a Hundred', 'Ceremony After a Fire Raid' and 'A Refusal to Mourn the Death, by Fire, of a Child in London'. Certainly these lines, with their ordinary, commonplace yet heroic lyricism, demonstrate this.

Then birds flying:
Suddenly easily, as though from another country, over and
around the still, still-living image in the dead middle of
the hit flat, burnt-black city areas killed at night;
and all the stones remember and sing the cathedral of each

blitzed dead body that lay or lies in the bomber-and-dove-
flown-over cemeteries of the dumb heroic streets.

And the eyes of St Paul's move over London.

Characteristically Thomas uses incidents and metaphors from the life of
nature – birds perhaps being its commonest living presence in the city's
streets – to embody roots of healing in contrast to war and destruction.
This excerpt is from Thomas's original script, before the cuts required for
the shooting scripts. (Comparison shows deletion of 'over and' (l2) and
lines 3 and 4. Alteration in some line divisions is also made.) City streets
and pavements become, as in the *Our Country* lines, the cemeteries for
the killed, while aspects of the world of nature, whether light or sea or
flying birds, become forms of redemption.

He dropped where he loved on the burst pavement stone
And the funeral grains of the slaughtered floor . . .
The morning is flying on the wings of his age.

This last line from 'Among Those Killed . . .' is echoed in *Our Country*'s
lines: 'Oh, walking through the streets in the morning would make you
nearly want to sing, though there were people dead under the stones'.

'Ceremony After a Fire Raid', written while Thomas was writing *Our
Country*, has several lines that echo this script.

Among the street burned to tireless death
A child of a few hours
With its kneading mouth
Charred on the black breast of the grave.

And later:

Child beyond cockcrow, by the fire-dwarfed
Street we chant the flying sea
In the body bereft.

In the poem's last section, 'steeples', 'statuary', 'weathercocks' 'luminous
cathedrals' etch war-time London's skyline at night, whether bombed St
Paul's luminous with searchlights or the poet's view from his high office
window in Golden Square (surely prompting the poem's image 'the
golden pavements laid in requiems'). This view was of 'the blitzed church
of St Anne's . . . the weathervane on the spire . . . still intact'.[71] His words
from 'A Refusal to Mourn . . .' – 'the unmourning water / Of the riding
Thames' – may have been a memory of that first evening of the Blitz.
Clearly Dylan Thomas's life, and work in films, in war-time London

brought about, and his our *Our Country* script signalled, the great civilian war poet of *Deaths and Entrances*.

Other lines cut from Thomas's earlier script include the eyes of St Paul's moving over London 'to a thousand histories of men and women on the tides of the platform' in the Waterloo Station section, and 'the faces of the fruit pickers, reflected in the mirror skin / of the orchard at peace / hold peace within them like the unkillable sweetness of / country summer' in the 'Apple picking' scene of the shooting script. *Our Country* has a pastoralism that is both refuge and touchstone of innocence and joy, in contrast to war's constant present and threat.

OUR COUNTRY

GLASGOW

To begin with
a city
a fair grey day
a day as lively and noisy as a close gossip of sparrows
as terribly impersonal as a sea cavern full of machines
when morning is driving down from the roofs of buildings
into stone labyrinths and traffic webs
when each man is alone forever in the midst of the masses
    of men

LONDON

              and all the separate movements of the morning crowds
(Big Ben)   are lost together in the heartbeat of the clocks
              a day when the long noise of the sea is forgotten
              street-drowned in another memory
              of the sound itself of smoke and sailing dust
(Piccadilly   trumpets of traffic signs and hoardings and posters
Circus)   rasp of the red and green signal lights
              the scraped string voices of overhead wires
              and the owl sound of the dry wind in the tube tunnels
              the blare and ragged drumroll of the armies of pavements
                  and chimneys

and crossings and street walls
the riding choirs of the wheels
the always to be remembered even through continual sea
    music
music of the towers and bridges and spires and domes
of the island city.

(*St Paul's*
Cathedral) There is peace under one roof.

And then birds flying
suddenly easily as though from another country.

(*Blitzed* And all the stones remember and sing
streets) the cathedral of each blitzed dead body that lay or lies
in the bomber-and-dove-flown-over cemeteries
of the dumb heroic streets.

And the eyes of St Paul's move over London:

(*Waterloo* To the crowds of the shunting flagged and whistling
Station)   cluttered cave-hollow other world under glass and
    steam
the loudspeaking terminus.

Going home now
going home to a quiet county
going to war now
going to that strange country
going away
coming back to the ten million-headed city
or going away never to come back.

Going out
out over the racing rails in a grumble of London-leaving
    thunder
over the maze track of metal
through a wink and a spin of towns and signals and fields
out
to the edges of the explosive the moon-moved man –
    indifferent capsizing sea.

DOVER CLIFFS

The shape of another country lies so near
the wind on Dover cliffs could touch it with its finger
and from this island end white faced over the shifting sea-
    dyes
a man may hear his country's body talking
and be caught in the weathers of her eyes
and striding inland be plunged again in the armoured
    floods.

THE HARVEST

(*Apple*   Nothing under the sun can change the smiling of sun on
picking)   harvest
the ripeness the sun dust.

War hangs heavy over the apple dangled acres
shadowing the small round hills of the heavy hanging
    fruit.
Only the fruit-loving birds flew once over these treetops.

(*Hop*   Summer is flying along plants and flowers
picking)   through harvest corridors
swiftly over the short country days of women and children
    from city smoke.

They come like a holiday every year
they come to work in the fields
and catch again the flying open Summer in their hands and
    eyes.

In the airless courts and alleys at home
it must last them a long Winter
and a leafless dark Spring.

(*The Fens*   A man may see on the roads he rides
and   Summer and war on all four fair sides.
Midlands) A man may hear on every hand
the voice of the rejoicing land
sounding together with the shout of the guns
and the swooping tons of the 'planes.

(*Harvest*) Outside the kitchens and music
the laughing the loving the midnight talking the resting the
    sleeping
in all the blind houses
outside
the searchlighted night is at war with another darkness
and men who were late at harvest stand cold and calm and
    armed
on hilltops under the punishing rush of 'planes.

THE ROADS

All night long the lorries have roared the long roads.
Now it is dawn.

All night through villages asleep
they grumbled past pond and school and green
oast house or windmill
the weathercocked church and the unseen wind-swung
    inn sign.

By orchard and cottage cluster
the drinking trough in the market square
and the lovers' lanes
they thundered through a hundred
all over the country's strangely singing names

Black Motley White Motley Paddon Hollow
Mintern Magna and Much Marcle
Finchingfield Corfe Sturminster Marshall
Shipbourne and Bredon
Walton in Gordano.

THE MARKETS

The journeying man from the sea may find some peace
(*Here-* and be at home again in the country towns
ford) among coops and hutches and stalls and pens
listening to the noises of farmers and horses and hens
breathing the smell of cattle and leather and straw
on the clucking quacking whinnying mooing market day
and going into the farmers' pubs

that once were all haggling and cider
and once a week news of the slow countryside.

WALES

And a man may journey still within the island gates

(*Aberdare*) through valleys and troules over hills slag-black or grey
as slates
or through fat lovely fields all lying green under their
flower folds
to where Wales waits

(*Rhondda* with hymns and coal and castles and tinplate
Valley) pithead and ploughland and ricketty streets
grit wind in the mine mounds
snow over the rough mountain hair
meadow and chapel and huge bitten sea coast
humpbacked irontracked bricked over smoked out
spreadeagled
bundle of valleys:
the valley's voice.

The voice of the pick in the hand hewn seam
the hunger born pit boy and blind pony
denial of defeat
the grief-fed country's furnace
the fire in men:
the valley's voice.

THE BUS RIDE

Take any direction any road up or down
the island alters round every village corner
at every turn of a town.
Take to the woods
or the slow lanes drenched with quietness and leaves
or to the climbing roads above the valleys
where the bright plaits of the rivers weave:
the weaving island leads all ways
calls a man down from the windblown sky-touching
island height
to the towns in the bowls of smoke

(*Sheffield*)   the clamorous galleries and metalscapes of mechanised
night.

THE GIRL'S STORY

Night after night, night after night, walking back from the
factory all alone, all alone, and then the warning going,
and looking up at the sky just like someone looking up to
see if it's going to rain to-night, quite calm you'd think
from looking at me but running home all the same because
you never knew you never knew if there wouldn't be a
whine and a scream and a noise like the whole town
blowing up and then suddenly all the houses falling down
on you and everybody you knew lying all dead in the street.
And suddenly the lights would be out, and then, this is the
end of the world I would say to myself, in case the others
heard, though they were thinking it too in the dark. This is
the end of the world. And you were dead as well.

And then we'd grow alive again, slowly, just like blind
people creeping out of a cave into the light at the very
beginning of the world. And you were alive. And when the
morning came it was like Spring in the middle of the
Winter.

Oh, walking through the streets in the morning would
make you nearly want to sing, though there were people
dead under the stones, or people not dead, sing because
the world was alive again in the daytime, and I was alive,
and you were alive.

THE TRAIN JOURNEY

(*Berwick*)   The train is racing the trees to Scotland
racing the towns that fly by like snowflakes
racing the rest of the world to the Highlands
sunrise and sunset over the rainy lakes.

(*High-*   TIMBER FELLING
lands)
Here near at one island end, the north fringe,
walk deep through the forbidding timber temples
count the Samson pillars fall

the thwacks of the wood-and-wind-splintering axe
crack of the trunk-shorn boughs
shuffle of leaves
the suddenly homeless birds' tree-call.

Forget for a second the beckoning sea
that lies at the end of the journey,
commanding your coming back
behind each fated tree.

ABERDEEN

To end with
a quayside
a fair grey day
with the long noise of the sea flowing back
as though never in factory or harvestfield
market or timber temple street or hill
it could have been forgotten
for a moment of the tidal movement of man's time
with the call of ships
the monotonous sea voice of the beautiful scavenging gull
the salt smell strong as sunlight
grease on the deck
the facing of the sea.

To end with
the faces of fishermen.

Fuel for Battle

Pit Production Committees were first set up soon after the fall of France, so urgent was the need to increase coal-production – an essential and key fuel for battle. In 1942 these committees were re-organised, consisting of 8–10 members, half from the management and half from the miners. They met weekly, discussing a previously circulated agenda. For the first time the miners' side had an opportunity to make suggestions for the improvement of output. This is the theme of Thomas's film.

John Eldridge, the director, and his film unit spent a day down a Durham pit, one particular coal-face at their disposal. The coal-face became a sort of studio for the day. They arrived before 5 am and left at 10 pm. At one point it seems the cameraman, Jo Jago, was lying on his stomach in several inches of water, shooting the coal-face. All around him the pit props were creaking and groaning as the roof gradually gave way. 'Don't worry', said one of the miners, 'the roof will last for at least five minutes!' It did, in fact it lasted another hour before it fell in.[72] Certainly the shots of working miners vividly convey the dangers and conditions of their work, implying their heroic contribution to the struggle for victory. That it is parallel to that of soldiers serving at the front is one of the themes of this documentary film: 'What's the good of having an army if you got no coals for munitions? What's the good of putting a gun in a boy's hand, when he can help the war better by using a pick.' Linked with this in the script is the fact that local young men preferred the adventure and glamour of joining the forces to working underground in the pit 'because that's the only work they've grown to understand. … How can we tell 'em they're doing a proper job of work? They want to be soldiers and fighter-pilots.' Many joined the Durham Light Infantry, a local regiment. In the film wives and mothers are encouraged to persuade their sons and husbands: 'they've got a job to be proud of … they're working … and fighting … as hard and as well as anybody anywhere … all their brothers and friends who are soldiers are proud of them, too'. The urgent need for coal brings to mind the 'Bevin-boys', the plan whereby young men could be drafted down the mines rather than doing national service.

In the opening scene of the film the young soldier Jim arrives home on leave and hears from his mother of Tom's excitement about the new Pit Production Committee. The conversation recalls the previous conflict between miner and manager during the pre-war years of industrial dispute and strikes. This is what they've been fighting for for years and, Ned argues, the miners must continue to have their say. As is usual in the documentary, the presentation of war-time reality in the setting up of Pit Production Committees is focused by reference to the wretched conditions of the pre-war years for miners – here through the experience of the younger miners now needed for war production: 'They're the youngsters that remember their own dads starving. They've been brought up on the dole 'alf of them.' The young soldier on leave confesses to his girlfriend the attachment he has now learned for his own mining community: 'You and me wanting to set up home after the war in this black old place. We were born 'ere, Mary. Not like strangers. You get used to the slag 'eaps and pit 'eads. ... All that's part of us', the script again turning to post-war life.

The film was made in collaboration with the Ministry of Fuel and Power, and its story turns on a special mines' week competition where the small, hand-worked pit – the one featured – challenges a neighbouring modern, all mechanical pit in a competition to produce the most coal. The small pit wins. Dylan Thomas may have remembered this script when three years later he wrote *The Three Weird Sisters*, a feature film set in a Welsh mining valley.

FUEL FOR BATTLE

NED: So long!

MAY: So long, Ned.

JIM: Hallo ... .. anybody at 'ome? Hullo May.

MAY: Jim! Why didn't you say you were coming 'ome lad? Eh, it's nice to see you. Now put you things down and we'll have a nice cup of tea. Now tell me all about yourself .... where you've been ... .. what you've been up to and everything.

JIM: No, no. You tell me. How's Dad and Tom? You're lookin' fine.

MAY: Oh everything's the same here .... Dad's still grumbling you know ... funny to call him Dad when he's only Dad-in-law. Tom's all P.P.C. – P.P.C. this and P.P.C. that –

JIM: P.P.C.?

MAY: Pit Production Committee. You know .... proper committee. Manager and a couple of under-managers and three of us. They're all together now, Dad, Mr Bradshaw, Tom and all the men.

JIM: Manager and Dad .... altogether? Dad'll .... Dad'll bite 'is bloody 'ead off ....

MAY: Oh, old Dad's awful. Mind they get on together. I don't understand it, but they have meetings and meetings and .... How long 'ave you got, Jim?

JIM: Seven days ..... seven whole days. Seven days with Mary. How is Mary?

MAY: Waiting for you.

JIM: Mary! Look down there Mary. Funny place to live in. And funny to want to live in it too, I suppose. You and me wanting to set up home after the war in this black old place. We were born 'ere, Mary. Not like strangers. You get used to the slag 'eaps and pit 'eads. Seeing that old smoke always. All that's part of us. And the people to speak to and know. To work with and live with, and know what they think about things. ... ... And seven days go ... just like that.

NED: Well .... the army's taught tha' summat, Jim. When tha' left here tha' couldn't 'it the parish tha' were born in. Could 'e Dad?

TOM: What's he doing in the army, anyway? What's he doing there? Production's down isn't it? They want more coal, don't they? So they say ... 'We'll take the best lads you've got, and turn 'em into soldiers.'

JIM: We've got to have an army, Dad .... to protect chaps like you. So's you can grumble your 'eads off.

TOM: I'm not a grumbler .... I'm a shouter. 'Bout time somebody shouted too. What's the good of having an army if you got no coals for munitions? What's the good of putting a gun in a boy's hand, when he can help the war better by using a pick. What's the good ......

JIM: What's the good of asking us questions? We can't do anything …. . Not Tom and me. That's for the others to decide.

TOM: What others? We're the miners ….. We're the chaps who stand to lose. Ah, but we got a committee now. P.P.C. we got a say now in not only what 'appens to us but the pits we work in. An' how we can put up production and help to win the war for us.

NED: You'd better come on home. Or there'll be no supper for us.

VOICES: Ay. Production's gone down alright. It's that damned Harton seam agen etc. etc.

MANAGER: And the next thing is an appeal from the regional fuel controller for a special drive in all Durham Pits for one week. You know … so's we can hit the target proper this time … Well, what about it?

CHATTER

MANAGER: Close the window will you?

CHATTER

MANAGER: Well, what about it? Floor's yours Tom. Go ahead.

TOM: Well, Mr Chairman. What I want to say is this: all of us here in this pit and all over Durham too – ay, and in every pit all over the country – we're going to do our best. We're going to see we get that target.

1ST MINER: Ay, Tom tha's right. But only if …… …

2ND MINER: Ay, we'll try to get the target but I think …..

TOM: It's no good – no good at all – just asking the chaps to slog 'arder. They'll do it alright, we all know that; they'll work like hell for the target. But we've got to see to it that they keep that output up for more than a week. We'll have reports on all the seams and the Harton Seam in particular.

MANAGER: We've got the figures on all the seams, Mr Davidson.

DAVIDSON: Harton Seam – 240.

NED: By gum, the tubs are running badly today. How many have you got full?

MINER: Five.

NED: You've done better than me – I've only got four.

MINER: We'll not get much pocket money out of that. It's always the same when we're working in Harton Seam.

NED: Nobody seems to care whether we get owt or nowt here. There's not another seam in the whole county where conditions are so bad. There's Busty and Brockwell and t'other seams ..... They're alright. They can get all the tubs they want. No wonder their output's well up.

MINER: We can't go on like this ... . working our legs off and getting nowt for it. It's about time production committee went into job.

DAVIDSON: Total output 10,440. 156 tons below target figure.

TOM: Well ... I propose that the Harton Seam be examined real thoroughly. No skimping. The chaps are complaining of shortage of haulage and shortage of belting and bad roofing. We think we could get another 500 tons out of the Harton Seam if these things and lots of other ones were seen to. So if the Committee agrees I'll call a meeting of all the men to discuss .... Investigations into all the pits here.

MINER: What about the Harton Seam? What power has Pit Production Committee got? Has it got any at all?

TOM: The Harton Seam's the one we're going to talk about most.

CHARLIE: Now I'm a filler .....

MINER: Well, who'd 'ave believed that!

TOM: Give 'im a chance. Give 'im a chance. He's as much right to talk as anyone.

CHARLIE: One of the chaps as earns big money.

LAUGHTER

TOM: Quiet .... quiet .... quiet please. Let's hear what he's got to say. Go on Charlie.

CHARLIE: I can't fill all the coals I could .... there ain't the tubs. Now I want to get out as much coal as anybody 'ere. But you can't send it up in buckets. Papers say we're afraid to fill too much coal in case we earn too much and have to pay Income Tax. Well Income Tax money's been getting less. Now I were idle half the shift this morning. We filled eighty tubs in the first half of the shift, and then no more. We could've filled another eighty tubs – Another thirty tons and more money in my pocket.

(LAUGHTER)

But you can't fill your pockets if you can't fill the tubs, can you? Gaffer says there's no room for more tubs on that face. Well I say there is if they'll put in more haulage power and make the set bigger. Perhaps it'd cost a bit to do it but if it's coals they want they can get more coals if we're given something to fill 'em in to.

NED: And I can answer t'other question. The one about what power our committee got. When I hear us pitmen talking like this I begin to think the things I've been believing for the last thirty years is wrong. There's been a lot of talk about miners not having their say. Well they got it. We all got it and we got to show that what we said all those years is right. We always wanted and shouted for a hand in the working of the pits, and now we've got the beginnings of it, we must show 'em how we can use it. We mustn't throw that away. And this is not the time to talk about 'If the Pit Production Committee's perfect – we know it's not. But what about the best and quickest way of getting the coals to win the war?

End of Reel One

TOM: Ay, everything's lovely here, isn't it. Except that the roofing's bad. You can't get the tubs up without a hell of a lot of trouble. Can't clear the loose coal off the face and cutter can't get on with his job.

MINER: Well what do you think we can do about it?

TOM: Take grippers off work that's not so important and get 'em to do some timbering. That's what.

MINER: You can't do that.

TOM: Can't do it! .... let me try. I'll get 'em.

MINER: O.K. You try.

TOM: Just a minute, lads ... I want to talk to you. Things aren't going so well in Harton, and we shall have to stop work unless we can get some more timbering done. Deputy says he can't get the men but what about us doing it? I know it's not our job, but somebody's got to do it.

TOM: That's where I want it Joe.

JOE: Oh, I see. Jock, you go under the face and set some timber. Jim, you go back to the landing and get some more props and planks.

TOM: That's the third time this week ..... just because those boys are so damned careless.

NED: Ay, I know it were only just a small fall but it held up everything for an hour. A whole hour. I know .... I know .... an hour doesn't sound much, but it might mean a 'undred tons or more. You say it was nowt, but a bit of carelessness. It's easy enough to say that. What matters is there needn't be any carelessness at all if only those lads'd take a bit of pride in their work. They've got to be craftsmen .... don't forget that ... Ay and proud of it too. Dad knows. They're the youngsters that remember their own dads starving. They've been brought up on the dole 'alf of them. And then in the pit, because that's the only work they've grown to understand. They don't go down because they want to. How can we tell 'em they're doing a proper job of work? They want to be soldiers and fighter-pilots. Why there's some of them think they're wasting their time, just heaving coal. Somebody's got to tell 'em they're not. I can't give them a bit of a lecture .... they'd spit in my eye .... and quite right too.

MAY: They would listen to us, Mary. Tom's going to say it's none of our business. It is .... it's our lives too. If only one of us could tell all the women in the town to ... to talk to the boys and ... and ... tell them they've got a job to be proud of. That they're working .... and fighting ... as hard and as well as anybody anywhere. That all their brothers and friends who are soldiers are proud of them, too. That they've got a real grand job.

APPLAUSE

MANAGER: I'll put it to the vote. Are we going to accept this challenge from the Walton Pit? That they can exceed the target figure during the special week by a higher percentage than us? Remember they're one of the smallest pits in the county. And they've no machinery .... it's all hand hewing there. But we're all pits. We're all in the war getting coal to win. In favour?

MINERS: Aye.

MANAGER: And next ..... so many of the younger chaps from

Waltons are away in the army serving in the Durham Light Infantry that they're going to call it a special D.L.I. week. Well ... we've got lads from this pit out there, too .... in favour?

MINERS: Aye, every one of us.

COLONEL: On this the first shift of the Competition week, I have a message for you from the County Regiment. It's because we have so many miners with us that the Durham Light Infantry has got the great fighting tradition that it has. Most of you now are older men and boys. We've taken many fine miners from you, but there are a grand lot of miners left to carry on with your battle, which is the same as ours.

CHEERS

MANAGER: Hey, lads, d'you want to hear results? Listen. I've got the final figures for the competition week. We've done alright. We've beaten our target by twelve hundred and fifty tons. Just over ten per cent. We can be damn' proud of that. However, Walton are 760 tons up. They're a smaller pit, so the beggars have run us to a near dead heat. The Colonel's been on the 'phone. Now he wants both pits to go along on Sunday for a joint celebration.

CHEERS

NED: Well, we reached the target. Give the bands a chance to come out and show what they can do.

TOM: Why not? There's nowt wrong in a bit of celebration so long as it doesn't stop at that. Now it's up to Pit Production Committee to go on and hit its target .... not only this week, and next week. And it's up to us miners to see they make a do of it, too.

NED: Aye, you're right.

A City Re-Born

It was in April 1944 that Dylan Thomas wrote to his friend Tommy Earp 'very disappointed I couldn't manage our Petersfield meeting. Donald [Taylor] wired urgently for my help on the rebuilding of Coventry Cathedral, so I had to hurry up and build it in Henekey's', characteristically joking when arranging a later meeting 'There'll be no cathedral-call this time.' But at the end of the following September a visit to Coventry was one of the many excuses for missing his close friend Vernon Watkins's wedding in London: 'I arrived in London [from New Quay] on Thursday, and was sent straightaway, that is, Friday morning, to Coventry: the city of Coventry where the company who pay me occasionally are making a film called *Building the Future*, a subject on which I particularly should have no say.'[73] The film on Coventry – both its war-time destruction and planned post-war rebuilding – was completed early in 1945 and was in fact named *A City Re-Born*. As we have seen, Dylan Thomas enjoyed his trips on location around the country, for all his quips and artful complaints in his letters. Certainly this script proved one of his strongest political texts. His visits to Coventry's bombed cathedral, together with St Paul's in London, also contributed to his poem 'Ceremony After a Fire Raid' written at this time, notably its religious images and feeling. As with *Our Country* there are strong links between the filmscripts and the poems in the evocation of the war-time bombing of cities.

Immediately the story and message of the script is struck: the people have suffered in war but heroically and selflessly struggle on, whether in the forces or factories, enduring the killing at home and overseas in the common resolve for victory. Then come the plans for rebuilding the city. Evidently Dylan Thomas's script of *A City Re-Born* followed the documentary pattern of integrating the immediate war efforts with urgent post-war social and economic change. After describing the war-time destruction of the city, the pre-war unemployment is contrasted with the financing of a full war-time economy, all workers, including the previously unemployed, contributing to the war effort. The theme of how after the war there must be social justice is emphasised in the commentary: 'In war we work together to destroy a common evil – in peace we must work with no less vigour for the common good.' Likewise the chess players in the newly built men's hostel quickly praise their new home in similar terms: 'They've got the proper idea in these places. Makes you think what a hell of a lot they can produce and make if it's for use and not for sale, doesn't it?' Clearly these documentaries provide the history and social concerns of our immediate past, that war-time sacrifice and idealism just within living memory. As the script suggests, such endeavour could not be left to private industry and private profit. In their conversation on the plans for rebuilding the city Dylan Thomas gives 1st Engineer, Arthur, the words and hopes common to his time: 'This is the People's City or anyhow it's going to be. Schools and roads and hospitals and houses and shops, all I've been able to do in my lifetime is to see a proper plan for them on the way. A proper people's plan.' The documentary concludes with a sketch for the planning of new hospitals, community welfare, schools – 'rebuilding the city after the war .... when people must have houses, and these worthy of their courage'. Dylan Thomas's script eloquently catches the spirit of the age:

> It must be, not every man for himself, but every man for the good and the happiness of all people living ... Every man must believe in the good and happiness that is to be shared ... to be shared, equally.

Historically this political and social debate belongs to the day before yesterday, but is resonant today.

The film opens in a railway train going to Coventry. The passengers we hear in chance conversation include a soldier going home there on leave after its destruction in the air raids, Mr Evans, an engineer 'directed' there for war work who was previously unemployed, and a girl also going to Coventry for factory work – her first job. The commentary initially sketches Coventry's beginnings as a monastery, then a medieval guild town celebrated for its mystery plays and pageants, then its modern fame as a great industrial town. The destruction of the city in November 1940 introduced a new word in the vocabulary of mass murder – to 'Coventrate'. But we learn that within a year the city was full of plans for rebuilding, and the city architect's model for the central section of the city is seen, the harmonious and rational plan is expounded.

In the company of the soldier and his girlfriend, who meets him at the station and comes home with him to his family, we see the city, including the blitzed areas and the bombed cathedral. They tour Coventry, giving special attention to finding a house when the war is over. A parallel is drawn with Mr Evans's needs. We see the factories, shots of narrow inner city streets and slums, Tudor buildings and the suburban areas, as well as the building of the new and quickly assembled prefabricated houses. Later we visit one of the new hostels for the homeless and redirected workers, where we see some friends playing chess, and also the Engineers' club where the older men delight in argument and discussion, especially on politics, and with that autodidact's enthusiasm so common to factory canteens, working men's clubs and social institutes of the time. And these, of course, were the places where such non-commercial documentary films were shown during these war years.

Thomas's script shows his mastery of easy, casual conversation, with its sociable humour, such as the war-time joke about 'spam' – (an often-mocked American tinned meat), the chess players with nicknames like Zhukov – a Russian general popular as one of our war-time allies, and the Engineer Arthur teased for his planning zest – 'replanning hell ... Better furnaces for all, eh?' It is a spirited, responsive script on the hardships and sufferings of civilian life in a city destroyed, its perspective heightened by the everyday aspirations for a job and a home of both the soldier on leave after three years on the battlefront and of Coventry's bombed-out civilian workers. It is an informed, vivid documentary, mirroring a time of heroism and called-for post-war reform. There were objections to some sections of the film which had the appearance 'of political propaganda'. These were cut out. The shooting script was revised in January 1945.

A CITY RE-BORN

SOLDIER: It's a game ain't it, excuse me, mind if I get by – Sorry – got half the army on my back!

MR EVANS: Tunnel coming.

SOLDIER: Like a Bank Holiday in the Black Hole of Calcutta, isn't it?

GIRL: I've been travelling since early this morning.

SOLDIER: Eh?

GIRL: I've been travelling since early this morning.

SOLDIER: Where you going?

GIRL: Coventry.

SOLDIER: Eh?

GIRL: Coventry.

SOLDIER: Oh, you'll like Coventry all right.

MR EVANS: Were you there during the blitz?

SOLDIER: No. I was called up before then. Hope they've left the King's Head. Where you going chum?

MR EVANS: Coventry, but not from choice. Been directed there.

GIRL: I'm directed too. Never had a job before. Hope they treat you all right or else they'll have my mother down on them.

MR EVANS: Sending girls all over the place like that. It's all right for us men – I'm a pretty good mixer and I can fit in anywhere.

SOLDIER: Oh, you'll like it all right. My Betty works in a factory there, she's my girl, we're going to get married on my next leave. She lives with my Mum and Dad since her people got killed in the blitz. She says these hostels are very nice places – there's plenty of good food, plenty of recreation and dancing and she says they're very helpful, you can go up and ask them anything you like.

MR EVANS: Oh I don't want to ask much at my age.

SOLDIER: Oh, yes – Betty will be at the station to meet me – she's got the afternoon off – anyway she'd better be – I haven't seen her for three years now – India, Africa, Sicily, Italy …

VOICE: Coventry … Coventry … the train which has just come in is from Birmingham and Wolverhampton. Coventry … Coventry … This is Coventry …

COMMENTARY: Coventry … the City of Coventry … In the middle of England. It grew out of a monastery in the eleventh century.
    It grew into a town that was famous seven hundred years ago for its trade in wool and cloth; into a town of mystery plays, and sacred plays and pageants.
    … Into a town famous all over Britain and in all trading countries for its silks and silk-dyeing, its cotton and carpets and watches, its blue-thread and ribbons; into a great industrial town in the industrial middle of the country.

Into a city of engineering, where motor cars were made, and aeroplanes, and radios and telephones.

A city of spires and towers, an ancient city which produced from its hundreds of factories the newest machines and engines in the world ...

On the 14th November 1940, it became a City of Destruction.

For three nights the German bombers attacked in their fullest force. This introduced a new word into the vocabulary of mass-murder; to – Coventrate.

Large areas of the City were devastated.

The hospital was destroyed.

Forty churches.

Fourteen schools.

60,000 houses were damaged out of a total of 75,000.

1,252 men, women and children lost their lives.

The monastery that grew into a little town. The little town that grew into a famous place of guilds and crafts and medieval ceremony, into a rich trade town, into a great centre of industry, into a burned, bombed city – it didn't die.

SOLDIER: Well they certainly made a mess of that didn't they? Knocked poor old Lady Godiva's statue too!

GIRL: It wasn't in there silly – it was in St Mary's Hall.

SOLDIER: Ah, but I'm sure I saw it in there.

GIRL: No, it wasn't.

SOLDIER: Oh, what difference does it make anyway. I'd sooner see you on a white horse – just the right hair cut.

GIRL: Uh-huh – come on – home ...

SOLDIER: Home, I wish it was our own home Betty – even a pre-fabricated one.

GIRL: What is fabrication?

SOLDIER: Prefabrication dear, you know, you must have read about it in the papers. The parlour comes along on Monday. The kitchen comes along on Tuesday – you hammer 'em together with a couple of nails and wait for the bedroom.

GIRL: And we'll have a car, won't we? One of those cheap ones – there's going to be millions of them after the war – and a nice little garage ....

SOLDIER: And a nice little nursery.

GIRL: You and your nursery! And a nice little garage –

SOLDIER: And a nice little nursery!

GIRL: We'll have our own home soon enough.

GIRL: Come on – let's surprise the others.

MOTHER: Wilf – oh Wilf –

SOLDIER: Hullo Ma!

DAD: How are you boy!

COMMENTARY: For the homeless workers of Coventry and for thousands of new workers directed to the city as war production was stepped up, hostels had to be built. In Coventry thousands now live in these hostels finding a new communal way of life.

SOLDIER: Well you're certainly not starving at home yet Ma – that was a good meal – what was it?

MUM: Spam – Dad says he dreams about it sometimes – says it comes up to him, makes faces and laughs.

SOLDIER: We had a chap in our mob once called Rudolph.

GIRL: What did you call him?

SOLDIER: Rudolph. He said he used to get nightmares about the fags they used to dish us out with. He said his lungs used to come out on his chest at night for fresh air.

MUM: You always could tell the tale couldn't you –

DAD: Where are you settling down after the war? Taking Betty back East?

SOLDIER: No – Coventry's good enough for me – I'm going to have a nice new house with a nice little nursery –

GIRL: Garage.

SOLDIER: And a nice little bit of garden – and who knows Mum – I might even keep a few chickens.

DAD: All right Mum – I'll give you a hand.

MR EVANS: Zhukov's move.

1ST PLAYER: Good evening. Just come? Could do with another player, couldn't we, Frank?

OTHER PLAYER: Ar.

1ST PLAYER: I could beat this bunch of Casablancas in the black-out couldn't I, Frank?

OTHER PLAYER: Ar.

MR EVANS: Nice little place you've got here. They seem to do you very well, mind you it's the first hostel I've seen – but if they're all like this ...

1ST PLAYER: They've got the proper idea in these places. Makes you think what a hell of a lot they can produce and make if it's for use and not for sale, doesn't it?

3RD PLAYER: Lot of good shells'll be after the war ... well, we hope not anyway ...

1ST PLAYER: Oh, well they can produce all the peace things they want to afterwards. Just the same way as food and clothes and houses here ...

4TH PLAYER: We don't want no economic arguments.

1ST PLAYER: I only made an ordinary social remark, didn't I, Frank?

2ND PLAYER: Hahugh – Check.

SOLDIER: This is the first time we've been together for three years – seven days in three years.

GIRL: And I've got to work in the morning – Oh Wilf.

SOLDIER: Ah never mind –

COMMENTARY: The city that didn't die had work and life but the destruction of the city still left a huge problem for the local authorities – the workers had shelter and food – the factories went on producing – but all this was only temporary. Plans had to be made immediately for rebuilding the city after the war – It had to look to a future when people must have houses, and these worthy of their courage.

1ST GIRL: How long have you been here?

2ND GIRL: Two years three weeks and four days – I'd keep a diary only I can't think of anything to put in it except 'got up at 6 o'clock factory 7.30 home again 5 pm'. You know just things like that.

1ST GIRL: Don't you go to the pictures? I like Cary Grant.

2ND GIRL: Oh, he's got dimples –

1ST GIRL: What are they doing?

2ND GIRL: Something to do with building houses after the war – you know – prefabrication. We're going to have a new house when we're married – and it's going to have a garage – a ...

2ND MAN: Where are you going to live. In one of those prefabricated houses?

SOLDIER: I don't know. I don't know much about them. Anyway it won't matter to me very much unless I get my job back.

2ND MAN: You'd all better get jobs when you come back otherwise there's going to be trouble ...

1ST MAN: Prefabricated houses! Chicken houses! A roost for the old woman, and a run for the kids. Pity we can't all lay eggs too.

3RD MAN: You don't know what you're talking about, Arnold. I seen 'em up at our place ... I know about 'em ... Now ...

COMMENTARY: After the war Britain will need millions of houses. After the war there can be no thinking of returning to the good old days, the days of cramped houses in crippling streets; of slums still living on, in a lingering death from the last century; of the sprawling, dull same-faced miles of suburbia, the pathetic attempts of people to escape from the city into the country which, acre by acre, they overcrowd and destroy. And this will happen again if we don't plan.

COMMENTARY: After the war a great number of houses must be built quickly and well. That is why within a year of the blitz Coventry had already begun to design houses which could be made in her factories – prototypes of which are being assembled now for everyone to see. The planners of Coventry know that in their great city there will be available all the skilled labour, the machines and all the facilities necessary to turn out factory made houses by the thousand. This they say will not interfere with the building of brick houses, but will be an additional contribution towards meeting the overwhelming demand for houses that will exist in bombed cities and everywhere else. People coming back from the war – the bombed out – the people newly married and the people of Coventry must have houses and they will get them.

PUB

3RD MAN: I tell you we've got to have them and why call them prefabricated houses – too much of a mouthful. Why not call 'em what they really are – factory-made houses. If you can make a good-looking motor car in a factory you can make a good-looking house.

SOLDIER: There's something in that.

3RD MAN: Here, Miss, that's my beer I haven't finished yet.

BARMAID: Sorry.

1ST MAN: Who wants to be cooped up in a mechanised soapbox? Give me old brick houses I say.

3RD MAN: When I hear chaps like you, Arnold, I says to 'em look at the houses you live in now. Blind back houses – slums and jerry-built little draughty holes where all the pipes burst in the frost and the waste-pipes get blocked up and you can't clean the sink and you got to burn the light all day long in the basement and perhaps there's beetles if you're lucky. Now look where I live, only don't look too hard it might fall down.

SOLDIER: Yes, all right, but what you going to have?

3RD MAN: Ta, Wilfred, a mild and bitter.

SOLDIER: Four mild and bitters please, Miss.

3RD MAN: Now I seen 'em working on some of these factory-made houses .... Got a bit of paper? Now, this'll give you an idea, see ... In most of the houses, the walls consist of a kind of light outer skin ...

1ST MAN: S'right living in a skin 'ouse now.

3RD MAN: And that keeps out the water.

SOLDIER: What's it made of?

3RD MAN: Oh you can make it out of lots of things. Plastic, clay tiles, concrete slabs, metal or plywood or asbestos, cement. Oh, lots of things. Then this outer skin or layer is fixed to a frame or kind of skeleton.

1ST MAN: S'right living in a sort of skeleton now.

3RD MAN: And another layer fixed to the inside of the skeleton, see, and that'll probably have the heat resisting material in it. Now stop me if I'm getting too technical ...

1ST MAN: Stop.

SERVICE GIRL: Well, what's the kitchen like?

3RD MAN: Oh come along, come along – there's real new methods of plumbing in these houses, all made in one piece ... I seen one of them with all the pipes, drainage pipe, flue pipe, fume pipe all grouped in one bloomin' duct inside the house, mind you not outside like the ...

1ST MAN: Now listen, she wants to hear about the kitchen. Leave your ducts out of it ...

3RD MAN: Well you've got two kinds of kitchens. One's more of a workroom, you'd call it, you see, just a place for cleaning up and getting in the wife's way.

1ST MAN: Where'd you shave then?

3RD MAN: In the bathroom, of course. You know, Arnold, you seen 'em on the pictures.

3RD MAN: ... and the other kind of kitchen is more of a place to have your meals in ...

3RD MAN: ... It's more of a kitchen to live in when you want to take your boots off by the stove ...

1ST MAN: I still don't like it.

SOLDIER: All I know is we want a new house to live in when we're married – It's not right for young people to go on living with their folks all the time.

SELLER: Safety pins?

3RD MAN: That's right, that's what I'm saying, you've come over to my side now. There's thousands of chaps like you want a home in a hurry after they come back.

3RD MAN: And that's the only way of giving 'em to 'em.

SELLER: Do you for a couple of hair clips?

3RD MAN: Coventry's going to be a great new city and there's going to be houses for everyone in it, and work ...

SOLDIER: Have you seen that new model of Coventry they're showing. I'm taking Betty there tomorrow.

COMMENTARY: Coventry was one of the first cities in Britain to have a complete plan for rebuilding – In this plan the centre of the city, largely destroyed – is to be rebuilt entirely – The planners of Coventry believe that cities only exist for the use of people – They believe that everyone should feel that it's worth his while to make his city or town or village a good decent, pleasant place to live in. In war we work together to destroy a common evil – in peace we must work with no less vigour for the common good.

1ST ENGINEER: ... and that's the real point I want to make, Mr Evans. THIS IS THE PEOPLE'S CITY or anyhow it's going to be. Any questions?

2ND ENGINEER: Arthur's off.

3RD ENGINEER: I told you, you'd come to the right shop, Mr Evans, if you want to know anything about Coventry, Arthur here's got the low-down on everything that's happened for the last – how many years?

MR EVANS: I'm very glad you introduced me Mr Jennings, I used to belong to an Engineering club at Wandsworth, and it's pretty lonely coming fresh into a city, without knowing anybody you can have an argument with, and I like a bit of an argument. Getting too old for pictures and dances.

2ND ENGINEER: You can argue till you're blue in the face here, chum. Religion, politics, sex ...

MR EVANS: Too old ...

2ND ENGINEER: ... nothing barred here ...

3RD ENGINEER: Mr Evans and me got talking in the Hostel about planning towns after the war; that's his – what you call it – well, what he likes discussing, isn't it? Give you a few tips too, Arthur.

MR EVANS: Oh no, Mr Jennings, I'm only an amateur and with bees in the bonnet too.

2ND ENGINEER: Plenty of humming round here.

MR EVANS: Now what's this new Coventry going to look like?

1ST ENGINEER: We've got all our plans for that; or at least some of us have. It's a real long-term plan and all I want is to be able to see things begin before I die.

2ND ENGINEER: And then he'll start replanning down there ...

1ST ENGINEER: Schools and roads and hospitals and houses and shops, all I've been able to do in my lifetime is to see a proper plan for them on the way. A proper people's plan ...

2ND ENGINEER: I can see old Arthur replanning hell, can't you?

3RD ENGINEER: Better furnaces for all, eh?

MR EVANS: Now what about the Cathedral, Mr Ibbotson?

1ST ENGINEER: We've got that taped. As town planners, we believe in every town having a focal point. We must have vistas. The people wherever they live must have something good to look at in the town if they want to be proud of it. Now in Coventry –

2ND ENGINEER: He's off.

1ST ENGINEER: ... in Coventry, to use a very good example, it's perfectly obvious that people will want houses looking at the Cathedral ...

3RD ENGINEER: Aye and every amenity too. Arthur's got the big view. I'm an old woman, when it comes to domesticity, I want a radio and a ...

1ST ENGINEER: All right, all right, it's only a minor point mind. Your house can have a radio and an electric washing machine, and a vacuum cleaner too, if you like. It stands to reason that a Council that's building twenty thousand houses, and that's what we're going to build, too – will find it easier to equip 'em with all those things than have them added separately, later and the rent will include all the amenities, too.

2ND ENGINEER: Well, what'll the houses cost?

1ST ENGINEER: About twenty million.

3RD ENGINEER: Told you he took the big view.

2ND ENGINEER: Well where will it come from? Not from us it won't.

3RD ENGINEER: Six pence on the rates only brings in a million and a quarter. Have a heart, Arthur.

1ST ENGINEER: That's all right. This is a national responsibility not only a local one.

MR EVANS: What about hospitals, then?

1ST ENGINEER: Now that's where you come into the idea of the New Coventry proper; there's a model been made of that; it's on show in the town now ..... and we're going to build a big thousand-bed hospital in the centre and all round the town there's going to be health centres – that's our idea for this town and then there's the ...

MR EVANS: What about schools?

1ST ENGINEER: ... that's just what I was going to say – schools – right, the school age is raised to fifteen, but here we've got a secondary school for girls and not a secondary school for boys. But there must be a secondary school for everybody.

MR EVANS: Roads?

1ST ENGINEER: Roads round the city of course – you can't have great big lorries roaring through the centre.

MR EVANS: Shopping?

1ST ENGINEER: That's part of it – no roads for traffic in the centre of the city – shopping done quietly, leisurely, no fuss and bother – no fear of being run over, no getting wet in the rain, arcade shopping – all covered – and all the stuff the shops want and the shoppers want – that's more important, they'll be delivered by road behind the arcade, see?

MR EVANS: Suburbs?

1ST ENGINEER: Self-contained – their own cinemas, their own shops, pubs, clubs, everything, individual communities.

SOLDIER: This is a good model, Betty, isn't it – the city'd better be good too, it's where we're going to live.

COMMENTATOR: Coventry is going to be a place to live in where people can believe how pleasant human life can be ...
It must be, not every man for himself, but every man for the good and the happiness of all people living ... Every man must believe in the good and happiness that is to be shared ... to be shared, equally.

GIRL: ... Goodbye darling ... don't be long.

SOLDIER: ... Don't worry, darling ... it can't be long now. We'll soon be together in our own little home with a ...

TRAIN WHISTLES

... with a nice little garage.

GIRL: ... and a nice little nursery.

A Soldier Comes Home

A Soldier Comes Home deals with the psychological readjustment necessary for wives and husbands after war-time separation. There were several earlier treatments of the original theme of 'The Development of Public Opinion in Britain' – interestingly the third by Pamela Hansford Johnson, Dylan Thomas's first serious girlfriend in the early thirties. When the war in the Far East ended a scene was added at the end of the film to fit the new situation. The MOI Monthly Release for November 1945 relates that now the war is over the thoughts of men and women in the forces are turning to the resumption of their lives in 'Civvy Street'. Particular problems arise for men who must remain in the forces for some time yet, since their wives will think this unfair while other men are being demobilised and returning to their peace-time work – as the film shows. Jack, the wife's husband, is sent back to England, given a month's leave but has to continue his service in another part of England. After the initial excitement of Jack's homecoming, his wife Cath becomes resentful though his young son delights in his stories and his talk of the achievements of our armies in the campaign, for Jack cannot forget his war-time experiences. But finally she accepts that she must await his turn to be demobbed.

The film opens with the train arriving on the station and the soldier walking home to meet his wife and eleven-year-old son again. We see father and son poring over the Atlas and he recounts his war-time experiences to the excited boy. Then the soldier and his son walk over the bombed ruins, the scene fading into a crowded steamship anchored at the quayside. Soldier, mother and boy watch the scenery from the side of the steamer as it makes its way under bridges up river, the moon shining on the Thames, Tower Bridge in the background. Finally we see Cath kissing her husband in the bedroom.

A SOLDIER COMES HOME

Reel 1

WIFE: Jack, oh darling, I was washing my hair to look nice for you.

SON: Dad, Dad, Dad, Dad, Dad!

HUSBAND: I thought it was a herd of elephants coming down stairs.

WIFE: Oh look, this is lovely.

HUSBAND: I picked that up in Calcutta at the bazaar. Aye, what a place. Goats and dogs and sacred cows, and chaps chewing betel. Betels are a sort of nut they chew and spit all over the place. Millions of beggars and what a stink.

WIFE: Sounds like Borough High Street Saturday morning.

HUSBAND: Now be careful you don't break that Jim.

SON: Did you see any elephants in Burma?

HUSBAND: The biggest elephant I ever saw. He couldn't bear the Sergeant. That was funny.

WIFE: And I did want to look my best, darling.

HUSBAND: You always do look your best.

SON: What happened to the elephant?

HUSBAND: Oh him, oh we gave him a big bun.

SON: Is this for cigarettes?

HUSBAND: Yes.

SON: I wish I could smoke.

HUSBAND: Ha – you wouldn't if you had what we were smoking.

WIFE: Oh dear, look at that table.

SON: When are you going back, Dad?

WIFE: Dad has only just come home, and he isn't going back to Burma either.

HUSBAND: Four weeks at home.

SON: I wish I could go to Burma.

HUSBAND: Oh, it's not all that lovely, it is stinking hot, and wet.

SON: May I go and show Dad my map?

WIFE: Ah no, dear, Dad has had enough for one day.

SON: It is only upstairs.

HUSBAND: And this is where we went back to them, Imphal and Kohima. I was at Imphal there, and the Japs on all the hills round us. Hell of a time but we got supply through alright, all from the air, the food and guns and some more fellows flown up from the south. Well we bust out of there.

SON: There?

HUSBAND: That's right and came down this valley to the river, the Chindwin River, see? Well the Japs had crossed the Chindwin only about four months before us.

SON: Why?

HUSBAND: Trying to break through into India, of course, but we didn't let them. This was the monsoon, now, and no one had ever fought in a monsoon before. We did, through all the rains and that's how we beat 'em. That's how we got to Mandalay. We had never seen a jungle. God, how you start hating. You hate the base wallers first, and then you start hating civvies and everybody at home except your own. Oh, then you feel you are alone and then it's all trees and the thousands of miles of stuff all round you. It is like living in a big steam laundry, full of enormous asparagus.

SON: What do Japs look like?

HUSBAND: Well, I have never seen what you might call an operational Jap. I have seen a few prisoners, dirty-looking bunch. Seen some dead too.

SON: What are they like when they are dead?

HUSBAND: Oh, like people dead.

WIFE: Come on Jim, it's past your time, bed now.

SON: Oh, must I. Alright then, goodnight Mum, goodnight Dad.

HUSBAND: Goodnight Jim.

WIFE: I'll be up soon.

WIFE: Bed now, Jack?

(LONG PAUSE)

SON: Goodbye Dad.

HUSBAND: Goodbye Jim.

SON: How do they say goodbye in Burma?

HUSBAND: Cor! So long or cheerio.

SON: Cheerio then.

HUSBAND: Cheerio. Can I give you a hand?

WIFE: No thanks.

HUSBAND: Come along and let me do something.

WIFE: Just stay where you are.

HUSBAND: I must do something. Does Jim talk about Burma all the time?

WIFE: Not to me, he borrows all the books about it from the library. Cuts everything out of the newspapers and sticks it in his scrapbook. He thinks you are wonderful.

HUSBAND: I should think so too.

WIFE: He thinks you are a hero.

HUSBAND: Don't you?

WIFE: I think you are a very good housewife. You couldn't even dry up a saucepan before without dropping it, now look at you. Did they teach you to cook too?

HUSBAND: Cook, yes, with a tin opener and a bayonet. All your Sunday dishes washed up by the rain before you started. Sitting in mud like brown porridge, eating mosquitos with your Sunday dinner. Well, what do we do now?

WIFE: Well, I'm going to make the beds, then I'm going to do the vegetables and tidy up a bit.

HUSBAND: What do I do?

WIFE: You just sit down and read the paper or listen to the wireless or something and don't be a nuisance. My dear, you don't want to do anything, no I mean that. I want to be lazy all the time and eat lots of food ... .

HUSBAND: And drink lots of ... .

WIFE: Oh you'll get plenty of your old beer tonight. Mother will be there, Janet and Peter.

HUSBAND: Looking forward to seeing your mother in the Railway Arms with a pint of beer and a clay pipe.

WIFE: You know she only drinks stout, and she doesn't smoke either.

HUSBAND: And Saturday I want to go up the Thames on one of those steamers.

WIFE: Do they run now?

HUSBAND: How would I know? Where do you think I have been? Oh, I can find out after tea when Jim and me can go for a walk – taking him down Cherry Garden Pier.

SON: Did I show you where the flying bomb came down Dad? There is one just over there, and you know that picture of Grandad when he was a little boy, the big picture in the flash frame with sea shells all round it, it fell on the floor when the bomb came and didn't break either.

HUSBAND: We were very far away. We had no idea it was as bad as this.

SON: Is the Irrawaddy as big as the Thames? I bet there are no barges on it. I wish there were crocodiles in the Thames.

Reel 2

HUSBAND: Ah, just like old times. Just like the nights we used to talk about in the jungle, sitting in the pub with all your pals, and talking a lot of rot. Plenty of drinks and a bit of singing. Didn't know your mother could sing. We used to talk about pubs and girls and grub, and how we met our wives. When you think of the chaps out there, just talking about home, and here I am, home. I feel I want to pinch myself sometimes. Might wake up – be out there again sweating like a pig and tomorrow you find you are out on a patrol and .... What is the matter sweetheart?

WIFE: It isn't fair, it isn't fair.

HUSBAND: Of course it isn't. What isn't?

WIFE: I can't even have you to myself when you are home. Not even for a few minutes. You are always talking about your pals, out there and what is happening to them. We have so little time. Can't you forget about it?

HUSBAND: It isn't easy sweetheart.

WIFE: Oh, I know, I know it isn't, but it isn't fair either. I haven't seen you for four years and now you are going back into the army. I shall be alone. Charlie in the pub talking about going back to his job, and Harry demobbed. Why can't you go back to your job?

HUSBAND: That is my job. I am not going back to Burma, and I will be home on leave again. It isn't as if I like it, it's just that it's my job to be in the army 'til my turn comes round. Somebody's got to do it and somebody's got to take my place out there.

WIFE: I'm sorry, I didn't mean to be selfish. I have got you still. There are lots of people ... I shouldn't complain. Anyway the war is over. I must try and be patient. I suppose somebody has got to be out there.

HUSBAND: And somebody has got to be here too.

WIFE: I'm sorry darling.

The Doctor and the Devils

The Doctor and the Devils was based on the historically factual incident of the body-snatchers Burke and Hare, who supplied the famous and eccentric anatomist Dr Knox with dead bodies for anatomical study and research. Dylan Thomas creates a drama of Jacobean horrors iridescent with his own poetic vision of death, corruption and terror. His provisional title 'The Business of Death' summed up both plot and morbid detail. The poet's attraction to his tale brings to mind the young Dylan Thomas's boast 'I'd prefer to be an anatomist or the keeper of a morgue any day'[74] and his interest in Beddoes, also an anatomist. Dr Rock's self-declaration as 'a *material* man ... , to study the flesh, the skin, the bones, the organs, the nerves of Man, is to equip our minds with a knowledge ... to search *beyond* the body' echoes Beddoes's 'I search with avidity for every shadow of a proof or probability of an after-existence both in the material and the immaterial nature of man.'[75] Obsession with the processes and metaphysics of death motivated Thomas's early poetry and prose. Here we are close to the macabre world of the early stories, though the discipline of filmscript makes him more deft in the swift evocation of atmosphere, character and the grotesque. Certainly the black-robed but bejewelled Dr Rock, the distinguished but amoral surgeon who mocks and flouts the conventions of respectable society, belongs to 'melodrama' – Thomas's description – when we first meet him (though there's something of Thomas's own sharp, mocking wit in Dr Rock's speeches).

> Closer now, we see that he is a youngish man in severe professional black; and his long cloak is the other darkness around him.

On changing the name of Salter to Rock, Thomas wrote to Donald Taylor: 'I think I forgot to tell you the new name I had thought for Dr Robert Knox: *Thomas Rock*. This is very near, in vowels and general feeling, to the original, and does I think satisfy Bridie's complaint: it does sound the name of a man who could be very distinguished and great in science.'[76] James Bridie had written a comedy about Burke and Hare, *The Anatomist*

(1930), and Taylor had been in touch with him. What interested Taylor was the theme of 'the ends justifying the means' in Dr Knox's behaviour, and Dylan Thomas does powerfully dramatise this in Rock's soliloquy of his Voices, young, old, gay and sad, that closes the play, prompted by a begging child's terror on hearing his name. But what distinguishes the script and provides Dylan Thomas's most original writing, poetically, visually and technically, is his depiction of the lives of the homeless, their poverty, suffering and cruel existence, young and old, on the Edinburgh streets. The dramatic power of his presentation is a notable stage in Thomas's development as a prose writer. Clearly the technique of film presentation here was remembered in the writing of *Under Milk Wood* with its reiterated 'Come closer now': we see and experience the horror of how children and adults sleeping in the streets become easy victims for the murderers. Thomas excels in what he called his 'descriptive-visual writing'. We see with a camera's eye the desperate low-life of tavern, lodging house or 'rag-and-bone alley', where the only comfort is cheap gin in the face of random cruelty and total squalor. And while there is a Jacobean horror and terror in the later detail of the murders, clearly Thomas's anger and compassion inspire his depiction of the suffering beggars and helpless victims of this society, his sketches at times reminiscent of Dickens and Mayhew. Thomas's concentrated verbal dexterity, both visually and emotionally effective, evokes the city market-place where 'the straw-strewn cobbles of the Market are crowded with stalls. Stalls that sell rags and bones, kept by rags and bones … There are many, many children, some very old.' At his dinner party Dr Rock mocks the cultured hypocrisies of the rich and successful of the city, declaring:

> Look any night at the streets of this 'cultured city'. Observe, with academic calm, the homeless and the hopeless and the insane and the wretchedly drunken lying in their rags on the stinking cobbles. Look for yourselves, sirs, at the beggars, and the cripples, and the tainted children, and the pitiful, doomed girls. Write a scholastic pamphlet on the things that prowl in the alleys, afraid to see the light; they were men and women once. Be proud of *that* if you can.

Leaving the house Dr Rock's colleague Murray walks through the humanity-littered streets and Thomas's 'every word and phrase bears an exact relation to the thing, and at the same time makes demands on the imagination',[77] as Dobrée's review noted.

> On both sides of the street are many ragged bodies, of men, women, and children. Some are stretched out asleep; some are sprawled drunk, their

hands still clutching a bottle; some are huddled together, like large, dishevelled birds, for company and warmth. A few have not managed to reach the comparative shelter of the sides of the street, but lie, ungainly outcasts, snoring scarecrows and men of garbage, across the cobbled middle.

Evidently then, though the filmscript ostensibly seeks to explore the question of ends justifying means through Dr Rock's character, Thomas most effectively touches the nerve of moral issues when confronted with the poor directly. We see this in Dr Rock's contempt for religious respectability (always a preoccupation close to Dylan Thomas), on giving Billy Bedlam some money one cold winter night in the dark street.

> Now he'll hurry as fast as he can on his bent bones to the nearest tavern, and fuddle his few poor wits ... Oh, how the pious would lift their hands to heaven to think of a man giving money to an idiot so that he could get drunk and be warm and happy for an hour or two. Let him die rather a frozen idiot in the gutter!

In this sombre world of suffering, gin is heaven. But throughout the script the anger and pity of Thomas's words ring with social and political voice and concern. 'As his shooting directions dwell on the violent life and cluttered squalor of the slums ... a subtle moral lesson takes shape. The hideous poverty of "Rag-and-Bone Alley", as Rock declares, is the result of a social crime, and the same crime has driven the murderers' starving victims into a kind of life that is next door to death. All the murderers do is open the door; these crimes are only small reflections of the greater one ... an indifferent society may be responsible for evil conditions for which it is entirely unaware'[78] wrote a 1953 reviewer. Thomas changed the murderers' names Burke and Hare to Fallon and Broom, and there is visual, cinematic horror in the murders, as in the wretched Billy Bedlam's (young and fresh corpses got a good price).

> FALLON (*slowly*):   You mustn't be frightened, Billy ... It'll all be over soon. No more bein' hungry ...
>
> Now Fallon, slow as a priest, is moving toward us and Billy. *Cut to* shot, from door, of Fallon moving towards Billy, and of Billy's bewildered, but still smiling face ...
>
> FALLON (*slowly*):   No more ... cold.
>
> *Cut to* shot, from Billy's angle, of Fallon moving, as though in procession, down the room.

And suddenly we hear the voice of Billy: screaming.

This perverse, evil atmosphere is echoed later in Fallon's blaming his hands for the murder, and the killing of the old, frail and lonely Mrs Flynn in their lodging house, 'gay as an old cat' in her last gin-induced fling of song and dance. There is Websterian intensity in the horror and pathos of this script. Dylan had listed Webster as an influence on his early verse and twice visited a London production of *The Duchess of Malfi*. Dr Rock's assistant Murray has a secret alliance with the beautiful and destitute 'Sweet Jennie Bailey', and her refusal to meet him anywhere but in the tavern strikes a note of personal and poetic pathos particularly reminiscent of Webster. 'Where else *could* you take me, sweetheart, except for a walk in the fields – and in winter too! Kissing in the hedge like two robins.' A final Websterian touch is the horrific discovery of her body by Murray when he opens the sack holding a newly delivered corpse for Dr Rock's dissecting table.

Demonstrably the discipline of his work in films not only widened Thomas's capacity for new forms of expression but importantly helped him towards extended prose work, as distinct from the short-story form of *Portrait of the Artist as a Young Dog*. It required, too, the adult's eye on the world projected rather than the looking back over his shoulder to childhood. Dylan Thomas is learning to sustain atmosphere, character and narrative in other and larger areas than previously. His description, seeing detail as a camera sees it, is also fruitfully allied to the wit of his own talk. The 1986 film of *The Doctor and the Devils* certainly has the horror-movie element in evoking the sombre scenes of the script, though it might more bitingly have caught the anger and pity of Thomas's words. Dora Bryan, nearly forty years after her role in *No Room at the Inn*, provides a vivid vignette as the merry but doomed Mrs Flynn.

THE DOCTOR AND THE DEVILS

1

Morning.

Music.
From a long way off, we see a deserted road winding downwards from a hill-top.
Huge sky, slow clouds.

A small black figure appears at the top of the road, and moves downhill. A small black figure with another darkness billowing around it.

Now we see the downhill-approaching figure as a top-hatted man in the wind. From our distance he is still the mystery of a man, alone in a blowing morning on a lonely hill-top; still the shadow, not the recognisably featured substance, of a man.

Closer now, we see that he is a youngish man in severe professional black; and his long cloak is the other darkness around him.

Closer still, we see his body and face as he strides down towards us. He wields his stick like a prophet's staff. We see the deep-set eyes behind the large spectacles; the wide sensual mouth tightened into its own denial; the wild fringes of hair blowing from under the sides of the stiff hat-rim; the coffin-shaped forehead; the insatiable, and even predatory, curiosity of the bent-forward head.

Suddenly he stops, looks down.

Now, with his eyes, we see the City that lies below him. An early nineteenth-century City, its crossing, twisting patterns of roofs at so many different levels, its streets and houses dangerously clambering, scaling, falling down from the steep hill, its patchwork of threading alleys, its compact wilderness of little archwayed courts and closes, sunless dead ends, market spaces surrounded by tumbling top-heavy tenements, hovels, cottages, pigsties ...

And now, from behind him, we see him stride on, top-hat and stick, towards the City; towards the rising sigh of city sounds, the mingling and slowly loudening voices of people and bells, the noise of hooves and wheels on cobble stones, and street cries unintelligibly distant. (*Dissolve to*)

2

City Market-place.

And up come the City sounds.

The straw-strewn cobbles of the Market are crowded with stalls. Stalls that sell rags and bones, kept by rags and bones. Stalls that sell odds and ends of every odd kind, odd boots, bits of old meat, fish heads, trinkets, hats with feathers, broadsheets, hammers. Stalls with shawls. Stalls like ash bins. Anything that is marketable, to the very poor.

Pigs and chickens grunt, root, cluck, and peck among the straw heaps and the refuse, getting in every one's way though no one notices or cares.

A heaped high hay-cart rumbles over the cobbles.

The doors of the shops and the public-houses are open on to the Market, and singing comes from inside some of them, and outside some of them stand men and women drinking.

And men and women lean, drinking, against the stalls.

There are many, many children, some very old.

Among the children, the butt of their noise, is a humpback with the smile of an idiot.

And across the Market the man in cloak and top-hat is walking: black and purposeful among all the turbulent laziness, among the talkers, the hawkers, the old leaners, the drinkers, the shrill children. We move with him.

Two men whom we see we will remember later. With earthenware tankards in their hands, they are standing almost in the middle of the Market. One is tall and very thin; the other squat, barrel-chested. The tall one is hollow-cheeked, corpse-pale, with jerky, inconsequent gestures; the short one full and ruddy-faced, knob-nosed, surly, slow-moving.

We see that the tall one is laughing: at nothing. We hear his laugh: a high-pitched snarl, an animal noise. The squat one pays no attention, but curses the whole Market with his scowling eyes.

We see a woman pushing a barrow heaped with rags and hucksters' scraps, and another woman trailing behind her.

We hear the first woman's cry as she turns into a side alley:

Rags and bones ... rags and bones ...

she cries.

And then the cry of the second woman:

... Cat-skin ... human hair ...

The faces of the two women also we shall remember.

Rags, rags ... rags and bones ...
Cat-skin ... human hair ...

The tall man mimics the cries.

A hawker passes, crying her cry of:

Fresh herrings ... fresh herrings ...

We hear behind her cry the high yelping mimicry of the tall drinker.

The man in cloak and top-hat moves on.
And the noises of the Market fade as we
(*Dissolve to*)

3

City square.

The man in cloak and top-hat is walking through the trimly treed garden in the Square towards a large building.
We follow him into the building.

4

Hallway of Rock's Academy.

As he walks through the Hallway, a Porter, in black coat, black trousers, and brass-buttoned waistcoat, approaches him. He is a little man with a very pale face.

PORTER: They're here, Doctor Rock.

Rock stops.

ROCK: Indeed, Mr Forsythe? Who or what are 'they', and where is 'here'?

PORTER: The specimens for the Anatomical Museum, sir, are in the Museum.

ROCK: How fortunate they are not in the gentlemen's Cloakroom. I should hate skeletons in all my cupboards. Thank you.

Rock walks to the end of the Hallway, opens a door, goes through.

5

Small Cloakroom.

Rock hangs up his hat and cloak, very neatly, puts his stick in a stand, and turns to look at himself in a full-length mirror.
We see, in the mirror, that he is wearing a long, dark coat, immaculately tailored, an ornate, embroidered waistcoat across which gold chains hang in festoons, a high cravat, higher than is the fashion of the gentlemen we shall see in future scenes, with its folds

passed through a diamond ring, a prominent shirt-collar, delicately plaited cambrics, watch-seals and pendants, dark trousers, shining boots, a gay waist-band.

At all this excellence he looks with approval; he preens himself, he flicks off invisible dust.

Softly he says to his reflection:

ROCK: Well, Thomas. To work!

And he crosses the Cloakroom to another door, and opens it, and walks through.

From the Cloakroom door we see into:

6

The Anatomical Museum.

It is a very large room.

Around the walls are anatomical specimens mounted and labelled.

There are specimens in glass cases, many unmounted specimens, and a great number of packing-cases of all sizes.

Assistants are unpacking the cases.

All over the floor are bones; the skeletons of birds, beasts, reptiles, fishes; odd fish; fossils; osteological curiosities; pickled monsters; brains in jars; the scattered treasures of a static, silent zoo.

Rock, some distance from his assistants, is opening a case and throwing aside the top layers of straw.

We (*track towards*) him.

He takes a little skeleton from the case: the skeleton of a baby or a monkey.

A man's voice is heard.

MAN'S VOICE: Good Morning, Thomas.

Rock looks round.

(*Pan round*) to door through which a heavily built, elderly man is entering. His hair is close clipped and iron grey, his demeanour severe, his face unaccustomed to smiling.

Now, from the door, we see him cross over to Rock.

They shake hands.

Rock still holds the little skeleton under one arm.

ROCK: Doctor Manson! You see me to-day, sir, with one foot in the grave. Now, where is a chair?

He looks around the Museum room.

ROCK: Perhaps you could make yourself comfortable on this case of ...

He glances at a label on a packing-case near him.

ROCK: ... stomachs of cetacea. I am *sure* there was a chair here yesterday. I remember it distinctly ...

MANSON: You probably talked its hind legs off. Don't fuss around me, Thomas. I shall sit here on your stomachs.

Manson sits on the near case.
Rock puts the little skeleton carefully down. He goes on unpacking specimens throughout the conversation.

MANSON: You look well. Odd, but well. How is your wife?

ROCK: Well, and not at all odd, thank you, sir. Oh, the doctors' wives still cut her in the street, but fortunately they resemble their husbands at an operation: they cannot cut anything properly. And you, sir?

MANSON: I am an old man. You should not ask old men how they feel, or they will tell you. I am old, like Doctor Hocking.

ROCK: Doctor Hocking was in his second childhood before he was adolescent. When he is your age, sir – a good age – he'll be old as the grandfather of a tortoise, take a week to put his boots on, a fortnight to suck his bread and milk, and a month to make up his absence of mind.

MANSON: You still do not approve of the distinguished Professor of Anatomy in our University.

ROCK: I still do not approve of stupidity and inefficiency, and sycophantic compromise, and pretentious, intolerable airs and graces.

MANSON (*unsmiling, as throughout*):   You speak too highly of him.

ROCK: He has become a professor on no wits at all. If he were a half-wit, with *his* self-assertion he would be known as a Scotch Sophocles.

MANSON: I am thinking of retiring, Thomas.

ROCK: If you leave your School of Anatomy, sir, you consign the medical reputation of the City to a man who reads his grandfather's lectures for his own and dissects like a labourer with a pick.

MANSON: I have no intention of leaving my students to *Doctor Hocking*. I would rather continue lecturing myself, toothless, on crutches, with my beard to my boots. I founded *my* School to keep the teaching of Anatomy away from hacks and drudges and medical impostors, crammers, and quacks. (*slowly, emphatically*) My successor must be a person of precision, method, vigilance, and expertness.

ROCK: In this City?

MANSON: I have found him.

ROCK: Oh, in heaven, sir, not here.

MANSON: In a museum.

ROCK: In a mummy-case?

MANSON: No, standing like a fool in front of me, with a leg under his arm.

Manson looks at Rock. And from his eyes we see Rock standing, a plaster leg under his arm, among the specimens he has unpacked from the cases; Rock staring back at Manson.
And we (*track back*) to see Rock and Manson still, silent, in the great room surrounded by bones and bodies, like men in a spilt graveyard.
(*Dissolve to*)

7

A Room in Rock's House (henceforward to be known as Elizabeth's Room).

It is an intimate, comfortable room.
A fire is blazing in the deep fire-place.
There is a table with sewing upon it.
And another small table with books.
Rock stands at the long window of the room, looking out.
Coming closer to him, we see, through the window, the roofs of the City.

It is dusk in autumn.

A woman comes in. She is young, small, fair, with a candid, tranquil face.

She is carrying a tray with biscuits and a glass of milk on it.

She stands for a moment, looking at Rock.

Then he turns.

ROCK: I never heard you come in, Elizabeth. You're a witch in a white apron. Downstairs you keep a little instrument, no bigger than a baby mouse, that can hear my brain ticking and my heart beating.

Elizabeth puts the tray down on a table.

ROCK (*gently*):   Shall I tell you my news now? Or shall I kiss you first ...

Elizabeth smiles calmly up at him.

ELIZABETH: Yes.

He kisses her.

ROCK: ... and ask you what you have been doing all day ...

ELIZABETH: Oh, the ordinary things.

ROCK: ... and how our little boy behaved ...

ELIZABETH: He's asleep now. He said his prayers, and then he said there was a tiger in his bed.

She smiles.

ELIZABETH: Tell me your news now.

ROCK: Do you remember Doctor Manson? Stern as a judge and solid as a mountain. When I was a student, he had the bearing and the voice of a god surrounded by the angels of logic.

Now he's old, and ill. He knows death. He can hear it growling and scratching around him now, like a dog after a bone.

He wants me to take his place. Do you know what that means? A whole School of Anatomy outside any influence but Manson's and my own. All the work I have ever wanted to do, I can do there. Can you see me as another St Hilaire, my dear, another Cuvier? ... Another old stick-in-the-mud, maybe, with bees in his bald head ...

This room is growing slowly darker.

ROCK: I said 'Yes' to Manson. Are you glad?

Elizabeth nods.

ROCK: When one burns one's boats, what a very nice fire it makes.

He looks out of the window, over the roofs in the gathering darkness, Elizabeth near him. He speaks almost as though to himself alone.

ROCK: What can spoil or hurt us now? Nothing, nothing, nothing. Nothing out there ...

He makes a gesture towards the dusky City.

ROCK: My future's here.

He raises his hands, palms upwards, then draws them back towards him, inviting Elizabeth.
She moves to him, and he takes her hands.

ROCK: And some of it is in your hands. Oh, I am happy to-day, Elizabeth, happy and tired.
I am tired of the dead! ...

He puts his arm around her, draws her close. Together they stand at the window. His hand moves along her bare arm.
(*Fade out*)

(*Fade in*)

8

Lecture Hall of Rock's Academy.

Rock is on the platform, lecturing.
Another younger man sits at a small table on the other side of the platform.
The amphitheatre is crowded with students.
Rock, as a lecturer, shows a rare felicity of movement, now reminding us of the slow and graceful minuet, then the quiet pose or soldierly *attention*; and these again are succeeded by the rapid gesture. After each diversion of his subject he readjusts his spectacles, draws up his gay waist-band and then, presenting a steady front to his class, resumes his prelection.

ROCK: I stand before you, gentlemen, as a lecturer in Anatomy, a scientist, a specialist, a *material* man to whom the heart, for instance, is an elaborate physical organ and not the 'seat of love', a man to whom the 'soul', because it has no shape, does not exist.

But paradox is inherent in all dogma, and so I stand before you also as a man of sentiment, of spiritual aspirations, intellectually creative impulses, social convictions, moral passions. And it is in my dual capacity of scientist and sociologist, materialist and moralist, anatomist and artist, that I shall attempt to conduct my lectures, to expound, inform, illustrate, entertain, and edify.

Our aim for ever must be the pursuit of the knowledge of Man in his entirety. To study the flesh, the skin, the bones, the organs, the nerves of Man, is to equip our minds with a knowledge that will enable us to search *beyond* the body. The noble profession at whose threshold you stand as neophytes is not an end in itself. The science of Anatomy contributes to the great sum of all Knowledge, which is the Truth: the whole Truth of the Life of Man upon this turning earth. And so: Observe precisely. Record exactly. Neglect nothing. Fear no foe. Never swerve from your purpose. Pay no heed to Safety.

For I believe that all men can be happy and that the good life can be led upon this earth.

I believe that all men must work towards that end.

And I believe that that end justifies any means ...

Let no scruples stand in the way of the progress of medical science!

Rock bows: a curt, but studied bow.

The students rise.

And Rock walks off the platform.

The other man on the platform makes a gesture of dismissal to the students, then follows Rock.

And all the students suddenly begin talking as they move down the Lecture Hall.

9

Hallway of Rock's Academy.

Rock and his companion on the platform are walking through the Hallway towards a door under the stairs. They open the door and go through. We follow them, through the open door, into a

10

Small Cloakroom.

It is a bare, dark room. A few pegs on the wall – Rock's cloak and top-hat hang from one – and a table with a water jug and a basin on it.

Rock rolls up his sleeves, very circumspectly, as his companion pours water into the basin.

We hear, from outside, the noise of the students.

ROCK (*with a nod towards the noise*):   What do they talk about afterwards, I wonder? Do they repeat one's words of golden guidance? Or make disparaging remarks about one's waistcoat? I think when I was a student we used to tell one another stories: they were anatomical, too. Ah, thank you, Murray ...

Rock begins to wash his hands in the basin. Murray takes off his coat.

MURRAY: You agree with all you said?

ROCK: But naturally.

MURRAY: 'The end justifies *any* means'? That is – to say the least of it – unscrupulous.

ROCK: Then do not say 'the least of it'. Say 'the most': that it is *honest*.

And Murray begins to wash his hands.

ROCK: You're coming to my dinner, of course? I can guarantee the cooking. Only the conversation will be half-baked and only the politeness overdone.

MURRAY (*smiling*):   Of course ...

ROCK: ... Do not trust an elder sister to choose one's company for one. Annabella will never believe I am properly grown up and so sits me down next to an elderly lady whose conversational ability would disgrace a defective three-year-old, or else closets me with a deaf historian so far advanced into the next world that he can only dribble and splutter in this.

MURRAY (*with a kind of tolerant affection*):   Dinner will be a monologue, as usual, Thomas. I can't think how you ever manage to eat or drink anything at all on those occasions ...

ROCK: I eat during the yawns.

Now he has finished washing. He adjusts his coat-sleeves. And Murray helps him on with his cloak.

ROCK: I *loathe* all Dinners with a capital 'D'. Why can't I have a *quiet* meal with a small 'm' and a large port?

MURRAY: Oh, but William! A Dinner to Celebrate the Opening of the New Session of Doctor Rock's Academy!

ROCK: I wish it were still Rock's and Manson's Academy ...

He puts on his top-hat. Murray passes him his stick.

ROCK (*as though to himself*):   ... Poor Manson ... (*suddenly in a different mood*) If Annabella hasn't invited at least one Duke I shall be so surprised that I shall have to ask one myself. And throw in a drunk baronet for bad measure.
Good night, Murray.

He walks to the door of the small, dark room.

MURRAY: Good night. Sleep well.

ROCK: Don't be a dam' fool ...

Murray smiles after him as Rock goes out.
And from Murray's eyes we see Rock walk down the Hallway towards the main door, which is opened for him by the Porter, Tom.

11

Dining-room of Rock's House.

On the large, shining table of the large and handsome room the candles are lit in their heavy silver candlesticks.
The curtains are drawn.
The furniture of the room is good and solid. There is little ornamentation.
At the table sits a woman, writing. There are coffee-things near her.
We (*track towards*) her, from the door.
And, close, we see that she is a woman of about forty, with black hair combed sternly back, strong features, straight unrelenting mouth: a woman of determination, who knows her own mind and, though she may not like it, will always speak it.

She is writing, with severe, upright pen strokes, on large white cards.
There is the sound of a door opening.
She looks up from her writing, and says:

ANNABELLA: Oh, Thomas. Can you spare me a moment?

And now, from a little way behind her, we look at Rock standing in the doorway, hesitant, top-hat in hand.

ROCK: A hundred, my dear Annabella. All my time is at your disposal, except when I am working or eating or drinking or sleeping. And so on.

ANNABELLA: Then come in and close the door.

ROCK: I *was* going upstairs to work. I had thought of completing my Observations on the Structure of the Stomach of the Peruvian Llama to-night.

ANNABELLA: I doubt if such a creature exists. I think you invented it as an excuse. And besides, if it does exist, it probably has no stomach.

Reluctantly Rock comes in and closes the door behind him. He approaches the table.

ANNABELLA: I want you to look at the invitations, that is all. I may have forgotten someone.

ROCK: Oh, fortunate someone!

Annabella hands the little pile of cards to Rock. He looks through them, idly.

ANNABELLA: There is no need to be contemptuous of a celebration in your own honour. It may well be the last if you continue to go around the City capriciously insulting every one, and writing absurd letters to the papers about every subject from salmon-fishing to astronomy, and preaching perverted nonsense to a lot of credulous youths and calling it the new philosophy.

ROCK: I smell vinegar in the air to-night.

But now he is looking through the cards again, and this time not idly. He speaks in a changed voice.

ROCK: Why are not Doctor and Mrs Gregory invited?

ANNABELLA: Mrs Gregory will not sit at table with *her*.

She makes a little gesture of her head towards the door. Rock gives no sign of having heard or understood.

ROCK: And the Nicolsons?

ANNABELLA: No self-respecting body would sit down at dinner in the presence of ...

ROCK (*interrupting, quickly, but in an expressionless voice*):   ... my wife.

ANNABELLA: You can't think that you can outrage every convention and not suffer for it. You married her for better or for worse; and it's worse. I have never understood why you didn't keep the girl as your mistress in some other part of the town.

But no, you have to bring your shabby amours back into the house and *legalise* them.

People have long memories. They don't forget that you disgraced your name, *and* mine, and defied every social decency when you married ...

But Rock, silent, is walking to the door, opening it, and going out. He pays no attention to Annabella. She is left standing at the table, her sentence unfinished.

12

Stairway of Rock's house.

Rock is climbing the stairs. As he climbs we hear the voice of his mind.

ROCK'S VOICE: ... When I married Elizabeth. When I said, cool as ice, one morning – cool as fire! – 'Elizabeth and I are married.' Oh, the shame and horror on the faces of all the puritanical hyenas, prudery ready to pounce and bite, snobbery braying in all the drawing-rooms and breeding-boxes, false pride and prejudice coming out of their holes, hissing and spitting because a man married for love and not for property or position or for any of the dirty devices of the world ...

We see him, from below, climbing up, disappearing round one winding corner, then appearing again out of shadow. And the voice of his mind grows softer and, slowly, fades.

13

Elizabeth's Room.

Elizabeth is sitting near the fire, nursing a young child, as Rock comes in. She looks up. She sees the controlled fury on his face.

ELIZABETH: Thomas. You have been losing your temper again.

He crosses to her, and looks down at her and the child.

ROCK: Not this time. No, my dear, society has been losing its temper with *me*. And you.

ELIZABETH: Society. That's a lot of people.

ROCK: Oh, Annabella is the priestess of the whole genteel rabble. She speaks for all the slanderers and backbiters from here to hell.

ELIZABETH (*gentle, as throughout*):   Was it you and me again?

ROCK: Again.

ELIZABETH: It makes people so angry, still. They think that if they don't *show* they're angry *all* the doctors and lawyers will be marrying market girls and housemaids ...

ROCK: It would do them good. I wish all the mummified lawyers would marry women of the streets and breed howling families of thieves and vagabonds. I wish the professors would marry their cooks and breed *proper* children, not more little scholars in diapers.

ELIZABETH: Oh no, that wouldn't work at all. You are famous. People want to look up to you. They can't do that if you insult them by marrying below you.

ROCK: Below me! Love is not below me! What am I? An insensible pedagogue, cold-blooded as a herring, with my nose permanently buried in a body? A mincing old maid of a man with ...

ELIZABETH: No, dear. Which of your friends have been refusing to meet me now? I've only met a few of them. I thought they were very nice and they got up when I came in and called me ma'am ...

ROCK: I do not need any friends. I prefer enemies. They are better company and their feelings towards you are always genuine. No, it is only that some overweening and underbred women, the wives and tormentors of unlucky doctors, have contrived to tell Annabella that they would not accept our invitation to dinner.

ELIZABETH: Oh, but they *must*. It's very important. You must be at your best. I want them to respect you. You must tell your sister to send off all the invitations, and at the foot of the ones to the ladies who won't accept because of me you must tell her to write, very nicely, that I won't be able to be present at dinner because I am indisposed.

ROCK: I shall cancel the dinner.

ELIZABETH: You'll do nothing of the sort, Thomas.

ROCK: Then I shall write to tell them that their inability to accept our invitation is obviously due to the fact that they suffer from swine-fever, and that I appreciate their delicacy in not wishing to spread it.

ELIZABETH: You'll tell Annabella exactly what I've told you. And now that subject is all over. You haven't asked anything about your son. He couldn't go to sleep to-night. He cried and cried. He was frightened. I've had to nurse him to sleep.

Rock kisses Elizabeth. He touches on the forehead the child in her arms.

ROCK: Good night, little boy.

And we (*track past*) Rock towards the window, out of the window and into darkness.

14

Music.

Night.
A graveyard.
Three muffled figures skulk down the graveyard path. One carries a lantern. By the lantern-light we see the shapes of the gravestones on either side; some of the graves are thickly spiked and railinged round. And by this light we make out the appearances of the silent, shadowy figures.
One is very tall and thin; he wears a top-hat. One, also top-hatted, carries some heavy implements; the lantern, for a moment, flickers his way, and we see the shape of a spade, the coils of a heavy chain. The lantern-carrier is a very short man.
Now the lantern-carrier stops at a new grave, and lowers his light.

The grave is only a tidy heap of newly turned earth; no stone stands at its head.

We hear the whisper of the lantern-carrier:

Here it is. This is the one.

The spade-bearer puts down his implements. We hear his whisper:

Hallelujah.

And the tall, top-hatted man whispers:

Go to it, Mole.

The short man begins to dig at the end of the grave earth.
And the tall one, looking carefully, slyly, around, whispers again:

Quiet as death to-night.

And the one who carried the spade whispers in return:

Praise be the Lord.

The short man digs on. Then, putting down the spade, he whispers:

The chain!

The tall man hands it to him. We see that the chain has a large hook at the end. We see it thrust into the hole the spade has dug. And we hear the noise of steel knocking on wood.

The chain, in the hands of the short man, wriggles above the earth like a snake.
Steel grates against steel.
The short man whispers:

It's a hard clasp they've put on the coffin.

His companion whispers:

... The unbelievers.

And the tall man whispers:

Break it with the spade, then. Hurry. The cold's got into my bones.

The short man pushes his spade through the earth. Spade against steel. The ripping of wood.
The tall man whispers:

Careful.

And the chain is lowered again.

And slowly, out of the earth, comes the head of a man, and then the shrouded shoulders, hauled up by the hook of the chain.

The tall man whispers:

Easy, easy. Don't wake him.

Slowly the three men raise up the fourth.

The arm of the dead man drops, stiff, against the lantern.

The lantern goes out.

And suddenly, to loud gay music, we (*dissolve to*):

15

Interior of Tavern A.

On a bench in a corner sit three men. No one sits quite next to them, though the tavern is crowded. We recognise them as the three men of the graveyard. All three are drunk, though solemnly as befits men whose business is death.

The very tall top-hatted man (Andrew Merry-Lees) is a cadaverous clown; a deacon of the drinking-cellar, a pillar of unrespectability.

The other top-hatted man (Praying Howard) has an almost benevolent, almost sweet and saintly, appearance run to seed and whisky.

The short man (Mole) is very hairy; almost furry, like a mole.

They raise their tankards to each other.

ANDREW MERRY-LEES: To the dead!

PRAYING HOWARD: To the Surgeons of our City!

They drink.

Now we see, sitting quite close to them, the two men of the Market-place. They are listening hard, but cautiously, to the other three.

MOLE: It's been a good month. I'm thirsty.

PRAYING HOWARD: A blessed month.

ANDREW MERRY-LEES: Subjects like penny pies. Plenty of 'em. I'm thirsty too, Mole. I've drunk three pints o' gin. And I'm goin' to drink *three pints more ...*

PRAYING HOWARD: Careful, careful, Andrew, you'll get the taste for it.

And the three of them croak and laugh, without smiling, like three carrion-crows.

And the two men of the Market are listening all the time.

The short, squat man beckons, secretly, with a stubby black finger, to an old woman, all rags and bones, standing drinking near them.

Coming closer, we hear his whisper:

Who would they be with all that money for the drink?

The woman looks, with frightened eyes, at the croakers in the corner. Then she whispers:

Andrew Merry-Lees, and Praying Howard, and (*her voice goes softer*) ... the Mole.

And the squat man questions her again, in a rough, Irish whisper:

And what do they do for a living, my lovey?

She answers, in a sharp whisper full of fear:

Body-snatchers.

He makes a movement as though to cross himself, then lets his hand fall, and looks at his companion.

We see the thin side-twisted lips of his companion frame the syllables:

Body-snatchers.

They look at each other as the camera (*tracks back*) to show the whole tavern and the three solemnly croaking, laughing men in the corner.

(*Dissolve to*)

16

Dining-room of Rock's house.

There are eight gentlemen at table.

The port is being passed.

Through the general conversation we hear:

GREEN: I was sorry to hear that Mrs Rock was indisposed, Thomas. Only once I had the honour ...

FIRST GENTLEMAN: Nothing, I hope? ...

ROCK (*shaking his head*):   ... Serious ... The child ... The weather ...

SECOND GENTLEMAN (*nodding in the direction of Murray across the table*):   I was asking Mr Murray, purely out of academic interest, why body-snatchers are known as Resurrectionists. He was polite enough to excuse my morbidity so soon after dinner, but ...

MURRAY: I'm afraid I was rather uncertain myself. Thomas can tell you.

GREEN: Thomas knows *every* answer. I sometimes suspect him of prearranging the questions so that his encyclopaedic information can come rolling 'spontaneously' out.

ROCK: You overestimate me, Doctor Green. I can answer every question only *after dinner* when people are usually not in a position to verify my facts. But Mr Sinclair's question is too simple. The removal of a body from the walled precincts of God's Acre was viewed by the superstitious and the credulous as nothing less than an interference with the plans of Providence and the Great Resurrection. So the poor ghoul of a body-snatcher became a 'Resurrectionist'.

THIRD GENTLEMAN: If by the superstitious and the credulous you mean believers in Christianity, Doctor Rock ...

ROCK: Sir, I did not say a superstitious and credulous Christian any more than Brahmin or Buddhist or Worshipper of Elephants. If I say, in conversation, that I know a woman who is opinionated, vicious, and ugly, I *do* distrust the man who immediately says: 'Sir, you are talking about my mother!'

THIRD GENTLEMAN: If Logic itself came to dine with you, you would give it an excellent dinner and then try to strangle it. All I wanted to say was that as a Christian I deplore the sacrilege of digging up the dead for anatomists to dissect.

FIRST GENTLEMAN (*to no one in particular*):   I wish I had retired with the ladies.

ROCK: I am no platform drummer, no hawker of slogans, but I say that the Resurrectionists who dig up the dead and sell them to the Anatomical Schools are a direct result of the wrongness of the Law. The Law says that surgeons must possess a high degree of skill. And a surgeon cannot acquire that skill without working upon dead human beings. But the Law also says that the only dead human being we *can* work upon must come from the public gallows; a very uncertain, and meagre, supply. Legally, the hangman is our one provider. But he would have to hang all the *liars* in the City or all the men who are unfaithful to their wives, before there would be sufficient subjects for us. Therefore, we have to obtain our bodies illegally.

I myself, last term, had to pay out five hundred guineas to the Resurrectionists.

Rock drinks.
Murray passes the port to the Second Gentleman. The Second Gentleman fills his glass.

SECOND GENTLEMAN (*aside*):   What very good port they provide in a mortuary these days ...

But Rock now has the attention of the whole table.

ROCK: Do not suppose for a moment that, even after dinner and in one of those mellow, argumentative moods in which one would try to prove that black is white or that politicians are incorruptible, I regard the Resurrectionists as anything but the vicious human vermin of the gutters of the city; in fact, a pack of devils.

But as the Law says 'No' to our need, to the need of progressive science, so up crawl these creatures to satisfy that need *against* the Law. The same applies to every city, though *ours* is rather more fortunate than most; it is *full* of perverted blackguards.

GREEN (*provokingly*):   If you dislike so much the Law that applies to your own science, Thomas, why did you become an anatomist rather than anything else?

ROCK: There was more body to it.

FIRST GENTLEMAN: You would make our City sound to a stranger like Sodom or Gomorrah ...

GREEN: It *is* a seat of learning, after all, Thomas ...

ROCK: And the bowels of squalor. Look any night at the streets of this 'cultured city'. Observe, with academic calm, the homeless and the hopeless and the insane and the wretchedly drunken lying in their rags on the stinking cobbles. Look for yourselves, sirs, at the beggars, and the cripples, and the tainted children, and the pitiful, doomed girls. Write a scholastic pamphlet on the things that prowl in the alleys, afraid to see the light; they were men and women once. Be proud of *that* if you can.

In the silence that follows, Murray rises to his feet.

MURRAY: If you'll excuse me, gentlemen, I must try to brave this – *'terrible* city at night'. You'll excuse me?

At a smiling nod – for Rock has again, suddenly, changed mood – Murray bows and goes out of the room.

ROCK (*at his most jocularly donnish*):   And now, gentlemen, no more such talk from me.

SECOND GENTLEMAN: Oh, surely, not a little entertaining gossip about cannibalism, for a change?

ROCK: No, no, no, not another word. Or, as my friend Murray would say, 'Let us change the subject.'

(*Long shot*) of the dinner table, Rock at the head, waggishly professional.

17

City Street.

Music.
Night.
Murray is walking along the middle of the street. On both sides of the street are many ragged bodies, of men, women, and children. Some are stretched out asleep; some are sprawled drunk, their hands still clutching a bottle; some are huddled together, like large, dishevelled birds, for company and warmth. A few have not managed to reach the comparative shelter of the sides of the street, but lie, ungainly outcasts, snoring scarecrows and men of garbage, across the cobbled middle. Over these bodies Murray steps quickly, carelessly.
(*Cut to*)

18

Another humanity-littered City Street, with Murray walking along it.
(*Cut to*)

19

Doorway of Rock's Academy.

Murray is knocking at the door.
The door opens slowly, only a few inches at first, then we hear a husky voice from within.

VOICE: Och, it's you, Mr Murray.

MURRAY: Open up, Tom.

And the door is quickly opened wide. Murray goes in.

20

Hallway of Rock's Academy.

Murray stands waiting in the gloom of the Hallway while Tom closes the door.
Tom has a candle in his hand. He moves hurriedly in front of Murray and leads the way through the darkness down the Hall.

TOM: I thought it might be another *subject*, sir, at this time of night. There was one brought in only an hour ago ... (*in a whisper*) By you know who. Andrew and ...

MURRAY: Shut your mouth.

They reach a door at the end of the Hall.
Murray opens the door. Tom, with his candle, scuttles back into the darkness.

21

Dissecting Room of Rock's Academy.

Night.
A large room, cold, clean, and echoing.
Tables and slabs.
Anatomical diagrams on the walls.
On one of the tables we see an array of shining instruments: knives, saws, choppers, and long sharp steel tools.
The room is lit by one flickering gas-jet.
Two young men stand at one of the tables.
On it we see, half in shadow, a shrouded body wrapped in sacking.

Murray is coming into the room.

MURRAY (*brusquely*):   Evening, Brown ... 'ning, Harding.

Murray crosses to the table. He unwraps the sacking, flings aside a few soiled white cloths, lowers his hand in between them.
For a moment there is silence.

MURRAY: Stand out of the light, will you?

Suddenly he flings back the cloths, and straightens up.

MURRAY (*in angry undertone*):   Ugh! This is a week old! Why can't the fools bring something fresh? Don't they get paid enough? Might as well dissect a dog dragged out of the river after the fishes have been at it. Come on, let's go and have a drink in the Market. *That's* not worth pickling. Come on.

He walks towards the door, opens it, stands waiting.
Harding lowers the gas.
And out of the dim room the three of them walk into darkness.
And out of the darkness comes loud, gay music, and we are in:

22

Interior of Tavern B.

Shouts and laughter, and a wet dribble of singing.
The benches are packed tight with beggars, hawkers, cheap-jacks, drunks, street women, rogues, and slummers.
The rough tables are crowded with tankards and bottles, stained with spilt drink.
At the open doorway, children rabble together.
Moving slowly down the room, we pass the two women whom last we saw crying 'Rags and bones' and 'Cat-skin' through the Market.
In their bedraggled shawls and cock-eyed bonnets they look as though they might have been made out of their own wares.
Moving slowly down, we pass, near the two woman, a beautiful girl of about twenty years who has spent nearly half of them trying to defeat her beauty. She is giggling, half tipsy, at some unpleasantry.
Moving slowly down we pass Andrew Merry-Lees and Praying Howard. Sober as churchyard worms, in their corpse-dusty top-hats, they are trying to cure the hiccups of Mole – who sits, small and furry, between them – by pouring drink from a tankard down his throat.

Moving slowly down, we reach Murray and the two young students, Brown and Harding, with tankards before them. They are, all three, a little tight and talkative.

BROWN: Refined gathering to-night.

HARDING: Too refined for old Murray after his hurly-burly with the great. How did the dinner go?

MURRAY: Thomas was on top of the world.

BROWN: Gracious, loquacious, insulting, exulting …

HARDING (*overtopping him*):   … drastic, bombastic, charming, disarming …

BROWN (*not to be outdone, with extravagant gestures*):   … avuncular, carbuncular.

HARDING: What did he talk about at dinner, apart from sex and religion and politics?

MURRAY: Body-snatchers.

Harding, with a 'Sh!' of warning, gives Murray a dig with his elbow, and nods up the room to where Merry-Lees and the Mole are now solemnly pouring whisky down Praying Howard.

As Murray looks in their direction, so he sees the beautiful girl and beckons her over to him.

Beautifully unsteady, she approaches. Brown and Harding squeeze up to make room for her beside Murray.

MURRAY: Sit down and drink with us, sweet Jennie Bailey, my lovely charmer …

(*Cut to*) the two Market women looking with undisguised dislike at Jennie Bailey, Murray, and the two students, who are now drinking and laughing together.

The first of the women, she who cried the cry of 'Rags and bones', is soddenly morose, a coarse slattern and drab.

The second woman, she who cried the cry of 'Cat-skin', is a bawd and virago.

The first woman says:

Look at Jennie Bailey, the lady. Drinking with the doctors. Look at her, Kate.

KATE: I'd like to be putting my nails in her eyes ... I saw that Bob Fallon looking at her yesterday. Mind your step, Nelly.

NELLY: She won't be young for long. Another year and the men won't look at her. She's the sort that grows old in a night.
        I seen your Mr Broom looking at her, too. Showing all his teeth.

KATE: She wouldn't go with Fallon or Broom, not she. Look at her. Not when there's money.

(*Cut to close shot*) of Murray and Jennie. They are sitting close together. Brown and Harding have moved away from them, further down the table.

MURRAY: Why can't we meet in another place, sometimes, Jennie? Anywhere else, not always in this damned tavern, with all the sluts and drunks staring at us.

JENNIE: Where else *could* you take me, sweetheart, except for a walk in the fields – and in winter too! Kissing in a hedge in the snow like two robins.

MURRAY: We could find somewhere to be together.

JENNIE: Loving in the lanes, with all the trees dripping down your back and the thorns tearing your petticoats, and little insects wriggling all over you – oh no! Or sitting holding hands in your lodgings all the evening, and your brother studying books in the other corner! (*softly*) You know you could come home with me.

MURRAY: And you know that I won't. I *can't*! Don't you understand that I couldn't go back with you there. Not there, in that house. I don't want to think of you in that house, ever. I don't want to think of the others, and your smiling at them and letting them ...

JENNIE: Oh, the 'others' don't mean a thing in the wide world. They're *different*. I'm for *you*. Come back; now. I'll tell Rosie you're staying and ...

MURRAY: No. No, Jennie. Please. You're *beautiful*. Come away. Come away from everything here. Are you never going to say 'Yes' to me, even if I ask you a thousand thousand times! I'm asking you again, Jennie ...

JENNIE (*gaily*):   Oh, a fine young doctor's wife I'd make. Wouldn't the ladies love me? 'And from what part do you come, Mrs

Murray?' 'Number 23 Pigs' Yard. Your husband used to call on
Wednesdays.' ...

(*Cut to*) the door of the tavern, where the two men of the
Grass-market, the tall, thin, always half-dancing one, and the squat
one, are standing.
They look round the room.
They see Kate and Nelly, and make their way across the crowded,
swirling bar towards them.
The tall one crackles his way through the crowd, jumping and
finger-snapping, a long damp leer stuck on the side of his face.
The squat one elbows his way through, now sullenly truculent, now
oily and almost bowing.
They stand over their women.
And the squat man says, ingratiatingly and yet with an under-
menace:

Can you buy a little drink for us, Nelly darling? We're thirsty,
love.

And the thin man says, in his high, mad voice:

Can you buy a little drink for Fallon and Broom, Fallon and
Broom ...

He makes the grotesque movements of drinking, still finger-
snapping, one shoulder higher than the other.

NELLY: There's money for two more and that's all. Here, buy 'em
yourself, Bob Fallon.

She tosses Fallon a coin. And as he catches the coin and shoulders
the few steps to the bar, Broom reaches for Nelly's drink. Nelly makes
as if to snatch the tankard back, but Broom suddenly shows his teeth
and pretends to snap at her.

KATE: Ach, leave him be. Broom's got the devil in him to-night. He'd
bite your hand through. I know him.

By this time Fallon has returned with two drinks, and hands one to
Broom, who attacks it hungrily again.
Fallon, from under his heavy, hanging eyebrows, stares around the
bar. Suddenly he sees Merry-Lees and the two others.

FALLON (*to the women*): There's the three (*his voice lowers*) ...

snatchers we see in the 'Old Bull'. They're swillin' the drink again. Must've digged up another to-night.

He turns to look at Broom, who is staring at the three Resurrectionists with glinting, unseeing eyes.

FALLON: Fourteen pounds for a corpse they get when it's digged up new ... Fourteen pounds! ...

BROOM (*in his high, loud voice*):   Fourteen pounds for gin and pies ...

KATE: Hush! you mad dog ...

NELLY: There's no more left.

She gets up and goes towards the door. Fallon follows her, Broom and Kate behind him. As they move through the bar to the door, we hear Fallon whine:

FALLON: Come on, Nelly darlin', scrape up a penny or two for a drop for us ... There's plenty of ways, lovey ...

23

The Market-place, outside Tavern B.

Moonlight.
The noise of the tavern swirls in a hiccuping gust out into the street.
The Market stalls are shrouded like dead-carts.
And the doors of other pubs and houses are open, staining light out on to the cobbles.
People stand at doorways, up to no good.
People and other pigs flop on the strawed cobbles.
Nelly walks to a barrow just outside the pub and takes the handles. The barrow is heaped with rags.
Fallon, Broom, and Kate follow her as she begins to push the barrow through the moonlit Market.
Suddenly, with a yelp, Broom leaps on to the barrow, sitting bolt upright among the rags.

BROOM (*in a high, gay snarl*):
Broom
In his carriage and pair ...

Nelly takes no notice but doggedly pushes the barrow on.

And sullenly Fallon walks at the side, Kate trailing after him.

FALLON: Fourteen pounds for a corpse! ...

They move out of the Market, through the alleyways.

NELLY (*in a harsh grumble as she trundles the barrow on with its load of rags and one cackling man*): Why don't you dig one up yourself? You're frightened of the dark.

Over the cobbles of lonely alleys the barrow rattles, and the finger-snapping, dog-haired man squatting on the rags points his finger at one dark doorway, then at another.

BROOM: They're dead in there ... Dig 'em up, Fallon ... In there ... In there ...

Round a corner they come into Rag-and-Bone Alley.

24

Rag-and-Bone Alley.

They stop at the door of a tenement.
In a first-floor window hangs a sign:

CLEAN BEDS

Kate opens the door and goes through. Fallon follows her. Broom leaps from the barrow and is inside the dark doorway like a weasel into a hole.

25

Large Lodging-room.

The four of them are moving through the room.
Around the walls of the room are many narrow beds.
Some of these beds are occupied. By men, or by women, or by human beings at all, we cannot see, but we can hear the noises of unhappy sleep, the sodden snore, the broken sigh, the whimpering of breath.
The four move through the room towards a small open door.
The two women go through the door into the darkness of the adjoining room.

Fallon stops at the last two beds against the wall. He looks down upon them.

In each of them sleeps an old man covered with rags.

One old man is mumbling in his sleep the almost inaudible scraps and ends of prayer.

And as Fallon looks down upon him, Broom tiptoes to his side.

Silently Fallon and Broom look down upon the two old sleeping men, whose hideously haggard faces for a moment we see close.

26

Lecture Hall of Rock's Academy.

(*Close-up*) of Rock lecturing. He has a large volume in his hand.

ROCK: This, gentlemen, is a volume by Vesalius, the acknowledged father of our art. Look at its size, and bear in mind that its thousand folio pages ...

From Rock's angle we look down at the densely packed auditorium of his Lecture Hall. Among the faces of the students we recognise those of Brown and Harding.

ROCK (*continuing throughout*):   ... embrace only a special part of the human anatomy ... Now, gentlemen ...

From the auditorium we look up at Rock as, with a very small volume in his other hand, he continues:

ROCK: ... behold the advance of the age, the progress of science to-day, the *Pocket Anatomist*, said to contain the *whole* of Anatomy within the compass of three inches by two.

Reverently he lays down the large volume on his lecturing table.

With the greatest contempt he casts the small volume across the platform.

Laughter of the students.

27

Private Smokeroom in an Inn.

A snug little box of a room that could not hold more than four.

Two small oak settles facing each other.

A fire-place. A blazing wood fire.

A mantelpiece. A shining ebony clock. On either side of the clock, a tall silver candlestick. Candles burning.

A little counter. Behind the counter, bottles gleaming in candlelight. Two old gentlemen are seated in the room. They have an air of judicious, contented permanency. They seem part of the furniture; their baldness gleams like the silver, like the mellow bottles. Each holds a silver tankard.

FIRST GENTLEMAN: Now if I had a boy ...

SECOND GENTLEMAN: ... He'd be no boy now, John ...

FIRST GENTLEMAN: ... If I had a boy and he decided to enter the medical profession – against my wishes, needless to say; the legal profession has always been good enough for us – I would no more send him to Thomas Rock than I'd lay down the law to my wife. Your health!

SECOND GENTLEMAN: Health!

FIRST GENTLEMAN: They tell me, for example, that he openly condones the activities of the Resurrectionists ...

SECOND GENTLEMAN: He married a young person who was in domestic employment, too, I believe ...

FIRST GENTLEMAN: No, Richard, my wife tells me that she sold fish ...

SECOND GENTLEMAN: It is all the same – fish or dish-clouts.

FIRST GENTLEMAN: And I have heard he has a most scurrilous tongue ... Preaches Anarchy ... Ridicules the Law ... Has all his young men *laughing*, and spouting revolutionary doctrine ... Interpolates violent criticisms of the Constitution in the very middle of his supposedly scientific lectures ... He does not even try to live like a gentleman ... My wife says that they keep only *one* maid in the whole house ...

SECOND GENTLEMAN: Mrs Rock can do the rest of the work, I suppose. She is used to it.

FIRST GENTLEMAN: No, no, Richard, she sold fish ...

SECOND GENTLEMAN: Another, John?

FIRST GENTLEMAN: Thank you ... No more than a double ...

The First Gentleman raises his hand in a restraining gesture.
(*Dissolve to*)

28

Bright sunshine.

Students rushing pell-mell across the Square towards Rock's Academy.
A baker, carrying a big wooden tray of loaves across the Square, only just manages to avoid them.
We see the students race up the steps.

29

We see the students in the Lecture Hall of Rock's Academy.

Rock enters.
He enters like a great actor; he acknowledges the ovation of his audience; he bows; he steps to the platform table; he adjusts his spectacles and his cuffs; every movement is studied.

ROCK: Gentlemen ...
(*Dissolve to*)

30

Lecture Hall at night.

The hall is dimly lit.
Rock, in shirt-sleeves, is rehearsing a lecture to an audience of one solitary skeleton.

ROCK: ... And are we to be told that the Kafir is a savage because he lives in the wilds, and that John Bull is the happy creature of civilisation because he wears breeches, learns catechism, and cheats his neighbours? I say that ...

During this rehearsal, the door of the Lecture Hall opens slowly, and two very young students poke their heads around to watch the master in uncomprehension and awe.

31

(*Close-up*) of two elderly professors, in mortar-boards and gowns, standing against the background of a very large, ornately gold-framed portrait of another old professor.

FIRST PROFESSOR: I knew him when he was a boy. He was clever as a monkey, and he looked like one, too. But he was never *really young*.

SECOND PROFESSOR: Or sound.

FIRST PROFESSOR: No, one cannot say one likes him, or approves of him. But that is not the question. We must disregard personal prejudice.

SECOND PROFESSOR: Difficult, when *he* refuses to disregard it. He called me 'insipid booby' in the *Scientific Journal* ...

FIRST PROFESSOR (*with a side glance at his companion*):   Most uncalled for. No, my point is that one cannot look upon him as an insignificant opponent. His medical history is, unfortunately, brilliant. And they *do* think very highly of him on the Continent. Add to that, that he has five hundred students attending his classes, and that his nearest rival, our old friend Hocking, has less than a dozen ...

SECOND PROFESSOR: Nine, to be exact, and that includes three nephews ...

FIRST PROFESSOR: ... and we begin to see what a pernicious influence the fellow might have upon the whole scholastic life of the City; indeed, upon the trend of scholastic thought *everywhere* ...

SECOND PROFESSOR: A menace. A menace. So rude, too ...

32

Rock lecturing.

He holds a human skull high in his hands.

33

(*Close shot*), from above, of an Old Man lying in his coffin.

We recognise him as one of the two old men who were sleeping when Fallon and Broom looked down at them in Sequence 25.

The lid of the coffin comes down.

(*Track back*) to show that we are in the Large Lodging-room of Fallon and Broom's house.

A Coffin Carpenter is nailing the coffin which lies at the foot of a bed. The straw of the bed lies scattered round it.

In the next bed, the other Old Man, wrapped in his rags, is staring at the coffin, at the Carpenter, and at Fallon and Broom, who stand at the entrance to the small adjoining room.

The rest of the beds in the Lodging-room are empty.

BROOM: Hammer him in, hammer him in. Four pounds rent all dead in a box.

FALLON: Now who would've thought old Daniel could be so mean. Dying without a word, and owing us four pounds. He didn't even have a penny piece hidden under the straw …

BROOM: If only he was alive again so that I could kill him with my hands …

FALLON: And all he left was a bit of a broken pipe … And livin' here all these months on the fat of the land … Many's the night I've beaten the rats off him myself …

Fallon is slouched against the doorway in a kind of self-pitying gloom, but Broom is half dancing with rage …

The Carpenter goes on hammering.

BROOM: Four pounds gone! Whisky and gin and bonnets gone! No more money for Broom! Hammer him in – hammer him in!

COFFIN CARPENTER (*without looking up*):   And what do you think I'm doing? Pullin' him out?

The beating of the hammer on the nails of the coffin.

And slowly Broom's dancing fury dies; he swivels his eyes towards Fallon.

Fallon looks back at him, and slowly through his mulish bloodshot stupidity he seems to understand.

Now the Carpenter rises, collects his tools, goes out through the far door.

FALLON (*in a heavy whisper*):   Hammer him in, hammer him in …

BROOM (*softly*): … and what do you think I'm doing (*more loudly*) … pullin' him out?

Broom runs swiftly to the far door, looks out, turns back, slams the door, bolts it, runs back …

BROOM: Four pounds he owes us and ten pounds they'll give us for him …

FALLON (*with a kind of sodden horror*):   Body-snatchers!

But Broom is calling through the other door:

BROOM: Kate, Kate, come here!

Nelly and Kate come in.

BROOM: Here, take one end. Take his head.

Without understanding, the women obey, take hold of the top of the coffin while Broom takes the other. Together they drag the coffin through the door into the other room. Still Fallon does not move.

Then, suddenly, he draws back his heavy, muscle-bound shoulders, and follows them.

And the eyes of the Old Man in the bed follow *him*.

We hear whispering from the other room.

Then a scraping, screwing noise.

Then the door is shut.

34

City Street.

Late evening.

We see, in (*long shot*), Fallon and Broom moving up the street away from camera.

Fallon is carrying a tea-chest on his back.

By his side, at a zany trot, goes Broom.

We see two policemen coming slowly down the street towards them and towards us.

And Fallon and Broom move quickly and suddenly down a side street.

35

Another City Street.

Late evening.
Fallon and Broom walking along with the tea-chest.
Two students pass them.
Broom nudges Fallon, who puts down the tea-chest and follows them a few steps.

FALLON (*in his whining voice*):   Beg your pardon me askin', sirs, if it's not too much trouble for you, could you be telling me where the Academy is? We've a little matter of business ...

The students have paused and turned round.

FIRST STUDENT: What Academy do you want?

SECOND STUDENT: ... And what's the little business? Oh!

The Second Student has seen the tea-chest a little way off, with Broom, its attendant, winking and leering.
He draws the First Student's attention to the tea-chest.

FIRST STUDENT: If it's a subject ...

Fallon cringes, and nods, and nods again.

FIRST STUDENT: ... take it along to Doctor Rock's. That's over there. Round that corner. It's the second house in the square. He'll pay you a better price than Hocking.

FALLON: Oh yes, that was the name, sirs, Hocking, sirs, Hocking ...

FIRST STUDENT: You take it to Doctor Rock ...

FALLON: Oh, thank you, sirs, thank you, my humblest thanks to you, sirs ...

But the two students have walked off.
And Fallon rejoins the tea-chest and Broom, and lifts the tea-chest on his back and moves on ...

36

Doorway of Rock's Academy.

Broom raps at the door, then quickly steps back, ready to run.
Fallon, with the tea-chest, stands, bowed, near the door, stubbornly servile.

The grille in the door opens, and the face of Tom stares through: a face through a spider-web.

Through the grille, through Tom's eyes, we see the two men: the barrel-bulk of Fallon in the foreground, the lean lank Broom craning a little way behind him.

FALLON (*ingratiatingly*):   Two young gentlemen told us we could sell an article here ... We got it in the tea-chest ...

Now, from Fallon's eyes, we see the face of Tom at the grille.

TOM (*with a grunt*):   Wait.

The grille closes. Bolts rattle. The door opens slowly.

We hear Tom's voice from the darkness within the door, but we do not see him.

TOM'S VOICE: Come in. Walk quiet.

From behind them we see Fallon and Broom walk into the darkness. The door closes.

37

Hallway of Rock's Academy.

In the gloom, what stands within the tall, glass-fronted cases that line the Hallway cannot clearly be seen. But Fallon and Broom glance quickly, fearfully, at them, and we catch for a moment the glint of a bone, the shape of a stripped head.

Tom beckons, and walks down the Hall towards the door under the stairs.

TOM: Follow. Walk quiet.

Fallon and Broom follow him into the small, dark, bare Cloakroom.

TOM: Put it down there. Wait. Don't move now.

Tom goes out, leaving Fallon and Broom standing one at each side of the tea-chest in the dark room.

Tom walks into the Hall, climbs the stairs.

38

Corridor in Rock's Academy.

Tom walks along the Corridor. He stops at a door.
From within we hear the voice of Rock:

ROCK'S VOICE: ... It was Herophilus who first traced the arachnoid membrane into the ventricles of the brain and ...

Tom knocks three times on the door, and we hear Rock interrupt his sentence to say:

ROCK'S VOICE: Come in.

And Tom enters.
From the open door we see into:

39

Reference Library in Rock's Academy.

It is a smallish book-lined room, in which Rock is talking, informally, to a small group of seated students. He is walking up and down before them, his arms behind his back, but he stops at sight of Tom and raises his eyebrows questioningly.

TOM (*in a confidential voice*):   There's a couple of new hands downstairs, sir, they've brought ...

But Rock, turning to the students, interrupts him.

ROCK: Excuse me, gentlemen, you and Herophilus must wait a few moments.

And he walks out of the room, Tom stepping back to allow him passage.
Then Tom follows him.

40

Corridor in Rock's Academy.

We follow Rock and Tom along the Corridor, down the stairs, and into the Hallway.
They go into the Cloakroom under the stairs.

41

Small Cloakroom.

Fallon and Broom move aside nervously into the shadows as Rock, taking no notice of them at all, goes straight to the tea-chest.
Tom hurries to his side, cuts the ropes around the chest, drags away the straw and rags.
Rock looks inside.
Then he straightens up, takes out a purse, hands it to Tom.

ROCK: Give them seven pounds ten.

As Tom opens the purse and counts out the money from it, Rock, for the first time, looks at Fallon and Broom.

ROCK: What are your names?

Fallon steps, toadying, out of the shadows.

FALLON: Bob Fallon, sir.

Rock nods towards the shadows.

ROCK: And the other?

Broom comes out, like a ghost, smiling his long side smile, but he does not speak. His long fingers rap-rap-rap on his elbow.

FALLON: Broom, sir.

ROCK: If you have any more, let us have them.

Rock turns away and walks out of the room. And Tom hands over the money to Fallon.

42

City Square.

Music.
Fallon and Broom are moving through the moonlit Square towards us, Rock's Academy behind him.
Broom is half dancing, finger-snapping, his whole body one long lean grin.
Fallon, at his side clinking coins in his hands, is shambling an accompanying dance.
Nearer, nearer, they dance towards us until their faces fill the screen;

until all we can see is the thick snout-mouth and the thin fox-lips, the little glinting eyes and the slant slits.

43

Interior of Tavern B.

Closely we see, at a table, the faces of Fallon, Broom, Nelly, and Kate.

Coming closer, at the level of the table, we move past mugs and bottle to a pile of coins and Fallon's hands around them. The hands move, pushing some of the coins across the table.

FALLON'S VOICE: For you, Nelly love. All for yourself. For you, Kate.

Now, still closely, we see the four at the table.

FALLON: Broom and I share the rest.

And Fallon divides, in one movement of his broad fingers like big toes, the remaining coins.
Broom snatches his coins up.

BROOM: A bottle, a bottle, another bottle!

And he darts away from the table and brings a bottle back and pours whisky into each mug.

NELLY (*softly, in a kind of drunken, lumpish amazement*):   Seven pounds ten for an *old* man ...

And they all drink.

FALLON: Oh, the shame that he wasn't a *young* man ...

And, with their own kinds of laughter, they drink again.

44

Market-place.

Day.
Fallon and Broom are looking at the wares on a clothes-stall.
They plough and scatter through the clothes, while the stall-keeper, a fat woman smoking a pipe, looks on expressionlessly.
Fallon pulls out a shawl from a heap of oddments and tosses a coin

to the woman who, still expressionlessly but with the deftness of a trained seal, catches it.

FALLON: I'll have this ...

He pulls out another shawl, and a skirt, and a petticoat.

FALLON: ... and this ... and this ... and this ...

And Broom has decked himself with lace from the stall and is mincing around in the parody of a drunken woman.

Fallon, with a wide, extravagant gesture, piles all his presents under his arm, and tosses the woman another coin. She catches it.

And Broom still prances, now with a bonnet on his head.

BROOM: Look at me ... look at me. My *mother* wouldn't know me ...

And Fallon and Broom link arms and move away through the Market, Broom in his fineries, Fallon trailing a shawl behind him in the mud of the cobbles.

Arm in arm they move on through the Market, to the distant playing of a fiddle.

45

City Park.

Music.

A windy afternoon.

Rock and Elizabeth are walking down a path under the trees. Annabella walks a little way apart from them, stiffly, primly.

Some way in front of them two little children are running along and playing.

Through the music we hear the voice of Rock's mind.

ROCK'S VOICE: Oh, such a cold day for walking abroad, and the wind like a drunk beggar with his fiddle. Well, I suppose it does us good. It does *me* good to feel the family man again, walking through the respectable, gusty park with Elizabeth on my arm ... Oh, the years fly! Time with his wingèd chariot, hurrying near, and my life going true and even, and my children growing, and Elizabeth with me for ever, and books to write, and work to do ... Lord, but it's a happy time ... even in the unhappy times ...

Slowly, sedately, they move on through the cold afternoon.

46

Rag-and-Bone Alley.

Slowly, disconsolately, Fallon and Broom walk down the Alley towards the Lodging-house.

Broom is no longer dancing, finger-snapping, pirouetting, but walks like a wraith, holding his shabby thinness against the cold; and Fallon, head down, shambles without seeing or caring.

They reach the Lodging-house.

47

Large Lodging-room.

All the beds are empty, the earth-coloured blankets flung half off them.

All the beds except one: that bed nearest to the door of the small adjoining room, in which the second Old Man lies still under his filth and rags.

Fallon and Broom walk past the Old Man, open the door of the small room.

His eyes follow them.

The door closes.

48

Small Room in Lodging-house.

In one corner a straw bed.

In another, heaps of rags.

There is a table, a few broken chairs.

Straw and broken glass litter the foul floor.

Fallon throws himself on to the straw bed.

Broom walks about the room, caged, his eyes darting sharply at every squalor.

FALLON: And what d'you think you'll find? Prowling like a cat. D'you think there's money in the old straw?

Broom has stopped at the cobwebbed window and is looking out.

BROOM: There's fat pigs in the yard outside.

FALLON (*not listening*):   Drain the dry bottles, lick the floor, scrabble in the muck for a farthing. There's nothing, nothing.

BROOM (*still at the window*):   Fat, juicy porkers waiting for the knife to cut them ear to ear. Squeeeel!

FALLON: Shut your squeal. Ach, if old Daniel was here, dying again!

BROOM (*in a quiet voice, still looking out of the window*):   Geordie's dying.

Without turning from the window, Broom nods back at the door between the small room and the large room.
We move towards Broom.

BROOM: Geordie coughs all night. Krawf! Krawf!

We move closer to Broom.

BROOM (*softly, but clearly*): It's awful *tedious* waiting for Geordie to die ...

We are right up to Broom's face.
There is complete silence.
Then there is the sound of the rustle of straw. Then the sound of a door opening.
Still Broom does not look round.
Only when a cry comes from the next room, a cry like an old sheep's, half moan and half bleat, does Broom spin round like a dancer at a cue.
We see him, in (*close-up*), staring towards the other room.
Staring. And smiling.
(*Dissolve*)

49

City Street.

Music.
Late evening.
(*Long shot*) of Fallon and Broom walking away from camera. Fallon carries the tea-chest on his back.
Broom capers at his side.

50

Large Lodging-room.

Kate and Nelly walking through the room.
They stop at the Old Man's bed.

Nelly leans down to look at the empty bed. Then she straightens up with a little shudder.

And Kate looks.

Silently they pull up the rags and bits of blanket from where they have been pulled on to the floor, and cover the straw bed with them, carefully, like two housewives.

Suddenly, from outside, there is a loud knocking on the door.

The women start, look at each other.

NELLY (*whispering*):   Perhaps that's the ...

KATE (*whispering*):   Perhaps it's ... lodgers.

And straightening her dirty shawls about her, she walks down the room to see.

51

Hallway of Rock's Academy.

Tom is climbing the stairs. From the foot of the stairs we see him climb.

He is half-way up when Rock, with top-hat and stick, comes down. Tom stops.

As Rock approaches him, Tom speaks:

TOM: It's Bob Fallon and Broom again, sir. They've brought a new subject. It's an old man. He's not ... very long dead. They want ten pounds, sir.

ROCK: Give it to them.

He walks downstairs, down towards us. His face is expressionless, his attire immaculate.

52

City Church.

Organ music as the worshippers come out into the street.

Among the worshippers, distinguished by his loose-flowing cloak and his florid clothing, is Rock.

With him are four of his students, including Brown whom last we saw in Tavern B with Murray and Jennie Bailey. Other of the faces we recognise, too, as having been among those in the lecture classes.

Many of the worshippers stop outside the church, bow, raise their hats, gather in groups.

But Rock and his four disciples stride on down the street.

From outside the church we see how the eyes of many worshippers follow them; and a few black-apparelled heads come whispering together.

The organ music fades.

53

Hill above the City.

Rock and the students are walking up the Hill.
They stop. They look down at the City.
Rock sits on the grass, and the students sit at his feet.

BROWN: Did you ever hear such a mealy-mouthed sermon, sir? It made me ...

ROCK: Indeed? In my student days I fancied myself as something of a sermon-taster, but I cannot say that I was ever actually ill from it. I grew accustomed to the taste: a not too unpleasant mixture of boiled brimstone and the day before yesterday's sprouts ...

FIRST STUDENT: What was the sermon about? The Sanctity of Human Life, was it? I went to sleep.

ROCK: To sleep, Mr Duncan? I would not have known. You seemed to me to be wearing the same expression of studious concentration that you wear in my Anatomy classes. How strange and beautiful the City looks to-day. A city where good men walk in dignity and peace, and children play in green places, and girls are both pure and merry, and the hearts of young men are lifted with the aspirations of love, and scholars labour diligently with no other motive than the advancement of the knowledge and happiness of mankind. Dear me! Who would think that that lovely City below us is a Gibraltar of propriety and mediocrity, where the good men starve or are hounded into the dark, and the worthless thrive, and the scholars think only of material rewards, and the girls are born with their noses snobbed in the air and their eyes searching for a marriage bargain, and the young men's hearts are lifted only by the thought of easy success. And who would think, too, that within that Gibraltar lies an *inner* island of active evil ...

BENNET (*slowly*):   Yes. The Sanctity of the Human Body and the Human Soul. That's what the sermon was about, sir. It's my opinion that ...

ROCK: Ah! An opinion! Gentlemen, what priceless treasure is to be revealed to us now ...

BENNET (*blushing, and very confused*):   I was only going to say, sir, that I haven't got much of an opinion about it anyway ...

ROCK (*to the others*):   What did I tell you? A treasure! 'My opinion is that I have no opinion.' Excellent! ... But let us talk about other things ...

   That Rabelaisian *raconteur*, Mr Bennet, shall tell us some disreputable stories of his early youth.

And the very young Mr Bennet is confused again.
(*Dissolve to*)

Rock and students walking downhill.

   Music.
   Gathering darkness.
   At the foot of the hill, Brown and Students One and Two part from Rock and Bennet.
   We see them in (*long shot*).
   We hear none of their words, but only the evening music.
(*Cut to*)

54

Market-place.

   Music.
   Darkness gathering deeper.
   The lights are coming on. Lights in the windows of the taverns, and tallow-sticks flaring at the alley corners and outside a few of the Market houses.
   But the ordinary life of the Market does not cease with the dark and the coming on of the lights. Children still play on the cobbles; and from the alleys behind them, in the unseen courts and closes, come the voices of other children. And men and women stand about in shop and house and tavern doorways, drinking, talking, quarrelling. And a

horse and cart rumble out of darkness, over the cobbles, and into darkness again.

We see Rock and Bennet walking through the Market, towards us. And we see, too, the crippled boy with the idiot smile (whom we first saw in Sequence 2) playing among a little crowd of children.

He runs away from the children, over to Rock.

And Rock stops, and smiles at him.

ROCK: Good evening, Billy.

Billy smiles back delightedly, and bobs his head up and down.

ROCK: It's a cold night to be running about in the streets ...

BILLY: Not for Billy Bedlam ... Not cold ... (*And, like a taught parrot, he gabbles.*) He's never cold in September or November or December ...

ROCK (*patiently*):   Why, Billy?

BILLY: Because there's an ember in the month ...

Rock puts money gently into Billy's hand.

ROCK: Here's a present for you, boy. Hold it in your hand. Don't lose it.

Rock and Bennet walk on.

We hear, from behind them, Billy's voice crying:

BILLY'S VOICE: Night ... night ... Doctor Rock ...

And we move with Rock and Bennet through the night-time Market.

ROCK: Now he'll hurry as fast as he can on his bent bones to the nearest tavern, and fuddle his few poor wits, and crack his crazed little jokes half remembered from the cradle ... Oh, how the pious would lift their hands to heaven to think of a man giving money to an idiot so that he could get drunk and be warm and happy for an hour or two. Let him rather die a sober frozen idiot in the gutter! ... Would you care to join me at dinner, sir? ...

BENNET: Thank you, Doctor ...

ROCK: Don't call me Doctor. Do I call you Student? Come on, sir ...

And they walk out of the Market into:

55

Alleyway.

Rock and Bennet walk on down the Alley, away from us, into darkness.

And we (*track up*) the Alley towards a doorway with a tallow-stick burning above it.

Two figures stand in the doorway: a man and a woman.

And coming closer to them, we see that they are Murray and Jennie Bailey.

They are very close together.

They stand, their faces half illuminated and half shadowed by the burning tallow-stick, as though in a little island surrounded by a sea of darkness.

And from that sea come the cries of children at play in the dark; though far off now.

JENNIE: It's good night ... good night at the door again. Parting like strangers ...

MURRAY: You're close to me for a moment ...

JENNIE: Is a moment enough for you, then, my dear, my dear? And all the long night to go ... You're a sad, strange boy, saying you love me and leaving me all alone ...

MURRAY: It's I'll be all alone ...

JENNIE: Draw a pretty picture of me, then, to carry about with you so that you'll never be alone, and put it under your pillow at nights like a girl puts a lock of hair or a bit of weddin' cake to wish her sweetheart will come to her ...

MURRAY: I couldn't draw *your* picture, Jennie. You're never the same for a single minute. (*softly*) But you're always beautiful. I *know* you now; but sometimes I don't know you at all – when you're gay and *hard* and drinking and dancing ... And not caring ... It's the others that know you then ...

JENNIE: Oh, my sweet, you and your silly – others ... Come inside with me now ...

And Jennie opens the dark door beneath the burning tallow-stick.

And we see a little passage-way, lit by a gas-jet. And a curtain at the end of the passage-way.

ehind the curtain we hear the voices of men and women.
against the passage light, with the other light bright
.... ner head.

MURRAY: No. No, Jennie. Good night.

And he kisses her, and turns away quickly.
And she steps into the passage-way, and closes the door as the voices
behind the curtain rise ...

56

Dining-room of Rock's House.

From the angle of the door we see that under the light of the high,
many-branched candlesticks sit Rock, Bennet, Annabella, and
Elizabeth.
We (*track up*) to the table.
They are drinking coffee, but there is a decanter at Rock's elbow.
Annabella is frigidly angry.

ANNABELLA: ... And that is what I *believe*, and that is what is
right ...

ROCK (*pointedly to Bennet*):   Have some brandy ...

ANNABELLA: There can be, and there always has been, only *one* path
of virtue.

ROCK: Surprisingly I agree with you, Annabella.

ANNABELLA: Then it is only for the second time in your life.

ROCK: I can't remember the first. But I agree with what you say, not
with what you *mean*. *I believe in the virtue of following no path but
your own, wherever it leads* ...

ANNABELLA: And that is precisely the sort of statement that
antagonises you to the whole of the profession ...
For all your great successes and your famous friends, you do not
know how many people there are who would be delighted to see
you ruined ...

ELIZABETH (*to Bennet*):   Do you like this City, Mr Bennet, after the
Continent? I think you were very fortunate to have travelled
around so much with your parents in the holidays ...

BENNET: I like France, ma'am, very much indeed. Of course, I like this City, too ...

ANNABELLA: Mr Bennet, do you, as a student, find that my brother's language and attitude are congenial to the other students?

ROCK: How d'you find the brandy, Bennet? Not mellow enough for you?

BENNET: No, sir ... it's ... excellent. Yes, Miss Rock, we all find Doctor Rock's language and ... er ... attitude ... most ... congenial and, and ... and *stimulating*.

ANNABELLA: Like brandy on persons of weak health, physical or mental.

ELIZABETH: I should very much like to see Paris, Mr Bennet ...

ANNABELLA: My dear Elizabeth, is this a geographical conversazione? I merely wanted to know ...

ROCK (*to Bennet*):   Without embarrassing you further, and allowing you no opportunity of savouring, let alone swallowing, the brandy you were kind enough to call excellent, may I explain to you that what my sister really wishes to know is whether you agree with her that the medical profession, with some notable exceptions, consider me a seducer of youth and an atheist? (*in another tone*) You have no need to answer, of course ... (*gently*) Has he, Elizabeth, my dear? I would far prefer to talk about Paris ...

BENNET (*in an agony of embarrassment, but still determined to defend his master*):   I can't pretend to know what the medical profession thinks of Doctor Rock, Miss Rock, but *we* all think that most of the other doctors and professors are enormously *jealous* of him. (*to Elizabeth*) Jealous because he's a great anatomist, ma'am, and a great — (*He breaks off.*)

ROCK: H'm! I know Paris well, especially the cafés. I always used to wear a yachting cap in France, I can't think why ... I wish you'd been there with me, my dear ...
(*Dissolve to*)

57

Small Room in Lodging-house.

Nelly, at the fire, is stirring a wooden spoon in a black pot, and something is being fried. We hear the sizzling.
Kate, with an almost bristleless broom, is brushing the broken glass into a corner.
The broken table has been laid: there are four pewter mugs on it.
Suddenly there is a noise of singing and stamping from outside.
The door is crashed open and Broom dances in, a bottle under each arm.
He winks and leers at the women, nods and jerks his fingers at the open door.
And in through the door Fallon staggers, singing, with a little old woman hanging, half falling, on his arm. She too is trying to sing.

FALLON: And look what I've brought home, my doves. A pretty old woman with nowhere to sleep ... have you, Granny? Nowhere to sleep but with us. Shall we give her a bed?

NELLY: Where d'you find her?

Broom is opening a bottle and pouring whisky into the mugs. He gives the Old Woman one.

BROOM: Drink with Broom!

FALLON: She was lying in the gutter like an old cabbage, weren't you, Granny? Her poor grey hairs dragging in the mud. And who should pick her up but kind Bob?

Fallon lifts the Old Woman up and places her on the bed.

FALLON: There. The place of honour. Nothing's too good for her.

KATE: What you're going to do?

BROOM: Do? Drink!

FALLON: Do? Drink with Granny. All night long.

The Old Woman titters and drinks. She nearly falls off the bed, but Fallon catches her and lays her down gently.

FALLON (*softly*):   No harm must come to you now. You might have bumped your head. Then what'd the doctors think?

Broom skips over and takes the Old Woman's mug from her hand and pours whisky down her throat.
She coughs and gasps.

FALLON (*in a different voice, to the women*):   You two be running off on an errand.

Broom points at the Old Woman who is now almost unconscious, spread on her back, her black mouth open.

BROOM: You needn't be long.

FALLON (*slowly*):   Go now.

And the women, without a word, and without looking at the Old Woman, fasten their shawls and go out.

FALLON (*to the Old Woman, as though to a child*):   Up you get, dear. Don't you want no more whisky? (*into her ear*) Whisky, whisky!

And, trembling, the Old Woman manages to regain some consciousness. As soon as she does, Broom, ready all the time, pours more whisky down her throat.
She falls back.

FALLON: Give me the bottle.

Broom hands it to him. Fallon drinks from it. He passes the bottle back. He rubs off the sweat from his forehead. He moves, unsteadily, but heavily, to the head of the bed.
And Broom crouches at the foot.
From above, we look down on to the Old Woman's face.
Her eyes open.
Suddenly her face is frightened.

58

City Square.

We see Fallon and Broom through the grille in the door of Rock's Academy, as through prison bars.
Fallon carries the tea-chest.
Now, from behind Fallon and Broom, we see the door opened by Tom.
We follow Fallon and Broom as they enter the Hallway.

59

Hallway of Rock's Academy.

Without any need for instruction from Tom, Fallon and Broom move with the tea-chest into the Cloakroom under the stairs.
As they go in, so Murray, in evening dress, comes down the stairs and sees them.
In the Hallway he beckons Tom over to him.

MURRAY: Who are the dapper gentlemen?

TOM: Bob Fallon and Broom, sir. They're new hands ... but they're getting pretty regular. They ask for ten pounds.

Murray goes into the Cloakroom and comes out a moment later. He nods his head.

MURRAY: That'll do.

Now, from the back of the Hallway, at the foot of the stairs, we see Tom opening the door wide to Murray.
In the street outside we see a stationary coach.

MURRAY (*at the door*):   If any more bodies call, tell them I'm at the theatre with Doctor Rock. Good evening, Tom.

And we see him, in (*long shot*) from the back of the Hallway, walk out, down the steps, and into the coach.

60

Vestibule of Theatre.

At the door leans Jennie Bailey, with a gay shawl round her shoulders.
We see, outside the Theatre, coaches waiting.
There is a great burst of applause, and she turns round to look towards the door of the auditorium.
The audience pours out.
Down the stairs at the side come Rock, Elizabeth, Green, Murray, and Annabella.
From Jennie's angle we see them stop to talk to other members of the audience.
We see Murray looking round him.
We see Hocking.

(*Track up*) close to Rock's party.

HOCKING: Good evening, Doctor Rock.

ROCK: Good evening, Doctor Hocking.

HOCKING: I do not often see you at the play ...

ROCK: No, sir. I am able to find my entertainment elsewhere. The City is full of low comedians: it is a pity that the lowest of them all should also be a surgeon. Good night.

And Rock takes Elizabeth's arm, and leads his guests out.
The last of the party is Murray. He sees Jennie Bailey, and stops as the others walk out to the waiting coaches.
He looks round him quickly, then whispers to her, and hurries after the others.
Coaches drive off.
And Jennie goes out, too.
We follow her through the darkness until the Theatre lights behind us fade.
(*Dissolve to*)

61

Market-place.

Night.
We see the entrance to Tavern B from which light and voices pour on to the cobbles.
Jennie Bailey comes out of darkness into the light and into the tavern.

62

Interior of Tavern B.

The tavern is crowded.
Many of the faces are familiar to us now: That old bag of female bones over there, she was the one who described to Fallon and Broom the profession of Andrew Merry-Lees; that fat woman with a pipe there, who tosses down her drink as a tamed seal swallows a fish, she was the one who kept the stall where Fallon and Broom bought clothes for their women; that humpback there, looking at everything with an

idiot smile, he is the one called Billy Bedlam; one of those two very young men over there, being wise and waggish to a pretty girl of sixteen, is the student Bennet; that tall man in a scarecrow's top-hat, hiccuping solemnly, he is the one called Andrew Merry-Lees; and there are others we have seen before, in the tavern, in the street, in the Market, all of them, in their way, vice-residents of the tavern; and among them a few honest, very poor people.

We see all this through Jennie Bailey's eyes.

A dark, pretty young woman with a sulky expression, seated at the far end of the room, waves her hand.

And from her view we see Jennie Bailey, in her gay shawl, charming her way down the room, being familiar with every one (including Billy Bedlam) and over-familiar with some.

Now we see that Jennie Bailey is sitting next to the dark young woman.

And now we see them very close.

Jennie drinks from the dark girl's drink.

JENNIE: I been to see the play in the theatre, Alice.

ALICE: You didn't see no play, dear. You been up High Street.

JENNIE: I did. From the outside. Who shall we get to buy us a drink?

She roves her eye round the pub. She nods towards Billy Bedlam.

JENNIE: Him?

She nods towards Andrew Merry-Lees.

JENNIE: Him? Oooh, no!

She nods towards Bennet. He catches her glance, is about to blush, then, remembering his age, winks back.

JENNIE: Him!

She smiles at Bennet, beckons him over. He comes over.

JENNIE: Going to buy us some medicine, Doctor?

BENNET: Oh, of course I am, Jennie …

JENNIE: Some for Alice and some for me? It's a cold night for poor working girls like us …

Bennet goes off.

JENNIE: I saw my Doctor at the theatre. In my box.

ALICE: John Murray?

Jennie nods.

ALICE: Why d'you treat the poor creature so badly, Jennie?

JENNIE: Oh, but Alice darling, I'm so very very fond of him. I like him better than any man in the whole world ...

ALICE: Then why d'you carry on in front of his eyes and ...

JENNIE: Oh, but I don't, I don't ...

ALICE: ... and teasing him that he's a parson's son, and letting him see you walk out with any Tom, Dick, and Harry ...

JENNIE: ... I don't know any Harry ...

ALICE: ... No one could know you loved him, you're so *brazen*, dear ...

JENNIE: Oh, I want some fun before I die ... You're a parson's daughter yourself ... He must love me for what I am, that's all there is ...

Bennet comes back with two mugs.

JENNIE: There, you can always tell, he's got a sweet face ... I *do* like students and doctors and ...

ALICE: ... butchers and bakers and candlestick-makers ...

We hear a high yelping laugh, and then Fallon's voice.

FALLON'S VOICE: And there's my darling Jennie ...

BROOM'S VOICE: And mine, and mine!

And Fallon and Broom stagger to the table, pushing Bennet aside. Fallon pulls a bottle out of his pocket.

FALLON: Who's going to share a bottle with two county gentlemen?

Fallon and Broom sit themselves next to Alice and Jennie, Fallon next to Jennie, Broom to Alice. Fallon pulls two mugs across the table, and fills them.

JENNIE: I never drink with strangers except on Mondays ...

FALLON: And it's *Monday* to-night.
O the stars are shining, the bells are chiming, we'll drink to
Monday and Tuesday and ...

Fallon pours out another drink.

JENNIE: And I never drink twice with strangers before twelve
o'clock ...

FALLON: And Lord, it's *after twelve.*
O the moon is singing, the grass is growing. We'll drink to twelve
o'clock ... and one o'clock ... and two o'clock ...

(*Quick dissolve*) to the same table with more mugs and bottles on it.
Fallon and Jennie are now very tipsy.
Broom is smiling, leering, giggling, and clowning to Jennie.
Alice still remains comparatively sober, and still sulky.

FALLON (*wheedling*):   I got two more bottles in my little room, Miss
Pretty Bailey. Two great bottles of dancin' dew that'll make you
think the sun's shining in the middle of the night ... and satiny
shining couches for all the kings and queens to be lying on ...
And ...

ALICE: We're not going.

JENNIE: Will you give me a diamond ring and a golden bracelet
and ...

FALLON: I'll give you a bucketful of pearls. We'll sing and dance.
We'll be merry as crickets in Rag-and-Bone Alley ...

FALLON (*half laughing, half singing*):   We'll be merry as crickets in
Rag-and-Bone Alley ...

ALICE (*in an angry whisper to Jennie*):   You're not going with these
two creatures ... You must wait for John Murray ... Don't drink
any more with that Bob Fallon ...

BROOM: And I'll cook you liver and lights ...

JENNIE: Will you cook a partridge for me? ...

FALLON: And I'll put a peacock's feathers in your hair ...

JENNIE: Oh, listen to them both ... You'd think they were great rich
men with crowns and palaces, not a couple of naughty tinkers ...

ALICE: We're not going …
(*Quick dissolve to*)

63

Market-place in the dim moonlight.

Four figures move through the Market: Fallon, Jennie, Broom, Alice. Fallon and Jennie are singing.

FALLON AND JENNIE: We'll be merry as crickets in …

And Broom accompanies their singing, like a dog baying at the moon. Now they are moving through:

64

Rag-and-Bone Alley.

Their singing wakes up a shape that is lying in a dark doorway. Slowly, awkwardly, it rises to its feet. It is Billy Bedlam.
He follows the four, with his eyes, down the Alley, and sees them enter the Lodging-house.

65

Darkness.

Fallon, Jennie, and Broom singing and baying in the darkness.
A door is flung open.
We see, for a moment, the small room of the Lodging-house.
Nelly stands there at the dead fire.
Then Fallon and Jennie and Broom and Alice stumble into the light of the room.
Fallon lurches over to the table, opens a bottle with his teeth.
He makes an unsteady bow, offers the bottle to Jennie …

FALLON: You first, my Jennie, my merry, my cricket …

Jennie drinks.
Alice looks round the room with fear and revulsion.
Broom leaps on to the bed.
Nelly stands, drab and cross, before Fallon.

NELLY: Who told you you could bring your women here, you and that mad dog …

FALLON: Now, now, Nelly macushla, we've come to sing and drink …

But Nelly rushes across to Jennie and pulls the bottle from her lips.

ALICE (*urgently*):   I told you not to come, Jennie Bailey … Let's go, let's go!

FALLON: My Jennie's not going, she's not going, any one else in the wide world can go, not Jennie.

ALICE: Come on, Jennie, come on.

But Jennie is sitting, swinging her legs, on the table, and is trying to open the other bottle.

FALLON: If you don't like it here, go to your own pigsty.

Alice looks at Jennie, but Jennie has opened the bottle and is pouring from it into a glass.
And Alice goes. She slams the door behind her.

NELLY: And *she* goes, too.

Nelly, still with the one bottle in her hand, tries to tear the other bottle from Jennie.
Fallon suddenly lifts a glass and throws it in Nelly's face.
As she staggers, he takes the bottle from her. She puts her hand up slowly to her face, and feels the running blood.
And she goes out of the room like an old woman whipped.
Fallon takes Jennie's glass, drinks from it, puts it back in her hand. And Jennie drinks, swinging her legs.
And Broom is dog-creeping on the floor. As Fallon and Jennie drink he slips off the buckles from her shoes and leaps, lightly and silently, to his feet, and is out of the room, closing the door with no sound.
And Fallon's hand, as he looks at Jennie, slowly drops, and the drink from the bottle he is holding runs over her dress and down her legs.

66

Doorway in Alley (as in Sequence 55).

Alice is talking excitedly to a woman in the doorway.
The woman nearly fills the doorway. She is dressed in a long, loose shift. Her huge arms are bare.

ALICE: And I tried to tell her, Rosie, but she wouldn't listen, she was laughing and drinking with him … Oh, I didn't like the looks of him, Rosie …

ROSIE: Go and fetch her back.

Rosie has a voice deep as a man's, and heavy, and slow.

ALICE: But I'm telling you, Rosie, he's no good, he's like an *animal*; won't you send someone back with me? …

ROSIE: Go and fetch her back. There's persons waiting for her here …

Alice turns away.

67

Darkness.

The pattering of footsteps in the darkness.
A door is flung open.
We see into the small room of the Lodging-house.
But we see no one there.
Then Alice runs in, looks round. She sees Fallon lying stretched on his back on the straw bed in the corner.

ALICE: Where's Jennie?

FALLON (*in a dulled voice*):   Jennie? She went a long time ago.

ALICE: Where did she go?

FALLON: She went out.

And Alice runs out of the room, leaving the door open.

68

Alice is running down Rag-and-Bone Alley in the moonlight.

A dark shape leans against a doorway.
Alice stops.

ALICE: Which way did Jennie go?

Billy Bedlam shakes his head.
Alice points up the Alley.

ALICE: Did she go that way?

He shakes his head, and stretches out his hand.

BILLY: Have some snuff ...

But Alice runs on up Rag-and-Bone Alley.

69

Small Room in Lodging-house.

Fallon is still lying on the straw bed.
The door is still open.
Nelly comes in. The blood has dried on her cheek. She looks round the room.

NELLY: Where's Jennie?

He puts his hand down at his side, the side nearest the wall, and drags up Jennie's gay shawl, and holds it up to Nelly.
His face is hot and wet.
(*Fade out*)

(*Fade in*)

70

City Street.

Broad daylight.
Music and the ringing of church bells.
Fallon and Broom walking up street away from camera.
Fallon is carrying a sack on his back. Broom is holding the end of the sack mock-solemnly like a man at the end of a coffin.
We see, as they move, children coming out of the doorways, children scampering away from their play to sing and cry together:

CHILDREN'S VOICES: You've got a body in the sack!
  Body-snatchers!
  Dead!
  Dead!
  Dead!
  Body-snatchers!

And they dance around the sack.

And Broom snaps his teeth at them.
Fallon and Broom walk on. The voices fade behind them.
(*Dissolve to*)

71

(*Close shot*) of the sack on a table.

(*Track back*) to see that the table is in the Dissecting Room of
Rock's Academy.
There are many students. Some, with their backs to us, are bent over
the tables, cutting, probing, snipping. We see their movements but not
the objects upon which they are working. Some of the students are
talking together. None of them takes any notice of the sack.
Murray comes in and walks up to the sack.

MURRAY (*casually*): Let's see what we've got to-day.

He begins to untie the thick ropes about the sack.
Several students gather around him.

MURRAY: An old trull of eighty with bow legs and a belly like a Lord
    Mayor's, eh? A tramp from the gutter with cirrhosis of the liver and
    three teeth? What's your guess? ... An old ...

He opens the neck of the sack, and begins to draw the sack down
from the head.
Suddenly he stops talking. We see what he sees: Jennie's long fair
hair. Slowly he draws the sack down from the face, but we do not see
it. The students, silent now, gather around it, and we see only their
backs and the profile of Murray. We see that his face has hardened and
become grim, his lips are held very tightly together, as though he were
forcing himself not to utter a word.

BENNET (*in a long-drawn-out half-sighing whisper*): God!

FIRST STUDENT: Here, let me look.

The First Student bends closer over the table.

FIRST STUDENT: It's Jennie Bailey.

SECOND STUDENT: Sweet Jennie Bailey.

BENNET (*softly*):   Yes, it's Jennie! I saw her last night in the Market
    ... She was *singing* ...

But Murray does not utter a word.

THIRD STUDENT: How did she die? …

BENNET: She was *singing* … and *dancing* …

Suddenly Murray turns away and strides out of the room.
The students still stand around the body that we do not see.

72

Out in the Hallway Murray strides across to the door of the small
Cloakroom.

The door is open. Beyond it is darkness. Murray calls into the
darkness.

MURRAY: Tom!

And from the darkness we hear Tom's voice:

TOM'S VOICE: Coming, sir.

Tom comes out of the darkness like an underground animal. He
blinks at the light.

TOM: Yes, sir? I was … cleaning up.

MURRAY: Who brought the subject in?

TOM: In the sack, sir? That was Bob Fallon and Broom … Wasn't it
fresh, sir?

Murray turns away abruptly and, without a word, goes upstairs.
Now we see Murray walking along the Corridor.
He opens a door and strides in.

73

We see Murray stride into the Reference Library.

Rock is standing at a bookshelf at the far end of the room, his back
to us and to Murray.
He turns round as Murray comes in.

ROCK: You knock at the door very softly, Mr Murray.

Murray closes the door, and stands with his back to it.

Rock stands with *his* back to the bookcase. Murray speaks slowly, deliberately, like a man with a passionate temper who is afraid to lose control of it.

MURRAY: They've got Jennie Bailey downstairs.

ROCK: Indeed? Jennie Bailey? Oh yes, I think I remember the name. A beautiful slut with a bold eye and a tongue like a drunken horse-thief's.

And what might she be doing downstairs? I am sure, Mr Murray, that she is an expert in Anatomy, but her knowledge would be too specialised ... Or has she come merely to entertain?

MURRAY: She has come, sir, to be dissected.

ROCK: How very generous of her. I did not think that science was so near her heart. Does she wish to be dissected *alive*?

MURRAY: She is dead.

ROCK: That is carrying scientific generosity to its furthest limit.

MURRAY: She was murdered.

ROCK (*sharply*):   Who says so?

MURRAY: She was murdered.

ROCK: Are there signs of violence upon the body?

MURRAY: She was murdered by two paid thugs of yours: Fallon and Broom. I saw her last night after the theatre. She was well and gay. There are no signs of violence upon her body.

ROCK: Thugs of *mine*, Mr Murray? Do you remember that you yourself paid them for the last *three* subjects?

MURRAY: She was murdered. I saw her. (*slowly, rememberingly*) She had a red shawl on.

ROCK: Indisputable evidence that she was murdered. She should have worn a white shawl, for purity. And what if she *was* murdered, Mr Murray? We are anatomists, not policemen; we are scientists, not moralists. Do *I, I*, care if every lewd and sottish woman of the streets has her throat slit from ear to ear? She served no purpose in life save the cheapening of physical passion and the petty traffics of lust. Let her serve her purpose in death.

MURRAY: You hired Fallon and Broom to murder her as you hired them to murder the others.

ROCK: I need bodies. They brought bodies. I pay for what I need. I do not hire murderers ...

Rock walks over to the door. Murray still has his back to it. Rock stops. Their eyes meet. Then Murray moves aside. Rock opens the door and walks out. We see him walking down the Corridor.

74

(*Cut*) Dissecting Room of Rock's Academy.

Rock walks in.
Students are gathered round the table where Jennie's body lies. We do not see the body.
The students move aside as Rock enters.
He stands in the middle of the group. For a moment he is silent, his head held a little to one side, looking down at the unseen body.
Then Rock turns away from the table.
Murray stands at the door.

ROCK: Oh, Mr Murray. I think that before the body is put into the brine bath, a drawing should be made of it. Shall we not allow posterity to share our exhilaration at the sight of such perfect physical beauty?

I should be much obliged if you yourself would perpetuate on paper the loveliness of this poor clay, Mr Murray. We know your skill with the pencil. God should have made you an artist. He did the next best thing: he gave you a very vivid imagination.

And Rock walks out of the Dissecting Room.
Murray does not move.
The eyes of the students are upon him.

75

A City Street in the fashionable area.

Daylight.
Music.
Fallon and Broom are walking slowly up the middle of the street towards us, looking all around them with a nudging delight.

Broom wears a new extravagant cravat, but still keeps to his ruffian's coat.

Fallon has tied a gipsy-coloured kerchief round his neck.

We do not hear any of the street noises. This is a brief, silent scene, to music.

People are walking past them, up and down the street. An elegant old lady goes by. Broom side grins, points his finger after her.

A nursemaid with two children passes on their other side. And Fallon wags his head in their direction. For their own enjoyment, with winks and nudges, they point out in dumb show various of the passers-by, especially the elderly and the very young.

(*Dissolve to*)

76

Murray sitting, alone, in the Dissecting Room.

Night.

A drawing block is on his knees.

We see, over his shoulder, the drawing on the block.

It is a half-finished drawing of Jennie Bailey, lying as though asleep. Murray goes on drawing. Now, on the paper, we see take shape one arm that hangs over the edge of the table, over the edge of her last bed.

Now Murray is drawing the clenched hand of the hanging arm.

And from the picture we (*track up*) towards the real hand.

And suddenly the hand unclenches itself: an after-death jerk of the nerves.

And two pennies fall out of the now open hand, and drop on to the floor. We see them roll along the floor.

77

Large Lodging-room.

Nelly and Kate are tidying the room, sweeping dirt into corners, covering up tousled beds with mud-coloured blankets, stopping to drink from a bottle on the broken table in the centre of the room.

We hear, from outside, the sound of a knock on the door.

Kate wipes her lips on her shawl and tucks the bottle inside her cabby-like layers of clothes.

KATE: More lodgers!

She goes out of the room by the far door.

Nelly tipsily tidies herself, spits in her hand to help straighten a hanging lock of stiff hair.

And Kate comes back with a big, old, ragged beggar-man shuffling behind her, all dirt and hair, like a tame, tired, time- and whip- and weather-beaten bear.

KATE: You can sleep in any bed you like dad, for twopence a night. Clean and comfy.

NELLY: Are you alone?

The Old Man nods his head.

KATE: All alone in the world? Nobody to care about you at all?

The Old Man shakes his head.

KATE: Ach, isn't it a shame ... Nobody to care if you're alive or dead ...

Kate looks at Nelly.

NELLY: Let the old man have his bed for a penny, Kate.

And Kate takes the Old Man's luggage – which is wrapped up in a handkerchief – and they each hold an arm and lead him over to the bed near the small-room door: the bed where the other Old Man died.

78

Dining-room of Rock's house.

Day.

Elizabeth, in dust-cap and apron, is cleaning the silver.

Suddenly there is the long pealing ring of a door bell. And Elizabeth puts down her cleaning cloth, hurriedly takes off her cap and apron, and goes out of the room, leaving the door open.

We hear the opening of the street door, and then the voices of Elizabeth and Murray.

MURRAY: I hope I am not disturbing you, Mrs Rock.

ELIZABETH: Come in, please, Mr Murray. Do you want to see Thomas? He's lecturing. Oh, you'd know that, of course. My sister-in-law's upstairs ...

MURRAY: I want to see *you*, if I may.

And Murray follows Elizabeth into the room.

ELIZABETH: You shall see me cleaning the silver, then ...

She puts on her cap and apron again, and begins to polish the candlesticks on the table.

ELIZABETH: I thought it might be a stranger at the door ... That's why I had to take my cap and apron off. Miss Annabella would never forgive me if I went to the door dressed like this ... But it's only you. I needn't have worried, need I? ...

MURRAY: I'm afraid that after I tell you what I have to tell you, you will never want to see me again ...

ELIZABETH (*smiling*):   Oh no, no, nothing could be as bad as that ... What has Thomas been doing now? Writing terrible letters to the papers, or telling all the young men to put gunpowder under the City Hall?

MURRAY: No, ma'am.

ELIZABETH: *I* don't mind, you know ... It's only – some other people mind. Thomas can write or say anything he likes: I don't *understand* very much of it ... What have you got to tell me?

MURRAY (*slowly, deliberately*):   I believe that Thomas has instructed two men called Fallon and Broom to commit murder and to sell him the bodies.

There is a silence. Elizabeth stands still, half turned away from Murray. Then:

ELIZABETH: That is a – *horrible* lie. If Thomas hears it ...

MURRAY: He *has* heard it.

Elizabeth begins again to polish the candlesticks. She still does not look at Murray.

MURRAY: Yesterday the body of a young woman called Jennie Bailey was delivered to the Academy by Fallon and Broom. Less than twelve hours before, I had seen her outside the theatre, alive and well. It is not possible that she could have died a natural death.

ELIZABETH: Can't people die a 'natural death' in twelve hours?

And under Elizabeth's calm voice there is a new hardness. There is a tenseness in all her smallest movements as she cleans and polishes, not turning round. She is, quite suddenly, not a sweet and mild young woman but a protectress and an enemy.

MURRAY: She did not die a natural death.

ELIZABETH: Was this 'young woman' strangled, or stabbed, or shot, or poisoned, or beaten to death?

MURRAY (*in a slow, low voice, as though he had said the words over and over to himself*): There were no marks of violence upon the body ...

We see Elizabeth's relief expressed in the relaxing of the tenseness of the muscles of her shoulders. And now she turns round to face Murray.

ELIZABETH: And so you have no proof at all ... How could you? Why did you come to me with such a story? You should go to the police ...

MURRAY: I believe that she was smothered to death in such a way as to leave no signs ... I came to you first, because I want you to tell Thomas that he must go away. At once. Out of the country. I owe him a great deal. I would not care to see him hanged.

ELIZABETH: You are very kind ... Have you thought about yourself? Run out now and shout your lies in the streets, and they will lock you up because you are a madman. Or run to all the lawyers and justices, and they'll ask you for proof and you won't have any: and they'll lock you up because you bear false witness against your neighbour. Or go around in the dark, whispering all the foul things in your own mind to everybody that will listen, and you'll make such a panic and scare that Thomas's school will have to close and all the people who had anything to do with it will be stoned and spat upon and driven out. And you'll never, never, never again be allowed to work in any hospital or any school or anywhere. And nobody will ever speak to you again, or touch you, or be seen anywhere in the world with you ...

MURRAY: I have thought of that. I have thought of everything.

ELIZABETH: And if you call Thomas a murderer, everybody will call you murderer, too. They will call you murderer and butcher ...

MURRAY: All I know is that if Thomas did not *tell* these men to murder, he bought the bodies *knowing* that they were murdered.

ELIZABETH: I thought Thomas told me that it was one of *your* duties to buy the bodies. Will *that* help you very much when you accuse him? Will you go to the police now? Will you tell people what you've told me? It will be quite easy for you to wreck your life, and his, and mine! I shan't try to stop you.

MURRAY: What shall I do?

ELIZABETH: Keep quiet. You knew the girl – Jennie Bailey?

MURRAY: Yes.

ELIZABETH: What was she?

MURRAY: She was a girl from the market ...

ELIZABETH: Was she pretty?

Murray nods, slowly.

ELIZABETH: I think I remember her if she was the girl outside the theatre. She was – *beautiful.* You liked her very much?

MURRAY: Yes.

ELIZABETH: I think you liked her so much that when she died you – lost your head. You didn't know what you were doing or what you were saying. Do you understand? You *imagined things.* Do you understand?

Annabella comes in.

ANNABELLA: Good afternoon, Mr Murray. I didn't know any one had called. I see my sister-in-law is entertaining you ...

ELIZABETH: Mr Murray called to see if Thomas was here. He had something to discuss with him. But now he says it doesn't matter ... Does it, Mr Murray?

And Murray looks, without speaking, at the faces of the two women.

79

Interior of Tavern B, from the angle of the door.

Broom is standing in the middle of the room, looking around him. There are few customers.

In one corner, alone, wrapped up as though against the cold, we recognise Alice. She raises her head, sees Broom, clutches her shawl more tightly round her, and turns her head away to the wall.

And we see Billy Bedlam sitting, also alone, staring at an empty mug before him.

Broom flicks a coin in the air, catches it in the palm of his hand, looks down into his palm. Then he crosses to Billy.

(*Close shot*) of Billy and Broom.

BROOM: Would you be having a little drink, Billy?

Billy smiles up, trustfully, delighted.

BROOM (*without turning from Billy, in a high, loud voice*): Two gins. (*Then ingratiatingly*) It's you and me could drink the sea dry, Billy, and eat the fishes and cuddle the mermaids and dance a jig and play the penny whistle and ...

The potman comes up with the drinks. Broom pays as he talks, and the potman goes off.

They drink them off in a gulp.

BILLY: I've seen a shark ...

BROOM (*loudly*): Two gins. (*softly*) You could wrestle the shark and toss him over your head like a pound of cat's-meat ... *You're* strong, Billy ...

The potman comes up with the drinks. Broom pays as he talks, and the potman goes off.

They drink them off in a gulp.

BILLY: I know a riddle ...

BROOM: Tell Broom your riddle ... Two drinks!

BILLY: In what month of the year do the ladies talk least?

BROOM: Oh, that's a good one. And what month *would* it be, Billy?

BILLY: The month of February, because there wiz least days in it.

And Broom raises his head and yelps with laughter; and slaps his thigh, and cracks his fingers.

Delighted, Billy splutters and crows.

BROOM: Tell Broom a riddle, Billy ... another riddle ...

Broom beckons over his shoulder in the direction of the bar, then leans close to Billy again.

BILLY: I can tell you a riddle that nobody knows and nobody can guess it ...

BROOM: What is it, Billy?

BILLY: Though I black an' dirty am,
An' black as black can be,
There's many a lady that will come
And by the hand tak' me.
Now you can't guess that ...

BROOM: Ah no, Billy, I can't guess that fickly one. Who learned you all those fickly guesses?

BILLY: It wiz my half step-mither. Oh, she's a cunning old body! Oh, she's cunning as a kitten when we're all sitting beside her round the fireside. She tells us a million million million funny stories, but I don't remember them all ...
Though I am black an' dirty an' ...

BROOM: It's a tea-kettle ...

BILLY (*almost in tears*):   Somebody told you.

BROOM: Well, tell us another, *Royal* Billy ...

And he beckons over his shoulder, towards the counter, for more drink, and leans again across the table to listen to Billy.

BROOM: And we'll drink ... and we'll drink ... and we'll ...

And his voice softens and softens until it fades.

80

Small Room in Lodging-house.

Candles in bottles on the table.

We see, in a corner, the pile of old rags and bones. It is far higher than when we last saw it.

Kate lies half on, half off the straw bed near the wall.

Nelly is looking out of the window. The window is open. From outside we hear the squealing of pigs.

The door is flung open.
Broom and Billy lurch in.
Nelly turns from the window.
We hear her whisper:

NELLY: Not Billy Bedlam!

BROOM (*to Nelly*):   Shut the window. The pigs is too loud. It sounds like a killing ...

Nelly shuts the window.

BROOM: And bring out a bottle for Billy ...

Billy staggers to a chair in a corner, sits on it, tilts it back on two legs and smiles at Nelly, who is staring at him as she brings out a bottle from a cupboard near the window.

BILLY: He bought me snuff ...

Billy opens his box of snuff. Half of it spills over him. He scrabbles it off his clothes.
And Broom takes the bottle from Nelly and carries it over to Billy and gives it to him and watches him drink.
We see Billy's face as he drinks: drunkenly made beautiful.
But we see only the back of the watching Broom, and he does not turn round as he speaks:

BROOM: Go round the shebeens and find Fallon. Tell him there's business.

Nelly goes to the door; she looks over her shoulder at Billy.
From her angle we see Billy and Broom's back.

BILLY: He gave me snuff ...
He gave me snuff and whisky ...
He promised me a shilling ...

BROOM (*still not looking round*):   And a sleep ...

And, looking at Broom's back and at Billy, we hear the door close.

81

Interior of Tavern A.

(*Close shot*) of Fallon sitting at a table, a mug before him.
His face is covered with sweat.

And terror looks out of his eyes.
He raises his hands before him, palms upward. They are trembling.
His lips are moving, but no words come.
(*Track back*) to see Nelly sitting down next to him.

NELLY: Broom says you're to come.

Fallon stares in front of him.

NELLY: He says there's ... work.

FALLON (*without turning to her*):   My hands have worked enough.
There's devils in my hands.

NELLY: It's ... somebody we know Broom's got there ...

FALLON: I've known them all, all of them. They were my brothers ...
and my sisters ... and my mother (*in a horrified whisper*) ... All
dead ... dead ...

NELLY: Hurry up with you ... Broom's waiting ...

Fallon does not move.

NELLY: You've drunk yourself daft again ... like when you went on
your knees in the street, praying and shouting ...

FALLON: I wish I was workin' again, on the roads, on the canals,
anywhere ...

NELLY: D'you want us all to starve while you blather and weep your
eyes out ...

FALLON: Starving's better than these ...

And he raises his hands again ... and suddenly tautens them.
And Nelly pulls roughly, violently, at his sleeve, and drags him up,
and pushes him out of the door into the darkness.

82

Small Room in Lodging-house.

We see the room from the angle of the window.
Billy is still sprawling on the tilted chair in the corner.
Broom leans against the table, arms folded, watching Billy. He leans
with his head a little to one side, enjoying the spectacle: a freak
admiring a freak show.

Kate is still lying half on, half off the bed, her hand trailed in a puddle on the floor.

BROOM (*softly*): And when Mr Fallon comes back, oh, we'll have fun and singing ... It's he's got a voice that'll send you to sleep like your mother's ... And oh, the joking and riddles!

(*Pan round*) to the door as Broom speaks. Fallon is standing there. Behind him, almost in darkness, we see Nelly.

Fallon stands there at the door with his shoulders back and his head high. There is something almost of dignity about him: something that might suggest he is about to make a sacrifice.

And when he speaks, it is without the usual blarneying whine; a horror that has reached him has deepened the tone of his voice.

FALLON (*slowly*): Make Kate go.

Now, from Nelly's angle, behind Fallon, we see Broom move across to the bed in two cat-padded jumps and pinch Kate awake.

She looks round the room, thick with sleep. She sees Billy smiling at every one and no one; she sees the malicious face of Broom above her; she sees Fallon grim in the doorway. And, sober in a second, and frightened, she scrambles to the door.

Fallon does not move; she has to squeeze herself past him, keeping her body as far away from his as she can.

FALLON: Close the door.

(*Cut to*) shot, from behind Billy, over his crippled shoulders, of Fallon at the door and Broom by the bed.

Fallon's eyes are staring straight at us.

FALLON (*slowly*): You mustn't be frightened, Billy.

Fallon takes a step forward.

FALLON (*slowly*): It'll all be over soon. No more bein' hungry ...

Now Fallon, slow as a priest, is moving towards us and Billy.
(*Cut to*) shot, from door, of Fallon moving towards Billy, and of Billy's bewildered, but still smiling, face ...

FALLON (*slowly*): No more ... cold ...

(*Cut to*) shot, from Billy's angle, of Fallon moving, as though in procession, down the room.

And behind him, on tiptoes, comes Broom. Now they are almost upon us.

And suddenly we hear the voice of Billy: screaming.

83

Outside the door of the Small Room.

Nelly and Kate are standing close to the door.

A little light, as though from one candle, falls on their faces. Around them, darkness.

The women stand tensed, waiting, close together. And from beyond the door comes Billy's scream.

The scream mounts, breaks, and bursts out again. The crash of a falling chair.

And now it is not a scream that comes from beyond the door but a terrified howling; and with it the sound of a deeper voice: Fallon's voice – the voice of the damned inarticulately praying. And with it the smashing of wood, and glass breaking.

Then one scream destroys all other sounds.

The women put their hands over their ears, press their hands hard.

And the women are rocking slowly to and fro, as though at the side of a death-bed, as though at a wailing-wall.

Then the scream goes out.

Slowly the women grow still, and they move their hands down.

The door opens.

Light falls upon the white-faced women.

Fallon stands at the door with his back to the room, so that we cannot see his face or the room behind him.

Fallon raises his hand to beckon the women in.

He turns around, goes into the light.

The women go after him, so that the doorway is never unoccupied and so that we do not see into the room.

Then the door closes.

(*Fade out*)

(*Fade in*)

84

Birds flying over the City roofs.

Morning.

Music.

(*Pan down*) from the roofs to the Market-place.

As we (*pan*), we hear the voices of children rising.

And children are playing in the middle of the Market.

Then there is the clop-clop of hooves on cobbles. And down the Market comes a horse and cart.

As the horse and cart approach us, we see that Fallon is driving.

There is a large barrel in the back of the cart. Broom is thumping the barrel in time to the hoof-beats on the cobbles.

The children scatter as the cart drives down.

And then the horse stops.

Fallon raises a stick and beats the horse.

The horse will not move.

Broom stops his rhythmic thumping on the barrel and stands up.

He shouts at Fallon and the horse in his piercing voice, and the scampering children gather round the cart.

BROOM: Beat the hide off his back, skin the divil alive ...

Fallon beats the horse methodically, as though it were a carpet.

THE CHILDREN: Skin the divil alive.

BROOM: Oh, the mule of hell, the stinkin' gob of the knackers' yard, I'll tear off its tail ...

THE CHILDREN: Tear off its tail, tear off its tail ...

Fallon climbs off the cart and tries to drag the horse along by its bridle.

The horse will not move. And as Fallon drags and pulls, so Broom in the cart capers and cries, and so the children in delight caper and cry with Broom.

The people of the Market look on with little interest.

BROOM: I'll tear the bit out its mouth ... Give me a red-hot poker ...

THE CHILDREN: Red-hot poker, red-hot poker ...

FALLON (*solemnly*):   You'd think the old mare had risen in judgment against us ...

A Porter passes the horse and cart, pushing an empty barrow. He pays no heed to the caterwauling of Broom and the children.
Fallon sees the Porter.

FALLON: Hi, there!

The Porter stops.

BROOM: I'll kick it in the kyte ...

FALLON: Would you take a barrel with you for two shillings? It's only a little barrel ...

PORTER: Where to? It's a great big barrel ...

FALLON: My friend'll show you where.

Fallon beckons Broom, who has now stopped cursing the horse and is snapping like a dog at the children.

FALLON: Here's the shillings.

And Fallon, Broom, and the Porter lift the barrel down and put it on the barrow. As they carry it the Porter says:

PORTER: What you got in the barrel?

BROOM: Potatoes.

FALLON: Keep your talk in your mouth. You've got your money ...

And Broom and the Porter go off with the barrow.
And suddenly the horse, as soon as the barrow has gone, goes off himself down the Market, to the cries of the children, at a brisk trot.
Fallon shouts after it, but it trots on.

THE CHILDREN: Skin the divil alive ... Tear off its tail, tear off its tail ... Kick it in the kyte.

Fallon, after one shout, makes no attempt to follow the horse but walks back in the direction from which he had come; walks off heavy-shouldered and heavy-footed, his head sunken.
The voices of the children fade.

85

Rag-and-Bone Alley.

(*Track up*) to where a middle-aged man and woman are standing outside the door of the Lodging-house. The woman carries a baby in a shawl. The man holds a little child by the hand. They are dressed like beggars. The man is carrying a bundle in a stick over his shoulder. He knocks at the door.

WOMAN: It's a poor, dirty place.

MAN: It's got a roof …

WOMAN: I think I'd rather be on the roads, sleeping in the hedge in the cold …

The door opens.
Kate stands in the doorway.
She wears a new shawl.

KATE: You'll be wanting a bed? They're twopence.

MAN: Bed.

The man unwraps a piece of cloth from his pocket, and brings out a coin.

KATE: There's nobody sleeping at all here now … You can take your fancy where you sleep …

The man and the woman follow her into the house and into:
The Lodging-room.
Even in daylight it is half dark …
Kate walks down the room, and the man and the woman follow her.

KATE: You're strangers here …

MAN: Strangers everywhere …

KATE: You're from the roads?

The man nods.

WOMAN: I think we won't be troubling you for a bed … It's *dark* here …

KATE: It's darker on the roads. With no one you know in the world, and no one to take care of you … I'll make the beds a penny each. What names d'you go by?

MAN: Mr and Mrs Webb.

WOMAN: We're respectable people …

KATE: We're all respectable here. Just my husband and me. He's in the way of a merchant …

The man flings his bundle on a bed. And Kate looks at Mr and Mrs Webb.

86

City Street.

The Porter is pushing his barrow along, Broom at his side.

PORTER: You're sure you said it was potatoes in your – *little* barrel?

Broom winks.

PORTER: They're very heavy potatoes. Where do we go with them?

BROOM: Up the City Square. Doctor Rock's Academy.

PORTER (*with a sideways glance at Broom*):   He must be very fond of vegetables …

87

Hallway of Rock's Academy.

Night.
The Hallway is deserted.
The door to the small Cloakroom under the stairs stands open.
Murray comes out of the Cloakroom.
He looks around him, like a man slowly coming out of a nightmare and trying to grow accustomed again to the familiar things of the daytime world.

MURRAY: Tom! Tom! Where are you, Tom?

But it is only a whisper.
And now he walks up the Hallway past the glass cases slowly.
He opens the door, and walks out through the colonnade into the moonlit garden of City Square. And as he moves through the garden so we hear the voice of his mind, and the remembered voices of others.

MURRAY'S VOICE: Who brought the subject in, Tom? There's no need to ask.

TOM'S VOICE: Fallon and Broom, sir; Fallon and Broom …

MURRAY'S VOICE: What can I do?

ELIZABETH'S VOICE: Keep quiet ...

MURRAY'S VOICE: Keep quiet about Jennie or they'll lock you up ...

ELIZABETH'S VOICE: Keep quiet ...

MURRAY'S VOICE: Keep quiet about Billy Bedlam in the little room, or they'll call you a murderer and a butcher ...

ELIZABETH'S VOICE: ... stabbed or strangled, or beaten to death, or ...

MURRAY'S VOICE: There are no marks of violence upon the body.

ELIZABETH'S VOICE: ... You bear false witness ...

MURRAY'S VOICE: I swear that Jennie and Billy are murdered ...

ELIZABETH'S VOICE: It is quite easy for you to wreck your life ...

And he turns and walks back through the garden towards the Academy. Now his step is quicker and more purposeful.

88

Elizabeth's Room.

Rock, his coat off, but still immaculately dressed, is seated in a deep chair with his head against the back of it.
Elizabeth is curling what remains of his hair with curling-tongs.
Rock has an air of indolent luxury.

ROCK (*complacently*):   The sensual apotheosis of the intellectual animal ...

ELIZABETH: If you say so, my dear.

ROCK: The mind is relaxed, the body is pleasured and pampered, rancour has taken a holiday, and I am full of bliss, like a cat on the tiles of heaven ...

ELIZABETH: It must be very nice to talk ...

ROCK: It is comparable only to the pleasure of not having to think *as* you talk ... (*sighing*) I am a fool to-day.

ELIZABETH: Yes. Thomas ...

ROCK (*with a change of voice*):   But not so much of a fool as some I know. That rumour-breeder of a Murray! Falls in love with a pretty face and then won't cut it up once the little trollop's dead. Says she's murdered. Says, in effect, I murdered her myself.

ELIZABETH (*mildly*):   Oh, Thomas.

ROCK: When *I* take up assassination, I shall start with the surgeons in this city and work *up* to the gutter ... And now, to-day, along he comes with some fantastic rigmarole about a crippled idiot. Billy Bedlam. Says *he*'s murdered, too. Poor Billy's bed was the cobbles, rain or snow, and he ate like a rat from the garbage heaps, and swallowed all the rot-gut he could buy or beg. He was a consumptive and an epileptic. A wonder he hadn't been found dead years ago ...

ELIZABETH: What did you tell Mr Murray?

ROCK: I said: 'Mr Murray, go down and cut up the body and put it in the brine baths. Be careful you don't fall in yourself – you're wearing a good suit!'

ELIZABETH (*casually*):   And what did he do?

ROCK: What did he do? Why, what I told him to do, of course. No vicious-minded little prig with emotional adenoids is going to intimidate *me* with his whine and wail of 'Murder! Murder!' He suffers from hallucinations. My hands, to him, are red as Macbeth's ...

Rock raises his very white hands in an elegant gesture, and smoothes the palm of one hand along the back of the other ...

89

Music.

Pitch darkness.
Through the darkness, the laughter of Broom.
Then sudden light, and Fallon's hands, palms downwards, fingers stretched and tautened, murdering down the screen.
As the hands move we hear Fallon's voice, blurred in a distorting mirror of sound.

FALLON'S VOICE: There's devils in my hands. Let me go, my hands!

Then, close, from above, the upward-staring faces of old women and children, their eyes wide, their mouths open.

FALLON'S VOICE: Don't be frightened ... There's nothing to lose ...

Then Fallon's hands, palms upwards, fingers damp and limp, trembling up the screen.

FALLON'S VOICE: It's all lost ...

Then (*close-up*) of Fallon's face, drunk, arrogant, grinning. And we hear a voice questioning the face.

VOICE: And where d'you get all the money so quick? You're rich, you're *rich*, you're ...

FALLON'S VOICE: Ach, I done a little smuggling; a little bit o' drink on the sly ...

The questioning Voice continues through a (*close-up*) of Nelly in a new feathered bonnet. Nelly drunk, secretive ...

VOICE: And where d'you get all the money so quick? You're *rich*, you're ...

NELLY'S VOICE: Oh, I've been left a property in the country.

(*Close-up*) of Kate in a new bonnet.

VOICE: And where d'you get all the money ... (*The Voice fades.*)

KATE'S VOICE: Oh, Fallon's the favourite of a great lady ... *Twenty* pounds a visit she gives him ...

Then (*close-up*) of children's faces.

VOICE: Where's Billy? Billy Bedlam?

And the voices of the children answer as we see a (*close-up*) of Alice.

VOICES OF CHILDREN: Gone, gone ...

VOICE: Where's Jennie? Jennie Bailey?

And Alice's voice answers as we see a (*close shot*) of a sack put down and hands undoing the sack.

ALICE'S VOICE: Gone, gone ...

And out of the undone sack comes a human arm, and we hear the voice of the Porter.

PORTER'S VOICE: Doctor Rock is very fond of vegetables ...

(*Close shot*) of an Old Man, drooling drunk, his head capsized on one shoulder.

BROOM'S VOICE: Drink with Broom ... Drink ...

A hand with a bottle in it stretches across the screen towards him. (*Cut to close-up*) of the face of an Old Woman looking up at the bottle held across the screen.

BROOM'S VOICE: Drink ... drink ...

And, loudly, there is the noise of the pigs squealing.
(*Dissolve the picture to*)

90

Interior of Grocer's Shop.

From the end of the shop, opposite the door, we can see a section of the Market-place in daylight.

The Grocer, behind the counter, is a truculent man in a dirty apron, who seems to have given up hope a long time ago: a man always at the end of his patience.

And before the counter an Old Woman is standing, wrapped in pieces of the discarded clothing of the other poor.

GROCER: For the last time, I don't know a Flynn ...

OLD WOMAN: Timothy Boylan Flynn ...

GROCER: I don't know a Flynn, I've never known a Flynn, I never want to ...

OLD WOMAN: From County Donegal ... He came over two years ago and a half ... He's a tall, dark boy ... The lobes of his ears is pointed ...

Fallon comes in at the shop door. He stands, framed against the Market, listening.

GROCER: 'What's the time of the day?' 'Can you give me a wooden box?' 'My sister's fallen under a hay cart – can you lend me a penn'orth of brandy.' 'Have you seen a Flynn?' Will nobody ever *buy* anything? ...

OLD WOMAN: Could you spare me a bite o' bread, then?

The Grocer controls himself as Fallon, with a winning smile, comes to the counter.

FALLON (*to the Old Woman*):   Did I hear you say 'Flynn'? That was my mother's name.

OLD WOMAN: From Ardara, Donegal?

FALLON (*amazed*):   Ardara, Donegal! My mother's town! And would *your* name be – Flynn, too?

GROCER: *Her* name's Flynn, she's *looking* for a Flynn, and now your *mother's* name is Flynn ...

Fallon, still looking at the Old Woman, hands an earthenware jug over the counter to the Grocer.

FALLON: Fill it up with dew.

The Grocer disappears behind the counter.

FALLON (*affectionately to the Old Woman*):   Then you're my little cousin ...

He kisses her forehead ...

FALLON: Cousin Flynn ...
Faith, what a day of all days! I'm walking along gay as a thrush, I'm fragrant with the sweet smell of money, to-night's Hallowe'en when the witches fly and the whisky pours like rain, and who should I meet on top of it all but a Flynn from Ardara!

The Grocer returns to his place behind the counter; he hands over the earthenware jug to Fallon. Fallon, tossing coins carelessly on the counter, pays for it; but he does not take his eyes off Mrs Flynn ...

MRS FLYNN: It's my son for I'm looking all over, sir ...

FALLON (*emphatically*):   ... Cousin ...

MRS FLYNN (*hesitatingly*):   ... Cousin ...

FALLON: And we'll find your son for you if we have to pull the town down and scramble among the cobbles ...
You come with me, cousin ... you're welcome as sunlight ... I'll buy you a present for Hallowe'en, and I'll take you back to my fine house and we'll kick up a din like all Donegal drunk ...

Fallon, with the jug and Mrs Flynn, moves towards the door of the shop, towards the darkening Market.

As they go out we see a (*close shot*) of the Grocer.

GROCER (*with an awful resignation*):   Hallowe'en! ...

91

Rag-and-Bone Alley.

Late evening.
Music.
The Close is desolate.
We hear the dark noise of the wind blowing.
The noise grows, but the Close is emptily still.
The wind rises, to the rise of music.
And out of the gutters float the wind-driven shapes of witches and demons:
Waste paper flying out of the gutter, eddying into the air, fluttering, as though winged, past the shadowy houses:
Paper and rubbish gusted suddenly from the cobbles to flap and float about the street, to beat against the windows and scrabble there, to rise on the screaming breath of a wind and drift before the Lodging-house:
Straw blown in a squall, straw shapes and garbage shapes puffed through the growing, blowing dark:
Hay wisps and knotted straw, dust clouds and cloth shreds, small crumpled nameless shapes, light as paper and string, scudding through the narrowness:
All the inanimate furies of the Close alive suddenly, crying like the wind through telegraph wires, grotesque dancers from the dirt ...

92

Now we are standing at the end of the Large Lodging-room.

We are looking down the mostly dark Long Room and through the open door into the Small Room.

We hear laughter, and snatches of singing, and a jig tune played on a penny whistle.

Broom and Kate, arm in arm, come dancing out of the small room, turn in the narrow aisle between the beds, and dance, singing, back.

We (*track up*) slowly to the open door.

As we track we see that one of the beds is occupied: by a baby and a young child. They are the children of Mr and Mrs Webb. They are asleep. The child's arm is held protectingly around the baby.

Now we are near the open door.

We see, in the small room, Fallon leaning against the table, playing a whistle. There are cups and mugs on the table, bottles, and the earthenware jug.

Behind Fallon are a man and a woman: a squat and hairy man not unlike Fallon, and a slatternly young woman with wayward hair and smile.

And Broom and Mrs Flynn, arm in arm, come dancing out of the small room, towards us.

We see them close as they turn in the narrow aisle between the beds.

Mrs Flynn is gay as an old cat.

Broom is smiling and possessive.

They dance, singing, back into the small room.

We (*track*) right up to the open door.

In the Small Room we see that there are nine people: Fallon, penny-whistling at the table; the two strangers behind him singing the words of a jig; Kate and Nelly on the straw bed, beating jig-time on the littered floor; Broom and Mrs Flynn dancing between the table and the bed, dancing around the table; and Mr and Mrs Webb. Mr Webb, with a look of bemused contentment, is soaking pieces of bread in the earthenware jug and eating them; Mrs Webb, disapproving, sits on the edge of the one sound chair in the room.

Mrs Webb complains, through the singing, the dancing, the floor-beating, and the whistling.

MRS WEBB: Oh, the noise, it'll wake all the neighbours ...

THE MAN: They wouldn't wake to-night if you set their clothes on fire ... All the city's drunk ...

MRS WEBB (*to Mr Webb*): And stop eatin' bread and gin; it's bad for the stomach.

BROOM: It's Hallowe'en ...

THE MAN: It isn't us who's only making the din, you listen now ... Shh!

The Man raises his hand. For a moment the room is quiet. The dancers pause. From outside we hear the noise of drunken singing, and voices bawling and brawling.

Then Fallon begins to play again, and Broom and Mrs Flynn dance again, and the Man and the Woman sing, and Kate and Nelly, speechless on the bed, go on thumping.

MR WEBB: Bread and gin's good for the stomach.

MRS WEBB: You'll be waking the children, that's what'll happen next, with your caterwauling and your bang-bangs and your ...

Fallon stops playing.

FALLON: And can't a man have a party now in honour of his cousin?

MR WEBB: And rum and spuds is good.

FALLON (*to Mrs Webb*):   You're an auld spoil-sport, Mrs Webb, you'd stop the dead dancin' on Judgment Day ...

The baby, from the next room, begins to scream.
Mrs Webb jumps up and goes out.
But the screaming continues.

FALLON: Now that's a baby that likes good music ...

And he raises his penny whistle and plays again.
Mrs Webb puts her head round the door.

MRS WEBB: For the Lord's sake now, is this a lodging-house or a wake?

Fallon nods to Nelly.
And Nelly totters to her feet and goes out of the room.

93

In the Large Lodging-room we see Nelly and Mrs Webb at the bed of the screaming baby.
Through the open door we see the singers and dancers.

NELLY: Oh, the poor creature. It screams like it swallowed a pin ... And Fallon'll be playing his whistle all night ...

Through the open door we see Fallon whistling and dancing a lonely jig.

NELLY: ... and there'll not be a breath of peace ... (*wheedling*) Now why don't you take the children away for the night ... Fallon's brother there will give you a bed and a plate of food ... And Fallon and us'll stay singing with old Mrs Flynn till we a' fall down ...

The baby screams louder than ever.

MRS WEBB (*calling through the door*):   Come on with ye, Mr Webb.

Mrs Webb begins to lift the children out of bed and wrap clothes around them.

94

Through darkness we see a shivering candle move, and moving figures. The baby is still screaming.

MR WEBB: I don't want to go out in the cold ...

MRS WEBB: You and your bread and gin! ...

THE MAN: Only a couple of steps from here, Mrs Webb ...

MR WEBB: It's Hallowe'en! ...

NELLY: I think you're very wise to go, my dear. There's no knowing what pranks Mr Fallon'll be up to to-night ...

A door is opened.
We see Rag-and-Bone Alley in the moonlight.
And the Man and the Woman, and Mr and Mrs Webb and the baby and the child, go out into the moonlight.
And Nelly closes the door.
Pitch darkness. From the darkness a sudden swell of sound: the squealing and squeaking of the tin whistle, and the singing of Broom.
Then momentary quiet.
Then Broom's singing again, and, suddenly through it, a long, high, distant cry dwindling into silence again.

95

Snow falling in hard, bright morning light.

Nothing on the screen but the falling snow. We hear a cock crow.
We (*cut to*) a cock, on a wall, crowing in the middle of the snow, defiantly crying the morning up to the thick, falling flakes.
And now, as the snow drifts and drives past our eyes, we are looking, from the outside, through the Lodging-house window into the Small Room.

Isolated, behind the shifting wall of snow, sit Fallon and Broom, Nelly and Kate, at the table in the middle of the room. Only Fallon is not eating.

We move through the snow and through the window into the room and towards the table.

We see the details of the room very clearly now in the merciless morning snow-light: no shadows, no twisted shapes in half-darkness, but only the bed with its straw guts straggling out, and the fouled straw-heap on the floor at the foot of the bed, and the thrown-away bottles and the flung scraps of clothes, and the broken glass and the drying pools of drink, and the last and the snippets of leather, and the tin whistle cast near the straw, and the piled boots in the corner, and the iron pot near the smoking fire.

Then Fallon rises from the table and crosses to the window.

From behind him, looking over his tensed shoulders, we see the falling snow.

FALLON: The snow won't ever stop. It's like the last day.

And his voice, and his measured movements, and the concentrated stillness of the others, suggest the anticlimax after death.

And now, from the end of the room opposite the door, we see the door open and Mr and Mrs Webb come in. Their clothes are white with snow.

Broom leaps to his feet. Fallon turns, with a measured, deliberate movement from the window.

Nelly and Kate sit still at the table, looking up at Mrs Webb.

BROOM (*with a frightening smile*):   You frightened us.

And he goes out of the room, followed by Kate.

NELLY: You're early.

MRS WEBB: I been up and about since dawn; the baby wouldn't fall to sleep at all – it screamed like things were after it ...

Fallon stands still at the window, looking at Mrs Webb.

NELLY: What have you come for so early?

MRS WEBB: I come to look for the little boy's stockings. I left them here last night drying by the fire; and I come for our bits and pieces ... It's time we're moving ...

Mrs Webb is looking round the room.

She pulls out a clay pipe from her wrappings and lights it at the fire. With the blackened pipe burning like a little hayrick in her mouth, she bends down and searches among the scraps of clothes on the floor near the straw.

FALLON: Get away from that straw with your old pipe … You'll have the room blazing.

Fallon speaks so harshly that Mrs Webb takes an involuntary step backward and sits on the end of the bed.

MR WEBB: Where's Mrs Flynn? (*appreciatively*) She was a very gay old woman, dancin' like a nanny-goat …

NELLY: She was ow'r gay with Fallon. I tumbled her out of the house in the middle o' the night …

MR WEBB (*with a side look at his wife*): I like a gay old woman …

FALLON: Get out o' my room … Take your reeky scraps of rubbish and your yelpin' children and get out …

Fallon does not move from the window, but his stillness is more menacing than movement.

And Mr and Mrs Webb go out. As they go Mrs Webb whines:

MRS WEBB: I want my little boy's stockings …

Fallon is alone with Nelly.

FALLON: The snow's falling heavier.
    The world's cold.

He shivers, pulls his coat closer about him.

FALLON: It's cold in hell to-day.
    The fires are out.

Nelly looks at him in uncomprehending silence.

FALLON: Nothing can burn me any more.
    I'm a cold man, Nelly.
    I'm numb all over, like an old dead finger-nail.
    No more dancing.
    No more drinking and singing.

He shivers again, standing against the window and the snow.

FALLON: I got work to do.

And he goes out, followed by the strangely silent Nelly.
The door closes.
The room is empty.
Then the door opens, very slowly, and Mrs Webb puts her head round and looks at the emptiness.
She comes in, whispering over her shoulder.

MRS WEBB: They've gone.

And Mr Webb comes in, nervously glancing behind him and on every side.

MR WEBB: Find the stockings and let's be out of the house.

Mrs Webb is down on her knees now by the pile of old clothes; she rummages through them.

MRS WEBB: Who wanted to come to this house? I said it was bad. I could smell the badness as I come in. It's nothing but drinking and howling all night …

Suddenly she stops in her scrabbling search through the clothes and lifts up a crumpled dress.

MRS WEBB: It's the old woman's dress.

MR WEBB: How'd she be walking in the streets in the snow without her dress?

MRS WEBB: It's the old woman's dress. I mind the colour.

She starts to search among the clothes again, her hands nearing the straw.

MR WEBB: A body doesna walk in the streets without her …

Mrs Webb lifts up a ragged shawl.

MRS WEBB: And here's her little patchy shawl …

Now she is worrying the straw, like a dog on a scent.

MRS WEBB: And here's her …

And Mrs Webb screams.
A human arm lies naked in the parted straw.
Mrs Webb springs up and stands, with her back to us, looking down at the straw and the arm.
The scream stops.

Mr Webb bends down; facing us, he flings the rest of the straw aside. We do not see what he reveals, for Mrs Webb stands between us and it.

MR WEBB: The gay old woman! Her face is a' slimy.

Music.
Mrs Webb rushes out of the room.
And, as Mr Webb follows her, we see, for a flash, the dead white face among the straw.

96

In the Large Lodging-room Mr and Mrs Webb are frenziedly packing their bits and pieces into a sheet.

The music rises.
They rush, he with the sheet sacked over his shoulder, to the far door.
And suddenly Nelly is standing there, in the doorway.
The music stops.

NELLY: Where are you going? What have you seen?

MRS WEBB: Let me out, she's dead …

NELLY: She died in her sleep …

MR WEBB: Her mouth's blood …

MRS WEBB: For the love o' Mary …

NELLY: *She died in her sleep …*

MRS WEBB: … Let me out …

Nelly tears inside her apron, pulls out a purse, opens it. She pushes a handful of coins towards Mrs Webb.

NELLY: Nobody knows her, nobody'll claim her, you mustn't tell a word …

MR WEBB: Stand away …

NELLY: … she died like a baby …

MRS WEBB: You killed her in there last night …

NELLY: You mustn't tell a word, mercy, quiet, quiet … Fallon'll give you ten pounds, ten pounds a week …

Mr Webb thrusts Nelly aside.
Mrs Webb runs through the door, Mr Webb after her.
Nelly, at the door, cries out after them ...

NELLY: Ten pounds ...

97

Rag-and-Bone Alley.

Music.
Snow falling heavily.
Mr and Mrs Webb rush out of the Lodging-house.
The Webbs' boy, with the baby in his arms, stands, waiting, like a little snow man near the door.
Mrs Webb snatches the baby from his arms, hugs it to her shawls, and hurries on up the Alley.
Mr Webb takes the boy's hand and follows.
They keep to the right of the Alley.
And down the left of the Alley, coming towards the Lodging-house, we see Fallon and Broom and a Porter.
But, with the fierce snow driving upon them, upon their faces and their eyes, they do not see the wrapped-up figures of the hurrying Webbs.
And the Webbs do not see them.

98

Small Room in Lodging-house.

In the middle of the room is a tea-chest.
Fallon, Broom, and the Porter stand, snowy-coated, around the chest.
The Porter is the one we saw taking the barrel in his barrow.
He is pressing down the lid with all his weight.
And Fallon helps him.
Broom points a finger at the top of the lid.
A bunch of grey hair hangs out.
Fallon crosses to the last and the leather pieces and brings back a pair of cobbler's scissors.
The Porter cuts off the hair with the scissors.

99

Interior of Police Station.

Mr and Mrs Webb are talking to a Policeman.

MR WEBB: And there was blood all over her face ...

POLICEMAN: Aye.

MRS WEBB: And her poor lips were blue and her eyes were staring out as though somebody'd pressed 'em with his thumbs ...

The Policeman nods.

MR WEBB: She said she came from Donegal ...

POLICEMAN: The 'dead woman' told ye she'd come from Donegal?

100

City Street.

We see Fallon and Broom walking, in the slanting snowstorm, by the side of the Porter and his barrow with the tea-chest on it.

101

Interior of Police Station.

Mr and Mrs Webb are still pleading to the Policeman.

MR WEBB: No, no, sir, she said she'd come from Donegal when we was all drinkin' together last night ...

POLICEMAN: Drinkin'!

MRS WEBB: Mrs Flynn her name was, I've told you twenty times ...

Mr Webb, with hesitant, frightened fingers touches his own mouth.

MR WEBB: And now there's blood all over here ...

POLICEMAN (*placatingly*):   You sit down now. I'll come with you by and by ...

He turns away from them and moves towards the back of the room.

MRS WEBB (*dully, as though repeating a lesson*):   Mrs Flynn her name was ... They killed her ... Fallon and Broom ...

102

The always shadowy Hall in Rock's Academy, with its white secret witnesses staring from the glass cases.

Rock is mounting the stairs.
We follow him as he climbs, and hear the voice of his mind.

ROCK'S VOICE: Gentlemen ... Gentlemen, let us to-day dissect the human conscience. Lay it on the slab. Open it up.
You see? The liver of the conscience is knobbled by emotional excesses.
The veins of the conscience are full of bad blood.
The heart of the conscience palpitates like a snared rabbit's ...

Now he is walking along the Corridor, opening a door, to the small Reference Library.

103

Reference Library in Rock's Academy.

ROCK'S VOICE: In short, gentlemen, the conscience is a *very* unhealthy subject ...

And, at the end of these words, he is sitting in a chair behind a desk, facing us.
The room is empty.
And Rock, at the desk, addresses the empty room as though there were a gathering of students in it, turning from one invisible listener to another.

ROCK: There is right and wrong, gentlemen, just as there is right and left. Mine is the *right* direction. The fact that the majority would consider it the *wrong* direction, only substantiates my opinion that I am right ...

There is a knock on the door.

ROCK: Stay out.

Tom comes in.

ROCK: I see, sir, that to keep you out I should have said, 'Come in.'

TOM: Fallon and Broom, sir.

ROCK: Indeed? Must I laugh, weep, tear my hair, swoon for ecstasy!

TOM: They've brought a body, sir.

ROCK: I did not expect that they would bring a soul.

TOM (*suggestively*): They bring so many subjects, sir ... sixteen or more up till to-day ... and always fresh ...

ROCK: They are corpse-diviners. Or, as some have green fingers for gardening, so they have black fingers for death. Do you expect the dead to walk here, Tom? They need assistance. Fallon and Broom provide that assistance.
Have Mr Murray pay them.

TOM: Yes, sir.

Tom, with a side glance at Rock, goes out.
And Rock, alone, again speaks in a soft voice to his unseen audience.

ROCK: You see, gentlemen?

104

Small Room in Lodging-house.

We look at the room from above.
In the centre of the room stands the Policeman. Behind him, standing close together for protection, are Mr and Mrs Webb.
Fallon leans against the table, facing the Policeman.
And behind him are Kate, Nelly, and Broom.
They are frozen.
As, from above, we move down closer to them, they unfreeze.

FALLON (*smiling*): And where did the old fools tell ye they saw the body, sir?

Mrs Webb points to the straw.
The Policeman kicks the straw aside. Broom laughs.

FALLON: Maybe the mice, they dragged it down their little hole ...

The Policeman bends down, to stare at the floor-boards.

POLICEMAN: Blood on the boards.

A moment's silence.

FALLON: And has there ever been, for the love o' God, a Hallowe'en party with no blood spilt? We was all convivial; there was fightin' in every room of the house.

NELLY: And the old woman Flynn, she was so fashous I told her go with the toe of my boot ...

KATE (*pointing to the Webbs*):   And it's they were picking the pockets of the poor innocent persons that couldn't get up from the floor ...

NELLY: It's all lies, lies they said ...

The Policeman picks up the dress that Mrs Webb had found.

KATE: Don't you trust them, they're beggars, sir ...

BROOM: They eat dead cats ...

MRS WEBB: That's Mrs Flynn's dress ... I mind the colour ...

BROOM: Fur and all ...

NELLY: That's not hers, it's mine ...

POLICEMAN: Blood on the front.

NELLY: Fallon hit me with a glass in the face and the cut ran ...

MR WEBB: The old woman's face was a' slimy ...

And as Mr Webb speaks, so we hear the ringing of church bells ... (*Dissolve.*)

105

Policeman and Mr and Mrs Webb with their two children walking up snow-thick Street. Snow is no longer falling.

The sound of Sunday church bells rises.
And, black for Sunday, people hurry by over the white snow.

106

City Square.

Outside Hocking's Academy Mr and Mrs Webb stand shivering and waiting, the baby huddled in Mrs Webb's shawls, the little boy with his hands dug deep in Mr Webb's coat pocket.

The door of Hocking's Academy opens.
The Policeman comes out.
A Porter stands at the door.

POLICEMAN: If there's a new subject comes in to-day, let me know.

He walks towards Rock's Academy, beckoning the Webbs to follow him.
He knocks on the door of Rock's Academy.
The grille opens.
From the Policeman's angle we see Tom's face through the bars.

POLICEMAN'S VOICE: Have you had a new subject to-day?

TOM: Aye.

POLICEMAN'S VOICE: Open the door.

The door opens.
The Policeman walks in.

107

Small Dark Room off the Hall in Rock's Academy.

We see the figures of Tom and the Policeman, and the shape of the tea-chest.

POLICEMAN: Open the chest.

Tom opens the tea-chest.
The Policeman looks down into it.

POLICEMAN: When was it brought?

TOM: An hour ago.

POLICEMAN: Who brought it?

(*Cut to close-up*) of Mrs Flynn's face. With a sudden after-death jerk of the muscles, her mouth drops open, as though she were speaking.
And Tom speaks as the mouth opens.

TOM'S VOICE: Fallon and Broom.

(*Cut back*) to the Small Dark Room, the Policeman, and Tom.

POLICEMAN: Fetch in the old couple. They're waiting outside.

Tom goes out.

The Policeman looks round the Dark Room. We follow his eyes: we see, in a corner, what might be a body covered with a sheet: in another corner, what might be a cupboard or an upright coffin.

POLICEMAN (*in a whisper*):   Cold!

Mr and Mrs Webb come into the room.
The Policeman nods towards the open tea-chest.
Timidly they move towards it and look down.

MR WEBB: The old woman.

Mrs Webb nods and crosses herself.

POLICEMAN: What was her name?

(*Cut*) again to (*close-up*) of Mrs Flynn's face.

MRS WEBB'S VOICE: Mrs Flynn ...

108

Reference Library in Rock's Academy.

Rock, a sheet of paper in his hand, is walking up and down, in a characteristic lecture manner, behind his desk.
Some distance away, the other side of the desk, sits Murray.

ROCK (*gesturing with the paper in his hand*):   If this does not upset some apple-carts, I shall believe that the apples have been glued on like the coco-nuts in coco-nut shies; if this does not help to change the idiotic laws that apply to our profession, I shall run amok; I shall send Doctor Hocking a Christmas Greeting and sign it 'Yours in Homage'; I shall place my spiritual welfare in the hands of the Reverend Doctor Lever and have my seat *reserved* in hell.

MURRAY: I tell you, this isn't the time to attack.

ROCK: The national anthem of the rabbit world.

MURRAY: If you publish that letter now, attacking the system by which the medical schools get their bodies, you'll be raising a question you might have some difficulty in answering *yourself*.

ROCK: Am I still a Doctor Bluebeard to you, then, you terrified old lady? Do I spend my nights a-murdering?

MURRAY: I do not know, sir, what you do with your nights. I do not imagine that you can *sleep*. But I do know that *Fallon* and *Broom* are murderers. It is only my respect for you, and my great obligations, and my *cowardice*, that have stopped me from running out of this murder school and telling the whole City what I know and what I guess ... Even so, there are rumours. *I* have not spread them. But Jennie's death, and Billy's, have not passed *quite* unnoticed. Rumours are contagious.

ROCK: So are scabies. To destroy them you do not wear the armour of defence, you wield the weapon of sulphur ointment. And, by God, there's sulphur in this letter ...

Tom comes in.

TOM: The police have been here.

ROCK: What is yours, sir? A rum and bitters?

TOM (*bewildered*): Sir?

ROCK: Since you do not knock before you come in, I must assume that this is a public-house ...

TOM: I beg your pardon, sir, but the police came about the new subject. Fallon and Broom, sir.

ROCK: Am I never to hear the end of those men's names?

MURRAY (*softly*):   Never, perhaps ...

TOM: And they're taking the subject away ...

ROCK: Why didn't you call the police? ...

TOM (*more bewildered*):   Sir, I ...

ROCK: Go away and lock up the silver. If there isn't any silver, lock up Mr Mattheson: he has a gold tooth.

And Tom goes out.

MURRAY: Must you antagonise every one?

ROCK: Yes.

MURRAY: You heard? The police.

ROCK: Outside the gates of hell are not the words 'Abandon Hope All Ye Who Enter Here', but 'I Told You So'.

MURRAY: And if the police ask me questions, as they are bound to do, what shall I say?

ROCK: Say nothing. Squeak. They will recognise the voice of a rat.

Murray goes to the door. As he opens it Rock speaks.

ROCK: You will find cheese in the larder. Leave some for Tom.

The door slams.
(*Close-up*) of Rock. The sardonicism, the mockery, have vanished from his face.
(*Dissolve.*)

109

(*Long shot*) of Long Corridor in Rock's Academy.

We see Tom coming up towards us from the end of the Corridor.
We see him open a door, put his head round the door. We hear him speak into the room behind the door, but are too far away to catch the words.
He comes on up the Corridor, opens another door, puts his head round the door. We hear him speak into the room behind the door, but though his voice is louder now, we still cannot catch the words.
He comes on up the Corridor, opens the door of the Reference Library, puts his head round the door. And now we are close enough to hear the words.

TOM: Fallon and Broom. They've arrested Fallon and Broom. Murder.

He withdraws his head.
From the opposite end of the Corridor we now see, in (*long Shot*), Tom padding on, away from camera ...
(*Dissolve.*)

110

To another Corridor.

(*Track up*) the empty Corridor.
As we track we hear a mumble of voices growing louder. We reach a door marked 'Board Room'.
The noise rises.

111

Interior of Board Room.

Around the long table are attorneys, counsel, police officials, Hocking, and Green.

FIRST POLICE OFFICIAL: ... and if Doctor Rock did not know that these bodies were murdered, he's a far less canny gentleman than I supposed ...

FIRST ATTORNEY: He knew. One corpse might pass him by, but Fallon and Broom were in the wholesale trade ...

SECOND POLICE OFFICIAL: Indict him as accessory after the fact ...

HOCKING: I do not exonerate Doctor Rock, but I will not have the whole medical profession of the City put on trial.

GREEN: Accuse Rock, you accuse the integrity of all the surgeons in the City.

The Chairman (the Lord Chief Justice) nods in agreement.

HOCKING: Oh, more than that. The whole aristocracy of learning that has been so carefully built up would be tumbled to the ground. The stain upon his character would spread across the whole of our culture. There could be no more respect for us. Indictment of Rock would mean *the death of a class* ...

112

Private Smokeroom in an Inn (as in Sequence 27).

The two old gentlemen are seated there with silver tankards in their hands.

FIRST GENTLEMAN: A great pity his letter appeared in all the newspapers ...

SECOND GENTLEMAN: On the very day of the arrest. Your health!

FIRST GENTLEMAN: Health!

SECOND GENTLEMAN: It was so very untactful.

There is a silence during which they drink. They gaze at their tankards.

FIRST GENTLEMAN: 'We must have more bodies,' he said. Dear, dear.

SECOND GENTLEMAN: We must have more *murders*.

FIRST GENTLEMAN: An ugly word, Richard.

SECOND GENTLEMAN: Doctor Rock has endangered the dignity of the higher professions ... If he is indicted as accessory after the fact ...

FIRST GENTLEMAN: No, no, Richard, that must never be. Guilty or not guilty, his part in this affair must be kept in a decent obscurity, or Anarchy will be walking abroad in the land ...

SECOND GENTLEMAN: They should all be shot against the wall ...

FIRST GENTLEMAN: Who, Richard?

The Second Gentleman makes a vague, sweeping gesture.

SECOND GENTLEMAN: All of 'em ...

113

(*Close shot*) of two elderly professors in mortar-boards and gowns, against the background of a very large, ornately gold-framed portrait of another old professor.

FIRST PROFESSOR: I agree with you entirely. His whole attitude to society spelt ruin from the first. Attack Tradition, it always bites back; and its teeth are well grounded.

SECOND PROFESSOR: A man who could be so persistently and obnoxiously rude to his elders and intellectual betters would think *nothing* of murdering his *own children* for a penny piece.

FIRST PROFESSOR: That is, perhaps, a little extravagant. We *must* disregard personal prejudice, though I agree that to be called 'anaemic buffoon' could not predispose him in your favour. But Rock is a *symbol* ...

SECOND PROFESSOR: I agree. A symbol of scholarship. In a manner of speaking, we could regard ourselves as 'the royal family of the intellect', and ...

FIRST PROFESSOR: My dear Fraser! ...

SECOND PROFESSOR: ... and if a member of the royal family is accused of a commoner's crime, then it is the *whole family* that is accused. An elaborate simile – but you see my point?

And the two professors wag their chins in complete agreement.

114

Interior of Board Room.

Around the table the attorneys, counsel, police officials, Hocking, and Green.

FIRST ATTORNEY: Perhaps we are forgetting the murder of children and old women in our concern for our sacred society of autocratic schoolmen ...

CHAIRMAN: It is a very grave position ...

SECOND POLICE OFFICIAL: Rock is guilty of connivance ...

FIRST POLICE OFFICIAL: I am afraid we *will* have to use him as a witness, gentlemen ...

CHAIRMAN: Oh, certainly, certainly ...

The police officials rise.

CHAIRMAN (*in an undertone to Hocking next to him*):   But we won't call him, of course.

115

Corridor in Rock's Academy.

Tom padding up the Corridor.
He stops outside the Reference Library, opens the door.
From behind him we see into the Library.
Rock is seated at his desk.

TOM: Broom has turned king's evidence, sir.

ROCK (*without looking up*):   The king will be pleased ...

Tom closes the door, pads on up the long Corridor again, and turns a corner, leaving the Corridor empty.
We hear the very distant noise of a crowd ...

116

(*Long shot*) of narrow City Street.

Early morning.
The street is empty.
We hear, kept very low, the noise of a great crowd: the grumbling of a sea far off.

117

(*Long shot*) of another narrow, empty Street.

The noise of a great crowd rising, slowly.

118

(*Long shot*) of another narrow, empty Street.

Then, across the far end of the desolate tunnel of the Street, we see the crowd surging.
And the noise increases.
The camera moves down the narrow Street towards the surge of the crowd and the increasing noise.
It moves past empty doorways.
And out of the empty doorways, through the clamour of the nearing crowd, we hear chanted:

FIRST VOICE: Up the alley and down the street ...

On, on, past another doorway.

SECOND VOICE: Fallon and Broom sell bones and meat ...

Past another doorway.

THIRD VOICE: Fallon's the butcher, Broom's the thief ...

Now we are nearly among the crowd pouring past the narrow street end, but we hear a fourth voice through the noise ...

FOURTH VOICE: And Rock's the boy who buys the beef ...

And now, through and under the loud noise of the crowd, we hear many voices together taking up the chant.
The camera cranes with and over the heads of the crowd and up to the windows of the Court-room, and into the Court-room.

119

Court-room.

We see the backs of the judges.
We move past them, across the court, towards the dock.
As we move we hear the droning voice of the Clerk of the Court ...

CLERK: Robert Fallon and Nelly Connor, you are both and each of you indicted and accused ...

In the dock, facing us, are Fallon and Nelly. They are both more neatly dressed than usual. Nelly is in black. Fallon is clean-shaven.
We move past them.
Now from behind them, we look down at the Clerk of the Court, who is seated beneath the Judges' bench.
The Clerk has not stopped speaking. Now the sound of his voice rises.

CLERK: ... that albeit by the laws of this and every other well-governed realm, murder is a crime of an heinous nature, and severely punishable, yet true it is and of verity that you the said Robert Fallon and Nelly Connor are both and each, or one or other of you, guilty of the said crime ...

The sound of the Clerk's voice is lowered. Now it is a drone the words of which we cannot catch.
And, through the droning, we hear the muffled noise of the crowd outside.
We move, past Fallon and Nelly, towards the Judges.
(*Pan along*) the Judges' bench.
(*Pan down*) to the Clerk. The Clerk's voice rises.

CLERK: ... when she the said Jennie Bailey was lying in the said house in a state of intoxication, and did, by the pressure thereof, and by covering her mouth and nose with your body or person, and forcibly compressing her throat with your hands, and forcibly keeping her down, notwithstanding her resistance, or in some other way to the prosecutor unknown ...

(*Cut to close-up*) of Fallon.

CLERK: ... preventing her from breathing, did suffocate or strangle her ...

The noise of the crowd rises, then is dimmed into a background.
(*Dissolve to*)

120

Rock's Lecture Hall.

Evening.
The background of the crowd noise.
Rock is on the platform.
The candles are lit on the platform table.
The auditorium is crowded with students.
The noise of the crowd rises violently.
Through the noise of the crowd, we hear the percussive voice-beat of 'Rock! Rock! Rock!'
And, like a cymbal clashing, the sharp crash of smashed glass.
Stones hurl through the shattered window at one side of the Lecture Hall.
The students stampede to their feet.
And a heavy stone crashes at Rock's foot.
The students begin to rush down the gallery steps towards the doors and the platform, shouting.
Rock stands rigid.
He pales with temper, glaring at the rushing students as though they were his enemies.
In its intensity, his dignity is malevolent.

ROCK: Gentlemen!

Cold, controlled fury stops the rush.
The students stand frozen.
The noise of the crowd is still loud.

ROCK: I have attempted to teach you the dignity of man; I have succeeded in producing the degradation of a *mob*. Because the verminous gutter-snipes of the City snarl and gibber in the street, because the scum from the brothels and the rot-gut shops howl for blood outside my window, must *you* conduct yourselves, in return, as though you were born in a quagmire and nurtured on hog-wash?
     Take your seats. Pay no attention to *the mob*. The mob can never win. Remember that the louder a man shouts, the emptier is his argument.
     Remember that you are here to study osteology, syndesmology, myology, angiology, neurology, splanchnology: not bar-room pugilism or the morals of the crapulous bog-trotter and the tosspot.

(*In his usual lecturing voice*) The heart, gentlemen, is a four-chambered muscular bag which lies in the cavity of the thorax ...

(*Dissolve to*)

121

City Street.

Night.
The noise of the crowd is a distant, insistent background. We see, striding in front of us, the black-cloaked top-hatted figure of Rock with his heavy stick.
We follow him along the street.
Two figures, muffled against the cold, come out of a side-street.
They stumble into Rock.
He pushes them aside.
And suddenly one of them cries out:

FIRST MAN: Rock! Rock! Doctor Rock!

Rock strides on.
The men cry after him, and follow him down the street, though keeping a safe distance from him.

SECOND MAN: Doctor Rock! Rock!

And, from some way off, we hear the crowd take up the percussive noise of 'Rock! Rock! Rock!'

122

(*Dissolve to*) Rock, hatless, but still in his cloak, entering Elizabeth's Room.

Elizabeth, by the fire, is sewing.
Elizabeth looks up as he comes in, and puts her sewing down.
He crosses to her; kisses her; stands still then, looking down at her.
(*Close-up*) of Rock and Elizabeth.

ROCK: Oh, there's peace in here.

ELIZABETH: You didn't come home *alone* through the streets? I've been hearing the crowd everywhere, all the evening.

ROCK: Alone.

ELIZABETH: They might have hurt you …

ROCK: Hurt *me?*

With a flourish he opens his cloak. Stuck in a belt around his waist are two pistols and a long dagger.

ROCK: I'd fell them to the ground. I'd flood the gutters with their …

Elizabeth begins to laugh, though quite gently.

ELIZABETH: Take off your cloak. And put your silly knives and guns away. You're like a boy pretending to be a highwayman. 'Stand and deliver.' Oh, Thomas, my dear …

He takes off his cloak and flings it over a chair and places the belt, the knife, and the guns on a table near the fire: a small table covered with sewing and bales of wool and cotton reels.

ELIZABETH: Why do you have to go out alone at night, *now?* Why do you *always* have to be alone?

ROCK: If the crowd wants me, it can have me. I am not going to hide. I am not going to surround myself by a company of paid protectors …

ELIZABETH (*softly*):   I've always wanted to see another country. Couldn't we go away? Every one is against us here, now.

The distant noise of the crowd.

ELIZABETH: The women in the street didn't nod to me this morning. Not because I'm your wife – that's why they used to have nothing to do with me – but because *you're* my husband.

ROCK: We won't go away.

ELIZABETH (*gently, as throughout*):   I know why. You want to show them that they can't hurt you by calling you names. You want to show them that you don't *mind* when they say that you told those men to murder people. But they *do* hurt you.

ROCK: *Time's a wilderness.* (*Then, in a changed voice*) Do you remember walking in the park? Oh, not so long ago. It was very, very, very cold and windy, people were scudding along like ships in a gale, and I remember thinking: 'Here's my life going true and even, and my children growing, and Elizabeth with me for ever, and books to write, and work to do ... Lord, but it's a happy time ... even in the unhappy times.'

ELIZABETH: I'm with you for ever, that's true. And there's books to write, and work to do.

Noise of the crowd nearer.

ROCK (*suddenly in another mood*):   I was successful, I was established, I was standing in the light ... Then out of the mud of the darkness come two ignorant animals, and slowly, quite unknown to themselves, they set about the task of bringing my life and my work down, down, into the slime that bred them ... Perhaps from the very moment of their monstrous births, it was decreed, by some sadistic jack-in-office of the universe, that they should befoul and ruin a fellow creature they had never heard of: a garrulous, over-credulous, conceited little anatomist, in a city they had never seen ...

From outside the noise of the crowd rises. And as the noise rises, so the voices of Elizabeth and Rock become quieter and more intimate.

ELIZABETH: Let us go away.

ROCK: No, we must stay for ever.

ELIZABETH: I have never asked you before, Thomas, because I love you. Did you know that the bodies that those men brought you had been murdered?

The noise of the crowd rises. Now it is very loud.
And the night sky beyond the window is glowing.
Elizabeth and Rock turn sharply to look towards the window.

VOICES OF THE CROWD: Rock! Rock!
Hang Rock!
Burn him!
Burn!
Burn!
Rock's the boy who buys the beef ...

Annabella comes in. She is palely, composedly angry.

ANNABELLA: Do you know what those hooligans are *doing*, Thomas?

She crosses to the window.

ROCK: I gather that they are not subscribing to a testimonial to me ...

ANNABELLA: Look! Look!

She points accusingly out of the window.

And Rock and Elizabeth, he with his arm around her shoulder, cross to Annabella's side and look, through the window, down on to the street.

123

Street outside Rock's house.

We see, from the window, the crowd straining against the iron railings of the house; the crowd, in the middle of the street, dancing with torches in their hands; the crowd carrying an effigy of Rock, an absurdly top-hatted scarecrow; the crowd waving their torches, stamping, howling, making a witches' Sabbath in the decorous, graciously façaded street.

And then the effigy, the guy carried on a pole, is held in a position directly opposite the window.

And a young woman with wild hair thrusts her blazing torch into the belly of the effigy.

In the torchlight, in the light of the burning Rock, we see that the young woman is Alice.

And another torch is thrust into the burning body; and another; and another.

Soon the effigy is writhing on fire. And the crowd waves it, crying in a high, hysterical triumph.

And they carry it along the street; and the dark figures of the crowd, their torches above them like long streams of fiery hair, follow it down the street.

124

City Square.

Night.
Outside Rock's Academy stand Murray and Tom.
Crowd noise, in the not so far distance.

MURRAY: What's the light over there?

The sky beyond the Square is glowing.

TOM: They're burning an auld scarecrow of the Doctor in the streets.

(*Close shot*) of Murray. He says, softly:

MURRAY: Can that children's magic bring back the dead?

The crowd noise rises on the wind.

MURRAY: Here we are, Tom, the two of us: the two 'rats'! the two 'deserters'!

TOM: Aye, the Doctor was wrong again. We're no 'rats' or 'deserters'. He should have known we didna want to lose our jobs, eh, Mr Murray?

Murray draws a little way apart from Tom, then asks abruptly:

MURRAY: What's the time?

TOM: One after midnight. The trial's been nearly twelve hours now ...

(*Close shot*) of Murray.

MURRAY: It took a few short minutes to stop her breath ...

125

Court-room.

Broom in the witness-box.
We see him very close.
We hear the Prosecutor, but do not see him.

PROSECUTOR'S VOICE: What did he do then?

BROOM: He got on her with his breast on her head, and kept in her breath; she gave a kind of cry and moaned a little after the first cry ...

(*Cut to close-up*) of Fallon in the dock.

PROSECUTOR'S VOICE: Did he say anything while this was going on?

BROOM'S VOICE: No, he got up then and put his hand across her mouth and kept it there three or four minutes. She appeared quite dead then.

PROSECUTOR'S VOICE: Were you looking on all this while?

(*Cut to close-up*) of Broom.

BROOM: I was sittin' on the chair.

PROSECUTOR'S VOICE: Did you sit in that chair and see Fallon for ten minutes killing the woman, and offer her no assistance?

BROOM: Aye.

Broom smiles.

126

Newspaper Office.

Crowd noise from outside.
A room with a long, large window.
The First Reporter is writing at a table.
The Second Reporter is walking up and down the room and glancing, every few moments, out of the window.

SECOND REPORTER: Was he smiling when he said *that*?

FIRST REPORTER (*without looking up*):   If you call it smiling.

SECOND REPORTER: What did he look like?

FIRST REPORTER (*briefly, as he writes*):   Devil.

SECOND REPORTER: Fallon?

FIRST REPORTER: Quite quiet. Vurry polite.

SECOND REPORTER: And the woman?

FIRST REPORTER: Sober.

The crowd noise rises.

SECOND REPORTER: What are you calling the article? (*at the window*) They're running down the street now ... Thousands of them ...

FIRST REPORTER: 'Justice'.

SECOND REPORTER: 'Broom! Broom! Broom!' ... D'you hear them?

FIRST REPORTER: Broom'll go free.

SECOND REPORTER (*still looking out of the window*):   There's another fire over Newington way ... somewhere near Rock's place ... D'you hear them?

FIRST REPORTER (*writing, not looking up*):   They won't call Rock as a witness. That'll be taken care of ...

A great cry from the crowd outside ...

SECOND REPORTER: D'you hear that? ...

FIRST REPORTER: I'm not deaf. They're nearing the end now ...

127

Court-room.

(*Close shot*) of Lord Meadowbank. Camera (*pans along*) Judges' faces.

LORD MEADOWBANK: My Lords, I am confident that, although speaking in the presence of your Lordships, so much better instructed than myself, and so able to correct me were I in error, there is no chance of my being contradicted when I say that in the history of this country – nay, in the whole history of civilised society – there has never been exhibited such a system of barbarous and savage iniquity, or anything at all corresponding in atrocity, to what this trial has brought to light ...

128

Newspaper Office.

Night.
The two reporters.
The First Reporter flings down his pen.

FIRST REPORTER: Fallon guilty. The rest – innocent! And my title is '*Justice*'. I wrote the verdict *myself*, hours ago. Only the sentence now: I've written that, too.

129

Court-room.

LORD CHIEF JUSTICE: The Lord Justice Clerk and Lord Commissioners of Justiciary in respect of the verdict before recorded, determine and adjudge the said Robert Fallon, to be carried from the bar, and to be fed upon bread and water only until Wednesday, the 28th January, and upon that day to be taken forth to the common place of execution and then and there between the hours of eight and ten o'clock to be hanged by the neck until he be dead. And may Almighty God have mercy on your soul.
(*Dissolve to*)

130

Large (*close-up*) of Rock.

ROCK: I have no need of your sympathy. When I see a tear, I smell a crocodile.

(*Track back*) to show that Rock is standing on the platform of the empty Lecture Hall. Murray, a good distance from Rock, stands at the window, looking out.
Their voices echo in the Hall.

MURRAY (*turning round*):   For God's sake, Thomas, can you do nothing but – stand still and gibe?

ROCK: Would you have me death-dance and *moan*, like a Gaelic dipsomaniac at a distillery fire? Must tragedy go immediately to the feet and the tongue? Because I can observe my history *calmly* as it burns and topples around me, you emotional gluttons think yourselves cheated. 'Oh, he can't *feel* anything,' you say. 'When we told him his life was over, he did not tear the relics of his hair or address the travelling moon in blank verse. He blew his nose and called for Burgundy.'

MURRAY (*deliberately*):   Fallon is to hang.

ROCK: A quick end. If they wished his death to be longer and infinitely more painful, they should marry him to Doctor Hocking's daughter.

MURRAY: Fallon is to hang. Nelly Connor is 'not guilty'! Broom and his woman are free to murder again! And *you*?

ROCK: I shall stay here.

I shall listen to the voices of the crowd outside my window, *inside my head*; it will not be long before they forget me; I shall never forget them.

I shall stay here. The whispers of the slanderer and the backbiter will always be with me: mice behind the wall.

I shall stay here. I shall count my friends on the fingers of one hand, then on one finger, then on none.

Camera (*cranes back*), looking down at Rock and Murray all the time, over the empty tiers of the classroom.

Although Rock becomes further and further off, in (*long shot*), the sound, booming hollowly through the empty classroom, remains in full close-up.

ROCK: My lectures will be very well attended, at the beginning. I shall possess a sinister attraction to the young: dangerous and exciting, like dining with a vampire. But the attendance will diminish.

I shall stay here to see in the eyes of the passing stranger in the street cruelty and contempt; in the eyes of the poor the terrible accusation: 'You killed the lost, the weak, the homeless, the hopeless, the helpless. Murderer of the poor!'

God help me, life will go on ...

131

Condemned Cell.

Fallon on a chair in the middle of the cell.

His hair is shaven.

A Phrenologist is measuring his head. He speaks the measurements aloud to an assistant, who writes them down in a book.

Fallon submits, with interest, to the examination.

PHRENOLOGIST: From the ear to lower Individuality: 5 inches. From the ear to the centre of philo-progenitiveness: 4·8. From the ear to Benevolence: 5·7. From the ear to Destructiveness: 6·125.

Let us see:

Acquisitiveness: large.

Secretiveness: large.

Wit: deficient.

Cautiousness: h'm, rather large.

Sense of Tune: moderate.
Self-esteem: rather large.
Hope: small.

132

Exterior of Prison.

Night.
A coach draws up.
The driver is heavily shawled about, and his hat is pulled down over his eyes.
And two cloaked, muffled figures hurry Broom towards the coach.
Broom is wrapped in a thick coat, and hooded. It is hard to recognise him.
But suddenly, at the door of the coach, he pulls back his hood, looks up at the sky.
He shakes his shaven head, like a monstrous dog coming out of the water.
And he begins to laugh his high, clear, yelping laugh as the two cloaked figures smuggle him into the coach.
The coach moves off, out of picture.

133

Market-place.

Late evening.
The stalls closed down.
And a woman's scream, a scream of hate and anger, is coming from a Market tavern.
And with her scream are mingled the voices of men and women: voices shouting, cursing, and threatening.
Then a knot of people tangles inside the open door of the tavern.
A whirl of arms and a squall of voices.
And we see Kate thrown out of the tavern on to the cobble stones of the Market.
She stumbles to her feet, runs, squawking like a chased hen, down the Market.
But only the voices chase her.
People pour from the tavern, stand outside it, throw stones after her, manure, rubbish.

Kate runs on, huddled.
And windows, high up in the tenements around the Market, open.
And the contents of buckets are thrown upon her as she runs.

134

Road on the Outskirts of the City.

Night.
The road is long and winding.
We see Nelly Connor, with a bundle on her back, coming towards us, along the road, out of the distance.
She is pushing a hurly: a hurly with old boots upon it, and remnants of clothing, and odds and ends from the room in Rag-and-Bone Alley, and shapes one cannot identify in the night.
And we hear her voice as she pushes her barrow through darkness up the desolate road that leads out of the City.

NELLY'S VOICE (*softly*):
   Old boots to sell! ... Cat-skin! ... *Human hair!* ...

135

Newspaper Office.

Daylight.
We see the street through the tall window.
The Second Reporter stands at the window, looking out, his back towards us.
The First Reporter sits at the other side of the window, a pad on his knee. Through the window we see, at the end of the street, in (*long shot*), a scaffold.
The platform of the scaffold is raised above the heads of the crowd.
On the platform we see the gibbet; it is shaped like a T with one additional vertical on the right.
On the platform are several figures: clergymen, magistrates, hangman, and Fallon.
And we hear the crowd noise rise.
And looking through the window at the scene of execution, and hearing the cries of the crowd, we hear, too, the voices of the two men at the window.

SECOND REPORTER: Do you hear?

'Hang Broom! Hang Rock!'

FIRST REPORTER: Fallon's on his knees. He's praying.

The noise of the crowd rises. Then:

SECOND REPORTER: The rope's round his neck. They've put a cotton nightcap on his head.

FIRST REPORTER: Good night.

The noise of the crowd rises again.

CRIES OF THE CROWD: You'll see Billy Bedlam in a minute.

FIRST REPORTER: What are they shouting?

SECOND REPORTER: 'You'll see Billy Bedlam in a minute!' He's on the drop.

A great cheer from the crowd.

FIRST REPORTER: He was always one for dancing. He's dancing now.

136

(*Close shot*) of Alice and Murray at a table in a Tavern.

Around them the noise of the Market-place drinking. And pipes in the distance.

ALICE: Fallon's dead – why isn't the Doctor dead? Nobody remembers Jennie now.

MURRAY: Oh, there's lots of ways of dying. *I* remember.

137

(*Close shot*) of Annabella and Elizabeth; behind them, the window of Elizabeth's Room looking out on the wintry trees in the garden.

ANNABELLA: Do you *know* what it is to be lonely? I've always been lonely. I wanted to be mistress of my brother's house, I wanted to give dinner parties and dances and be charming and admired. I want to marry. But people wouldn't visit us because *you* married *him*. It doesn't matter now. Now nobody'll come ...

ELIZABETH: I married him because I loved him. But we're only a very little part of his life, Bella.
I've been lonely, too.

138

(*Close shot*) of Hocking and the Chairman (the Lord Chief Justice, whom we saw in Sequences 111 and 114) against the background of imposing bookcases.

CHAIRMAN: So, officially speaking, he's innocent as a lamb, the wolf.

HOCKING: We saved him from a criminal prosecution.

CHAIRMAN: Of course, of course. In order to save the good name of society. Fallon and Broom could have brought their bodies to *you*, of course. It just happened it was Rock they chose.

HOCKING: I would have none of their bodies.

CHAIRMAN: No?

HOCKING: But now it's all over. All over. We can speak our minds now.

CHAIRMAN: We save him from public ruin, so that we can ruin him privately. H'm, I'm sure he's grateful ...

139

Lecture Hall of Rock's Academy.

Rock is on the platform.
The auditorium is densely packed.
We see Rock from the back of the Hall, over the heads of the students.
And we move, slowly, over the heads towards him as he speaks.

ROCK: To think, then, is to enter into a perilous country, colder of welcome than the polar wastes, darker than a Scottish Sunday, where the hand of the unthinker is always raised against you, where the wild animals, who go by such names as Envy, Hypocrisy, and Tradition, are notoriously carnivorous, and *where the parasites rule*.
To *think* is dangerous. The majority of men have found it easier

to writhe their way into the parasitical bureaucracy, or to *droop* into the slack ranks of the ruled. I beg you all to devote your lives to danger; I pledge you to adventure; I command you to experiment. (*slowly*) Remember that the practice of Anatomy is absolutely vital to the *progress* of medicine. Remember that the progress of medicine is vital to the progress of mankind. And mankind is worth fighting for: killing and lying and dying for. Forget what you like. Forget all I have ever told you. But remember that ...

Now we see Rock in (*close-up*).
(*Dissolve to*)

140

City Street.

Gathering dusk.
We hear the thin, high singing of the wind in the street.
And, in the background, the sound of the voices of children drifting through the dusk.
Rock, from a grey distance, is walking towards us along the street. He is cloaked, top-hatted.
And as he comes closer to us a little girl runs out of the shadows of a side-street, runs barefoot through the wind, her black hair leaping.
She is grimed from the gutters of the city; her dress is thin and ragged; one shoulder is naked.
And she runs at Rock's side, crying out:

GIRL: Give us a penny, mister, give us a penny ...

The camera (*tracks back*) as Rock, and the little girl running at his side, move on down the street.
Then Rock stops, at a corner.
And the little girl stops; she stands still in a shadow at the mouth of a narrow tunnel-like street. She is almost lost in the shadow, her hair is mixed into the darkness, but we see her white face and white, naked shoulder.
Rock stands just outside the shadow.
He puts a penny in her hand.
He looks down at her, and is silent for a moment.

ROCK: It's a bitter cold night to be running about in the streets. You should go home.

The child in the shadows shakes her head.

CHILD: Granny says I can't come home till I got fourpence ...

Rock fumbles in his pocket for another coin.
The child holds out her hand from the shadow around her.

ROCK: What's your name, lassie?

CHILD: I'm Maggie Bell.

ROCK (*almost as though to himself*):   I'm Doctor Rock.

And the child runs screaming into the darkness.
And Rock walks on, away from us.

141

Hill above the City.

The dusk is deeper ...
The wind is blowing wilder ...
We look down the hill.
Out of the dusk, a long way off, Rock is climbing up towards us.
And as he climbs, we hear his voice. But it is only the little, wind-blown whisper of a voice, and we cannot hear a word of it.
And as he climbs on and up, so the windy whisper loudens and we begin to hear the words.
We begin to hear the fragments of sentences.
We hear some words and then the wind rises for a second and blows them away.
Then we hear more words, from the voice of his mind; the wind again will not let the words finish but blows them away.
And again; and again; and again.
Always the voice is the voice of Rock, but it is never twice on the same level: it is the voice of Rock young, then old, then gay, then sad; a high voice, a low voice.
And the sound of it rises as he climbs.

ROCK'S VOICE: And the child in the cold runs away from my
   name ...
   My name is a ghost to frighten children ...
   Will *my* children cry '*Murder*' and '*Blood*' when I touch them ...
   as if my hands were Fallon's hands? ...
   'Be good, be good, or the terrible Doctor will come with his knife.'

Poor Billy! I came to you with my knife.
Did I *know*, did I *know* from the very beginning?
Never answer, never answer, even to yourself alone in the night ...
All's over now ...
Oh, Elizabeth, hold my hand ...
'Oh, it isn't a hand, it's a pair of scissors! ...'
Did I set myself up as a little god over death?
Over death ...
All over ... over ... over ...
Did I set myself above pity? ...
Oh, my God, I knew what I was doing!

And he passes us and climbs up the long hill, and his voice climbs with him into darkness, into a whisper, into silence, into the climax of

(*Music.*)

Twenty Years A-Growing

Enclosing the words for *Our Country* Thomas noted in the accompanying letter to Taylor in October 1944: 'I am just starting to go through 20 years – the book, John's [Eldridge probably, the Strand/Gryphon director] selection of passages, and my own notes. I shd start on the real work this week.'[79] At the end of the month came the apology for slow progress, couched and lightened as usual with a humorous touch – 'though work on *20 years* has been going so slowly and badly that at one time I thought we'd have to alter the title to 40 years'. He adds: 'this little bungalow is no place to work in when there's a bawling child there, too ... & a friend arrived with another baby with a voice like Caruso's. Now, however, I have just taken a room in a nearby house: a very quiet room.'. It was of course a very busy time, with filmscripts, planning *Deaths and Entrances* and a burgeoning of new poems; broadcasts, too, were beginning to demand his attention. But he concluded: 'Will write again soon, with *much more encouraging "Twenty Years news"*.'[80]

Dylan Thomas's reading and research for filmscripts were certainly thorough, for the following February, while agreeing to do the script of the *Suffer Little Children* film, he adds in a postscript: 'I have just finished reading ... the autobiography, called *The Islandman*, of Tomás Ó Crohan. It is *the* very first book about the Blaskets ... "The Islandman", "Twenty Years" and Robin Flower's own book – the "West Island" is it? – represent all the available written literature of and upon the Blaskets. ... But we should be able, from those 3 books, to tell the story of life on the Island *in its entirety*.' Dylan concludes that 'I do not suggest we use the actual material of Ó Crohan's & Flower's books, but that we study them as background.'[81]

'Here is the egg of a seabird – lovely, perfect and laid this very morning' wrote E.M. Forster when Maurice O'Sullivan's *Twenty Years A-Growing* was first published in English, and certainly the unfinished filmscript of the first half of the book has kept the lyrical freshness. 'Thomas matched with admirable care the lyrical poignancy of that classic autobiography of a

childhood on the Blasket Islands'[82] observed Walford Davies. It is a
prose-poetry that Dylan Thomas has created, at its most beautiful and
delicate in such episodes as Maurice's dream when he sees the butterfly
coming out of his sleeping friend Mickil's mouth and flying over the sunlit
meadow. Maurice follows its flight leaving behind 'deep dusk, and the
note of the owl'. A few lines show we are near to the childhood lyricism of
'Fern Hill' – dusk and dark present too.

> We see a (*long shot*) of Maurice and Mickil walking in a meadow, picking
> flowers. Half of the great meadow is in sunlight, half in deep dusk through
> which we see the strange shapes of trees moving and strange hills.
> Closer now, we see the children sit down by a stream, their arms full of
> flowers. They sit in the sunlight. We hear birds singing above them, but,
> from a distance, we hear, too, the note of the owl as though it came from the
> dark half of the great meadow.
> And closer still we see a butterfly fly above Mickil sleeping.

Time and eternity, youth and age are themes reflected in seasonal change,
light and dark, movement and stillness in natural life, particularly birds
whose flight and migrations crowd these settings. There are some echoes
of such early prose as 'A Prospect of the Sea'. But this ubiquitous visionary
nature is there too in the almost contemporaneous 'Poem in October' and
'Fern Hill', and anticipates the fabled pastoralism of the later verse, such
as 'A Winter's Tale' – particularly in its narrative scenario. It is man,
childhood, happiness, that are transient against the paradoxically eternal
change of the natural world, whether migrations, tides, seasons – imaged
here with cinematic sound and sight: 'a flock of snowing', 'the sounding
of the waves', 'cries of birds … were falling'. In Thomas's Synopsis for the
second half of the script he relates 'And the (*camera*) reaches Maurice as a
youth. He is looking after sheep on the cliffside, the sun yellowing in the
west and a lark singing above. He sees lambs gambolling together,' an
eternal pastoral but unknowingly awaiting 'the appearance of the man
[who] now announces the beginning of doubt, introduces into the idyllic
timelessness of the island the first sound of the time-bound outer world'. I
think his work on this 1944/5 filmscript was seminal in the evolution of
his later narrative, visionary, sea- and bird-haunted pastoralism.

The script's opening picture of the market town of Dingle, a school bell
ringing, has the freshness and humour, too, of *Milk Wood*, as 'a large pig
crosses the road slowly, and enters a cottage'. The shots of landscapes,
'The Voice' which is the voice of Maurice O'Sullivan remembering the
lost childhood, remind us that Thomas was still writing documentaries,
which introduced him to this kind of structuring of his script. Describing

Maurice's schooldays, his friendship with Mickil and their sad parting – 'Mickil is still a child, and his eyes are full of tears' – when his father takes him to the Blaskets, Thomas uses the Voice to narrate episodes, a journey back to childhood. His life on the Blaskets includes scenes of dancing and song at home, to welcome him, and on such occasions as Hallowe'en; and walks with his grandfather who tells him 'Did ye never hear how the life of man is divided? Twenty years a-growing, twenty years in blossom, twenty years a-stooping, and twenty years declining.' Nor is the view of nature a sentimental one, for we see the hunting of thrushes and rabbits for food. Thomas vividly describes Maurice and Tomas enjoying their pints of beer when visiting Ventry!

The script pictures the wildness of the seascapes, the lonely but hardy peasant life of the Blaskets, in darkness 'the island thrown up black against the phosphorous sea', Thomas's rhythms and prose-poetry encapsulating sight and sound and feeling. In his Synopsis for the second half Dylan Thomas relates that his filmscript was to conclude with Maurice choosing a lonely, hard and poor life on the island: 'the enduring figure, the eternal peasant'. Blaise in *The Shadowless Man* is also redeemed by nature, albeit in the different circumstances of that tale.

TWENTY YEARS A-GROWING

It is morning in the market-town of Dingle. A cracked school bell is ringing. The main street is wide awake: a man leans at a corner, motionless, smoking. A woman stands at an open doorway, looking at the morning. A large pig crosses the road slowly, and enters a cottage. The school bell still rings.

Then, at the top of the street, appear a countrywoman and a little boy in a smock, hand in hand. They walk on down the street towards us.

And suddenly we hear a crying and shouting, and there appear, at the top of the street and behind the woman and the little boy, a helter-skelter of children who run down towards us. And as they run, so other children come out of the cottages, on either side of the street, and join them. And they all scamper past the woman and the little boy, making quite a noise, and past us and out of the picture.

And as the woman and the little boy approach us now, hand in hand, the little boy clinging, we hear the voice of Maurice O'Sullivan the man, gently, reminiscently talking, as a person to no audience but himself and a friend.

THE VOICE: And that's indeed the first thing I remember very clearly in all my life. It was in the town of Dingle, County Kerry, Ireland, and I was going on my first day to school, holding the hand of Peg de Roiste. For it was she who took care of me when my mother died, dear God bless her soul and the souls of all the dead. Faith, there in my memory still I see old Peg and myself, Maurice O'Sullivan, walking to school.

And Peg de Roiste and little Maurice O'Sullivan are walking now towards the entrance of the whitewashed village school. The cracked bell stops ringing. He clings hard to her hand, and looks up at her, and she smiles down, nodding and reassuring, as they go into the school.

Now we are in the schoolroom: a whitewashed room with rows of benches full of children and a little chair and table at the end, and a blackboard. At the end of the room, behind the table, stand two posts coming down from the roof to the floor. Peg de Roiste and Maurice sit close together on the back bench. He stares around the classroom, quiet as a mouse, his eyes wide. All the other children are making a power of noise.

The schoolmistress enters.

The noise is hushed.

THE CHILDREN: Good morning, mistress.

The schoolmistress sits at her table, opens a book, looks at the children, marks down their names, silently …

THE VOICE: I remember there was teaching us as schoolmistress a woman who was grey as a badger, with two tusks of teeth hanging down over her lip, and if she wasn't cross, it isn't day yet. She was the devil itself, or so I thought.

Close now to Peg and Maurice: we hear him whisper timidly.

MAURICE: Where are the nice sweets you said there'd be, Peg?

PEG: Go up now, she's for giving you the sweets.

Maurice shakes his head and clings harder to her hand. And Peg gets up with him and takes him by the hand to the little table.

From the back of the classroom now we see the backs of Peg and Maurice and the face of the schoolmistress.

MISTRESS: Who are you and what is your name?

MAURICE: They call me Maurice.

MISTRESS: Maurice what?

MAURICE: Maurice.

We hear Peg whisper to the mistress, who nods and writes in her book.

Then the mistress rises and goes to a cupboard and takes out a big tin of sweets and puts it on the little table before Maurice.

We (*track up*) towards the table. Maurice timidly puts his hand into the tin and takes out a sweet in the shape of a horse.

MAURICE (*with wonder*): A horse.

The mistress nods.

He puts his hand in again and takes out another-shaped sweet.

MAURICE (*a little louder*): A boat.

She nods.

He dips and takes out another two sweets, one in each hand. He raises his hands to show Peg.

MAURICE (*shrill with excitement*): Oh, a man. And a pig. [...]

THE VOICE: I was going to school every day, growing older and bigger and none the wiser at all, I am guessing, and it was the gentleness and the sweets had long grown cold. It seemed to me there was nobody in the world had a worse life than myself. I did not know what I wanted, but I knew it was not to be kept indoors all day, like a baby or a girl. I wanted to be, oh, I knew not where ...

And we see, as the Voice speaks, that Maurice is not joining in the speaking-aloud of the lesson but is lost in a world of his own mazy making. Suddenly the mistress's voice cuts across the voices of the children, and they stop.

MISTRESS'S VOICE: Maurice O'Sullivan.

He raises his eyes. We do not see the mistress, but only, close, the benches of children.

MISTRESS'S VOICE: You are dreaming again. Come here.

Maurice rises and crosses out of the picture.

MISTRESS'S VOICE: Put out your hand.

We see the intent faces of the children staring at the invisible punishment. One child nudges another, smiling. But most are dead quiet. We hear the sound of a stinging slap.
Mickil, next to Maurice's empty place on the bench, winces and involuntarily draws back his hand.
Another stinging slap.
Mickil's face is set and white.
Another slap.
Maurice returns; takes his place; sits stiffly, staring in front of him with very bright eyes.
And the children begin to recite together again.
Maurice moves his lips. We hear very softly, through the voices of the children, the voice of the child Maurice.

MAURICE: Your soul to the devil, you old herring ...

Now Maurice is coming out of a Dingle cottage – a cottage not in the main street we have seen before but in a country road. He carries his school-books hung over his shoulder. With him is Mickil. And once more the cracked school bell is ringing, but farther off than before.
They dawdle down the road together, their school-books swinging, slashing off the tops of the roadside ferns, idly kicking the stones.

MAURICE: I don't know why in the world we are going to school, on a day like this, Mickil.

MICKIL: We could be having the day under the hedge ...

MAURICE: We could be playing the devil up on the Hill of the Cairn, or making shapes out of sticks ...

MICKIL: Or snatching the bags of sugar out of the hands of the old men in the poor-house ...

MAURICE: Or dabbling in the boghole, by God ... Oh, when will I be a grown man, Mickil, with a pony and cart and a clay pipe maybe ... Whisht! Who's that there?

Up the road towards them come two women and a man. They wave at Maurice and Mickil and walk on straight towards them. Maurice turns and runs in the other direction, and hides in the hedge.
From the hedge we see what he sees: the man and the women talking

to Mickil and pointing up, smiling, towards the hedge. One of the women puts an orange in Mickil's hand, and the other woman gropes in her bag for a present. And, still from the hedge, we see Maurice run back towards them, stopping shyly a yard away.

WOMAN: Why did you run away just now?

MAURICE (*bashfully*): Nothing ...

WOMAN: Do you know who I am?

MAURICE: I do not.

WOMAN: I am your aunt, my treasure.

She takes Maurice up in her arms and kisses him, then puts him down again but holds him close to her.
And the other woman kisses him also.

WOMAN: That is another aunt, too, and this is your uncle.

MAN (*An elaborate greeting in Irish.*)

The school bell stops ringing.

MAURICE: What sort of talk has that man?

WOMAN: That's Irish.

MAURICE: What's Irish?

WOMAN: Oh, wait now till you go home, that is the time you will have the Irish.

MAURICE: Where is my home? We have no Irish at all in this home here.

WOMAN: This is not your home, Maurice. Your home is in the Blasket.

Maurice looks, without understanding, at the faces of his aunts and his uncle.

MAN: ... (*A speech in Irish.*)

And the speech is softened so that, through it, we hear:

THE VOICE (*softly*): But I was as blind to what he was saying about the Blasket as the herring leaping in the Bay of Dingle ...

MAURICE (*to the woman, who still holds him close*): What is the Blasket?

WOMAN: It is an island.

MAURICE: Is it a long way away? Over the sea?

WOMAN: It is ten miles from Dingle ...

MICKIL: Ten miles, God be with us ...

FIRST WOMAN: Oh, hear him. You were born on the Blasket, Maurice, asthore, and because you were only half a year old when your mother died ...

SECOND WOMAN: Dear God bless her soul and the souls of all the dead ...

FIRST WOMAN: ... your father sent you to Dingle to be cared for by Peg de Roiste. Has she never been telling you that? ...

WOMAN: And your father is for coming out before long to take you home at last. Would you like that, Maurice?

MAURICE: Who is my father?

WOMAN: Isn't it often your father was talking to you? You should have known him long ago ...

MAURICE: I don't know which of the men he is, for many come ...

WOMAN: Oh musha, youth is a queer thing ...

And the women give Maurice and Mickil sweets, apples and oranges.

And the man comes up to them both, and, talking Irish, solemnly shakes their hands. As he talks, Maurice and Mickil look at one another in wonder. Then he takes money from his pocket and gives Maurice a half a crown and Mickil a shilling ...

And the two aunts kiss Maurice again.

FIRST WOMAN: Now we go to see Peg de Roiste. Farewell, and a blessing (*in Irish*).

SECOND WOMAN: Farewell, and a blessing (*in Irish*).

MAN: Farewell, and a blessing (*in Irish*).

And they go up the road.

(*Close-up*) of Maurice and Mickil. Mickil outs his shilling for Maurice to see.

MICKIL: I never saw a penny as bright as that ... Where is yours?

MAURICE: Look, mine is bigger.

MICKIL: I don't know what we had better buy with them ...

MAURICE: Marbles and boats and ... Oh, Mickil, the bell has stopped!

And they race down the road.
The classroom.
The mistress is chalking on the blackboard, her back to the children.
The door creaks open and Maurice and Mickil creep in to their places on the bench.
They look up fearfully at the blackboard and the mistress, who has not turned round. [...]

(*Cut to:*)
(*Long shot*) of Maurice and Mickil running up the hill of the Cairn, past the black bog, into the dusk. And as they run, calling to each other in the still evening, we hear:

THE VOICE: And the end of it was we had the rest of the day off, and we played, I remember, on the Hill of the Cairn till the dark came ...

We follow the boys up the hill, and as the dusk grows deeper we hear:

THE VOICE: Was it that night, I wonder, that I dreamed a dream I have never forgotten? That night or another, who cares, for the tale of a man's life is beyond the bother of the clock and he must try to remember it the best he may ...

And Maurice and Mickil have vanished into the darkness, and now there is nothing but darkness, and now again the darkness lifts and we are in a cottage room lit only by firelight. We move down the room, past dresser and table and chairs, and come to a bed where Maurice and Mickil lie together awake but silent. The voice is talking throughout.

THE VOICE: I only know it was a winter's night, very wild, with the patter of snow on the window panes, and myself stretched out on the flat of my back in the fine cosy bed, and ever thinking of the Blasket.

We come closer and closer to Maurice and Mickil, and their eyes close and they fall asleep, the firelight moving their faces.

THE VOICE: But falling asleep, I was dreaming all of a sudden not of the Blasket at all but that Mickil Dick and I were walking through a fine green meadow, gathering flowers. When we had gathered our fill of them, we sat down, talking of school and brilla-bralla, as is the habit of children.

After a while it seemed that Mickil fell asleep – and I asleep that was dreaming it all. While I sat thinking what a strange thing was that same sleep, what would I see come out of his mouth but a pretty butterfly.

Through this we see a (*long shot*) of Maurice and Mickil walking in a meadow, picking flowers. Half of the great meadow is in sunlight, half in deep dusk through which we see the strange shapes of trees moving and strange hills.

Closer now, we see the children sit down by a stream, their arms full of flowers. They sit in the sunlight. We hear birds singing above them, but, from a distance, we hear, too, the note of the owl as though it came from the dark half of the great meadow.

And closer still we see a butterfly fly above Mickil sleeping.

We see the butterfly fly away down the meadow.

Still it is flying.

Maurice is running along the sunlit meadow.

Still the butterfly is flying.

Maurice is running along the sunlit meadow towards the dusk. And as he runs, so the sunlight behind him grows suddenly dusky and the dusk before him lightens.

Still the butterfly is flying.

It flies on to a gate.

Birds are singing.

Beyond the gate with the butterfly perched upon it is a sunlit meadow.

Maurice is running towards the gate and the butterfly. And behind him is deep dusk, and the note of the owl.

He reaches the gate and the butterfly flies away, into the sunlit meadow.

And Maurice climbs the gate. And climbing the gate, he is suddenly in deep shadow.

With a spring he is over. Over into the sunlight.

Still the butterfly is flying.

In the meadow lies a horse's skull.
Maurice kneels by the skull.
The butterfly flies through the eyes of the skull.
The sunlit field is darkening, dusking.
The butterfly flies out of the mouth of the skull.
The butterfly is flying.
Maurice rises and runs through dusk towards the gate which stands
at the entrance to a sunlit meadow.
The butterfly is flying.
Maurice climbs the gate, in deep shadow.
With a spring, he is in sunlight.
He runs along the sunlit meadow.
Mickil is lying asleep. The butterfly flies over his face, and is gone.
Maurice sits by his side, looking into Mickil's face.
Mickil wakes, yawns, stretches.
And we hear the voice of Maurice the child saying, as he sits by
waking Mickil in the sunny meadow, by the stream:

MAURICE: It seems, when a man dreams, a white butterfly do be
coming out of his mouth …

The meadow is sunlit no longer, but in deep dusk. The deep dusk
deepens into darkness.

Then it is light again, morning light, and we are in the cottage room
again, by the bedside of the two boys. Mickil is awake, sitting up,
looking at Maurice, who is still speaking:

MAURICE: … and walking away; and when it comes again it is then
he wakes.

And Mickil burst into a shout of laughter. And Maurice awakes.

MICKIL: Och, listen to the way he is talking in his sleep …

And he bursts into laughter again …
(*Close-up*) of the two boys.
(*Dissolve to*):
(*Close-up*) of the two boys in the classroom, sitting on the bench …
We hear in the background a boy reciting his lesson.

MICKIL (*whispering*):   And a butterfly was after coming out of my
mouth. Faith, it was my tongue! – like this …

Mickil puts out his tongue.

MAURICE: Put in your tongue or the pooka will bite it off. […]

FIRST AUNT: This is your father, Maurice.

And Maurice walks slowly up to his father, and his father embraces him.

FATHER: Would you like to go home with me today?

MAURICE: I would indeed, what sort of place is it?

FATHER: Oh, a fine place.

MAURICE: Will we be going now?

FATHER: As soon as you have dressed in this nice suit of clothes here, we will be going in the name of God.

MAURICE: Will there be trousers?

FATHER: Trousers, indeed, and a jacket, and a shirt, and a collar and a cap and …

MAURICE: We will be going, surely … I will go in now so, and say goodbye to Mickil.

He walks into the school: quietly, a little stiffly and self-consciously: a small dignified boy in a child's smock.

In the classroom he stretches out his hand to Mickil. They stand for a few seconds, without speaking. We see them close. Then:

MAURICE (*in a formal way, as befits a small boy about to become a man, but gently still, and with affection*):   Goodbye, Mickil, I am going home to the Blasket today and I hope I shall see you again in health and happiness.

But Mickil is still a child, and his eyes are full of tears.

MICKIL: Oh, so do I, so do I, Maurice … […]

And the father points to the north-west, to the Blasket Islands.

THE FATHER: There to the north-west. Over there.

And, from the cart stopped at the high, windy edge, we see the island, and hear:

THE VOICE: I could not speak, a lump came in my throat. I saw little white houses huddled together in the middle of the island, a great wild hill straight to the west with no more houses to be seen, only a tower on the peak of the hill and the hillside white with sheep. I did not like the look of it.

MAURICE: But how will the horse and cart get over there?

THE FATHER: We will go in a curragh.

They all climb down from the cart.
A little way away from them.

MAURICE: But what sort of thing is a curragh?

They stand now on the cliff edge, looking out to the island: Maurice small and still between the two tall men.

And suddenly the head of a man appears over the cliff edge, then his shoulders, then his body, then he is all there, standing on the very edge, the wind blowing his hair and his clothes. There is no sign of a path for him to have climbed. He appears just like that: a man, suddenly, comes up over the cliff.

MAURICE: Oh, look, look, the man has come up out of the sea.

The man walks towards them. There is a post-bag on his back.

MAURICE: Oh, who is that, Father? Did he fly up like a bird?

THE FATHER: Faith, he is the King of the Island ...

MAURICE (*in wonder*):   Do all kings come up like that?

And the King – a 'fine, courteous, mannerly, well-favoured man' – approaches the two men and the boy. And he greets the boy first.

THE KING (*in Irish*):   Musha, how are you now?

MAURICE (*in English*):   Thank you very much.

THE KING: The devil, I think you have no understanding of the Irish ...

MAURICE: I have not.

THE KING: You will. And how does it please you to be going to the island?

MAURICE: It does not look too nice altogether ...

THE KING: It does not neither, just a rock torn off the land and sitting down in the sea. But there is no place like it in the world. Come down now.

And the King takes Maurice's hand and they walk to the very place on the edge of the cliff where the King had appeared, and the uncle waves his hand and gets into the cart and drives off, and the father follows Maurice and the King.

Maurice and the King stand on the cliff edge, the wind tumbling their hair and gusting about them.

Maurice looks down at the sea. [...]

THE VOICE: Oh, the island that day said Welcome, and Welcome.

And behind the voice we hear, softly, the echoing sound of Welcome, Welcome, in Irish, called by many voices.

The crowd closes round the King, the father and Maurice, but it is the children who come most close to Maurice and they stare at him without speaking.

Now an old man, the grandfather, comes out of the crowd and walks towards Maurice, and the close circle of children is broken, and the grandfather embraces Maurice.

THE GRANDFATHER: Musha, God bless your life, my heart and my blood.

MAURICE: Who are you?

THE GRANDFATHER: Och, isn't it a strange thing that you would not know your own grandfather. You shall call me Daddo. Come up with me now ...

The grandfather takes Maurice by the hand and together they climb up the path from the quay. The children follow them, dancing and calling. From the top of the path we see them climbing towards us. First one woman, then another, darts out of the crowd and kisses him, and we hear:

THE VOICE: Oh, the kisses they gave me then, the women of the island, I might have been a soldier returning from the holy wars but I would rather the frost than that to be done to me.

Now the grandfather and Maurice are walking past the village houses: long, low, narrow houses, many of them dug into the steep slope of the hill for shelter from the wind. [...]

A young man is squatting near the hearth, playing a melodeon ...

Boys and girls are dancing; Maura the sister is dancing alone among them.

The father and the grandfather sit at a table at the end of the room; there is a bottle on the table; all around them is the smoke of their pipes, and we see them through smoke; cloudy, immemorial peasant figures.

And the dancing goes on.

Then the boys and girls sit down on the floor, and clap their hands.

And shyly the sister Eileen steps out of the smoky darkness near the end table, and sings.

At the end of a verse, we hear, from the cloudy table, the voice of the grandfather crying:

GRANDFATHER: My love for ever, Eileen.

And as she sings, so children dance, we move again, and we move slowly, around the room, to sad-and-gay music, round the firelit hearth, the player, and the corner seat where Maurice, alone, half dreaming, half awake, watches and listens, and the table of smokers and drinkers, and Eileen's voice fades.

And then, out of that smoky end of the room, comes the voice of the grandfather singing 'Eamonn Magaine'.

And moving away again, towards Maurice in his corner, we hear:

THE VOICE: I would feel a shiver of delight in my blood as I sat listening that first evening of my homecoming, and it was no wonder, with the sweetness of the song and the tremor of the voices. I did not understand the meaning of the words, but the voice and the tremor and the sweetness were clear to me.

Very slowly the room is growing darker, but the music goes on. And Maurice's head is nodding.

THE VOICE: ... no wonder with the sweetness and the singing and the noise of the sea and the darkness and the sweetness and the singing and the darkness ...

And the voice fades slowly on the last words, and Maurice is asleep in his chair in the darkening corner, and with the singing and the music of the melodeon mingles the surging of the sea.

And, as the picture (*fades out*), we hear only the surging of the sea.

(*fade in*):

To the sea breaking on the island cliffs.

Now a seagull is flying over the sea.

We follow the flight of a seagull over the sea towards the island.

We follow the flight of a seagull through the sky above the island.

We (*pan down*) the sky, from the flying seagull, to see, in (*long shot*), a man, a boy and an ass moving away towards Hill Head ...

Closer now we see that the man and the boy are the grandfather and

Maurice. And we hear Maurice's voice, and the grandfather's voice closely, clearly, as though they were near us, though they are still in (*long shot*).

MAURICE: Oh, it is a grand day to be on the island, Daddo.

THE GRANDFATHER: There is no place like it ...

And now the (*camera moves*) around the island. We see the Great Skellig and Skellig Michael, and Iveragh to the south-east, and herring-gulls around the trawlers in the bay. And over the sea sounds we hear the singing of larks.

MAURICE: Shall I be living here always and always, going after a load of turf with the old ass in the morning, or up at the sparrow's chirp to go lobster fishing with my father, or gathering the birds' eggs, or dragging the sea for herrings, or after the seals and the rabbits ... ?

THE GRANDFATHER: Och, the day will come ...

And as the grandfather speaks, we (*cut to*) him and Maurice, close, standing on Hill Head.

MAURICE: What day, Daddo?

We see them now from a low level so that they are great simple figures against the moving clouds.

THE GRANDFATHER: Let it be gone from your head now. It's a fine, grand day today, praise to God on high!
There was music of birds flying over
the green grass
and little fish in hundreds
frolicking in the nets ...

MAURICE: Is that from a song?

THE GRANDFATHER: It is indeed, from an old song. Come now, boy ... Come.

He turns away ...
(*Cut to*) the grandfather and Maurice loading turf on to the ass.

MAURICE: Were you ever away from the Blasket, Daddo?

THE GRANDFATHER: My sorrow, I spent a great part of my life going out to the islands all around, and it is little shoe or stocking was worn in those days, not even a drop of tea to be had, nor any thought of it.

MAURICE: No tea at all!

THE GRANDFATHER: There was no flour to be bought, no tea or sugar. Upon my word, it wasn't bad for that time. We had our food and our own clothes – the gathering of the strand, the hunt of the hill, the fish of the sea and the wool of the sheep. The devil a bit was there to buy some tobacco, and you could get a bundle of that for threepence ...

Many was the day we would leave the house at sunrise and we would not come home again until the blackness and the blindness of the night, myself and Stephen O'Donlevy ...

And Pad Mor and Shaun O'Carna, dear God bless their souls, for they are all on the way of truth of now ...

Close, we see him straighten up from the loading of the turf, and look out at the sea. There are tears in his eyes.

THE GRANDFATHER: Did ye never hear how the life of man is divided? Twenty years a-growing, twenty years in blossom, twenty years a-stooping, and twenty years declining.

MAURICE: I never heard that before.

The grandfather smiles.

THE GRANDFATHER: Indeed, it is many things you have never heard before. Go on with you now ... Be happy when you can ...

And now we see, in (*long shot*), the grandfather, Maurice and the ass on the path towards the village. Maurice is running, scampering and dancing on all sides of the slow patiently moving old man and loaded ass.

Now Maurice is running along the strand of white sand towards the harbour. We hear, loud, the noise of the waves; and the barking of dogs we do not see, hollow, as though in caves; and the cries of the gulls.

Now with another boy, Tomas Owen Vaun, he is striding along the hill path towards Horse Sound, two dogs with them. The dogs run off into the deep grass and ferns and begin to bark: the high eager bark of the hunter. The boys run after them.

Now Maurice and Tomas are striding on towards the Scornach; they both have rabbits slung over their backs. And we hear:

THE VOICE: In a man's life there are twenty years a-growing. And here on the island, for me, they were growing slow to the din of the sea and the singing of ten thousand birds as I was up in the morning with Tomas and the dogs hunting the rabbits in the ferns after the shippens, the fat little puffins, and the seagulls' eggs on Scornach cliffs.

And, while the voice speaks, we see Maurice and Tomas reaching the top of the Scornach. We look down, from their eyes, at the great cliff sickening to the sea. They put their rabbits in a hole, and Tomas begins to climb down the cliff, light as a goat through the screes. Maurice climbs, slowly and fearfully, after him: a long way after him.

And we look down from the clifftop and see Tomas far below us, and Maurice clinging on not so far below, staring up at us, the blue sea below him and all around him the great noise of birds. We hear, through wind, sea and birdery, the blown voice of Maurice crying.

MAURICE: Oh, holy Father, isn't it a dangerous place I am in?

He moves cautiously, along a cliff ridge. Great numbers of birds fly all around him.

Now, from below, we look up at the little figure of Maurice on the cliff face, and hear:

THE VOICE: Oh, kittiwakes, herring-gulls, puffins, guillemots, sea-ravens, razorbills, black-backed gulls and petrels, you frighten the life out of a sinner with your crying and flying ...

And now, closer to Maurice, we see him groping in a burrow between the rocks, groping and digging and scratching. Suddenly he pulls out his hand. There is a baby puffin in it. And, holding the puffin out, he turns, perilously, and calls down the cliff:

MAURICE: Tomas ...

And the echo answers:

ECHO: Tomas.

And another echo, and another, and another; each farther off.

He moves about the face of the cliff, thrusting his hand into the hidden nests of the puffins.

Now on the cliff edge, we see Maurice climbing up, and over his shoulder is hanging a rope on which many puffins are tied together.

He reaches the clifftop, and flops down there, his puffins at his side.

Then he whistles down the cliff. And the echoes take the whistle and multiply it and throw it about in the wind and lose it.

And, after the echoes, comes:

TOMAS'S VOICE: I'm coming ...

And soon he has climbed up to the clifftop, dirty and smiling. He has made a sack of his jersey, and hung it, heavy, over his back.

MAURICE: What have you got?

TOMAS: I have guillemots' eggs, razorbills' eggs and seagulls' eggs, my boy ... why didn't you come down with me?

MAURICE (*slyly*): Och, I was frightened. I got nothing at all.

And he rises and lifts up his bundle.

TOMAS: What have you there?

MAURICE (*in a casual voice*): Oh, puffins. Just puffins. Just thirty-six puffins, that's all ...

And his casualness drops away from him, and he begins to dance, whirling his rope of birds. Now we see only the roped birds whirling. Now we see only a skein of birds whirling through the sky.

TOMAS: Upon my word, you're a great hunter.

(*Cut back*) to Maurice.

MAURICE: I'm the happiest hunter on the hills of Kerry.

Now his birds are still.

TOMAS: Come to see if my eggs are clean now ...

And he moves away, Maurice following him after he takes up the rabbits from the hole where they were left.

MAURICE: Can't you see they're clean, you little blind man.

Tomas stops at a big pool in a bog hole.

TOMAS: Look now, if this egg is hatching it will float on the water, but if it is clean it will sink.

He throws in an egg.

(*Cut to*) the pool, the egg floating on it.

TOMAS'S VOICE: Och, the devil take it, there is a chick in that one.

Another egg lands on the water, and floats.

TOMAS'S VOICE: It is a good beginning.

Another egg lands, and floats. And another, and another.
Now the surface of the pool is covered with red-and-black-spotted eggs floating.

TOMAS'S VOICE: The devil a clean one among them.

Now Maurice takes his rope of puffins and cuts it in half, and hands over half the puffins.

MAURICE: Look at us now! Half apiece ...

Tomas begins to laugh as he takes his share.

TOMAS: Look at us now, indeed.

MAURICE: I don't know why in the world you are laughing at me ...

TOMAS: Because anybody would think you were an ape, you are so dirty ...

MAURICE: Faith, if I am dirty as you are, the yellow devil is on me.

Tomas, still laughing, begins to strip off his clothes; and Maurice likewise.
We see them dive, naked, in the pool.
Now they are lying, half dressed, on the grass.
Tomas takes out a pipe and tobacco, and lights the pipe and puffs it and passes it, silent, over to Maurice.
And Maurice takes it and puffs it and hands it back.
He lies flat on his back staring up at the sky.
There is music through bird and wind and sea noise.
Looking up, from Maurice's eyes, at the sunset sky, we see gulls lazily wheeling.
We hear Tomas's voice singing softly ...
Now the sky becomes blurred, and blurred birds seem to lurch across it.

MAURICE'S VOICE: I'm thinking the tobacco is strong, Tomas, or a most queer storm is a-coming up ...

(*Cut to*) Maurice and Tomas, Maurice now smoking. Slowly he hands over the pipe to Tomas and rises to his feet.
Now the two boys are walking back towards the village, their dogs

quiet at their heels, through the sea-sounding sunsetting evening. Maurice is a little unsteady on his feet.

Now we see the reflection, in water, of the houses of the village, trembling with little spots of light.

Now we see the village itself, Maurice and Tomas walking through it.

It is night nearly. Lamps are lit in every house.

An old man stands at his doorway.

TOMAS: Are you well tonight, Puncan?

OLD MAN: Oh, musha, I was never so bad as I am today.

The boys pass on, laughing.

TOMAS: Isn't he always bad? Good night, Maurice.

(N.B. Insert two more greetings with two villagers whom we will be seeing later.)

Tomas goes in at a cottage door.

MAURICE: Good night, Tomas.

Maurice walks on, one dog at his heels, and reaches his cottage.

The grandfather stands outside.

And Maurice stands by him. He looks up at the climbing moon.

MAURICE: What a night it is, Daddo ...

THE GRANDFATHER: And a fine gold moon over Cnoc-a-comma. Come in now before the potatoes get cold.

And he goes in.

And the moon climbs.

(*Fade out*).

(*Fade in*):

To the calm sea in the full light of morning.

Over the sea a bird is flying.

The bird is flying towards the island.

The bird is flying above the harbour.

(*Panning down*), we see that the quayside is crowded with people and that more are flocking down towards it on every path from the village.

We see, from the quay, a curragh coming in.

Now down a path run Maurice and some boys, and we hear:

THE VOICE: It is the custom of the island for everyone to be on the quay when the King is coming with the post-bag from Dunquin ...

Maurice joins the crowd. He sees Tomas in a group of children.

MAURICE (*calling*):   Tomas ...

Tomas runs over to Maurice, and a little girl, Mauraid, with him.

THE VOICE (*continuing, even through Maurice's cry*):   ... with news from the mainland and stories from the length and breadth of Ireland and the rumours that do go about of what is happening in the wide world beyond ...

Now the King is standing on the quay, people all around him, making a deal of noise, chattering, arguing, questioning.
Now we see him, as he talks, from where Maurice and Tomas stand, the little girl Mauraid shy by their side. [...]

MAURICE'S VOICE: Good morning, Shaun Teague and Tomas. How will be the mackerel tonight?

They go on setting the nets.

SHAUN TEAGUE: Och, there'll be plenty, with all the gannets about, there was never such a day for them ...

We move on. Outside a cottage two women are washing clothes in a tub.

MAURICE'S VOICE: Good morning to ye, Kate O'Shea and Kate Joseph ...

They go on washing.

KATE O'SHEA: Good morning to ye, Maurice. (*to Kate Joseph*) Did you ever see such a shirt in all your life? ... I'm thinking all the dogs in the island have been after chewing the tail ...

We move on, the words trailing after us. Outside a cottage Padrig O'Dala and Tomas's father and Paddy Tim are mending their lobster pots ...

MAURICE'S VOICE: Good morning to ye.

TOMAS'S FATHER: Tell Tomas not to be forgetting the turf after school now ...

We move on. Outside a cottage, Mauraid is scattering food for the chickens which cluck and peck all around her …

MAURICE'S VOICE: Good morning, Mauraid …

She looks up and smiles.

MAURAID (*shyly*): Good morning to ye, Maurice … Will you be on the cliff tonight to see the fishing?

We move on.

MAURICE: Arra, I will.

MAURAID: Shall I look at the fishing with you, Maurice?

We move on, her words trailing after us, on along the clustered village with its men working at pots and nets, sharpening tools, cutting wood, and a clatter of pots and pans and the sound of women's voices coming out of the open cottages …

THE VOICE: Or on days when there was no school, maybe I would be lying with my daddo, stretched out on the turf, gazing down at the fish-filled sea …

And as the voice speaks, the picture (*dissolves to*) the cliffs, and we (*pan*) along the cliffs to where the figures of Maurice and the grandfather are lying. Closer to them, we see that the grandfather's eyes are closed in sleep. Maurice is lying on his belly, looking out to sea. It is afternoon.

MAURICE: Do you know where I am looking, Daddo? I am looking at America. Oh, it is a fine place surely, all its chimneys touching the sky and everybody rich as captains … Do you think that I will ever be going to America when I am a young man, Daddo?

The grandfather does not answer.

MAURICE: Daddo, Daddo …

Maurice turns around and looks at the old man sleeping, and we hear:

THE VOICE: I remember thinking, looking down at the face of the old man asleep …

MAURICE'S VOICE: You were one day in the flower of youth, but, my sorrow, the skin of your brow is wrinkled now and the hair on your head is grey. You are without suppleness in your limbs and without pleasure in the grand view to be seen from this hill. But, alas, if I live, some day I will be as you are now ...

As Maurice gazes at the old man asleep, and as we hear his voice, his lips do not move.

Now Maurice puts out his hand and gently pulls the old man's beard. The old man opens his eyes.

THE GRANDFATHER: Oh, Mirrisheen, I fell asleep. Am I long in it?

MAURICE: Not long at all.

THE GRANDFATHER: And were you speaking to me in my sleep? I seem to have heard your voice, a long way away ...

MAURICE: I was letting on I could see America across the water but all I could see were the waves and the old gulls ... Shall I ever be going to America, Daddo?

THE GRANDFATHER: Upon my word, it is likely. The young are ever after going away over the water, and they leave the old country cold and poor as a house without children ...

MAURICE: Then I shall stay on the island then, and be a fine fisherman ...

THE GRANDFATHER: Musha, my heart, a man of the sea never had a good life and never will ...

MAURICE: Och, where I shall go then?

THE GRANDFATHER: I don't know what way you will go but only to follow your nose in the end of all.

And as he speaks the grandfather is filling and lighting his pipe. And when it is alight Maurice takes out of his own pocket a blackened clay and lights it, bowl to bowl, from the grandfather's pipe. He draws the smoke down deep, and the old man smiles. They lie together, over the noisy sea, smoking and smiling ...

(*Dissolve to*):
The sea. It is evening.
A bird is flying over the sea.
A bird is flying over many, many curraghs out on the sea.
A bird is flying over the cliffs of the island.
We (*pan down*) on to the cliffs above the strand.
All the women of the village are sitting on their haunches on the edge of the cliff, looking out at the curraghs.

Behind them along the cliff stand old men and children, Maurice and the grandfather and Tomas among them. And we hear:

THE VOICE: And on a night of mackerel fishing I would stand among the children and the old men of the village on the cliff over the strand, looking out at the curraghs and hearing the women calling and crying across the water to their men ...

Close now to the women on their haunches, we hear:

ONE WOMAN: Your soul to the devil, throw the head of your net behind them ... [...]

And we are outside the house now, on the wild island: the island thrown up black against the phosphorous sea.
We see the bobbing pinpoints of lanterns on the stormy cliffs.
Now we are closer to the cliffs. Three lanterns bob towards us, and then stop. In their light we see the faces of Maurice and Tomas and a youth, Padrig Peg ...
Padrig lifts his hand out of his oilskin pocket.
We see the hand close, in the lantern light. It is full of dead thrushes.

PADRIG: Six.

Tomas puts out his hand.

TOMAS: Three here.

Maurice puts out his hand.

MAURICE: One. I had my hands around two more but they pecked me like puffins.

A bird's cry – giog-giog-giog – comes out of the darkness.

MAURICE (*whispering*): What is that?

PADRIG: It is a peewit ... It's blinded in the light ... What did you think it was ...?

Padrig thrusts his hand into a sparse and wind-blown bush and pulls out the bird still crying. The crying stops.

PADRIG: Now we will go down Seal Cove ... Quiet! Dead quiet! Take it fine and easy. Don't be afraid.

(*Cut*):
Now we see, from the cliff edge, the three lanterns bobbing down the

cliff. The noise of the sea shouts up to us. Blackness, and the three lights bobbing. Blackness, and the hollow shouting of the sea.

(*Cut*):

Now we are close to the three boys standing in the cove. They move their lanterns slowly in half-circles, illuminating the great rocks and the sea breaking upon them, and we hear:

THE VOICE (*softly*):   You would think the living and the dead were there with the roar of the waves and the hiss of foam ...

PADRIG: Don't be afraid. And don't speak a word till we get across to the patch of soil there. The thrushes are all sleeping now ...

Now we see the lanterns bobbing across the cove, and across the crevice and the patch of soil.

Close, we see Padrig thrust his hand into the crevice and draw out a thrush. And again. And again. And again. As he is capturing the sleeping birds, so Maurice and Tomas, moving their lanterns to light the battering sea, speak fearfully:

TOMAS: Are you afraid at all?

MAURICE: The devil a bit ...

TOMAS: It's often my father told me that people had been heard speaking here ...

MAURICE: Oh, whisht, Tomas, do not say that ...

TOMAS: But they were not people indeed.

MAURICE: Faith, it is I know they were not ...

Now from another part of the cove we see the wavering lanterns, we see mighty waves roaring in and crashing on the rocks.

Now the three lanterns' lights move up the cliff.

Now from the edge of the cliff we look down on to the three lights climbing up towards us. They come closer. We see, in the lantern light, the three boys scrambling up and clinging on to one another's coat tails.

Now the light is blindingly near us.

And now we are back in the bright cottage, at the end of the room farthest from the door. It is full of boys and girls. The girls are beginning to pluck the sparrows heaped on a table.

The door is flung open. The wind hurling in, and then Maurice and Tomas and Padrig, spindrift-wet and wild-haired.

There is a noise in the house, of the voices of children merry together, and a boy calls out, and his cry is taken up by other voices, as the three enter.

A BOY: How many have you?

ANOTHER BOY: How many now ... ?

ANOTHER BOY: Oh, look at them all ...

A BOY: I got twenty ...

PADRIG: Faith, we have twenty-eight ...

The three throw their thrushes on to a table ...

(*Cut to*):
The thrushes roasting on the fire. We hear the music of a melodeon. (*Pan along*) the room slowly from the fire.
A young man is sitting on the floor, back against the wall, playing the melodeon ...
Four girls and four boys are dancing a set, which is a dance like the old quadrille.
Boys and girls are sitting at the table, eating. Some stand, eating the little roasted birds with their fingers, watching the dancing.
A girl is sitting on a boy's knee.
Boys are leaping up at a big apple hung by a rope from the rafters, trying to take bites out of it.
Now we are close to a tub of water and a little group of boys and girls, Mauraid and Maurice among them, kneeling around it.
A boy and a girl, at the same time, throw a bean each into the water.

MAURAID (*softly, looking at Maurice*):   If the beans sink in the water, it is a sign that Michael and Brigid do love one another ...

THE GIRL BRIGID: Och, they are floating ...

Mauraid puts a bean in Maurice's hand.

MAURAID: Will you try?

Maurice throws the bean into the water, and, as he does so, Mauraid throws one in also.
We see the beans sink in the water ...
Now we see close the faces of Mauraid and Maurice.
And now nearly all the boys and girls are dancing. The melodeon is

playing a gay tune. Maurice is dancing with Mauraid ... the music rises.

(*Fade out*).

(*Fade in*):
On the sea.
The sea is violent.
The sea is still.
The sea breaks against the rocks.
The sea laps the rocks.
A bird is flying over the rough sea.
A bird is flying over the calm sea.
A bird is flying over the sea.
A bird is flying over a single curragh on the sea.
And through this we hear:

THE VOICE: The life of a boy a-growing
    on the little island
    was a great coming and going;
    sea loud or silent
    as a flock of snowing –
    a great coming and going
    of the weathers and the birds
    and the seasons and the tides
    and the singing of the Irish words
    and the love of the world besides ...

And behind the words of the voice, and through the changing voices of the wind and the sea, we hear the same words very softly spoken in Irish.

And now we are close to the curragh, and Maurice and Padrig Peg and the grandfather are sitting and rowing there.

THE VOICE: Fishing for mackerel or herring
    in the Great Sound
    or out after pollock on the Wild Bank
    where the cries of a million birds were falling –
    riding the wild waves in a Samhain wind
    or turning in spring time
    to the island of Inish Vickallaun –
    There was so much to be done
    under the moon and the sun
    I cared for nothing

save the island people and the island ways
and the great passing of the days
to the sounding of the waves ...

Through the words of the voice we see the curragh in the Great
Sound, and on the Wild Bank; we see the nets raised, empty and full;
we see the curragh moving on choppy and on glassy water.

Now we are close to the curragh again, Maurice and Padrig and the
grandfather there with dogs at their feet.

THE GRANDFATHER: Do you see the house on the Inish now?

The grandfather points out to the Inish Island.

MAURICE: I do not.

THE GRANDFATHER: Look carefully at the middle of the island and
you will see the sun sparkling on something ...

From the curragh, we see the house high on the Inish, caught in
the sun.

PADRIG: It was there I was born, but only the birds and the beasts do
live there now.

THE GRANDFATHER: It was once a fine place; now the weeds grow
over the paths and all the houses but the one are fallen in the wind
and the rain.

Now the curragh is closer to the Inish.

MAURICE: Oh, listen, listen.

And we hear from the Inish a noise which takes an echo out of the
coves. Gurla-gu-hu-hu-golagon! Gurla-gu-hu-hu-golagon!

THE GRANDFATHER (*smiling*):   Have I not told you often that spirits
are to be seen and fairy music to be heard above the Inish?

MAURICE: What is it, Daddo?

THE GRANDFATHER: Row on, row on ...

Again we hear the noise of Gurla-gu-hu-hu-golagon! And its echo in
the coves.

Now the curragh is closer to the Inish.

PADRIG: Look in now, and keep your eyes on the shingle ...

And we see, from the water, a great number of seals stretched at full length, sunning themselves on the strand.

MAURICE'S VOICE: Och, the seals are sleeping in the sun ...

THE GRANDFATHER'S VOICE: And do you think they are sleeping? Look, boy ...

We hear the grandfather and Padrig give a great roar.
The seals raise their heads.
Then away with them to the water, at a wonderful swiftness.
They are spouting in the water.
Now we are close to the strand; not a seal to be seen, save only the rings they have left in their wake.
Now Maurice, the grandfather and Padrig are climbing an old path up the Inish cliff.
Now they are within sight of the house at the foot of a little hill.
The dogs are barking and chasing in and out of the ferns, the tall grass and the bracken. We see rabbits running.
Now we are near the house: a little low hut with a felt roof, ruins in plenty around, weeds and nettles growing among them. The dogs, each with a rabbit in his mouth, run up to the two men and the boy, who take the rabbits away from them.
The men and the boy stand alone on the island in the setting sun.

THE GRANDFATHER: The house of Shaun O'Carna stood there.

We see a few pieces of rotten wood in the deep and tangled grass.
And we (*pan along*) the nettled and weedy wilderness ...

PADRIG'S VOICE: Here my father was born and his father before him – there was the schoolroom there – here were the fine paths where we climbed up to the sheep on the hills – there was singing and dancing and great story-telling in all the fine stone houses – nothing now, nothing, nothing ...

(*Cut back*) to the three.

THE GRANDFATHER: My sorrow, the day will come when the Blasket is empty too and the houses in ruin and nothing to be seen but the green grass.

MAURICE: Faith, never, Daddo.

THE GRANDFATHER: The young will be going away from the island, as they went away from this place – over the sea to America, into the towns and the cities …

The sun is setting behind the Foze Rocks, and nothing to be seen beyond them but the sky like a great shining wall.

Now the three are moving up the little hill, the grandfather's voice continuing.

GRANDFATHER'S VOICE: … the young will go and the old will be left. And after the old are dead and are on the way to truth, there will be no more fishing nor hunting nor fowling on the island and all will be ruin …

We are in the churchyard half way through the grandfather's words, by the old chapel. The two men and the boy are standing in the middle of the churchyard. Above the ruin is a cross.

THE GRANDFATHER (*softly*):   Maybe it will come that *all* the little islands, *all* the little places where men do make a livelihood together out of the gathering of the strand and the hunt of the hill and the fish of the sea will be empty and forgotten …

MAURICE: I shall stay on the island …

THE GRANDFATHER (*smiling*):   You will be most lonely, for you will be the only one … Come now, let us go down to the little house …

And they move away out of the darkening churchyard.

(*Dissolve to*):
The entrance of the Inish house. The grandfather opens the door. Maurice peers past him into the room. We see the room from Maurice's angle. The walls are whitened with flaking lime. A rabbit scampers out of the room through a hole in the wall.

Now, from the end of the room opposite the door, we see the grandfather enter, followed by Maurice and Padrig.

The grandfather crosses to the hearth, his arms full of ferns. He kneels and begins to make a fire of the ferns, saying over his shoulder:

THE GRANDFATHER: You be going out and laying traps for the morning, Padrig. Maurice, open two of the rabbits now and hang the other two outside the house …

He lights the fern.

(*Cut to*) Padrig sweeping the floor of the room with a brush of ferns.

(*Cut to*) Maurice skinning the rabbits with his knife.

(*Cut to*) two rabbits hung on a nail outside the window in the deepening darkness.

(*Cut to*) the grandfather, Maurice and Padrig sitting, the old man in a broken chair, the others on fern-heaps on the floor, near the fire, eating from a steaming pot. A lantern is lit. Moonlight streams through the window on to the fire and the seated figures. We hear the noises of the wind and the sea.

They have finished eating. The two men light their pipes.

MAURICE: I think I can hear the seals. Olagon olagon.

And we hear, through wind and sea, the far noise of the seals.

MAURICE: I wonder, Daddo, would you believe that the seals are people put under magic?

He looks up at the old man, his face white in the moonlight.

PADRIG: I have heard it, and upon my word I would believe it, for they are just like old women keening.

THE GRANDFATHER: Some years ago there was a man went from the Blasket hunting the seals, about the month of November, because the young seals were born. It was back in Bird Cove it happened …

In moonlight and firelight Padrig and Maurice on the ferns stare up at the old man speaking, his pipe a-glowing.

THE GRANDFATHER: When he came out of the boat he saw a young seal up in the head of the cove. He went up after it, stick in hand, as was the custom when they went seal-hunting …

MAURICE (*in a whisper*):   Yes, yes …

THE GRANDFATHER: And the cow-seal leapt straight at him, snarling. But he clambered up on the ledge on the side of the cove, and when he had reached it, would you believe it, the cow-seal spoke out to him. 'If you are in luck,' said she, 'you will leave this cove in haste, for be it known to you that you will not easily kill my young son'; and she went back again to her young one. 'For the sake of the world,' the man cried out to his mate in the boat, 'back her in as quick as you can.' And they were off. And from that day till the day he died, that man never saw a day's health …

MAURICE (*softly*):   Faith, I believe it …

Now in the moonlit room – the fire and lantern out – the two men and the boy lie, each in a corner, on a bed of ferns …

Close to Maurice, we see that he is not sleeping but that his eyes are wide open ... He is looking up at the moonlit night through the cobwebbed window.

We look up at the night from Maurice's angle. The two rabbits hang on a nail outside, at the side of the window, moving slightly in the wind, half dancing on air.

We see a hand, an arm, pass across the window to the rabbits. The hand lifts the rabbits off the nail.

Very close to Maurice, we see his eyes strained wide, his mouth rounded. We hear his terrified whisper: 'O Lord, save me from the fairies.'

As the hand, dangling the rabbits, slowly draws back across the window and vanishes, Maurice screams.

He leaps to his feet, runs over to Padrig, kicks him.

Padrig turns in bed.

PADRIG (*sleepily*):   What ails you?

MAURICE: Oh, oh, Padrig, it is something I saw outside going off with the rabbits ... a long hooking hand ...

PADRIG: Musha, my pity for your brass head. Go to sleeeep ...

He turns back to sleep.

Maurice creeps to the corner where the grandfather lies.

The grandfather is lying on his back, his hands folded across his chest like those of a dead man, his lips smiling.

And Maurice creeps back to his own corner and burrows under the ferns and heaps them over his head until not an inch of him can be seen. [...]

Now, in (*long shot*), we see the grandfather, Maurice and Padrig walking through the thigh-deep grass of the Inish.

We hear the dogs barking.

We see the three figures bending every now and then and lifting up a rabbit and tying the rabbit on to the pole which Padrig carries across his back. The pole is hung with rabbits like dark, furry washing on a line.

We see them on the edge of the cliff.

One by one, they go over the edge of the cliff.

Now there is nothing to be seen on Inish Vickallaun but the wild fern and grass blowing and the birds flying and crying over.

Betty London

(An excerpt from *Suffer Little Children*)

This excerpt is from the 196-page draft of *Suffer Little Children* which Dylan Thomas wrote in 1945. He wrote to Donald Taylor: 'I do want to say again that I think *Suffer Little Children* a superlative idea, and I am longing to talk about it in detail and around it, to discuss it at great length with you ... and to produce the completed script more quickly than any other we have done. I'll come up as soon as you want me.'[83] But Taylor visited Dylan in New Quay a few weeks later and on his return Dylan wrote jokingly: 'Today, limp in the hut, watching the exhausting sea, lost in our Betty – Betty dark? – drowned in our Sophie – Sophie fair? – but writing little until tomorrow, first, cold thing in the morning, with dew on the grass, and the Captains in bed, and the trees talking double rook.'[84] Betty and Sophie were two main characters in the projected script. Some of the dialogue was used in the Diana Dors film *Good Time Girl* when Gainsborough bought the script. The comic touches in this excerpt, where Betty has been placed in a guest house, anticipates such comedy in *Under Milk Wood*. *Suffer Little Children* was another instance of the feature film Donald Taylor hoped to produce after the war. As with *Twenty Years A- Growing*, it was not made.

BETTY LONDON (AN EXCERPT FROM *SUFFER LITTLE CHILDREN*)

The Steamy Basement Kitchen of Mrs Foster's Boarding House.

It is a big, dark, overcrowded, stone floored kitchen, with a very large range and an old-fashioned bell-indicator over the door: a kitchen that can have changed in no essential since the more gloomy basement days of the last century. The cook, a faded, doleful woman, is making pastry at a table. Betty is busy at a wash tub, up to the elbows in suds. Betty wears a long stiff white dress, white cap, big apron. We see her close. A bell rings, loudly. Neither Betty nor the Cook looks up or turns around.

BETTY: I bet it's Mr Dibdin the author – oh why does he live so high up ...

COOK: Perhaps it's Mr Chatterjee.

And Betty begins to giggle.

COOK: What'd he call you when you took his tea up?

BETTY: My little passion flower ...

The bell rings again.

COOK (*without turning round, in a high, sad voice*): It's only Mrs Foster again ... always ringing, like a fireman ...

Betty turns to look at the bell-indicator. We see the rows of names, and a star coming into place on Mrs Foster. Betty sighs, wipes her suddy hands, takes off her wet apron, pats her clothes into place, and goes out. When she is at the door, the Cook calls out after her in a doleful voice:

COOK: Look out for Mr Chatterjee ...

(*Cut to*) Betty going up the creaking uncarpeted kitchen stairs. We see only her feet and legs.

(*Cut to*) Betty's feet and legs climbing another, shabby-carpeted, flight of stairs.

(*Cut to*) Mrs Foster's Bedroom.

It is a large, heavily Victorian room; the curtains are drawn. A figure is sitting up in bed. From the end of the room opposite the door, we see the door open and Betty come in.

BETTY: Good morning, ma'am.

Betty curtsies in the half dark, towards the bed. She crosses to the window, pulls open the heavy curtains. Morning light comes into the room. We see, clearly, the figure sitting up in bed: Mrs Foster, with a nightcap on. We see the solid, inconvenient furniture, the dark cupboards, the screens, the trinkets of every kind on the laced dressing table, the pictures on the wall of men with beards, women with bosoms, cattle with sunsets. Betty stands, facing Mrs Foster, in the middle of the room. Mrs Foster is fat, and has some difficulty in breathing.

MRS FOSTER: Good morning, Betty. Has Miss Seymour Carr had her Russian tea?

BETTY: Yes'm.

MRS FOSTER: And Indian tea for Mr Chatterjee?

BETTY: Yes'm.

MRS FOSTER: Mr Dibdin the author?

Betty nods.

MRS FOSTER: Captain and Mrs Bottral?

Betty nods.

MRS FOSTER: Now first I want the stairs dusted from top to bottom – and no pushing the dust under the carpet. And after breakfast you dust the dining room. Other guest houses, I am told, have vacuum cleaners to encourage idleness among the servants. There were no vacuum cleaners in my day. And there were no idle servants! Then, you clean all the rooms on the second and third floors, not forgetting the offices. Then you scrub the front steps *and* the area steps, and then carry on with your washing. Now, there must be no dust and no noise. Dust is an enemy. I am *down* on dust. My mother was down on dust. Dust and noise and Fosters cannot live in the same house. That is all.

BETTY: Yes'm.

She turns to go out.

MRS FOSTER: Have you forgotten something?

Betty turns again.

BETTY (*puzzled*):   No, mum.

MRS FOSTER: Think again, Betty ...

And Betty curtsies.

MRS FOSTER (*graciously*):   That is correct. We mustn't forget the little civilities that help to turn the wheels around ...

And Betty goes out.

(*Dissolve to*) Betty dusting the stairs.

(*Dissolve to*) Miss Seymour Carr's bedroom.

There are some Eastern pictures on the wall, and a few oddments of Chinese furniture. Betty is cleaning the room. From a door off the room, Miss Seymour Carr comes in: a middle-aged lady dressed in the art-nouveau fashion of some years ago: long dress, peasant blouse, fringe, heavy necklace and bracelets.

MISS SEYMOUR CARR (*brightly*):   Poor child! Work work work ...

She crosses to an Eastern objet d'art – an inlaid thing of little drawers and shelves – and unlocks it.

MISS SEYMOUR CARR: Don't you ever feel you *must* have some colour in your life? Something gay, and ... strange?

BETTY: Yes, Miss Seymour Carr ...

MISS SEYMOUR CARR: I know. You are like myself – you are one of those who *feel*! I *knew* it the first day you came here.

BETTY: Yes, mum.

Miss Seymour Carr takes out a string of garish beads. She crosses to Betty, holds them for a moment against Betty's throat.

MISS SEYMOUR CARR: There! You see? But of course you don't, how silly I am ... Look in the mirror ... Yes, take them for a moment ...

Betty turns to a mirror, holds the beads against her throat. We see her in the mirror.

MISS SEYMOUR CARR'S VOICE: I *live* for colour ... and shape, of course. There, give it to me.

Betty turns from the mirror. Now we see Miss Seymour Carr take the beads, put them away.

MISS SEYMOUR CARR: I'd rather part with my right hand ...

She looks at her right hand.

MISS SEYMOUR CARR: I should have been a pianist ... Yes I'd rather part with *anything* than my little treasure trove ... Look ...

Betty looks at the shelves of Miss Seymour Carr's inlaid treasure-trove.

MISS SEYMOUR CARR: These ear-rings – like blood drops ...

We see the ring. Miss Seymour Carr takes it out, lifts it up, shows it to Betty.

That ring was a gift from an admirer. 'Savage beauty to sav—' well, I mustn't tell you *all* he said. (*looking at Betty who is looking at the jewellery*): You haven't had an admirer yet, Betty? No, no, how could you, I am *so* silly. I'm always being told by my friends how *silly* I am – they seem to like it, for some reason – how could you in that dreadful place ...

Miss Seymour Carr carefully locks up the cabinet.

Do you ever *read*?

BETTY: I used to read, mum, when I was young ...

MISS SEYMOUR CARR: 'When I was young!' O my dear child, you must think of *me* as old as the hills ... Ah, but then it was only fairy stories wasn't it? You haven't read any real love stories?

BETTY: No ...

Miss Seymour Carr crosses to a desk, takes out a paper backed book.

MISS SEYMOUR CARR: Then you must start straight away ... Take this, and when you've finished it, you can have another ... I've got *heaps* ...

Betty takes the book.

No, don't thank me, don't thank me ... Take it with you ... They're beginning a new serial in it ... You'll get to *love* Rex Trent ...

Betty takes up her mop and dust pan and paper backed book.

(*Dissolve to*) Dining Room of Boarding House.

Miss Foster at one end of the table, an elderly man, Mr Dibdin at the other: Miss Seymour Carr also, and a few other nondescript people. Mrs Foster rises and rings an old-fashioned bell-pull.
(*Cut to*) Basement Kitchen.
Betty is loading a tray. The Cook is sad at the long range. We hear the bell ringing.

COOK: Clang, clang, another fire …

BETTY: Don't they eat quick … And then Mrs Foster said, 'Dust's an enemy. I'm down on dust. My *mother* was down on dust, too,' she said …

COOK: That's where her mother is now alright …

Betty takes the tray out.

(*Cut to*) Betty's feet and legs going upstairs.
(*Cut to*) Betty going into the Dining Room. She puts the tray down. The plates rattle.

MRS FOSTER: Quiet, quiet! No noise in the house, please …

(*Cut to*) the kitchen.
Betty is scrubbing the floor. The Cook is about the kitchen, sadly banging at pots and pans. There is quite a lot of noise.

COOK: I'd like her to have my feet …

BETTY: Miss Seymour Carr lent me a book, I'll show it to you tonight …

COOK: I'd like her to have them for one day, that's all. What sort of a book?

BETTY: It's a love story.

COOK: Perhaps Mr Chatterjee upstairs wrote it. Is it about passion flowers?

BETTY: No, it's about someone called Rex Trent and he's a Captain in the Army …

COOK: He wouldn't be if he had my feet …

The Shadowless Man

'I have rather a good film idea, which might also interest Redgrave: a dark and fantastic romance of the German 1830s. I'll try and type out a reasonable synopsis,'[85] wrote Dylan Thomas in September 1947, soon after he moved into the Manor House, South Leigh. It tells the story of a young sailor, Blaise, who sells his shadow for a 'Bottomless Purse' of gold to a man without a shadow. This idea is probably taken from the German film *Student of Prague*, which Thomas includes in his 1934 list of films he particularly enjoyed and which is about a student who sells his reflection for great wealth and marriage, but after much anguish shoots himself. In the 1926 version Conrad Veidt gives an excellent performance as the student Balwin and this may have been the one Dylan saw since he gives the name Conrad to the wealthy owner of the magnificent country house with its Pleasure Gardens and rich guests. It is a fluently told, haunting tale and when Blaise ends up a penniless beggar he is redeemed by taking on the pain of animals, for he has the gift of healing the wounded. 'A circle of shining eyes watches' as he makes his decision to stay with them as healer. In his redemption he seems a Christ-like Pan figure, who has taken on the pain and suffering of the animal world. Clearly there are links with the animal kingdom of Thomas's last poems. He regains his shadow when he dies on taking on the pain of Mary, whom he had once loved in vain.

Three years after its composition Thomas wrote to a production manager who had read it: 'I did, of course, realise at the time how impracticable a subject it was in the light of Wardour Street's reaction to it. Your suggestion that I should try it out on Cocteau, I shall certainly do something about.'[86] But there is no evidence he attempted to promote this 'film idea' further.

THE SHADOWLESS MAN

An Idea for a Film
Period 1850
Somewhere in England

SHADOWS · PART 1

There are *shadows* in bright sunlight.
Shadows of tall trees on dusty roads
Of Village bright church towers, the bells ringing.
Of cattle drinking, their shadows on the midged and
hazy, lazy summer water,
Of sheep angled on white cliffs
Of lambs about their mothers
Of cows in shallow streams, drinking
Of peasant lovers in deep and idle early evening lanes,
Of the jutting and hanging roofs of old houses in
narrow sunbaked streets,
Of children's hoops bowling along the cobbles of sunny squares,
Of the piled fruit and striped canvas of open-air
markets, the balloons of street vendors, the awnings
over little shops.
Of large cottage loaves, and large tea pots on white
tea cloths spread on tressel tables under garden trees,
Of the wheels of carriages rolling along a sunlit quay.
Of fishermen making sails on the strand.
Of the sails of boats and ships on sparkling water.
Of the sails and masts of one slowly moving
three masted ship.
And now that ship with its great white sails is rounding
a cliff point towards us. The high cliffs stand white
against a cloudless sky. There are long white beaches.

The ship is coming into the harbour of a small town, past twin
lighthouses, serenely moving among the crowded fishing boats.
    From the ship is heard: a young man's voice, singing carefreely
and gaily.

His shadow is cast on the deck of the ship.

The shadow moves across the deck to the side of the ship.

And now we see that the shadow is that of a tall and wellfavoured young man dressed as a sailor.

He leans on the shiprail next to another young sailor, cheerful and sturdy and impudent.

They look at the bright approaching town, and talk of all the happy times ahead of them in their shore leave in this new port and new district.

The tall young sailor is Blaise. The other is Johnny.

On landing, Blaise and Johnny go to a quayside Public House, and on a bench in the sun, drink beer and talk of the future.

Blaise says that he has with him a letter of introduction, from his brother, to a very rich citizen in the neighbourhood, Mr Conrad, who might help him in his fortunes.

And Blaise says that after they have eaten, he will leave his seaman's chest at this public house and go to seek Mr Conrad, why does not Johnny come with him.

But Johnny says that, for his part, he will remain awhile in the little town and see what pleasures it has to offer.

Blaise and Johnny are served at table by a shy pretty young girl, Mary, who has come up from the country for a holiday and to help her uncle who is the owner of the Public House. Blaise and Johnny pay some attention to her.

When the meal is over, Blaise, promising to return to Johnny that evening, sets out, in an old shabby quayside carriage, to find Mr Conrad's house.

The carriage drives through pleasant country, full of orchards and harvesting.

After some time, the carriage stops and the driver tells Blaise that he will go no further. He gives no explanation, only points to the country before them and says that if Blaise intends to travel on there, he must go by foot.

And Blaise walks the hot country roads.

At last he comes to the great gates of Conrad's house, and walks up the long drive, bordered by exotic trees, and strangely shaped plants and bushes, to an enormous and fantastic house.

Here he asks for Conrad, and is conducted through seemingly endless galleries, halls and courtyards, magnificently appointed dining halls, ballrooms and State Chambers, into the Pleasure Gardens.

These gardens look down upon wide sunbrilliant Valleys and rivers, winding down to the distant fishing-sailed sea. And in the gardens wanders a large company of guests.

The are all rich and splendid, but take no notice of Blaise as, in his sailor's dress, he moves among them. Occasionally he stops to enquire of one or another group of guests the whereabouts of Mr Conrad, but either they take no notice or vaguely they point in some direction and, turning away, forget him.

He comes, at last, to one large company of guests in the middle of a great lawn overlooking prosperous Valleys and hop fields. Here he finds Conrad in the centre of this company, but so preoccupied with his guests that he cannot approach him.

He stands at the edge of this company and listens and watches. Conrad is a fat, loud, middle-aged man, extravagantly clothed, his fingers dazzling with rings, his wrists bangled, carrying a walking-stick of gold. And to his guests about him, he boasts of his wealth and his property, of the unrivalled beauties of his estates.

About his listeners, Blaise remarks an air and appearance of excited apprehension.

Greedily they hang upon Conrad's words, and their eyes glisten as he describes the wonders of his wealth. Among those who listen most avidly is a young and very beautiful girl. She interrupts Conrad, in a glowing description of the prodigies of his Pleasure Gardens, and the wonderful mazes and labyrinths, parks, pleasances, lakes and luxuries of the Valleys below him, to wish that she could see it all from the lawns on which she stands. If only, she says petulantly, she had a telescope.

Standing near Blaise, on the outskirts of the company, is a very tall, thin man, clad in very perfect and correct grey clothes and a grey top hat.

His face is very white, shining white.

On hearing the young woman's request, he steps forward and produces out of his breast pocket a telescope. An enormous telescope. And no-one is surprised. The young woman takes the telescope and looks through it and urges the rest of the company to do the same. Only for a moment does she notice Blaise.

Blaise looks about him in amazement.

Servants bring out a great picnic repast, and again the young woman complains that she wishes there were carpets to sit upon.

And the grey man again steps forward and produces from the same breast pocket a vast Turkey carpet which is then spread out for all the guests to sit upon.

None of the guests, but Blaise, looks at the grey man.

He and the Man in Grey stand at opposite sides of the great carpet, gazing at one another.

Then the young woman complains of the heat, and the grey man produces a huge marquee complete with poles and ropes, and this is erected over the guests.

Then suddenly Blaise turns and makes his escape, and rushes down a steep path and through a wood in the direction of the far sea and the tinily distant harbour town.

He runs on and on. Behind him all the time is the sound of running footsteps.

He stops. The footsteps stop also. Again he runs, through wood, over meadow, past many of the wonders of Conrad's estate, the hanging gardens, the lake, the rockeries, the pagodas and summer houses. Behind him is the sound of running footsteps. He stops, looks behind him. The footsteps stop. There is nothing to see. And again he runs on. He runs into an ornamental Maze, and the footsteps follow him. He runs down the paths of the Maze, around and around between the tall impenetrable grotesque hedges. And the slow deliberate footsteps run just behind him.

Along the winding paths of the Maze he and the footsteps run until he reaches: the centre of the Maze. The centre of the maze becomes an extensive and barren plain strewn with monolithic Stonehenge stones. Blaise runs behind the shelter of one colossal stone and stops still. This time the footsteps do not stop but continue, growing louder, towards him. Nearer and nearer they come drumming. Then they stop.

And around the stone, silently, comes the tall very white-faced man with the grey suit and the grey top hat, his hand in his breast pocket.

He removes his hat and bows very low.

Blaise does likewise.

Blaise's shadow is cast on the ground.

The Man in Grey has no shadow.

Hatless, they face each other, like duellists.

Then the grey man speaks. He speaks slowly with a deep toneless voice, with downcast eyes as if begging, supplicating. He asks Blaise to sell him his shadow. Blaise does not understand. And wheedlingly the man in grey repeats his supplication. It is only his shadow he wants. Such a very little thing. Only his shadow. And for his shadow he will give him the Purse of Fortunatus, the Bottomless Purse.

Blaise becomes seized with temptation. He sees gold pieces floating in the air and falling in showers about him. The Man in Grey brings out of his breast pocket an old leather purse tied with strings and holds it out to Blaise.

Blaise as if without thinking stretches out his hand to take the purse. And the man in the grey top hat kneels down, gathers up Blaise's shadow from the ground, folds it neatly, puts it in his pocket, bows, turns around and walks away, stiffly and slowly, from the huge stones and along the great gaunt plain.

Blaise clutches the purse and runs in the opposite direction, out of the plain, into the woodland, on to the highway. Beyond him, the sea shines. And as he runs, night comes slowly down.

Now Blaise is entering the harbour town. There is a bright full moon.

As he walks along the moonlit street, he passes an old woman begging, and from the purse he takes a gold coin and drops it in her bowl. He walks on. The old woman looks after him as he moves down the moon-shadowed street.

Everything casts a shadow except himself. And, frightened, the old woman throws away the gold coin.

Blaise walks quickly through the deserted streets.

He bumps into a drunkard lurching out of a lighted Inn. The drunkard sways and staggers in front of him, not letting him pass. And the drunkard's shadow sways and staggers too! The drunkard laughs at his shadow. Then suddenly he stops laughing. He sees that Blaise has no shadow.

Now Blaise runs away from him, down another street towards the sound of the sea. The masts of ships finger up above the low roofs. Coming down the street is a gay drunken group of young students playing 'catch your shadow' or 'cut your shadow' with duelling swords. They challenge Blaise. But he has no shadow, and they all are seized with fear.

Now Blaise rushes, terrified, to the quayside inn. He enquires of the shy young girl who had served them earlier, where Johnny is, but she does not know. He pays his bill with gold, collects his seaman's chest, goes out on to the moonlit quay.

One horse and carriage stands near on the desolate quay, casting a still shadow. He calls the carriage over. It is the same carriage which drove him into the country.

He orders the driver to take him to the best hotel in the town.

In the Hotel he takes the finest room and locks himself in. Alone, he unties the strings of the purse and takes out gold piece after gold piece. Deliriously he burrows in the bottomless purse, piling the gold around him. Ceaselessly he pulls out gold from the purse. And now the room is almost full of gold, heaps, mounds, and mountains of gold, and he falls back exhausted on the gold hills and sleeps.

He awakes the next day and is horrified at the mountain of gold. He must somehow get rid of it like a murderer left with his victim's body. He pulls the bellrope in his room. A servant knocks at the locked door. Without opening up, Blaise calls for strong wooden chests to be brought to him and left outside the door. Secretly he opens the door, after he has heard the arrival of the chests, pulls them into the room and fills them with gold. His chief concern now is somehow to be rid of it and to regain his shadow. He goes downstairs and enquires for a servant. Various men come to interview him, the riff raff of the harbour, drunken, dissolute, brutal, knavish. But the last man is Johnny, who has gambled away all his money. Blaise pretends he has won his wealth in the same way: each is delighted to see the other.

Blaise sends Johnny to Mr Conrad's house to spy out the land and to see if he can find out anything about the man in the grey clothes and grey top hat. He describes to Johnny the incidents of the telescope, the carpet, and the marquee.

Johnny finds the house. The great iron gates at the entrance are broken and rusty and on their last hinges. The great drive up to the house is thick with weeds. The once ornate bushes are overgrown and bedraggled. And the house itself is roofless and in ruins, the mere shell of the fabulous building where Blaise walked through endless corridors and galleries.

Mice run over the rotten floors.

Johnny goes out into the weedy neglected Pleasure Gardens. In the middle of the lawns he finds the telescope, the carpet and the ragged marquee.

There is no-one at all. No guest – no servant.

Coming out of the broken gates of the house, Johnny meets a tall, thin man in a grey cloak.

The man says 'Tell your master he will not see me here again. But in a year and a day I shall have the honour of paying him a visit, when in all probability I shall have a proposal to make him of an agreeable nature.'

Johnny returns to the hotel and recounts the meeting to Blaise who immediately recognises the grey man from his description. Blaise then filled with despair tells Johnny about the selling of his shadow, and they decide to make the best of the situation. They are both young and are fantastically rich and have a whole year in which to enjoy themselves. Johnny devises means and skill to hide Blaise's secret from the world.

Blaise remembers the spoilt young beauty of the party in Conrad's garden, and sets about finding her. He finds his fellow guest in the hotel, he courts her, gives feasts and hunting parties – careful to arrange these on dull and shadowless days. But when she tells him that she desires a midnight party during the full moon, he is unable to refuse.

Luckily, the night of the midnight party is cloudy, and, thinking himself safe, Blaise follows her into the garden. Suddenly, there is a great gust of wind, the moon sails full and bright into the sky.

In the moon drenched garden, the trees and the garden statues cast shadows on the smooth grass, she turns to confront him, smiling and waiting to be embraced.

She sees he has no shadow.

But, to his horror, he sees that she has no shadow either. He rushes back into the house, calls for Johnny, for his coach, his servants, his chests. He flings himself with Johnny into the coach and they drive away, like a fury, out of the town into the night.

Also on the coach is Blaise's new servant, Nick, a sly and saturnine fellow who now seems to have taken charge of Blaise, his affairs and his fortunes. (Possibly the same quayside driver, who took Blaise to Conrad's house?)

The coach drives on, into the dawn, Nick driving.

Now in full daylight, the coach approaches an old cathedral town. A little distance from the town, the coach stops before a large crowd of people on the road. The crowd splendidly dressed in country Sunday fashion, sing and carry banners.

PART 2

A young girl steps out from the crowd and coming to the window of the coach, presents Blaise with flowers.

They recognise each other immediately. She is the young girl who served Blaise and Johnny at the quayside Inn.

Blaise asks her to enter the coach with him and drive into the town. She tells him, as they drive on through the singing crowds, that this is her home-town where she has returned from her holiday.

In the cathedral town, the Mayor receives Blaise with honour, and offers him the Mayor's Palace for his stay. The Mayor addresses Blaise as 'Count Peter'.

In his apartment in the Palace, Nick explains to Blaise that a visiting royalty under the travelling name of Count Peter was expected in the city. Nick says that, as he had heard that the royal party had taken another route and would not be visiting the town after all, he made so bold as to send warning to the town that 'Count Peter' – in reality Blaise – was on his way.

Blaise is furious at this deception and is about to dismiss Nick when a demonstration is heard outside his window. He steps on to the balcony and accepts the homage of the crowds. Now he cannot reveal himself or claim his true identity because he has placed himself in a false position by having accepted the popular ovation.

But his main reason for wishing to stay in the town is the young girl Mary, with whom he has fallen in love. And so he continues to live as 'Count Peter'.

But he does not repeat the ostentatious display of wealth with which he courted the petulant young beauty of Conrad's garden party. He escapes from those entertainments he is forced to give, in order to be with Mary.

And incognito, he joins with her in the happy life of the country fairs, the village dances, the travelling Circus.

And in the fields and the woods he makes love to her in the evenings and on cloudy days.

And, as time goes on, impatiently he waits for the coming, at the end of the year, of the terrible grey Man. Then on his arrival he can confess his deception, renounce the Purse of Fortunatus, and set up as an honest man with Mary as his wife.

Meanwhile, Nick is stealing large sums of money from Blaise, and making mischief against him.

Johnny warns Blaise of Nick's theft and treachery, but Blaise will not listen to him and he and Johnny quarrel so bitterly that Johnny leaves him.

The day arrives when Blaise, expecting the return of the Man in Grey, sets out to ask Mary's parents for her hand. But Mary's father receives him coldly and sternly tells him that he will not allow her to marry Blaise and that he has promised her to another.

Blaise goes into the next room and finds Mary in the arms of her mother. They are weeping. He learns from them that Nick has told Mary's father that he, Blaise, is not Count Peter, that he has acquired his wealth by evil means, and that he has sold his shadow to the devil. And Mary's father, in return for Nick's unveiling of Blaise's secret, has promised him Mary as his wife.

Blaise leaves Mary in misery, and wanders out of the city on to the sea shore.

It is a long wide pebbly beach with high white cliffs.

Blaise sits down near to where some boys are throwing stones at a cairn they have built by the edge of the sea.

Soon the boys go away, drifting in couples over the dunes, and Blaise is left alone, staring at the sea.

Idly, for want of better to do, his thoughts elsewhere, he takes up a handful of pebbles and throws them at the cairn.

And, suddenly: the cairn becomes the tall grey man standing there at the sea's edge, still and silent, staring at Blaise. And frenziedly, Blaise throws stone after stone at the grey Man round whose feet the sea waves lap.

But none of the stones strike him.

And then, slowly, the grey Man makes his way up the foreshore towards Blaise.

He tells Blaise that this is the day on which he had promised to come. And he offers Blaise his shadow back if he will sign away his soul at the day of his death.

The Grey Man tempts Blaise with the picture of Mary in love with him but forced to marry his betrayer. Not only will the Grey Man restore his shadow, but he will also expose Nick as a thief and see that Blaise and Mary are married.

And, as the Grey Man tempts him, he and Blaise are walking from the foreshore towards the town.

They approach Mary's house. Outside the house the feast for the betrothal is already in progress, the long benches and tables in the sun stacked with food and fruits and wine, and Mary sitting in the place of honour dressed as a bride and a statue of grief.

Slowly they walk away from the house towards the cliffs again. And suddenly, torn between temptation and fear, Blaise asks 'What bargain did Conrad make with you?'

And the Grey Man pulls out of his breast pocket the terrible manikin form of Conrad corrupted.

Blaise flings himself on the Grey Man, and together they wrestle on the very edge of the cliff. Blaise is overcome and left creeping on his hands and knees with only enough strength to take the Purse of Fortunatus and fling it over the cliff into the sea.

PART 3

And now Blaise is a beggar wandering from place to place, doing menial jobs for food and lodging but never for money which he now refuses to touch.

One day he comes upon the same Country Fair that once, in the days of his happiness, he had visited with Mary. He goes to the tent where various animals are tethered. All the animals are deformed: a sheep with six legs, a two-headed dog, monstrously maimed and crippled creatures. Around them stands a curious crowd, mocking and jeering them.

Blaise, filled with pity for their sufferings and with anger against the crowd, challenges the biggest mocking brute, and they fight in the crowded tent. Though his opponent is ferociously strong, Blaise gets the better of him and drives the crowd away. He is left alone with the animals. He strokes the head of the deformed sheep, and immediately it is made whole. Blaise is filled with amazement and a certain fear, but he goes to each animal in turn and touches its deformity and each time the miracle occurs. His fear turned to joy, and, accompanied by a dog whom he has healed, he sets off again on his journeys, stopping whenever he finds a sick animal to touch it and make it well.

On the outskirts of a country town, he comes across the Circus which he and Mary once, long ago, had visited together, and here he offers his services as a man in charge of certain of the animals whose friend he becomes.

One night, at a crowded performance, a fierce fire breaks out in the Circus. The audience stampede in panic, and the people of the Circus abandon the animals.

Alone, Blaise makes his way through the blazing tents to the cages of the frightened animals and releases them and pacifies them and leads as many as are hurt out of the circus-ground and on to a deserted heath. Here he finds an abandoned outbuilding and sets about repairing it. Here he attends to the sick animals.

And now sick animals come to him from all over the country and he heals them and cures their illnesses and he becomes famous through the length and breadth of the country, and the people of the country bring their beasts to him for his miraculous healing.

But, very gradually, there grows a very strange change in his appearance. He begins to take on upon himself, the sicknesses and diseases from which the animals, whom he cures, suffered. His whole shape becomes most grotesque and fearful, and he suffers great torments, and he is near to dying of his pain.

It is at this time, on the edge of death, his appearance monstrous now and his pain well nigh insufferable, that on a night of wind and storm, thunder and lightning, the Grey Man once again appears and offers his final temptation.

In exchange for his soul, he offers Blaise release from his pains and the return of his shadow. He tells him that Mary is a widow still living in the country town where Blaise had left her.

Blaise, now hideous and in great agony, fights with his desire for life. He is on the point of acceptance when he asks what will happen to the animals he has healed and cured, and the Grey Man explains that each creature must again be inflicted with its torments. But what are animals!

In the half darkness, a circle of shining eyes watches Blaise for his decision.

And his decision saves both them and his soul.

He commands the Grey Man to go *away forever*. And he turns to the pilgrims who come to him from all over the land bringing their animals for healing.

The animals come, by themselves to him.

In darkness, for his shape is now too horrible to be seen, he receives them.

His fame spreads to the town where Mary lives. The travelling circus has returned and Johnny, now the faithful guardian of Mary who herself lies dangerously ill, meets some of the clowns and acrobats and animal trainers in a local tavern, who tell him of the Healer, his skill, his renown, and describe his poor dwelling, the heath, and the animals that live with him and of those that visit him for cure.

Johnny hurries home to Mary, bringing news of the famed healer, who lives in darkness on a heath in another part of the country. Perhaps he can cure Mary he says.

And he persuades her to journey with him.

Johnny brings Mary to Blaise.

Supported by Johnny she enters the darkness where he lies.

She speaks to him.

He recognises her voice.

Suddenly the dark room is dimly filled with moonlight. And gradually, and at first indistinctly, Mary sees an enormous shadow appear on the wall behind the head of Blaise.

Fantastic and marvellous it is at first the shadow of his terrible appearance, horned and trunked.

And the voice of Blaise, under the shadow, says to Mary: 'Yes, I can cure you. I can cure you as I cured the animals. I took their pain. You are dying and I can take your death to myself.'

And he takes her death to himself and dies.

And the Shadow slowly changes to the shadow of Blaise.

And she recognises him and knows it is Blaise, and that he has regained his Shadow, and with tears of grief and joy she bends over him as he dies.

The Three Weird Sisters

'Land of my Fathers. My fathers can keep it!' is one of the many arresting comments in *The Three Weird Sisters*, based on the book of that name by Charlotte Armstrong, an American thriller writer. But Dylan Thomas took little more than the title, plot, the three elderly spinster sisters and their rich half-brother and his secretary, whom they try to kill. He transferred the scene to the political and cultural conflicts of a South Wales mining valley in the 1930s, dropping Armstrong's retired academic detective Professor MacDougal en route to visit an American Indian reservation near Ogaunee and coming upon murder and mayhem in a ghost town in an iron-mining area in Michigan. In translating the thriller-style plot to a Welsh mining community, now largely derelict, Dylan Thomas brings his own preoccupations with relish into this Welsh melodrama. He delights in giving expression to his private Welsh themes of religion – particularly nonconformity, radical politics, and the cultural cross-currents with which he himself grew up in what he once called his 'semi-proletarian, bourgeois, provincial upbringing'.[87]

The plot centres on the sisters – Gertrude who is blind, Isobel who is arthritic, and Maud who is deaf – who are trying to keep up appearances as Ladies of Morlais House, standing above the village of Cwmglas. In the opening scene violent and sudden pit subsidence destroys several cottages and the ladies, led by the dominant and domineering Gertrude, promise to rebuild them. They approach their rich brother. Owen comes down from London with his secretary Claire Prentiss, who is a primly efficient middle-class lady in contrast to both Armstrong's self-declared gold digger and Maud's salacious and prurient slanders, in order to prevent Gertrude's sponging on him in the family name. Early on, the sisters' unrelenting formality acquires a tone of threat, as does their unbreakable calm. Their attempts to murder Owen for his money, and later Claire Prentiss when he wills it to her, are suitably 'B' movie thriller in this film of jokey menace. Morlais is very much a gothic horror film haunted house, where Beattie the cook, in her basement kitchen, and her simple-minded son Thomas, general servant to the ladies, also live, as well of course as that Dylan Thomas familiar the owl. An influence may be one of Thomas's favourite thriller films *The Old Dark House*, adapted from the J.B. Priestley novel *Benighted*, about stranded strangers subjected to the odd behaviour of its sinister inmates. Dylan knew much of this film by heart and loved playing his favourite parts, as Theodora FitzGibbon remembered.

However, it is the tirades and set speeches that provide real passion in this very Welsh film, whether Owen's cowardly blustering in his dismissal of his sisters' patronising lifestyle in the village on his money or his anti-Wales outbursts. Thomas's comic vituperation, as in Owen's dismissal of the solicitor as a 'forensic ferret' and the description of Gertrude, after a failed murder attempt, as looking like 'a cheated vulture', is written in a poet's vivid phrase. As so often, Dylan Thomas observes life and parodies it as he goes along, for much of the social and political comment is veined with parody, such as Mabli Hughes's speech of political 'dialectic' to the assembled dogs on the mountainside, the pit nearby and the attentive dogs wagging their tails in friendly support. In this way the points are made about South Wales valley politics, albeit that Thomas prefers the role of jester – as so often in his prose – to 'didactic' tones. Against Claire Prentiss's disparagement of Cwmglas for its poverty and ugliness, the doctor, whose training and education were paid for by the sisters after his father was killed in the pit, rebukes Prentiss as 'Miss London'. He calmly but cogently defends the miners for keeping their own truths – of love and dignity – despite their scarred lives and hardship. He firmly points out, too, that their truth is not the truth of the chapels or of the Morgan-Vaughan sisters' patronage or that of 'trippers' to the valley. This of course is a directly political and social comment, and one of the most appealing on Welsh mining communities.

Similarly Dylan Thomas parodies as he describes the 'hwyl' (a chanting, persuasive, emotional tone) and the sanctimoniousness of the Baptist minister Mr Price, Gertrude's family Bible-reading and parodied parable in her instructions to the simple-minded Thomas to effect the killing of Owen by misdirection, and in the memorial chapel service after the deaths of the sisters, 'the dear ladies', Mr Price referring to the congregation as 'my people'. Dylan Thomas is here deliberately echoing the title of the famous book by Caradoc Evans, the satirist who first blazed the trail of Anglo-Welsh writing and whose satiric jibes are not far away in this film. Dylan greatly admired him, and as a young man visited him in Aberystwyth.

It was fascinating to discover in this film the source of 'Land of my Fathers. My fathers can keep it!', first quoted by Suzanne Roussillat in the *Adam* memorial issue, but with no reference. She met Dylan Thomas, however, while he was living in South Leigh, where he worked on this script. It was also in 1948 that he made his fiercest attack on Wales and why he left it in his talk to the Scottish PEN centre in Edinburgh, saying mockingly that in Wales a writer 'reads Caradoc Evans only when alone and by candlelight'. Referring to this talk Roussillat writes: 'an echo of the severe accusations at the beginning is found in *The Three Weird Sisters*, whose script was written by Dylan Thomas', adding 'This film is bitterly resented by Welsh people.'[88] It is likely that Dylan mentioned the 'Land of my Fathers' comment in their conversation.

The names of the villagers such as Polly Probert, Daddy Waldo, certainly anticipate *Under Milk Wood*, as do their exchanges, and after Morlais House (echoing Dylan's middle name Marlais) collapsed in the mining subsidence, evidently the owl flew straight to 'Milk Wood'! I wonder, too, whether his dog Mably prompted Dylan's idea of Mabli Hughes's audience of dogs in the film!

As in *No Room at the Inn*, I have transcribed the dialogue from the soundtrack of the film. It was the dialogue, always his forte, he was particularly employed to write. I have suggested settings, action, and movement of the characters when needed.

THE THREE WEIRD SISTERS

The film opens with noises of pit disaster as the old workings of the now disused mine give way and village houses and road collapse in the sudden, dramatic subsidence. There are noises of panic and terror at the earthquake-like scene in the village street, and some cries can be heard by the three sisters in their house, Morlais, above the village.

VOICES: Sergeant bach! Sergeant bach!

(*Calls from the village below.*)

MAUD: I don't know what's happened! I was nearly thrown out of my bed!

ISOBEL: Look at all the lights moving in the valley!

GERTRUDE: Where in the valley?

ISOBEL: Down at the bottom of the valley, down by Zion.

(*Thomas, mentally retarded, their servant, enters.*)

THOMAS   (*His simple-minded excitement breathlessly relates events.*):   It's the old mine workings. Lion street's gone – and Alban Garage! And they're all down there digging, and Dr Davies and Mr Price, and Mrs Jones Mount-Pleasant was screaming like a pig until the Doctor slapped her face and then – and then –

GERTRUDE: Thomas! *Try* and answer my questions. Now listen to me carefully. You say the old Vaughan workings have collapsed?

THOMAS   (*excitedly*):   Yes!

GERTRUDE: Is the old road gone?

THOMAS: Yes!

GERTRUDE: How many cottages in Zion street?

THOMAS: They're all gone! Mrs Griffiths's, the Bevans's, and old Daddy Waldo's – you can see his rocking chair stuck on Mrs Probert's chimbley. They all slide down together!

GERTRUDE: Lord have mercy!

ISOBEL: You must go and get dressed!

(*Scene moves to the village devastation, terror, and excitement.*)

MRS BEVAN: Dr Davies! Dr Davies! Is it broke bad Doctor?

DR DAVIES: Well, it's not broke good Mrs Bevan.

MAN'S VOICE: Dr Davies! Quick man!

MRS BEVAN: Leave me alone now! Go on now! Go on you – get someone hurt proper!

DADDY WALDO: And a chest of drawers on top of him! He was swearing and cursing!

QUIET VOICE   (*sadly*):   Jack Richards. Jack Richards! He's got his pipe still in his mouth.

WOMAN: There, there, boyo, we'll find Mam soon.

(*A child cries.*)

DADDY WALDO: Yes, Mam won't leave you. No!

GERTRUDE   (*now joining the scene*):   And how are you this terrible night, Mrs Lewis?

MRS LEWIS: Oh, I'm okay, Miss Gertrude. Mrs Bevan's broke her arm, and they can't find Olwen Harris. She's buried.

MABLI HUGHES (*aggressively to the Rev. Price*):   So this is one of your acts of God, Mr Price! He moves in a mysterious way his wonders to perform, I will say that.

MR PRICE (*with touch of hwyl in his voice*):   It is all part of the pattern. Why did the workings cave in, you ask? We do not know. Only God knows. Why did the cottages crumble and tumble in thunder-clouds of dust and little bits of brick. We do not understand. Only God understands! He understands everything!

MABLI HUGHES: Well, he didn't understand Jack Richards. Old Jack wanted to live, why he'd just done his pools, mun.

MR PRICE: It is not for us to say who shall be called, Mabli Hughes. And mind your spade, man!

MABLI HUGHES: Hm! Ours not to reason why, I suppose. Well, I am reasoning see. I'm reasoning that the gallery should have been filled in before the Vaughan pit was abandoned. You can't blame God for these ruins. These aren't his blunders. All you can blame is the criminal negligence of profit makers who don't care a damn in hell about the people that make their profit for them. It's the Morgan-Vaughans and all their sort who smashed this street and left old Jack Richards to die all mucked up in his blood. Hm! Ours but to do or die! Ay, die for the Morgan-Vaughans.

RESCUER: Dr Davies! Dr Davies!

DR DAVIES: She'll do. She'll be all right (*examining woman*).

MAN'S VOICE: There, there, what did I tell you, boyo, Mam's home now.

GERTRUDE: Here's Mr Price. How many souls have we lost, Mr Price?

MR PRICE: Only two! It is a miracle Miss Morgan-Vaughan. We have much to be thankful for. Perhaps more for the help and guidance you give us, than for anything else.

GERTRUDE: My sisters and I will of course take personal responsibility for the re-housing. The old workings of the Vaughan mine are the cause of the disaster. Naturally we *must* see justice done ...

(*We return to the house. Gertrude is phoning her bank manager.*)

BANK MANAGER: I'm sorry Miss Morgan-Vaughan, but your account can't even begin to meet this liability.

GERTRUDE: Our bare securities.

BANK MANAGER: Your overdraft is already slightly in excess of the value of your securities.

GERTRUDE: In that case our brother Owen, as head of the family, will undoubtedly honour the obligation. The rebuilding of the these cottages is our responsibility. Will you please speak to him on the telephone?

BANK MANAGER: If you wish it, Miss Vaughan. (Telephones Owen.)

OWEN MORGAN-VAUGHAN (*angrily*):   Listen, Williams, if you let those old harpies think they can get another penny out of me I'll take every penny of my business out of your hands. (*calls secretary*) Prentiss! I don't care whose idea it was! Your duty is to say no. And go on saying no! Yes, of course I understand the position. As far as I'm concerned the whole village can fall in the mine! She's there with you now isn't she? All right, you tell her here and now that I'm coming down this afternoon to stop this *head* of the family nonsense once and for all. Good day! (*to his secretary, Claire Prentiss*) I'm going down to Cwmglas after lunch. We go by car.

CLAIRE PRENTISS: Me, Mr Morgan-Vaughan? You mean you want me to come?

OWEN MORGAN-VAUGHAN: That's what I said. I've had enough of coping with my sisters by myself.

CLAIRE PRENTISS: Oh but, well I can't be of much use, I don't know them.

OWEN MORGAN-VAUGHAN: Exactly! This is a business interview, and as my secretary you know as much about my business as I know myself. You'll be able to support my statement that I can't afford to throw away another penny on this philanthropic nonsense. Right, ring up this garage and see the car's on time.

(*Owen Morgan-Vaughan and Claire Prentiss driving into derelict mining village of Cwmglas.*)

CLAIRE PRENTISS: How do you pronounce it?

OWEN MORGAN-VAUGHAN: Cwmglas.

CLAIRE PRENTISS: I find it all rather sinister.

OWEN MORGAN-VAUGHAN: No, it's just derelict. Dead as mutton. Nothing sinister about it. Except my grandfather's statue.

(*Stone thrown at car window as it arrives, breaking window. Car careers to halt.*)

MAN'S VOICE: Look, William, the gentleman is bleeding.

(*Commotion on village square.*)

OWEN MORGAN-VAUGHAN: Cwmglas! (*contemptuously*)

VILLAGE VOICE: Who's been throwing an apple?

BYSTANDER: A little stone, mun.

MAN'S VOICE: It looked like an apple.

OWEN MORGAN-VAUGHAN: I don't care what it was! I want to know who tried to kill me!

DADDY WALDO: I seen it all! I was outside the Morning Star, and I seen him lift up a stone.

OWEN MORGAN-VAUGHAN: Who?

DADDY WALDO: He lifts it up.

OWEN MORGAN-VAUGHAN: Who did?

DADDY WALDO: It was –

POLLY PROBERT: Who was it, Daddy Waldo? You didn't see his face did you? You couldn't have seen his face, you was too far off.

DADDY WALDO: No, no! I didn't see who it was.

MR PRICE: Mr Morgan-Vaughan, what do you think of us? There's never such a thing happened in Cwmglas before.

DADDY WALDO: In the middle of the afternoon too!

OWEN MORGAN-VAUGHAN: What the hell does it matter what time of day it was!

MR PRICE: Well, well it was an accident now. Thank heaven you're not hurt proper, Mr Morgan-Vaughan.

MABLI HUGHES: Oh, Mr Morgan-Vaughan, what will you think of us, Mr Morgan-Vaughan, *Emperor* of Cwmglas. Shall we kiss it better for you, Mr Morgan-Vaughan? (*Makes rasping sounds. Baby cries.*)

MR PRICE: You keep to your place Mabli Hughes.

CLAIRE PRENTISS: Can you tell me where we can find a doctor, please?

VILLAGER: Yes, the house up at the corner there, Dr David Davies.

(*Car sets off.*)

DADDY WALDO: But why shouldn't I say what I seen, Polly Probert?

POLLY PROBERT: Daddy, listen I tell you!

DADDY WALDO: I tell you I saw Thomas throw that stone, mun, clear as clear.

POLLY PROBERT: Do you want to make trouble for him, Daddy. He's twp. He don't know what he's doing.

DADDY WALDO: But I see him!

POLLY PROBERT: Oh, come on you old teapot!

(*Scene in Doctor's surgery.*)

DR DAVIES: It should heal in a day or two. You may have a headache for a bit though. I should get him to rest as much as you can Miss Prentiss.

CLAIRE PRENTISS: I'll do my best. Is this the normal way of greeting visitors in Cwmglas?

DR DAVIES: They've always been very nice to me.

CLAIRE PRENTISS: Well, maybe they didn't like my face.

OWEN MORGAN-VAUGHAN: It's *my* face they threw stones at! Oh! Come on! Come along for heaven's sake!

CLAIRE PRENTISS: Sure you're all right?

OWEN MORGAN-VAUGHAN: Yes.

CLAIRE PRENTISS: Thank you very much, Doctor.

OWEN MORGAN-VAUGHAN: Have you paid him? ... I could have learned to collapse and brought down the cottages! (*driving again*) If it wasn't my own village ...

(*Arrival at the House, a gaunt, baroque 'horror movie' mansion set apart and above the village. Owls hoot.*)

CLAIRE PRENTISS: You don't look too good, Mr Vaughan, why don't you lie down for a minute or two.

OWEN MORGAN-VAUGHAN: No of course not, I'm not going to lie down. That young Doctor can't even tie a bandage properly.

CLAIRE PRENTISS: No. I'll fix it.

(*Isobel, one of the sisters, enters.*)

ISOBEL: I trust I'm not intruding (*insinuatingly*).

CLAIRE PRENTISS: Mr Vaughan had an accident.

OWEN MORGAN-VAUGHAN: This is Isobel, Claire, my sister. She has a genius for putting unpleasant interpretations on things.

ISOBEL: Still your old delightful self Owen. May I ask who this *young* person is?

CLAIRE PRENTISS: I'm Mr Vaughan's secretary, Claire Prentiss.

ISOBEL: How do you do Miss Prentiss. Please sit down. My sisters will join us in a minute. How did this accident occur, Owen?

OWEN MORGAN-VAUGHAN: When the committee of welcome threw a stone at the car.

ISOBEL: Oh! Oh! How dreadful! They wouldn't do such a thing. They couldn't have known who it was.

OWEN MORGAN-VAUGHAN: I don't care whether they knew or not. I've had my head cut open (*angrily*).

MAUD (*enters*): What? (*Maud is deaf.*)

OWEN MORGAN-VAUGHAN: I've had my head cut open.

MAUD: Oh, I'm so sorry. I didn't know we had a visitor (*seeing Claire Prentiss*).

ISOBEL: This is my sister, Maud. Miss Prentiss, Owen's secretary.

MAUD: Oh how charming! And when am I to congratulate you?

CLAIRE PRENTISS: I don't understand.

ISOBEL: *She* doesn't understand. I'm afraid you'll have to mouth your words Miss Prentiss, my sister's stone deaf.

CLAIRE PRENTISS: Oh, I'm so sorry.

ISOBEL: There's no need for sympathy, Miss Prentiss. We're quite content to have mastered our afflictions sufficiently to lead busy and useful lives.

MAUD: Perhaps Miss Prentiss would like to wash after her journey?

OWEN MORGAN-VAUGHAN: Oh, cut the social stuff, I'm here on business. Claire, where's my dispatch case? You had it last.

CLAIRE PRENTISS: Oh, I left it in the hall.

OWEN MORGAN-VAUGHAN: It's never there, is it! (*grumpily*) ...

GERTRUDE (*enters*):   Who are you? (*in the hall*)

CLAIRE PRENTISS: I'm Claire Prentiss, Mr Morgan-Vaughan's secretary. I'm sorry if I startled you, you see I –

GERTRUDE: I can't see, I'm blind ... (*they return to sitting room*) Miss Prentiss tells me that she's your secretary Owen, *very* interesting. Does she always travel with you?

OWEN MORGAN-VAUGHAN: Certainly when I'm on business.

GERTRUDE: Are you on business? In *this* house?

OWEN MORGAN-VAUGHAN: What else do you think I came for? I've been waiting for you, that's all.

GERTRUDE: Oh I see, you've come to discuss family affairs?

OWEN MORGAN-VAUGHAN: I've come to stop the indiscriminate spending of my credit.

GERTRUDE: I may be old-fashioned, but I always thought family affairs were discussed only among the family.

CLAIRE PRENTISS: You put me in a very embarrassing position Miss Morgan-Vaughan.

GERTRUDE: You must blame my brother for that. It was wrong of him to imagine that we should discuss our private affairs before – you. Forgive me – any stranger.

OWEN MORGAN-VAUGHAN: You'll break your neck on that high horse of yours one of these days, Gertrude.

GERTRUDE: Owen, please. Maud!

MAUD: Yes.

GERTRUDE: Will you take Miss Prentiss into the library.

MAUD: Very well.

GERTRUDE: I'm sure she won't mind. You won't think me very discourteous. But we're a very old and proud family. I'm sure you'll understand.

CLAIRE PRENTISS: You've made it only too clear! You wish me to leave Mr Vaughan?

OWEN MORGAN-VAUGHAN: Yes I – I'd better stay here. Look up the Morgan-Vaughan account while you're waiting, will you?

GERTRUDE: Mr Williams tells me you were regrettably rude to him on the telephone, Owen.

OWEN MORGAN-VAUGHAN: Now look here, Gertrude. I can see through these tactics of yours. I'm a small boy again, eh? You're the big sister telling me I'm uncouth. I've had a different mother. What can you expect from the son of a cook!

ISOBEL: If you insist on behaving like the son of a cook what other treatment do you expect?

GERTRUDE: Isobel, please. Since you came of age we've always regarded you as head of the family, Owen.

OWEN MORGAN-VAUGHAN: That's right, the golden goose. Maybe it's my common blood that made me a good businessman. I've made money, which is more than the old man ever did. He lost it hand over fist. Well I'm not throwing good money after bad, not for the doubtful compliment of being called the head of the family.

GERTRUDE: Owen!

OWEN MORGAN-VAUGHAN: Don't try and stop me, I've been wanting to say this for years. Head of the family! Head of what family? The Morgan-Vaughans, owners of a derelict mine with a sycophantic peasantry!

GERTRUDE: Owen, I warn you!

OWEN MORGAN-VAUGHAN: I'm ready for a showdown.

ISOBEL: Charming phraseology!

OWEN MORGAN-VAUGHAN: That's what's wrong with you, all three of you. You're antiquated, you're living in the feudal system, particularly you, Gertrude, with your beastly owls hooting all over the place. *They* ought to be shot for a start. I'm fed up with the whole lot of you. Ladies of the manor bravely conquering your infirmities with the lickspittle of a lot of down-and-outs.

MAUD: You beast! You low beast, coming here to insult us with your fancy lady.

GERTRUDE: Maud! Control yourself!

ISOBEL: Maud's right, Gertrude, that horribly painted young woman!

OWEN MORGAN-VAUGHAN: The charitable Morgan-Vaughans. Poor little Claire. So it's an idea.

GERTRUDE: You're all behaving like very unpleasant children. Abuse achieves nothing. Owen, you came here to discuss business, the question of these cottages, and the Morgan-Vaughan responsibility.

OWEN MORGAN-VAUGHAN: I tell you there's nothing doing.

GERTRUDE: We've given our word the cottages will be re-built, and nothing will induce us to go back on that word.

OWEN MORGAN-VAUGHAN: You'll have to find another gold goose, Gertrude. You've had up to £20,000 out of me in the last five years.

(*Scene moves to library.*)

CLAIRE PRENTISS: What are you doing here? ...

THOMAS: I'm Thomas, my mother told me to bring in the coal.

CLAIRE PRENTISS: Where is your mother?

THOMAS: Beattie? She looks after the ladies.

CLAIRE PRENTISS: You – you live here?

THOMAS: They let me. They're good.

CLAIRE PRENTISS: If you think that, why did you throw the stone at Mr Morgan-Vaughan? Tell me, Thomas, why did you throw the stone?

THOMAS: Mr Owen isn't going to give money to all the people that have lost their homes. He's bad. Miss Maud says he isn't fit to live. Miss Maud is good to me, so I didn't want him to live, and so I threw the stone.

CLAIRE PRENTISS: How did you know Mr Owen wouldn't give the money?

THOMAS: My mother heard the ladies talking after they'd seen Mr Williams at the bank. Mr Owen hit me when I was little. He hit me on the face.

BEATTIE (*enters*): Thomas! Go back to the kitchen ... Tea is served in the drawing room (*to Claire*).

DR DAVIES: Hello, I've come to fetch you to tea.

CLAIRE PRENTISS: Well, you never know who you're going to meet in this house.

DR DAVIES: I'm glad you feel one of the family.

CLAIRE PRENTISS: Family! I should never have thought that.

DR DAVIES: Well, perhaps I've given the wrong impression. What I meant was that the Morgan-Vaughans have done so much for me that I feel this is my real home.

CLAIRE PRENTISS: I see.

DR DAVIES: My father was a miner in the Vaughan pit. He was killed. The Morgan-Vaughans paid for my education and looked after me until I qualified.

CLAIRE PRENTISS: Oh yes, Thomas has told me how good they are. Now, I think I'd like some tea.

DR DAVIES: Oh, I'm so sorry ...

(*They return to sitting room.*)

GERTRUDE: I'm sure you must be ready for your tea, Miss Prentiss.

CLAIRE PRENTISS: Thank-you, I'm ready for anything. (*to Owen*) How's your head?

OWEN MORGAN-VAUGHAN: Terrible!

CLAIRE PRENTISS: Oh, I'm so sorry. I do hope you've got no more business to do.

OWEN MORGAN-VAUGHAN: No, no, that's settled.

ISOBEL: Your tea. You take sugar?

CLAIRE PRENTISS: Yes, please. It looks as if you'll have to let me drive you back.

GERTRUDE: My brother will not be leaving tonight, Miss Prentiss. Dr Davies is most insistent that he should have a night's rest after that blow on the head.

CLAIRE PRENTISS: I see. Where can I get a train?

OWEN MORGAN-VAUGHAN: You cannot get out of this god-forsaken place this time of day without a car.

CLAIRE PRENTISS: Maybe Dr Davies will drive me to the station.

DR DAVIES: Well, I'd love to but –

ISOBEL: Dr Davies has patients to see at five o'clock.

GERTRUDE: It seems that you'll be forced to accept our hospitality Miss Prentiss.

CLAIRE PRENTISS: Oh thank-you. It's a little awkward you see. I have no night things with me.

GERTRUDE: We can discuss those matters later.

OWEN MORGAN-VAUGHAN: Of course you'll stay, Claire. You'll look fascinating in white flannel.

DR DAVIES: You'll excuse me, but as Miss Isobel says I have patients to see at five. I'd like to change that dressing before you leave in the morning Mr Morgan-Vaughan.

OWEN MORGAN-VAUGHAN: You will stay the night too. Let's have a party (*with sarcasm*). I'm leaving here at six o'clock in the morning (*sternly*).

MAUD: I'm perfectly capable of changing a dressing. You should know that, David.

DR DAVIES: The Morgan-Vaughan sisters are almost qualified Doctors, Miss Prentiss.

ISOBEL: Dr Davies exaggerates, of course, but we learned a great deal of medicine when we were helping him with his studies.

OWEN MORGAN-VAUGHAN: If anyone's going to fiddle about with my bandages *she* can do it (*pointing to Claire*). She's a genuine trained nurse.

DR DAVIES: A nurse? ...

OWEN MORGAN-VAUGHAN: Yes, part time, during the war. Does that surprise you?

DR DAVIES: No, I don't think so, really. I think you could do anything you wanted to.

ISOBEL: Maybe now you want to see your room? I'm sure you'd like to freshen up.

CLAIRE PRENTISS: How very thoughtful. Goodbye, Dr Davies, it's been a most interesting experience meeting you.

DR DAVIES: Au revoir, please.

CLAIRE PRENTISS: Has your clock always been like that? (*on way upstairs, to room, seeing hall landing clock somewhat askew*)

ISOBEL: No, that happened at the time of the subsidence. Although it looks dangerous they assure us it's perfectly safe for the time being. It would need a structural alteration to put it in position again. And we don't feel justified in using the labour when so many people need a roof to their heads. Would you mind going first Miss Prentiss? First door on the right, past the chest of drawers, Miss Prentiss. I'll be with you in a moment. (*sounds of owls and night birds*) Here is a night dress, Miss Prentiss (*entering Miss Prentiss's room*) – not flannel. You must be on very intimate terms with my brother to allow him to discuss such things in mixed company.

CLAIRE PRENTISS: I resent that remark Miss Morgan-Vaughan. I'm Mr Vaughan's secretary, no more and no less.

ISOBEL: I'm afraid we've had no previous experience of the duties of secretaries.

CLAIRE PRENTISS: All my concern is you must have very unpleasant minds. I am sorry, Miss Vaughan, after all I am your guest. But, you know, you're not making things easy for me. Mr Vaughan's your brother, you must know as well as I do that he says whatever comes into his head.

ISOBEL: And he usually regrets it afterwards. I am glad you realise that trait in him, Miss Prentiss. Since you're concerned with him in business you must know how generous he's always been to his old sisters. And because he thinks generosity is unmanly he puts himself in the worst possible light. Sometimes he makes us feel like the daughters of the horse-leech, but we understand him and appreciate him.

CLAIRE PRENTISS: I'm glad.

ISOBEL: He has an unswerving loyalty to the family. Nothing can shake that.

CLAIRE PRENTISS: Nothing?

ISOBEL: I hope not. We should be most distressed. Dinner is at seven o'clock, Miss Prentiss. (*She leaves.*)

OWEN MORGAN-VAUGHAN (*shouting from room*):   Now, clear out, Gertrude! Now leave me alone!

GERTRUDE: Must you shout, Owen?

OWEN MORGAN-VAUGHAN: Now don't you start. I told you I want to be left alone. My head's splitting.

GERTRUDE: But you're still determined to leave at day-break, Owen?

OWEN MORGAN-VAUGHAN: There are two things I've never been more determined of in my life. One is that I'm leaving at daybreak, and the other is that I've said my last word about money. Not another penny do you nag out of me, any one of you. I can't make it any plainer. So now clear out and leave me alone …

MAUD: As you wish. Dinner will be served at seven. Is there anything else you require? Your secretary for instance?

OWEN MORGAN-VAUGHAN: You wicked old bag (*slowly*).

ISOBEL (*calling*):   Miss Maud! Miss Gertrude would like see you in her room. (*The sisters leave.*)

(*Scene in Owen's bedroom. Claire Prentiss comes in.*)

CLAIRE PRENTISS: There, that's better.

OWEN MORGAN-VAUGHAN: Yes. (*Locks door.*)

CLAIRE PRENTISS: Why did you do that?

OWEN MORGAN-VAUGHAN: One's got to lock doors if one wants to be alone in this house.

CLAIRE PRENTISS: Why do you want to be alone?

OWEN MORGAN-VAUGHAN: Because I want to talk to you. So you know why I brought you here?

CLAIRE PRENTISS: It's becoming more obvious.

OWEN MORGAN-VAUGHAN: I've brought you here because I haven't got the guts to face those women alone. You know me as a businessman, don't you? Well, I've had to appear hard to get through, but maybe I'm like a crab. I'm soft inside. You've seen this house, you've seen *them*. Okay they're the genuine article all right. Highborn mother and all. But I'm the son of their father and his cook. Legitimate but – beyond the pale. Gertrude was seventeen when I was born. She spent the next seventeen years impressing how the only way to press out that shame was to follow in Viola's footsteps. Not down the kitchen stairs of course, but up the steps to heaven. Gertrude's heaven, mind you. The place where one gives all to the poor, and thanks God one was born a Morgan-Vaughan, and able to do it.

CLAIRE PRENTISS: What happened to your mother?

OWEN MORGAN-VAUGHAN: Oh, she did what was only fitting. She died when I was born. I stuck it out for seventeen years, then I cleared out. But it was too late.

CLAIRE PRENTISS: Why?

OWEN MORGAN-VAUGHAN: Because they'd got their grips on me. They got me so tied up I didn't know the difference between duty and – oh feeblemindedness.

CLAIRE PRENTISS: Ha! Ha! Well you know now. You stick it out this time.

OWEN MORGAN-VAUGHAN: Do you think they'll let me do it? They'll go on and on and on till they convince me I'm wrong.

CLAIRE PRENTISS: What do you want me to do?

OWEN MORGAN-VAUGHAN: Stand by me. See, you're normal. You're – you're part of the outside world. Just stick around, and let me look at you sometimes, and remember that there is an outside world. Will you?

CLAIRE PRENTISS: Of course. (*A knock at the door.*)

OWEN MORGAN-VAUGHAN (*nervously*): Who is it? What do you want? (*He opens door.*)

MAUD: I *thought* you were locked in here Owen. Gertrude wants you to take a glass of sherry wine before dinner. She's asked Miss Prentiss to join us. She's in there with you, isn't she?

OWEN MORGAN-VAUGHAN (*to Claire*):   Take no notice of her. You will come, won't you? You promised, didn't you?

CLAIRE PRENTISS: I promise ...

(*Scene returns to sitting room.*)

GERTRUDE: Come in, Miss Prentiss, come and sit down by me, won't you? (*speaking in formal, stiffly friendly tone*) I'm afraid I've been very neglectful in my duties as hostess today. You must excuse me and let me try to make amends. Isobel, will you get the sherry, please?

ISOBEL: I'll serve Miss Prentiss first, Owen.

OWEN MORGAN-VAUGHAN: No, let me take this tray for you.

ISOBEL: No, you're our guest, you sit down and let me wait on you.

OWEN MORGAN-VAUGHAN: Oh, there's nowhere to sit!

GERTRUDE: I'm sure you'll appreciate this wine, Owen. It's the last bottle of father's Amontillado.

OWEN MORGAN-VAUGHAN: I feel very honoured.

GERTRUDE: I hope you will always be honoured in this house, Owen.

OWEN MORGAN-VAUGHAN (*to Isobel*):   Aren't you having one?

ISOBEL: Much as I should like to drink to your health, Owen, one can't play tricks with rheumatoid arthritis.

OWEN MORGAN-VAUGHAN: Oh well. (*tasting*) Mmm, it tastes of cork to me.

CLAIRE PRENTISS: That's sacrilege, Mr Vaughan. It's wonderful sherry!

ISOBEL: I've never met a self-styled connoisseur of wine who hadn't some fault to find. To prove a sensitive palate, I presume.

GERTRUDE: You know Wales, Miss Prentiss?

CLAIRE PRENTISS: No, not very well. I don't know the South at all.

GERTRUDE: It has a curious and arresting quality all of its own. We very much hope that Owen will allow himself – and you – to stay with us for at least a couple of days so that you may see something of it.

OWEN MORGAN-VAUGHAN: Can I have another glass, Isobel?

ISOBEL: I'm afraid not, Owen, there's hardly time.

OWEN MORGAN-VAUGHAN: Oh! (*Sound of dinner-gong ... they go in to dinner.*)

(*After dinner they go into the baronial sitting room again. Beattie and Thomas with them.*)

BEATTIE: It's late for you, Miss Gertrude.

GERTRUDE: Yes, it is, Beattie. We'll have our reading now.

OWEN MORGAN-VAUGHAN: I'm going to bed. I've had enough for one day. I've been driving for hours and hours, slag heaps and pit heads and vile black hills. Huh! How vile was my valley! I'm sick of all this Celtic claptrap about Wales. My Wales! (*mockingly*) Land of my Fathers! As far as I'm concerned, my fathers can keep it. You can tell he's a Welshman by the lilt in his voice. Huh, little black back-biting hypocrites, all gab and whine! Black beetles with tenor voices and a sense of sin like a crippled hump. Cwmglas! Full of senile morons and vicious dwarfs, old poles of women clacking at you like blowsy hens, self-righteous little humbugs with the hwyl, old men with beards in their noses cackling at you, blue gums and clackers. Oh the mystical Welsh – huh! About as mystical as slugs!

GERTRUDE: You must forgive my brother Miss Prentiss, he sees in Cwmglas so many of his own endearing qualities.

MAUD: He looks just like his mother (*sneeringly*).

OWEN MORGAN-VAUGHAN: I don't know who's got the dirtiest mind, Maud. You or the devil.

MAUD: He's religious too! (*mockingly*).

OWEN MORGAN-VAUGHAN: This is a nightmare, Claire, only one never wakes up from it!

GERTRUDE: Have you finished all you want to say, Owen?

OWEN MORGAN-VAUGHAN: Yes, Gertrude.

GERTRUDE: Then please sit down. Shall I read a passage from the Psalms, Thomas?

THOMAS: Yes! (*excitedly*)

GERTRUDE (*reading*):   The Lord shall destroy thee. He shall take thee and pluck thee out of thy dwelling. Thou shalt cry but there shall be none to help thee. Yea, even unto the Lord shalt thou cry, but we shall not – (*cries from Owen*) hear! (*more cries, Gertrude looks up sternly*) Please remain where you are! That's all for tonight, Beattie. You can go now. Good night.

BEATTIE: Good night, Miss Gertrude.

CLAIRE PRENTISS: What is it, Mr Vaughan? (*alarmed*) Please clear the couch, Mr Vaughan's very ill. Miss Vaughan I want blankets and as many hot water bottles as you have and I want them at once.

GERTRUDE: Miss Prentiss asked for blankets and hot water bottles. Will you fetch them, please!

CLAIRE PRENTISS: What's the Doctor's telephone number?

GERTRUDE: Are you really a trained nurse, Miss Prentiss?

CLAIRE PRENTISS: Tell me the number, otherwise I shall ask the exchange.

GERTRUDE: Cwmglas three.

CLAIRE PRENTISS: Cwmglas three, please. Will you bring a glass of water? Don't argue, Miss Vaughan! Please do as I say! (*telephoning*) Dr Davies, this is Claire Prentiss. Can you come over right away? Mr Morgan-Vaughan's been taken very ill. Hm? No, this is nothing to do with his head. Please listen to me, this is an urgent case with violent convulsions and stomach pains. I suggest you bring a hypodermic and strychnine.

(*Scene changes to Gertrude alone in her bedroom.*)

GERTRUDE: Must I lift up my hand against my brother? I am beset with doubts; acquainted with darkness; there is none that cares, no not one ...

DR DAVIES (*entering house*):   Good evening, Beattie, where's Mr Morgan-Vaughan?

(*Scene changes to sitting room.*)

CLAIRE PRENTISS: Are you feeling better now?

OWEN MORGAN-VAUGHAN (*irascibly*):   I'm still alive if that's what you mean. My stomach's full of hyenas.

DR DAVIES: Good evening, Miss Prentiss. How's the patient now?

CLAIRE PRENTISS: Oh, he's much easier.

OWEN MORGAN-VAUGHAN (*mocking*):   Oh, he's fine, he's dandy, he can breathe. Huh! He's in agony and he wishes you all dead – you're thinking?

DR DAVIES: I think you'll be all right now.

OWEN MORGAN-VAUGHAN: All right? I vomited like a hippo.

DR DAVIES: What have you been eating?

OWEN MORGAN-VAUGHAN: Brimstone, white ants, ground glass, rat poison, what's it matter?

DR DAVIES: You'll have to take it quietly for a day or two, you know.

OWEN MORGAN-VAUGHAN: Hanky-panky, hocus-pocus, professional soft-soap and treacle. Old Gertrude looming there like a cheated vulture! I'm clearing out in the morning!

GERTRUDE (*enters*):   I'm glad you're feeling more yourself, Owen (*sardonically*).

DR DAVIES: Suppose we get you up to your bed now Mr Vaughan? Feeling strong enough?

OWEN MORGAN-VAUGHAN: I'm staying here. I'm quite comfortable, I'm tired, I'm sleepy. So you all just clear out and leave me alone.

DR DAVIES: All right, Mr Vaughan, so we'll leave you alone. There's nothing else you want?

OWEN MORGAN-VAUGHAN: Peace, sleep. No sisters, no doctors, no Wales.

CLAIRE PRENTISS: I'll be around if you want me. Now try and sleep. Remember, I'm here.

GERTRUDE: You're not really going to allow him to leave in the morning?

DR DAVIES: No, but there was no use arguing. He'll find out soon enough that he isn't in a fit state to stand up, let alone travel. If you don't mind, Miss Vaughan, I'd like to stay here tonight to be on hand just in case he does try to leave.

GERTRUDE: That's very kind of you, David, I'll tell Beattie to make up a bed for you. (*Leaves.*)

DR DAVIES: Thank you. I've just got to make a phone call and then I'd like a word with you. Will you wait for me in the library? ... (*to Claire*)

(*Scene in hall.*)

MAUD: Miss Prentiss, how is Owen? We're so worried about him.

CLAIRE PRENTISS: He's much better, thank-you. Dr Davies is with him now.

MAUD: I thought he was going to die. When his mother died – she was the cook, you know – she screamed! (*spoken with relish*) (*Claire leaves.*) Oh, David, how is Owen really? (*Dr Davies comes in.*)

DR DAVIES: I think he'll be perfectly all right now.

MAUD: You mustn't let him go in the morning.

DR DAVIES: He will if we don't stop him. He's a strong-minded man. Did Miss Prentiss go into the library?

MAUD: Miss Prentiss is in the library. She likes books (*with sarcastic relish*).

DR DAVIES: I want to ask her a few questions about this attack of Mr Vaughan's.

(*Scene moves to library.*)

CLAIRE PRENTISS: Extreme stomach convulsions, and he said his throat was burning too.

DR DAVIES: What time did the attack start?

CLAIRE PRENTISS: It was when Gertrude said 'Yea, even unto the Lord shalt thou cry'. About nine o'clock.

DR DAVIES: What did he have for dinner?

CLAIRE PRENTISS: We all had the same, boiled mutton.

DR DAVIES: It would be boiled mutton (*smiling*).

CLAIRE PRENTISS: And suet pudding (*laughing together*).

DR DAVIES: Earlier in the day?

CLAIRE PRENTISS: We both had sandwiches.

DR DAVIES: Did he have anything to drink?

CLAIRE PRENTISS: None, till just before dinner. We all had a sherry, all except Isobel. Yes, I remember! He said it had a funny taste.

DR DAVIES: You asked me to bring the hypodermic and strychnine injection.

CLAIRE PRENTISS: I know ...

(*Scene moves to Gertrude's room. She is speaking to Thomas.*)

GERTRUDE: Thank-you Thomas, but it was wrong of you to throw that stone at Mr Owen. Just as it was wrong of him to hit you when you were a little boy. Very wrong. I know you didn't forget that. Are you listening Thomas?

THOMAS: Mm! Mm!

GERTRUDE: You know the two roads that lead out of this village – You're a clever boy, a very clever boy. One is straight and clear and leads to a busy, happy place, the place your mother takes you when you're good (*in sanctimonious preacher's tone*). The other is dark, dangerous, full of great holes and leads to death. I hear someone has set up a board warning against this. Have they Thomas?

THOMAS: Yes! Yes!

GERTRUDE: Supposing someone were to remove that board, anyone might be misled. But if they were good the Lord would lead them along the straight, safe way, even though the board had been removed. But if they were not good they would take the road that leads to death. I described the two roads to you to make it easier for you to understand ... Getting late! You must be up early, so that you can help Mr Owen and Miss Prentiss along the road *they* must take. You must go to bed now.

THOMAS: In the morning! I'll be up early in the morning!

GERTRUDE: Clever boy! Very clever boy!

(*Early morning light, Claire calls at Owen's bedroom door.*)

CLAIRE PRENTISS: Mr Vaughan! Mr Vaughan! It's half past five. You wanted to leave by six remember! You wanted to leave by six!

OWEN MORGAN-VAUGHAN: I wanted to leave ... (*half asleep, confused*)

CLAIRE PRENTISS: Yes, yes!

OWEN MORGAN-VAUGHAN: What time is it?

CLAIRE PRENTISS: Half past five.

OWEN MORGAN-VAUGHAN: Oh, my mouth tastes horrid, like a dog's basket! I'd like some champagne! I'd like some brandy! I'd like the brandy *in* the champagne. I'd like vodka in the brandy. I'd like schnapps – will you make me a cup of tea?

CLAIRE PRENTISS: Where's the kitchen?

OWEN MORGAN-VAUGHAN: Down the steps.

CLAIRE PRENTISS: All right! You go and dress while I make the tea and then I'll get the car round ...

(*Scene in kitchen.*)

BEATTIE: What are you wanting in my kitchen?

CLAIRE PRENTISS: Oh, is Thomas here? I want to see him.

BEATTIE: He don't want to see you. Nobody wants to see you here ... (*Scene in Owen's bedroom, Beattie takes in the tea.*) Good morning, Mr Owen. You'd like a cup of tea wouldn't you?

OWEN MORGAN-VAUGHAN: Yes, but don't wake the whole house up. Don't let the three furies know.

DR DAVIES (*entering room*):   So you are going!

CLAIRE PRENTISS: Mr Vaughan's going. I'm going with him.

DR DAVIES: Sorry about that.

OWEN MORGAN-VAUGHAN: Did you bring the car round? (*to Claire*) I'll be with you now. Where's the tea? (*Owen comes downstairs, Woman's voice cries 'Get out!' The clock falls from the balcony above, narrowly missing Owen. It crashes to pieces on the floor near him.*)

DR DAVIES (*rushing over to Owen*):   Are you all right? Come and sit down!

OWEN MORGAN-VAUGHAN: I'm not sitting anywhere. I'm going home! Home! Poisoned! Hit with clocks!

GERTRUDE (*entering*):   What is it? What's happened?

DR DAVIES: Miss Maud leant on this clock. Miss Prentiss warned her but she took no notice.

GERTRUDE: I think you forget she's stone deaf. Are you questioning that statement, Miss Prentiss? (*sharply*)

CLAIRE PRENTISS: You ready to go Mr Vaughan?

OWEN MORGAN-VAUGHAN: Yes.

GERTRUDE: Owen, you have a Doctor and a house here. They both know that you ought not to go, that you're not fit to go. Please, don't go!

OWEN MORGAN-VAUGHAN: Balderdash!

DR DAVIES: I'd better come with you.

CLAIRE PRENTISS: No, thank-you Dr Davies. You see I don't trust you either. (*They leave.*)

(*Owen and Claire driving in car later and leaving village.*)

OWEN MORGAN-VAUGHAN: Where are we now? Hell or Wales?

CLAIRE PRENTISS: I think we're on the wrong road!

(*Car crashes ... the doctor arrives on the scene of the crash.*)

DR DAVIES: Are you all right?

CLAIRE PRENTISS: Yes, I think so.

DR DAVIES: Can you open the roof?

CLAIRE PRENTISS: I'll try. Have you got the car?

DR DAVIES: Left it at the fork. You're on the wrong road. I tried to warn you.

CLAIRE PRENTISS: But it wasn't the wrong road. The other only said –

DR DAVIES: No road!

CLAIRE PRENTISS: Let's get him to hospital.

DR DAVIES: There is no hospital.

CLAIRE PRENTISS: There's only that house (*bleakly ... owl hoots*).

Blind, deaf, and warped. Owen was right. He said it was a nightmare. But the nightmare's worse because you don't understand. Thomas threw the stone at that car. *She* told him to do it. The three sisters told him to do it. I know they did. They wanted to kill him and Thomas couldn't kill him. You know what they did, Dr Davies? They tried to poison him. The blind one put the poison in. The one with the claws, have you seen her hands? The one with the claws gave it to him, and the deaf one – wanted to hear him scream. Who pushed the clock Dr Davies?

DR DAVIES: I wish you'd never come here. Oh don't misunderstand me, I know you're charming, cool, clever, efficient, cultivated, but you're – you're stupid, Miss Prentiss.

CLAIRE PRENTISS: The sisters are evil.

DR DAVIES: You're wrong! You're wrong! I know you're wrong.

CLAIRE PRENTISS: And I know. I know they're not going to let him get out of that house alive.

(*Scene moves to police station.*)

SERGEANT FLOWER: Of that house (*slowly*) alive. Now, Miss Prentiss, take the stone what Thomas chucked. There is sane people and there is insane people. Well, you couldn't rightly call Thomas either, and he hates Mr Owen. Take the sherry, what he drunk. You've seen Cwmglas. It's a *little* place. There isn't room for two doctors in it. One doctor, one policeman, and we accept each other's *expert* opinion. Stomach ache says Dr Davies, stomach ache agrees Sergeant Flower.

CLAIRE PRENTISS: But any doctor will tell you that without a proper analysis it's practically impossible to tell arsenic poisoning from a stomach ache.

SERGEANT FLOWER (*in slow pedantic voice*):   Take the clock what fell, who was leaning on it? Miss Maud! Mis Maud is what? Miss Maud is deaf. She didn't hear you when you shouted. And last of all, take this morning, take the road barrier what was moved, and you say you suspect Thomas. But you have no proof. There is no proof for any of your accusations, no proof, and no motive against the Misses Morgan-Vaughans.

CLAIRE PRENTISS: No motive? They can't go back on their word. That's their motive. They promised to provide the money to re-build Zion Street, but they haven't got the money. Owen's got it.

(*End of scene, Claire Prentiss walks away and down village street.*)

CLAIRE PRENTISS: Do you know where Mabli Hughes lives?

WOMAN: Yes, No 29.

CLAIRE PRENTISS: Thank-you. (*Walks down terraced valley street, knocks on door.*) Does Mabli Hughes live here?

MAN AT DOOR: He's over at the colliery. (*smiles*) You *look* a fly bit too!

(*Scene at the colliery. Mabli is revealed as addressing assembled dogs on the hillside. Tone of humour and parody.*)

MABLI HUGHES: The social system, gentlemen, is iniquitous. It stinks to heaven. Consider, from the depths of your not inconsiderable intellects, the position of Cwmglas. Here in Cwmglas all social evils are condensed and crystallised. This one village may be regarded as the hub, the nucleus of a microcosm of all plutodemocratic inequality! (*Shot of listening dogs.*) You see my point? (*Dogs happily wag tails.*) Where is injustice? Cwmglas, mun. Where does social chauvinism flourish? Cwmglas, mun. Where do hate and hunger lope like wolves through the nasty streets? Cwmglas. Who is to blame? I ask you gentlemen, you gentlemen with tails. (*Tails wag happily, and dogs sit contentedly watching Mabli Hughes.*)

CLAIRE PRENTISS: Mr Hughes, I must speak to you at once. You don't know me. I'm Claire Prentiss, Owen Morgan-Vaughan's secretary, I saw you in the street the day we came. The day Thomas tried to kill him.

MABLI HUGHES: I know you madam (*sternly*). Nice weather we're having (*dismissively*).

CLAIRE PRENTISS: Nobody *listens* to me! Nobody believes me, the Doctor, the policeman, anybody in the village. They're all the same. The Morgan-Vaughans can do no wrong. They can only try to *murder* their brother!

MABLI HUGHES: Hmm. (*looking up at hillsides*) Plenty of sky about! (*again dismissively*)

CLAIRE PRENTISS: Then I remembered you, I remembered the way you looked at the other people. *You* don't believe the Morgan-Vaughans are good. You know that –

MABLI HUGHES: You confuse, madam, my dialectic approach to the rudimentary errors of the capitalist system with my own personality. (*coughs*) *There's* clouds like – like semolina (*mockingly*).

CLAIRE PRENTISS: Won't you please listen to me? (*in desperate appeal*)

MABLI HUGHES: It is fundamental deep-rooted schism. I hate the relevance of the Morgan-Vaughan fraternity to the body politic, but they're okey-dokey. I abominate the principles that motivate their charity, but they're *nice*. The fruition my dear young lady of the seeds that are socially implanted in their bosoms – if you will pardon my expression – (*She runs away. Dogs breathe heavily.*)

CLAIRE PRENTISS (*meeting Dr Davies in village*):   You're always where you're not wanted here. Tell me, Dr Davies, have they killed your patient yet!

DR DAVIES: I've only got two serious patients, you and Mr Owen.

CLAIRE PRENTISS: How is he?

DR DAVIES: Oh, he's the kind of man who needs a vet. But if you're not careful you're going to have a nervous breakdown.

CLAIRE PRENTISS: No cheek from a country doctor, fawning and toadying to those three old witches! Oh, I know they found you. They dug you up, they sent you to school, they made you a Doctor! They made you into a little snivelling provincial snob! They made you blind, too, blind to poverty and filth and dirt and ugliness and – and murder.

DR DAVIES (*calmly*):   People often come down to the mining valleys (*in steady, firm voice*), just like you. They see it's bare and ugly! Look where they live, isn't it grim and grey and horrible! I can't understand how they can put up with it. *I can.* You can be honourable, Miss Prentiss, Miss London, even when you're scrutting like a rat in the guts of the earth. The old men are scarred and twisted, but *they* haven't lost – I don't care what you call it, love or dignity or anything else. But when a man works hard for himself and for other men – it's the truth, and it isn't the truth of the chapels, or the Morgan-Vaughans, or the trippers.

CLAIRE PRENTISS (*reflectively*):   I know. It's true. David, you mustn't hate me too much. But it's not true of this place, not here. The place is dead ... (*end of scene*)

(*Scene moves to Owen to bed.*)

OWEN MORGAN-VAUGHAN: No, we're not very well thank you, we're not (*in usual tone of irascibility*) looking on the bright side, we're not feeling very chirpy this morning, and we hate the sight of your nice, hygienic faces. We're poorly!

DR DAVIES (*cheerfully*): He's improving. I think you both need a good sound sleep. I'll bring you something – you need some food young lady – may I call you young lady?

OWEN MORGAN-VAUGHAN: You may call her duck face as far as I'm concerned!

CLAIRE PRENTISS: I *would* like to eat. You couldn't bring something up, could you David! I can't face those sisters. I want to stay with old sunshine too! (*David goes downstairs.*)

ISOBEL: How is he?

DR DAVIES: Oh he is much better. I was just going to get some food for Miss Prentiss, if I may.

ISOBEL: Can't she come down here herself?

DR DAVIES: Well, I think I'd rather she stayed with Mr Vaughan, I want him to get to sleep again.

ISOBEL: You mean she can't trust him out of her sight! So she's turned you round her little finger, too. I am disappointed in you, David.

DR DAVIES: Please, Miss Isobel.

(*Scene in kitchen.*)

THOMAS: But Miss Gertrude said if they were good God would lead them on the straight, safe road, even if the sign had been changed.

BEATTIE: She shouldn't have said it then.

DR DAVIES (*entering*): Oh, Beattie?

BEATTIE: Yes, Mr David –

DR DAVIES: Will you take some food up to Miss Prentiss. I want her to stay with Mr Owen for a while.

GERTRUDE (*entering*): Is that you David?

DR DAVIES: Yes, Mr Vaughan is more comfortable now. He should be asleep again soon.

GERTRUDE: We have no intention of disturbing him (*sternly*).

DR DAVIES: You see, I want him to be as quiet as possible, to see as few people as possible.

GERTRUDE: You have made your wishes perfectly apparent.

(*Scene moves to surgery, Doctor and Dispenser.*)

VISITOR TO SURGERY: I heard Mr Morgan-Vaughan had an accident this morning. Was he hurt bad?

DR DAVIES: No, couple of ribs broken, that's all. Had a very lucky escape, though! Is there anything?

VISITOR TO SURGERY: Yes, Mrs Roberts again. At her age too!

DR DAVIES (*to Dispenser*): Put me out twenty-five one grain luminol tablets, will you? And check through this bag. I'll be back as soon as I've seen Mrs Roberts.

DISPENSER: Very good, Dr Davies.

(*Scene changes to Owen's bedroom.*)

OWEN MORGAN-VAUGHAN: Claire! Claire! Come quickly!

CLAIRE PRENTISS: What's the matter?

OWEN MORGAN-VAUGHAN: I have a nightmare! And I've been thinking too! You see, if they don't get any money when I die, there's no point in their killing me. So I – it came in a flash! I'm going to leave all my money to you. Phone me up that solicitor of mine, what's his name? Amos Blackguard? No, no, Beynon – Beynon, that's it! Tell him it's urgent. Tell him to stop whatever he's doing and come over here. I don't care who he's chiselling. It's a matter of life and death.

(*Scene changes to dispensary.*)

DR DAVIES: Mrs Roberts will be another couple of hours at least. I've time to take that luminol over to Vaughan's. You got it ready?

DISPENSER: Doctor, did you use strychnine last night?

DR DAVIES: No.

DISPENSER: There were seven tablets left in the bottle. I know because I checked them. There's only six left now.

DR DAVIES: You perfectly certain of that?

DISPENSER: Of course. I thought you ought to know. It's a dangerous thing to leave lying about.

(*Scene returns to House.*)

CLAIRE PRENTISS (*phoning*): Mr Beynon? Mr Emrys Beynon? I'm so glad to have got hold of you. I'm speaking for Owen Morgan-Vaughan who's just met with rather a serious accident. He's at his sister's house in Cwmglas. Do you know? Oh good, because he'd like you to come over here right away. He wants to make a new will. Yes, I'm afraid it's most urgent. When can we expect you? This afternoon? Oh thank-you very much, Mr Beynon. Goodbye.

GERTRUDE (*overhearing*): If Owen is awake and able to make a new will I am going to see for myself how ill he really is.

CLAIRE PRENTISS: Well, it's against Doctor's orders.

GERTRUDE: David's?

CLAIRE PRENTISS: Against Dr David's orders.

GERTRUDE: I accept no orders from anyone in my own house ...

MAUD: Isobel, we're being shut out.

ISOBEL: Why are we being shut out?

(*Scene moves to Owen's bedroom.*)

OWEN MORGAN-VAUGHAN: I'm not going to die. I'm not going to die! That's why I'm making a new will. I've planned it. Anything happens to me, everything goes to Claire. I am making her my sole heiress.

DR DAVIES: When did he wake?

CLAIRE PRENTISS: Just now.

DR DAVIES: He shouldn't have visitors, Miss Vaughan, the quieter he keeps the quicker those ribs are going to mend. Are you sleepy? (*to Owen*).

OWEN MORGAN-VAUGHAN: No. Never.

DR DAVIES: Give me a glass of water, please. Oh, um, perhaps I'd better leave these with you (*gives tablets to Claire*). Give him two now and two more tonight. And, Miss Vaughan, I think we'd better leave him now.

GERTRUDE: Dr Davies, I'm not at all pleased with your behaviour, will you wait for me downstairs? Miss Prentiss, I'd like a word with you in my room ...

(*In Gertrude's room.*)

ISOBEL: We came in here, Gertrude, in case you wanted us.

GERTRUDE: You were quite right. What I have to ask Miss Prentiss concerns us all. Am I to understand, Miss Prentiss, that my brother has sent for his solicitor in order to make a new will, and that under the terms of this will *you* are the sole heiress to the Morgan-Vaughan property?

CLAIRE PRENTISS: Yes.

GERTRUDE: Do you think that we are going to allow this? Do you think that we will allow it? Do you? Do you?

(*Scene returns to sitting room.*)

DR DAVIES (*to Claire*): Are you cold?

CLAIRE PRENTISS: Yes.

DR DAVIES: Could she have a hot water bottle, Miss Vaughan?

GERTRUDE: Of course.

DR DAVIES: The luminol. What happened to it?

CLAIRE PRENTISS: I don't know. I had the box in my hand.

GERTRUDE: I'll find it. (*goes out*)

CLAIRE PRENTISS: David! She's mad! Please don't leave me alone.

DR DAVIES: I'm not going to, not until you're safely asleep.

CLAIRE PRENTISS: Not when I'm asleep, either. Please, not! I'm so frightened!

DR DAVIES: But there's no need to be, my dear.

CLAIRE PRENTISS: David, you must listen. (*Maud comes in.*)

MAUD: Oh I do hope you're better, Miss Prentiss. We were so surprised when you fainted. I liked you when you fainted.

DR DAVIES: Did you find the pills Miss Prentiss had in her hand?

MAUD: Yes, I've got them. Here.

DR DAVIES: Could I have a glass of water please.

MAUD: Shall I take those?

DR DAVIES: No, we'll leave Miss Prentiss now. I want her to get some sleep.

BEATTIE (*entering*):   You're wanted on the phone, Dr Davies. It's the surgery.

DR DAVIES: Thank you, Beattie ... (*on phone*) Yes! Oh tell them I'm coming right away. No, I've got my bag with me. Yes, I have, I've found it. All right, goodbye. Oh, Miss Vaughan, I'm called away on a case. I'm afraid I shan't be back until this evening. They should sleep for some time.

GERTRUDE: I shan't disturb them. It's cold and dank upstairs, I've told Thomas to put on the heating.

(*Scene moves to surgery, Dr Davies talking to the Dispenser.*)

DR DAVIES: You got those strychnine tablets?

DISPENSER: Yes. Do you want them? ... Have you found it?

DR DAVIES: Yes, I'd like to see the last prescription I gave Miss Isobel Morgan-Vaughan.

DISPENSER: The arsenic for rheumatoid arthritis?

DR DAVIES: Yes, I want to check the strength we are giving her at the moment.

DISPENSER: How's she responding to the treatment?

DR DAVIES: Oh, very well, thanks. I'll be up at Morlais House, if I'm wanted.

DISPENSER: Very good, Doctor.

(*Doctor returns later to the house.*)

BEATTIE (*talking to Doctor at Morlais House*):   The ladies are at the Institute, Dr Davies. It is their afternoon. I think Mr Owen and Miss Prentiss are still sleeping. I was told *not* to disturb them.

(*Sounds of coughing. Doctor rushes off to rooms.*)

BEATTIE: What is it Dr Davies? What has happened?

DR DAVIES: These two rooms are chock full of fumes from humidity. Make some strong tea quickly ... (*in basement boiler room, talking to Thomas*) Why are you burning coke?

THOMAS: Miss Gertrude told me to. She said it would be quicker.

(*In Beattie's kitchen.*)

DR DAVIES: Who's been playing around with this stove? Someone's been playing tricks with the heating, dangerous tricks, coke fumes were flowing directly through to Mr Owen's and Miss Claire's rooms. They were asleep, under a sleeping draught, both of them. If I hadn't come back when I did they'd have been dead in an hour, who did it, Beattie? I need to *know*. Was it Thomas? Thomas who threw the stone at Mr Owen? Thomas who moved the barrier this morning? You're going to tell me, one of you.

(*Thomas breaks down, sobbing and in tears.*)

BEATTIE: You think because I am tied to this house with a son who's simple that I am one of them. Poor Beattie that nobody will take in because of him! Miss Gertrude went down to the stove.

CLAIRE PRENTISS (*enters kitchen*):   Beattie, may I have a cup of tea, please?

BEATTIE: Yes, Miss, I'll bring it in to you! ... Do you believe me now?

(*Gertrude returns to the House.*)

GERTRUDE: Beattie? No, David. Oh you're back much sooner than you expected.

DR DAVIES: Yes, a good deal sooner than any of us expected.

GERTRUDE: Oh, you've managed to persuade Miss Prentiss to leave her sick bed. That was clever of you. Now we can all have tea together (*calmly*).

CLAIRE PRENTISS: Do you mind if I sit down?

MR PRICE (*with Gertrude*):   There's a nasty shock it must have been. All of us in the village were *so* distressed to hear of the accident. We *bled* for you and Owen Morgan-Vaughan. You cannot understand how beloved the Morgan-Vaughans are! Our stay and salvation! (*sanctimoniously*)

CLAIRE PRENTISS: I think I'll now lie down a bit.

GERTRUDE: Beattie was just going to bring tea.

DR DAVIES: She can take it up to her.

GERTRUDE: As you like. (*leaves*)

CLAIRE PRENTISS: David, I'm trapped! Can't stand it!

DR DAVIES: No we're not. As soon as I've taken you upstairs I'm going out. I can't telephone from here, but I've got to get an ambulance for Mr Vaughan. You'll have to look after him while I'm away. Mr Price will go on talking in there for hours, I know him, and they can't do anything to either of you while he's still here. Remember that. (*leaves*)

(*Three sisters together with Mr Price.*)

ISOBEL: Thank you, Gertrude (*taking tea*).

GERTRUDE: I've seen the Borough Council, and sat through interminable meetings. They flatly refuse to re-build the cottages.

MAUD: Gertrude went for a walk this morning all by herself, right down to the gates.

MR PRICE: Ah yes, and what was their attitude?

GERTRUDE: They say that the village is finished now that the mine is worked out. They say it's dead. It's no place to live in at all. It's only for old people to die in. Therefore it's not worthwhile re-building. They will find accommodation for the victims in another parish.

MR PRICE: So the old are to be deprived of their last privilege! They will not be allowed to spend their declining years in their own valley.

(*Solicitor arrives, and is ushered in with his clerk.*)

GERTRUDE: I'm afraid he's far too ill!

SOLICITOR: He can't be too ill to see me, Miss Morgan-Vaughan. He wants me to alter his will. It's going to cost him something too!

CLAIRE PRENTISS: I'm Claire Prentiss, I spoke to you this morning.

SOLICITOR: I recognise that very charming voice. Soprano!

CLAIRE PRENTISS: Mr Vaughan would like to see you right away.

SOLICITOR (*pompous and precise of speech*): Soprano, like a madame … Now about witnesses. This is Evan Evans, Miss Prentiss, one of my clerks. I took the precaution of bringing him along to act in that very capacity. Usually do in a case of this kind. Client's last will and testament may be in the bosom of his family. That can be awkward, you understand. You are an outsider aren't you, Miss Prentiss, so we'll use you as second witness.

CLAIRE PRENTISS: I'm afraid not. You'll soon understand why.

SOLICITOR: Beneficiary?

GERTRUDE: That's one of the reasons why I've been trying to prevent you from seeing my brother in his present condition. Owing to his accident, I am afraid he's not quite normal.

SOLICITOR: You mean he's not in his right mind?

GERTRUDE: I think that is so.

SOLICITOR: Where's the Doctor?

CLAIRE PRENTISS: He'll be back any time now.

SOLICITOR: Excellent! If I have any doubts as to his mental condition I can expect the Doctor?

CLAIRE PRENTISS: Oh yes.

SOLICITOR: Who's that fellow?

CLAIRE PRENTISS: Oh that's Mr Price, the baptist minister.

SOLICITOR (*with satisfaction*): Baptist! Well, well.

GERTRUDE: Mr Price, will you be so accommodating as to accompany me upstairs. Mr Owen Morgan-Vaughan's making a new will. (*They go upstairs.*)

(*In Owen's bedroom.*)

OWEN MORGAN-VAUGHAN: No! Who said I'm not in my right mind? You? You forensic ferret?

SOLICITOR: It's a point, Mr Vaughan. The will might be contested on those grounds.

MR PRICE: I for one contest your decision now, Mr Owen. I beg you to take thought before you make this will. Your sisters will be left destitute.

SOLICITOR: Now, have you ever known Mr Vaughan refuse his sisters any reasonable request? Has he ever left them destitute? Has it never occurred to you that in making this will they are still his foremost charge? You know nothing about his business affairs. Suppose he were in disastrous financial circumstances and this was the only way of saving his sisters from becoming involved? I'm disappointed in *you*, Mr Price. You are the last person I should have suspected of harbouring uncharitable thoughts, and a Baptist Minister too!

MR PRICE: I apologise, Mr Owen.

(*Scene in hall.*)

CLAIRE PRENTISS: Is it all right?

DR DAVIES: No! We can't go before tomorrow morning. We'll have to stay the night.

MAUD: Oh, David, I am so glad you've come. We are desperately worried about Owen. You said he was too ill to see us, yet Miss Prentiss has sent three men to his room to talk business with him. Go and send them away at once! It's your responsibility.

(*In Owen's room.*)

DR DAVIES: I must ask you gentlemen to leave this room at once. Mr Vaughan is a very sick man.

SOLICITOR: We are just leaving, Doctor, Good day, Mr Morgan-Vaughan.

EVAN EVANS (*clerk*): Good day, Mr Owen.

DR DAVIES: You don't obey my instructions, Mr Vaughan!

OWEN MORGAN-VAUGHAN: No, but I've saved my life.

SOLICITOR (*leaving*): I'll give you a lift to the village, Price.

GERTRUDE: We'll excuse you for leaving us, Mr Price. I am quite aware it must be very embarrassing for you. I hope you found where your duty lay.

MR PRICE: I did, Miss Gertrude. I am convinced your brother is acting for the best. Good night, Miss Gertrude. (*leaves*)

GERTRUDE: Now, Miss Prentiss, I am going to take you to your room. You must be worn out. Come with me. (*takes her to room*) I suggest you take off your clothes and get straight into bed.

CLAIRE PRENTISS: No! I only want to rest for an hour or so. I'll be all right.

GERTRUDE: As you wish. I'll see you're left undisturbed.

(*Scene in hall.*)

DR DAVIES: But I couldn't get any sense out of any of them. What were you all doing in Mr Owen's room?

MR PRICE: Mr Owen was making a new will. I was one of the witnesses. I must admit I had some serious misgivings at first. It seemed strange he wished to leave all his money to his secretary.

DR DAVIES: Miss Prentiss?

MR PRICE: Yes.

DR DAVIES: So that's what he meant when he said he'd saved his life. He's made safe at her expense! It's her life that's in danger now. She mustn't be left up there alone!

GERTRUDE (*upstairs*):   Miss Prentiss! Miss Prentiss! Miss Prentiss!

CLAIRE PRENTISS: Yes.

GERTRUDE: Come here, it's Owen! ...

OWEN MORGAN-VAUGHAN: Claire!

CLAIRE PRENTISS: Owen! Owen, what's happening? (*screams*) Owen! Owen!

(*Violent sounds, screams, explosions, cries of 'Down! Down! Down!' Upper part of the house begins to crumble and collapse, and the whole house begins to give way and disintegrate in the renewed subsidence. The three sisters, still upstairs, are killed in the collapse of the building ... The rest safely flee the disaster.*)

(The final scene in chapel, with the congregation singing a Welsh funeral hymn, which grows fainter but continues as background. Welsh chapel hymn singing during Mr Price's speech, which is both funereal, sanctimonious and plangent, and not without the emotional chanting hwyl.)

MR PRICE: And we are gathered here on this most mournful occasion to pay our last respects to the departed, for the sins they have committed. And none of us is free from sin! *(taking on the Welsh hwyl)* My people! We can only pray for their forgiveness. But let us never in Cwmglas forget the dignity, the great dignity, the great love, the genial warmth, and the *profound* humanity of those dear ladies, Gertrude, Isobel and Maud. Now with us no longer.

No Room at the Inn

In *No Room at the Inn*, adapted from Joan Temple's 1945 stage play, Dylan Thomas's vivid and realistic dialogue re-creates the vernacular of war-time, its slang and common language, and the time of the Blitz, rationing, sweet coupons, spivs getting round the shortages, and the disrupted lives of civilians as well as those in the forces. It is war-time social drama that focuses on the sometimes grim plight and victimisation of child evacuees, themselves often Blitz orphans like Ronnie. Virginia Graham's *Spectator* review declared that: 'Miss Joan Temple's tormenting play, about war-time evacuee children billeted on a drunken slut has been turned into an equally tormenting film. *No Room at the Inn* gives Miss Freda Jackson ample scope to be as savagely nasty as she pleases, and I must say she is alarmingly successful. Miss Hermione Baddeley [as Mrs Waters] blowsily supports her and Miss Joan Dowling is admirable as a pert blackmailing adolescent.'[89] This perhaps overplays the torment, and fails to note the occasional humour, as in the children's dialogue and fantasies at play, the flirtations between Mrs Voray and her various shopkeeper friends and callers like the billeting officer Mr Burrells and Terence O'Rane, the evacuee Mary O'Rane's father, on a few days' leave from the navy. Indeed, O'Rane soon proves less interested in Mary's complaints than in Mrs Voray's sexual advances.

In his film version Dylan Thomas makes significant changes, mostly in widening the social world of Market Norton, which sounds like a small town set in Oxfordshire, where Thomas was then living. We meet Mrs Voray as she goes shopping and the local butcher, grocer and tobacconist are keen to please her with whatever extras they can provide in this time of rationing, and there is amusing flirtation and chat. Dylan Thomas's adaptation is also very conscious of class difference and the vivid, not to say racy, lifestyle and dialogue of Mrs Voray and her men friends contrast with the genteel concern for the children of such people as the vicar, Reverend Allworth, and Mrs Jarvis. Dylan Thomas's film adaptation focuses strongly on the reiteration of the theme implied in the title *No*

Room at the Inn, with its strong New Testament echoes chiming through the film. Mrs Voray is a hard-drinking, good-time girl who accepts a houseful of children for the money and ration coupons they bring in, but she does in fact give them a home, in contrast with the middle-class do-gooders who feel sorry for the children but find excuses not to have their daily lives disrupted by taking evacuees. They shed crocodile tears of sympathy but complain of the children's rough behaviour and language.

Thomas's dialogue is very responsive to class differences at this time, as in the comic bumbling figure of Reverend Allworth, reluctant to be disturbed from his alpine garden plants and his delight in their Latin names; while the snobbery of the middle-class Market Norton schoolgirls, as in their exchanges with the orphan Ronnie from Camberwell, is also a thread in this pattern of war-time life. In its opening up of the social life of the town the film also includes the lively debate among the town councillors, including Mrs Voray's gentlemen friends who aid and applaud her calculated contribution to the Council debate; her cunning in easily out-manoeuvring the schoolteacher Miss Drave's sincerity. In her anger she uses the word 'Judas' at the children's betrayal, Dylan Thomas again using New Testament analogy. Relatedly, in contrast with the play's opening 'Prologue' where police are investigating the death of Mrs Voray, seemingly suffocated with a pillow by the children, the film begins on a future Christmas Eve where the carol 'Once in Royal David's City' rings through a busy London store. The sales assistant, Mary O'Rane, recognises Norma Bates being arrested for shoplifting, and the introduction to the film turns strongly on the Christmas theme of the homeless child and Mary's memory of that childhood evacuation that made petty thieves of them both.

In the children's scenes Thomas's dialogue is particularly effective, as in Norma's story of Cinderella and the handsome prince played out in a south London setting of cockney slang 'down the Borough'. Interestingly, too, Mary O'Rane arrives as a rather priggish girl but becomes more attractive and likeable as she mixes with the other children and learns their ways of survival, especially in her friendship and loyalty to Ronnie. Again the dialogue in the pub when Mrs Voray arrives late and is ditched by her spiv friend for his newly picked-up girlfriend, splendidly played by a young Dora Bryan, shows Dylan Thomas's quick evocation of scene and atmosphere in this vivid war-time story.

NO ROOM AT THE INN

(A large crowded store, busy with Christmas shoppers, the carol 'Once in Royal David's City', its tale of the manger as bed for the child aptly introducing the opening scene as the words and music ring out.)

MARY O'RANE: I'm an assistant here. There was one evening I will always remember. It was Christmas Eve, just before closing. There was the usual crowds of last-minute shoppers. In that last hour everyone in the world wants to come in, and they all want to be served at once. I had just gone away from my counter for a moment when I looked back and saw that a crowd had begun to collect around it. Probably someone caught shoplifting I thought. And then I saw who it was, Norma, Norma Bates, and I shuddered to think how easily it might have been me. The detective was marching her away to the manager's office. Yes, Norma is a thief. I know that. I know much more than that. I know *why* she is a thief. You see, once I thought stealing was quite unimportant. How well I remember, years ago, walking with Mr Burrells through the railway arch, and catching my first glimpse of that dreadful house (*sound of train rushing*). Poor Norma, I remember ...

(*Mr Burrells arrives with the child Mary O'Rane, knocks and Mrs Voray comes to the door.*)

MRS VORAY: Oh, it's you again is it? Now, now children, quiet. (*calls into the house*) Quiet! I like to see them enjoying themselves, I like having children about the house, you know, especially other people's. Shut up! (*shouting*) can't yer! (*House becomes quiet.*) Wonder what a bit of control can do, isn't it! You ought to try it some times.

MR BURRELLS: Oh, well really, Mrs Voray.

MRS VORAY: Oh, Mrs Voray, ay! Very high and mighty this morning, aren't we, very cut glass!

MR BURRELLS: Alright then. Aggie.

MRS VORAY: That's more like it, cockle. (*looking at Mary*) Who's she?

MR BURRELLS: That's the young girl I –

MRS VORAY: Oh, you don't say. What d'you think I thought she was, a monkey on a stick? Hm, quite the little lady, isn't she. Still got the young madam by the looks of her.

MR BURRELLS: Shall I bring her in?

MRS VORAY: No, she can stop where she is. Do her good to take a back seat. (*Mr Burrells comes into the house.*) Put yourself down. Take the weight off your watch chain! 'Ere, we don't want you sat there, Perce, that's the old woman's sofa, the springs'll give way.

MR BURRELLS: Well, what about this girl? Come on, Aggie, be a pal.

MRS VORAY: Be a pal, what for? Why should I have all your waifs and strays? Don't tell me. I'm not a doss house.

MR BURRELLS: I know but –

MRS VORAY: Now don't try and boss over me. I don't want no more kids.

MR BURRELLS: Only this one.

MRS VORAY (*mockingly*):   I know, I know. You're the only one wot'll take her in Mrs Voray. You've got a heart of gold, Mrs Voray. Well, you can't feed the kids on a heart of gold.

MR BURRELLS: I know but (*whispers*) her mother died yesterday.

MRS VORAY: Alright, her mother died yesterday. So what? Hasn't the kid got no father?

MR BURRELLS: He's at sea in the merchant navy. Oh come on now, there's a good girl.

MRS VORAY: Well! I've been called some *things* in me time! Hasn't she got any relations that'll take her?

MR BURRELLS: Well, from what I heard, her mother married beneath her (*confiding*).

MRS VORAY: Ah? Now I did the same meself. Remember Herbie? Nobody bothered about his family tree except the dog. What's her name?

MR BURRELLS: Mary O'Rane.

MRS VORAY: Hm! You can see me waiting on her hand and foot can't you? As if I 'aven't got enough on my plate with these four.

MR BURRELLS (*in confidential tone*):   I believe her mother left a bit of money. We can't touch that yet, of course. But later on. If you take her in now, it'll stand you in good stead with the council too.

MRS VORAY: Oh, alright, bring her in.

MR BURRELLS: Mary! Mary, come in m'dear. Mrs Voray, this is Mary O'Rane.

MRS VORAY: Pleased to meet you, I'm sure. Pleased to meet you, I'm sure.

MARY O'RANE: Pleased to meet you, Mrs Voray.

MR BURRELLS: Mrs Voray's the lady who's going to give you a new home, Mary.

MRS VORAY: Now don't you be so previous, Mr Burrells. Anyway if I do take her in it means I'll have to put myself out quite a good deal, I might tell you.

MR BURRELLS: Oh, I've tried everywhere else.

MRS VORAY: I see, just making a convenience out of me, eh? (*turning to Mary*) Well, do you want to stop here or don't you? … Alright then, you'd better move in straight away. Is that all the luggage you've got? Well, well, well. Quite a wardrobe, isn't it!

MR BURRELLS: I'm sure we're very grateful to Mrs Voray.

MRS VORAY: Come on Mr Burrells, I'll take you to the front door …

MRS VORAY (*returning*):   Nobody'll take you in only me, eh. Well, well, well. Nice coat you got on though.

MARY O'RANE: Mummy had it made out of one of hers (*proudly*).

MRS VORAY: Oh, did she. I thought it didn't look like utility stuff. I'm afraid I can't let you wear it you know. It would not be fair on the other kids.

MARY O'RANE: Oh, but I *must* wear it. It's my best coat.

MRS VORAY: I dare say, but I'm afraid I can't let you. It would make the other kids jealous – you having a nice coat like that. No, I'm afraid I shan't be able to let you wear that coat. (*knock on door*)

JUDITH DRAVE: Good evening, are you Mrs Voray?

MRS VORAY: I am.

JUDITH DRAVE: I'm from the school. Norma Bates is in my class.

MRS VORAY: Oh, come inside.

JUDITH DRAVE: Why, Mary, what are you doing here?

MRS VORAY: Her mother's dead.

JUDITH DRAVE: Mary, my dear, I know. I'm so sorry. I was going to see you today.

MRS VORAY: Nobody else'll take her in only me.

JUDITH DRAVE: Oh, my dear!

MRS VORAY: Well, what's the matter with that?

JUDITH DRAVE: Nothing. I've brought you a note from the headmistress.

MRS VORAY: Oh, thanks.

JUDITH DRAVE: Don't worry, my dear, it won't be for long – I promise.

MRS VORAY: Now that's what I call funny, very funny indeed. I was just thinking I might go round to the school about this very thing.

JUDITH DRAVE: So you think the best line is to take the offensive?

MRS VORAY: Are you insinerating that I'm offensive? Now look here, I work myself till I'm fit to drop. Try it, try it, mark you, to keep these kids clean and decent. But if the children have been brought up like little hooligans you don't change them into angels by evacuating them.

JUDITH DRAVE: Even if they're rough in their behaviour it's up to you to keep them clean.

MRS VORAY: For God's sake, what d'you think this is – a creech?

JUDITH DRAVE: What time do the children leave the house in the morning?

MRS VORAY: In time to get to school punctual.

JUDITH DRAVE: Then why do they arrive so filthy if they've started out clean?

MRS VORAY: 'Ere, 'ave you got any kids of your own?

JUDITH DRAVE: No.

MRS VORAY: No, I thought not. Well, there ain't much you can tell me about kids. I've buried some of my own.

JUDITH DRAVE: Doesn't look as if you're a great success, does it?

MRS VORAY: Now look here Miss, you don't think this place is good enough for Mary, do you? Alright, take her away. *You* give her a home.

JUDITH DRAVE: I wish I could, but I've only got a small room in a hostel.

MRS VORAY: Alright then. Now get this. I'm standing no interference from the likes of you. You'll see.

JUDITH DRAVE: Goodbye, Mary dear. I promise.

MRS VORAY: Good afternoon. *Miss.*

(Mrs Voray in living room, Judith Drave has left.)

MRS VORAY: Hm! Norma! Norma! Come you down 'ere. I want you. Interfering lot, these teachers, aren't they, ducks! All lot of old maids and all – never could abide old maids meself (*with contempt*). Gimme the 'orrors.

MARY O'RANE: But Mrs Drave's awfully nice (*in middle-class voice*).

MRS VORAY: Oh, I dare say – but I'm the only one with the grain of decency wot took you in. Aren't I?

MARY O'RANE: Yes.

MRS VORAY: Well, I only hope you're going to behave yourself, that's all. Just help with the housework. And you'll have to learn to keep your trap shut. Get my meaning?
       Well, what you looking like a wet week for? (*to Norma, who has just entered*) Takes all sorts to make a world, doesn't it?

MRS WATERS (*shouting from front door*):   Only me, Mrs Voray!

MRS VORAY: Oh, come right inside, Mrs Waters.

MRS WATERS: Hello ducks! (*seeing Mary*) Oh, so you're taking her in are yer?

MRS VORAY: Ay, she's another little bit of Gawd'elp-you.

MRS WATERS: But I thought you was having *my* friends for a couple of nights?

MRS VORAY (*to children*):   Out now, kids. Go and play in the street – and if you cut yourself on that broken glass I'll crown yer.

MRS WATERS: It is alright about my *friends* then?

MRS VORAY: Of course it's alright. (*She brings a bottle of gin and two glasses. Mrs Waters sits down.*)

(*Scene moves to children playing on ash tip, near the gas works and the house.*)

LILY: Look at me! Look at me! Look at me, Rene – I'm king of the ash tip.

IRENE: Garn, you can't be king. You ain't a man. You're a woman, you are.

NORMA: Oh, let her be king if she wants to.

IRENE (*seeing Mary*):   Who's she?

NORMA: Oh, she's Mary O'Rane. In my class in school. Huh! Stuck-up little faggot!

LILY: Well, what's she doing 'ere? …

MARY O'RANE: But I'm going away again.

LILY: Where to, ducks?

MARY O'RANE: I'm going to friends.

NORMA: Huh! Lord and Lady gobstopper!

IRENE: Oh, shut up Norm! Can't you see she's been crying? What's the matter?

MARY O'RANE: My mother died.

LILY: My ma's gone off with a soldier (*proudly*).

MARY O'RANE: Oh, I wish I could go away!

IRENE: So do we!

MARY O'RANE: There's nowhere else to go. No one will take me in.

IRENE: Nor us!

LILY: We ain't respectable ...

(*Ronnie appears.*)

IRENE: He's Ronnie.

LILY: He's a blitz orphan ...

MARY O'RANE: I'm frightened of her.

NORMA: Nothing to what you will be, ducks.

MARY O'RANE: Does she hit you?

IRENE: Oh no, she don't hit yer.

LILY: Last week she shut Ron up in the coal hole all night.

MARY O'RANE: In the coal hole?

NORMA: That's where the rats live. As big as guinea pigs they are.

LILY: Bigger ...

MARY O'RANE: Had you been *very* naughty, Ronnie?

RONNIE: I wanted my mum, and I kept crying.

MARY O'RANE: Oh, we must go away from here, please. There's five of us now – they'd *have* to take notice!

NORMA: They'd only take us back here, instead of up the police station. What's the good?

IRENE (*dancing on ash tip*): 'Ere, my mum's a dancer. I'll be a dancer too, one day!

NORMA: Perhaps you won't be so stuck-up now, Mary O'Rane, wouldn't mix with me at school because you thought I was dirty. Now you got to sleep next to me in bed. Next to all of us. See, like sardines in a tin ...

(*Scene moves to sitting room, breakfast.*)

MARY O'RANE (*children at table*): Where's Mrs Voray?

(*Mrs Waters is getting the breakfast.*)

MRS WATERS: Oh, her ladyship, she don't get up till twelve.

NORMA: Except when she's got an hangover.

MRS WATERS: Then she don't get up till tea-time!

NORMA: Then she don't drink tea! (*Children laugh.*)

RONNIE: 'Ere you do yer'self alright don't yer (*sees Mrs Waters preparing herself a large cooked breakfast*).

MRS WATERS: You shut your trap and go off to school. Go, all of you!

(*Scene in classroom, teacher addressing children.*)

JUDITH DRAVE (*in deliberate, correct voice*): I've been correcting the essays you wrote last week, when I gave you the choice of two subjects, 'My Home Town' for those girls who have always lived here, and 'My Impressions of Market Norton' for our war-time guests. Shelley Greenwood, your essay's particularly good and I am going to read it out at the end of this lesson if there's time because I think it may help all of us to understand each other better. Some of the new girls don't really understand us yet, alas! For instance, here's one – and she doesn't like Market Norton a bit. She says 'I think that all the girls are a lot of swanky, stuck-up' – I can't quite make out this word – 'and they think we don't know anything – and they don't want us here. The whole place is dull as dishwater, and there isn't any fun and it's full of a lot of' – I can't – er – quite make this out either.

NORMA: 'Stinkers' is the word Miss (*some of the class breaks into laughter*). Stinkers!

(*Mrs Voray out shopping. Goes in to Mr Green's, the Grocer.*)

MR GREEN: Hello, Mrs Voray! Good afternoon, Mrs Voray!

MRS VORAY: Good afternoon, Mr Green, how's the lumbago keeping, Mr Green?

MR GREEN: Very troublesome, thank you!

MRS VORAY: Here we are, here's the ration books.

MR GREEN: Thank you. Yes, I think we can manage that (*looking at her ration books and grocery list*). Now, did the vicar's wife have the last tin I wonder. Oh, never mind! (*in friendly manner*) I'll see what I can do!

(Scene of children playing in the house and watching the heavy rain through the window.)

MARY: *(in sing-song voice)*:   Rain, rain, go to Spain, never show your face again. Specially on Sunday – we could go to the park, we could, if it wasn't raining.

RONNIE: 'Ere, I got a catapult! I swopped it in school. I hit a cat with it.

MARY: What you swop it for?

RONNIE: Told him three new swear words.

MARY: Who told you?

RONNIE: Nobody told me 'em. *She* called me 'em.

MARY: You shouldn't swear, Ronnie. You shouldn't hit cats either.

RONNIE: It was only a little cat!

MARY: Oh, why is it raining!

(Later children are looking in sideboard drawers for sweet coupons. Norma finds some money. Also letters.)

NORMA *(pocketing money)*:   Finding's keeping's, eh! ... 'Ere! Love letters!

NORMA *(reading letter)*:   'You're a bit of alright Aggie, and whenever I see you I feel' – Oh, this is better! 'And when I see you I feel' –

(Scene of children listening as Norma reads letter changes again to Mrs Voray shopping. She goes into butcher.)

BUTCHER: Hello stranger!

MRS VORAY: Hello!

BUTCHER: Haven't seen you round the usual lately, where you been putting yourself?

MRS VORAY: I'll tell you later *(smiling)*. Well what you got? *(They talk flirtatiously.)*

BUTCHER: Got a nice bit of tripe – under the counter for you, Agg.

MRS VORAY: Oh, I know you have! I read it in your letter.

BUTCHER: Aggie, you're a caution! And I got a drop of what you fancy at the back an' all.

MRS VORAY: You never 'ave!

BUTCHER: I have! (*laughs, and calls to butcher's boy*) Here, Gilbert! Come along m'lad, and look after the shop a minute, will you? This way lady!

(*Scene changes to children reading letters.*)

NORMA: 'I like a woman who is a woman. I like a woman of the world. I like you, Aggie!'

LILY: He's barmy.

IRENE: Who is it?

NORMA: It says at the end 'must stop now, Harold'. Cor blimey! What's he got to stop for now! 'E's better than *Pam's Paper*! (*putting letter aside and searching drawer*) Oh, where's them coupons? What she do with them? (*looks through window*) There's old Charlie! Wotcher, Charlie! 'Ere! You got any sweet coupons? What's that on the rubbish heap, Charlie, your mother-in-law? (*singing*) Charlie, Charlie, I can smell your breath, Charlie, Charlie, who's been drinking meths? 'Ere there's a man coming up the hill. He's a sailor! Sober too!

RONNIE (*sadly*):   Her dad's come to take her away!

(*Scene changes to Mrs Voray still shopping, entering tobacconist's shop.*)

TOBACCONIST: Hello, Mrs Voray.

MRS VORAY: Good afternoon (*rather stiffly*).

TOBACCONIST: And of what can I have the pleasure? Anything in the fancy goods? I got a nice little line here. A friend of mine up in Nottingham recommended them to me last week. It's garters *with* initials (*confidentially*).

MRS VORAY: No thanks, not my style.

TOBACCONIST: I didn't see you at Palais last Saturday, Mrs Voray. Not a bad little hop, a bit tame though. They've got Al Ace and his Joysticks this week.

MRS VORAY: How much on these? (*showing sweet coupons*)

TOBACCONIST: Oh, there's half a pound 'ere, and there's mmm ... three quarters here.

MRS VORAY: I'll take half a pound of satin crunchies.

TOBACCONIST: Sweets for the sweet! I'm not much of a one for the Palais, you know. Especially on me own. Not that there isn't plenty of girls, mind you. Fly bits too, some of them! But I don't know, a man gets tired of that sort of thing. I mean it's experience that counts. You know what I mean?

NEW CUSTOMER: You got any cigars? (*A stranger, but clearly well-off. Mrs Voray shows interest.*)

TOBACCONIST: Excuse me, sir, I'm serving the lady.

MRS VORAY: Oh, that's quite alright, you can serve the gentleman first, if you like, I don't mind, I'm sure.

CUSTOMER: Well, give me the best you've got. I'll take three.

TOBACCONIST: That'll be fifteen shillings. (*Customer leaves briskly.*) Some people have got the manners of pigs! I'd like to have a few words with him alone.

MRS VORAY: Who is it?

TOBACCONIST: I don't know, he's a stranger to me, I'm glad to say. (*looking at Mrs Voray's sweet coupons*) There's still three quarters here.

MRS VORAY: What? Alright, give me some of them liquor chocolates.

TOBACCONIST: Oh, I've seen plenty of his sort in Nottingham. I seen plenty of the right sort, too. You know what I mean? I was going past 'The Black Boy' one day – you know the old 'Black Boy' – and there was one of the smartest bits of homework.

MRS VORAY: Come on, get a move on!

(*Scene closes. Next scene back in the house, Mary O'Rane's father has just arrived.*)

TERENCE O'RANE: Well, tell me, darling, why don't you like this place? Looks alright to me.

LILY: You ain't seen old ma Voray!

TERENCE O'RANE: Who's she? The lady that keeps the house?

NORMA: That's her.

MARY O'RANE: Dearest Daddy, she's got claws, and I think she's got a fork tail, too. Don't you, Ronald?

TERENCE O'RANE: As bad as all that! We'll have to do something about this.

MARY O'RANE: I knew you would! (*showing him Ronnie*) He's nine years old, Daddy, and they dropped a bomb on his house. Everyone was killed except him. He's an orphan now, and, Daddy, I've promised he can come and live with us forever and ever!

TERENCE O'RANE: Of course he can one day. One day soon. Please don't think I'd let you stay here if you don't like it. And we'll have a *proper* home too.

MARY O'RANE: One day? But I've been waiting *every* day for you to come and take me away. And Ronnie too! You can't leave us here, Daddy. Mummy wouldn't have ever let us stay. She'd have taken us away. Anywhere!

TERENCE O'RANE: But what's the matter with the place, honey? The old girl doesn't knock you about does she?

MARY O'RANE: No. But she frightens me.

TERENCE O'RANE: I'll put the fear of God into that one. I'll give her *one look*.

(*Mrs Voray enters, and O'Rane is taken aback by her appearance and manner, not at all the woman he expected.*)

MARY O'RANE: This is my daddy!

MRS VORAY: Pleased to meet you, I'm sure.

TERENCE O'RANE: How do you do, Mrs—?

MRS VORAY: Voray – a gentleman once told me it was French, not that my husband was French, of course. Well, glad to see your dad, Mary?

TERENCE O'RANE: Yes, well, Mrs Voray, Mary feels that ...

MRS VORAY: Sit down, Mr O'Rane. Make yourself comfortable. It isn't often we have a sailor in the parlour, you know. Oh, she's been a brave girl. It hasn't been easy for her as you might guess. But she's been a brave girl. I'll say that for her. Of course some people might say she didn't show much feeling, but I know different. You soon learn to hide your feelings, don't you, when people shut the door in your face and refuse to give you a home? I suppose Mary told you I was the only one what'd take her in.

TERENCE O'RANE: Yes, she did say something of the sort.

MARY O'RANE: Oh, Daddy, please.

MRS VORAY: Make yourself comfortable. I've got a drop of the thing in the scullery you'll like – make yourself at home now.

TERENCE O'RANE: I'll tell you what, Mary, go out with your friends and get some sweets, the lot of you.

MRS VORAY: What's that I hear?

NORMA: No, thank you, Mr O'Rane, you see we can't buy sweets without coupons. (*Children leave, apart from Mary.*)

TERENCE O'RANE: Nice little chap, Ronnie.

MRS VORAY: Well, Mary, what are you waiting for?

MARY O'RANE: If you're going to talk to my daddy, I'm staying here.

TERENCE O'RANE: Perhaps I'd better have a little talk with the lady, first, and then you can –

MARY O'RANE: When shall I come back?

TERENCE O'RANE: Well, about ten minutes.

MARY O'RANE: Five minutes, please, Daddy. (*leaves*)

MRS VORAY: There, that child never ought to be wearing her mother's watch. She'll only break it one of these days when she's out playing. Wouldn't it be better if you were to keep it for her?

TERENCE O'RANE: Well, maybe you're right.

MRS VORAY: Well, happy days, Jack – and nights! How long you got? (*They drink.*)

TERENCE O'RANE: Just the weekend.

MRS VORAY: And where you stopping?

TERENCE O'RANE: Oh, I'm not particular.

MRS VORAY: Oh, aren't you? Well, I am. I'm very particular who sleeps on *my* sofa.

TERENCE O'RANE: Is that where I'm sleeping?

MRS VORAY: Well, it just depends (*suggestively*). It depends on your promise to behave yourself. You see, I know what you sailors are when you come ashore.

TERENCE O'RANE: Oh, no, I'm different.

MRS VORAY (*smiling and flirtatious*):   Are you really! Well I never did! (*calls to children, in other room*) Go on now! Run out and play! The rain's stopped. (*Children go out.*)

NORMA: Cor blimey, if this ain't rain, what is it then? Somebody spitting! Huh! (*looking back through window*) Look at the orphans of the storm! Bet old mother Nasty's got her dad where she wants him. He hasn't got a chance. He's putty in 'er hands – I read that in a book.

(*Scene returns to living room.*)

MRS VORAY: Let's have a fag, shall we?

TERENCE O'RANE: Thank you, Mrs Voray.

MRS VORAY: You can call me Aggie, if you like Jack.

TERENCE O'RANE: That's mighty friendly of you, Aggie.

MRS VORAY: Of course I know I'm easy-going and all that. Only if you stop here for the weekend, you might perhaps think I was *too* easy-going. Your wife thought she was a superior sort of person?

TERENCE O'RANE: She was that.

MRS VORAY: A bit difficult to live with, perhaps? I hear that your wife give out that she'd married beneath her.

TERENCE O'RANE: Well ...

MRS VORAY: It's awful what folk will say about you behind your back, isn't it? Oh, you don't have to tell me, Jack. I know just what you had to put up with. I do really. (*Mary returns.*)

MARY O'RANE: It's more than five minutes, Daddy.

MRS VORAY: That child never ought to be wearing her mother's watch. She'll only break it.

TERENCE O'RANE: That's right.

MARY O'RANE: I'd never break Mummy's watch!

TERENCE O'RANE: Well, you'd better give it to your dad, he'll take care of it for you.

MARY O'RANE: No! Mummy said I could keep it – always.

TERENCE O'RANE: By rights it's mine, honey. I sort of gave it to Mum, you know.

MARY O'RANE: But it's mine!

TERENCE O'RANE: Ah, there's a good girl, give it to Daddy.

MARY O'RANE (*sadly*): Alright. But I *will* have it back when I grow up, won't I, Daddy?

MRS VORAY: What d'you think your dad's going to do with it, Miss Suspicious?

MARY O'RANE: He might give it away. (*turns and walks from room*)

TERENCE O'RANE: You know, I expected someone quite different from you!

(*After a few drinks they go to the pub, and scene moves to children in bed.*)

IRENE: Come on, tell us a story, a funny story.

NORMA: Oh, don't know no stories.

LILY: Oh come on Norm, tell us a weepy one.

NORMA: Oh why don't you ask *her*? She's top of our class ... of course – she knows all the stories.

MARY O'RANE: Oh no, you tell it Norm. You tell them beautifully. Red Riding Hood, Babes in the Wood, Gone with the Wind, Cinderella.

NORMA: O alright then, Cinder-blooming-rella. You asked for it didn't yer! Well once upon a time, and a long time ago it was ... so long ago you could pop in a shop and ask for an a'porth of Dolly Mixtures – and they'd give you a bag as big as a barrage balloon – no coupons either. The three sisters, they lived right next door to the pawn shop.

LILY: That's where you lived Norm!

NORMA: One was called Dirty-Gertie, one was called Cosy-Rosie, and the third was –

RONNIE: Cinderella!

NORMA: Who's telling this 'ere story, you or me! Well, Dirty-Gertie and Cosie-Rosie were a couple of artists down the Borough. Little Cinderella, she was a char on the side. One day a feller called the Prince – 'course he wasn't a real prince really – that was because all 'igh up he was, he own'd a string of barrers, he 'ad a boozer and a pawn shop next door. Well, he was 'aving a bit of a party for his clicks. Dirty-Gertie and Cosie-Rosie were going, but he didn't ask Cinderella, 'cos he didn't know 'er. Poor Cinderella, she had to help them for this do. Both had a perm – and a bath *each*. And she put the wireless on, and it was playing 'Ah Sweet Mystery of Life' with Grace Moore. Then she 'ad a bit of a cry to do her good! Then she looked up. And there, in the middle of the kitchen, was her fairy godmother in tights. Kind of all-white combs, all sparkling. And she said 'what are you?' And the fairy godmother says 'I'm your fairy godmother!' And Cinderella says, 'blimey!' And the fairy godmother does her stuff!

(Scene changes to pub, where Mrs Voray and O'Rane are getting drunk.)

MRS VORAY *(rather drunk)*: And I've been keeping her on seven-bob-a-week, seven-bob-a-week. What d'you think about that? I've had to work my fingers to the bone for seven-bob-a-week!

TERENCE O'RANE: Oh, never mind. Tell you what, I'll put some money in the post office in Mary's name.

MRS VORAY: Oh, no, you don't! She'd take it out and spend the lot! Let me take care of her.

(Scene returns to children at home, Norma telling her story.)

NORMA: There goes Cinderella in her pumpkin coach ... and the fairy godmother standing at the door waving her wand and calling

out 'Goodbye, Cinders, I hope you enjoy yourself!' And the
pumpkin coach gets to the pub where they're having this big ball –
and out gets Cinderella very chic ... and it's all in technicolour and a
couple of guest stars, and Dirty-Gertie and Cosie-Rosie shaking
their cups. And the prince himself with an eyeglass, just like a film.
And when he sees Cinders he whistles with his fingers in his mouth
(*sound of whistling*). She goes over to him and he says 'What's
yours?' he says. 'I'll 'ave the best in the house!' she says. He bows
very low and he says 'You *are* the best in the 'ouse', he says, 'and
that's that.' Well, he gives her a gold tipped cigarette and a port.
And then they're 'opping around the floor for always and always.
And the MC gets up and he says there's a special competition
tonight for dames. Very special – for the smallest feet ... and he
holds a glass in his hand and says who can get her chopper in it.
Well, Dirty-Gertie and Cosie-Rosie has a shock, for they've got feet
like choppers. Cinderella, she has a go, and it suits her like a
sausage skin. 'Put your hand' says the Prince Charming, smiling
and showing all his gold teeth. She could marry him for the asking!
And suddenly she remembers that her fairy godmother said to her
'keep your peepers on the clock, Cinders love!' she says. And
cinders looks at the clock. And lo and behold the clock struck the
witching hour.

(*Scene returns to pub as landlord calls 'Time, gentlemen, please!'*)

(*Scene of schoolchildren playing, including Mrs Voray's evacuees and
Mary's local friends.*)

MARY O'RANE: This is my new friend.

FIRST FRIEND: What's his name?

SECOND FRIEND: He's one of the kids from Mrs Voray's.

THIRD FRIEND: He's been combing his hair with the leg of a chair.

RONNIE: I'm Ronald Tilbury and I come from Camberwell. And I'm
nine ...

THIRD FRIEND (*mocking*):   I'm Ronald Tilbury and I come from
Camberwell and I'm nine. I never to speak to girls –

RONNIE: The bomb fell on our house, and I'm the only one what's
left.

MARY O'RANE: Yes, and I'm one of the kids at Mrs Voray's too! And

Ronnie and me are friends forever and ever! And if you want to be my friends still, like you used to be, you've got to be Ronnie's too! 'Cos I'm never going to leave him!

FIRST FRIEND: We didn't mean it, Mary, honest we didn't. We were only joking.

SECOND FRIEND: He's a nice boy really, and I like his hair like that.

THIRD FRIEND: Of course we're still friends, Mary, and you can have my new sweet coupons, if you like, Ronnie – well, half of them anyway.

(*Scene of Judith Drave calling on Mrs Jarvis.*)

MRS JARVIS: Oh it's you. Good evening, Miss Drave.

JUDITH DRAVE: Good evening, Mrs Jarvis. You told me you'd have your answer ready for me, if I called this evening after school. Can you take in Mary O'Rane or not? Oh, do say yes.

MRS JARVIS: Well, really, my husband and I –

JUDITH DRAVE: Oh, please, you see this is important – it's the girl's whole life. She's been days and days in that dreadful house. You haven't seen it. You wouldn't, you *couldn't* let any girl you know live there.

MRS JARVIS: I know, Miss Drave, I know. I mean I've heard that Mrs Voray's a disreputable person, and I'm sure that Mary's a sweet girl. But you see –

JUDITH DRAVE: I see.

MRS JARVIS: Oh, no, you're not to think we don't *understand*, we'd do anything we could. But you see my husband and I are not as young as we used to be. We are not accustomed to young children, and my husband has his little fads and fancies, you know. We live a very quiet life. And now he's retired from the bank. *You do* see what I mean.

JUDITH DRAVE: Yes, I do see what you mean. *There's no room for Mary.*

MRS JARVIS: I'm so sorry.

JUDITH DRAVE: Yes, I see what you mean, Mrs Jarvis. Yes, I know you're very sorry. We are *all* so sorry. Would you like your daughter, Mrs Jarvis ...

MRS JARVIS: Now, Miss Drave, we've got to take these things quietly.

JUDITH DRAVE: Why?

(*Scene returns to children playing in the living room.*)

NORMA (*trying to recite poem*):   Bring me my bow of burning gold! Bring me – Mary, what are they to bring me now?

MARY O'RANE (*coarsely*):   Oh, get on with it you fool!

NORMA: Bring me, oh get on with it you fool!

MARY O'RANE: Get on with your poem, when I tell you.

NORMA: It's so sloppy that's why I can't get it into me head. Why can't Miss Drave give us something with a story in it? Irene's got a nice piece to learn. She said it's called how they brought the good new to the Gents.

MARY O'RANE: You mean how they brought the good news to Ghent. (*seeing Norma unwrap a sweet*) 'Ere, you can't say your piece with a sucker in your mouth. Your jaws will get stuck. And I want to hurry up so we can find Ronnie. I want to go out.

NORMA: Alright, I'll just have to suck now to keep up me strength. Now where was I? I know –
'Bring me my arrows of desire'
O! – O what?

MARY O'RANE: 'O clouds unfold'.

NORMA: Cor, in'it tripe?

MARY: No it isn't, it's lovely (*in something of her former middle-class tone*).

NORMA: Not *my* style, dearie.
'O clouds unfold'.
Bring me – blimey what do you want to bring me now?

MARY O'RANE: 'Chariots of fire'.

NORMA: Gawd, the things I want! Here, there's a kid pushing a barrer (*looks out of window*) – what yer got in yer chariot of fire? ...

NORMA: 'Ere, here's old Ma Waters coming in ... Oh, good evening, Mrs Waters.

MRS WATERS: Is Mrs Voray in?

NORMA: No, think not. Can I take a message for you?

MRS WATERS: No, just tell her I can let her have a spare room for two nights, if she's interested.

NORMA: I *might.*

MRS WATERS: And what does might mean, I ask?

NORMA: I don't do things for nothing, dearie.

MRS WATERS: Oh, yer don't, don't yer? (*handing Norma a coin*)

NORMA: Huh! A penny! Thanks for nothing. There's a Miss Bates at school, she's always asking questions.

MRS WATERS: That has nothing to do with me. Where does she keep the bottle now?

NORMA: In the grate, I think ...

MRS WATERS (*puts her hand up chimney*):   Oh, ho! Oh, look where she kept it hid! (*laughter*) Up the chimbley! Now I call that a suspicious nature! And what did you tell Miss Nosey Parker?

NORMA: Cross me palm with silver first, lady.

MRS WATERS: I'll cross you with a flat iron!

NORMA: She wants to make a stink about the house. But she don't know how. Mind you, I could tell 'em unless I'm paid to keep me trap shut. It's worth a bob to you.

MRS WATERS: I wish your mother could see you now!

NORMA: You're lucky she can't, she'd ask half a quid. Now come on or do you want me to pop out this house next Wednesday and bring back someone you'll be sorry for!

MRS WATERS: That's blackmail!

NORMA: Have a swig! (*takes gin bottle*)

MRS WATERS: Can such things be! They'll be hotting up the fires down below for you, my girl!

NORMA: Huh! More'n they do here, anyhow. (*Enter Mrs Voray.*)

NORMA: Waters wants to see you.

MRS VORAY: Does she? What for?

NORMA: Says she's got another let.

MRS VORAY: OK.

MRS WATERS: I've been waiting for you, Aggie.

MRS VORAY: Oh, there you are. Young Norma just told me. You got another let for me, or summat?

MRS WATERS: That young Norma's a bad lot!

MRS VORAY: Oh, she's alright.

MRS WATERS: Told me her schoolteacher's been asking questions.

MRS VORAY: Let her ask! She'll not get 'owt out of Norma. I give Norma a tanner now and then to keep her mouth shut.

MRS WATERS: Oh, but she's just gone and 'ad a bob from me.

MRS VORAY: She never 'as.

MRS WATERS: She 'as!

MRS VORAY: That young madam, would you believe it! I'll crown her when she comes in. (*knock on door*) Go and see who's that, Mrs Waters, will you?

NORMA: I saw Miss Drave walking up the hill. Thought she must have been coming here. I brought her in.

MRS VORAY: Alright, you clear out now young Norma.

JUDITH DRAVE: I'd rather she stayed, Mrs Voray. I want to ask you some questions. Norma, too.

NORMA: Can I have the coupons? And I want some money for the sweet rations.

MRS VORAY: Oh, you do, do yer? Alright dear, there's the coupons, and there's a ten bob note. Bring me back some change!

NORMA: Yes, Mrs Voray. (*turns to leave*)

MRS VORAY: Oh, come back! Teacher wants to ask you some questions – I forgot.

NORMA: Oh?

JUDITH DRAVE: Norma, how do you children sleep here?

NORMA (*abruptly*):   Quite well, thank you.

JUDITH DRAVE: I mean, how many of you sleep in a bed?

NORMA: Well, me and Lily sleeps in the big room, and Mary and Ronnie sleeps in the little one.

JUDITH DRAVE: Why does Mary sleep with Ronnie?

NORMA: Well, he's afraid of the dark, and he always clings to Mary.

JUDITH DRAVE: Norma, does Mrs Voray ever take in visitors?

NORMA: She really hasn't the room, has she?

JUDITH DRAVE: Why are you scratching your head?

MRS VORAY: I expect a flea jumped off the cat. Norma attracts them. She's funny that way. Well, have you got anything else to say before they show you the door?

JUDITH DRAVE: Yes, I've found a home for Mary O'Rane.

MARY O'RANE: Oh! (*delightedly as she comes in*)

JUDITH DRAVE: Mary dear, I promised I'd find you a nice home didn't I?

MARY O'RANE: Yes.

JUDITH DRAVE: You know Mrs Harper, don't you, and Granny and Brigid? Well, the cousin's gone back, and Mrs Harper's willing to take you in for as long as you like. Do you want to go away?

MARY O'RANE: Oh yes, *please*. Ronnie'll come too won't he?

JUDITH DRAVE: Well, not for a little while, but I'll try to find him a nice home somewhere else. Don't worry, Mary dear, we'll find him a good home. Will you come?

MARY O'RANE: *No*. I can't leave Ronnie, *never*. I promised.

MRS VORAY: Well? ... That's that, isn't it? And now perhaps you'll get out of *my* house. Get out, and stop out!

(*Schoolroom scene, Mary and Norma looking through Miss Drave's desk as she enters.*)

JUDITH DRAVE: What are you two doing in here?

NORMA: Oh, nothing, Miss Drave, I'm only looking for me pencil. Come on, Mary!

JUDITH DRAVE: Mary, Norma! Come back!

NORMA: What's the matter, Miss Drave?

JUDITH DRAVE: Have you been looking through my desk?

NORMA: Oh no, Miss Drave!

JUDITH DRAVE: Have you been looking through my desk?

NORMA: Oh no, Miss Drave!

JUDITH DRAVE: Mary, have you?

MARY: No, Miss Drave, I never! I *never* touched your gloves!

(*Scene in the Rev. Allworth's garden, where he is tending his plants. Judith Drave has just called at the house.*)

BEATRICE: Mr Allworth!

REVEREND ALLWORTH: Yes, Beatrice?

BEATRICE: There's a lady to see you, Miss Drave. Are you at home?

REVEREND ALLWORTH: Well, where do you think I am? (*good-humouredly*)

BEATRICE: Shall I send her in the garden?

REVEREND ALLWORTH: Yes Beatrice ... Morning! (*to Judith Drave*)

JUDITH DRAVE: Good morning!

REVEREND ALLWORTH: A radiant morning! Good to be alive! I'm planting Alpines – rock plants, you know. This is a Campanula Pusilla, it will flower between June and August. This –

JUDITH DRAVE: You read my letter? (*cutting in on his chatter*)

REVEREND ALLWORTH: Oh, indeed I did, Miss Drave. Most distressing! I'm also *very amused* by these (*turns to discussion of flowers and horticultural names*) ... I once had a sweet pea call Mrs Jelly. Very amusing!

JUDITH DRAVE: What are you going to do about these children? (*rather sharply*)

REVEREND ALLWORTH: I really don't see, Miss Drave, what I *can* do. You see it's all *rumour.* Rumour isn't evidence.

JUDITH DRAVE: Mary O'Rane was a sweet and gentle girl. Now she's coarse and savage and sly. That's not rumour! She was pretty – I thought she was beautiful. Now she's dirty and uncared for. And that's evidence.

REVEREND ALLWORTH: You said in your letter, Miss Drave. Now where is your letter? Bills – bills. Ah! (*shuffling through papers*) A little poem!

JUDITH DRAVE: Often all the children have to sleep together, four girls and a boy.

REVEREND ALLWORTH: Did they tell you that themselves?

JUDITH DRAVE: Whenever Mrs Voray lets out one of the children's rooms they all have to crowd into one bed – (*with mounting passion and anger*)

REVEREND ALLWORTH: I must have left it in my wool-work –

JUDITH DRAVE: I said that when Mary's father came to see her –

REVEREND ALLWORTH: Oh yes, the father.

JUDITH DRAVE: He and Mrs Voray got drunk together.

REVEREND ALLWORTH: Oh, dear!

JUDITH DRAVE: I said the little boy was locked up at night in a cellar full of rats. I said the children had lice and sores and that they are half starved. What are you going to do about it? Are you going to let them stay with Mrs Voray?

REVEREND ALLWORTH: Will nobody else take them?

(*Scenes of people declining to help.*)

VOICES: We are grieved for the poor. But I am full up with summer visitors … Of course we'd take them in, but the children, Miss Drave, are so rough!

JUDITH DRAVE: Doesn't that sound familiar? *There was no room for them at the inn!*

REVEREND ALLWORTH: Really, Miss Drave, I find all this *infinitely* distressing! And I really fail to see what I can do! It's all so unlikely!

And it's all so much outside my province. Let me sleep on it, Miss Drave. We must consider what is the best thing to do all round! We mustn't be precipitate. We must use reason. We must ... (*Judith leaves.*)

(*Scene of Council Meeting.*)

CLLR WORDSWORTH: Mr Chairman, I move we discuss the next item on the agenda. The question of the evacuee children, now resident at the house of Mrs Agatha Voray, Number 1 Pleasant Street.

CLLR TROUNCER: Ay, the vicar's being playing hell about that.

CLLR MEDLICOTT: Ringing up the Town Hall day and night!

CHAIRMAN: He told the Town Clerk that a schoolteacher at the Elementary School, Miss Judith Drave, had complained to him about Mrs Voray in very strong terms. He said that as a Minister of the cloth he was forced to bring this to our attention and to beg us that Miss Drave be granted a personal interview, *here* in the Town Hall.

CLLR GREEN: It's a scandal Mr Chairman! The woman should be driven out of the town.

CLLR TROUNCER: What are the complaints? (*looking at his papers*) Drunkenness. Children ragged, hungry, lousy. If all this is true, Mr Chairman, I agree with Cllr Green for once. She should be driven out of town.

CLLR GREEN: Councillor Trouncer misunderstands me, as usual. I mean it is a scandal that these unfounded accusations should be brought against Mrs Voray. And that this mischief-making school-marm should be sacked. And sent off!

CLLR WORDSWORTH: Mr Chairman, why does Councillor Green assume these accusations are without foundation?

CLLR GREEN: I know the facts of the case. I know Mrs Voray.

CLLR PARKIN: Good old Aggie. Ha! Ha!

CLLR MEDLICOTT: I suggest Mr Chairman we see Miss Drave at once, without any further prejudice or comment.

CLLR TROUNCER: Ere! Ere!

CHAIRMAN: Miss Drave, please!

CLLR PARKIN: Ten to one she's got rimless glasses and a beak like a poll parrot! (*laughs*)

(*Miss Drave comes in, formally but smartly dressed.*)

CHAIRMAN: Good morning!

JUDITH DRAVE: Good morning, gentlemen.

CHAIRMAN: Now, Miss Drave, the accusations you bring against Mrs Voray are extremely serious.

JUDITH DRAVE: I realise that bestiality and torture and swinish filth, and spiritual corruption are quite serious matters, Mr Chairman.

CHAIRMAN: Those are very strong words, Miss Drave. I hope you can substantiate them.

JUDITH DRAVE: I've *been* to that house, time after time. I've seen the squalor and the tyranny and the evil – the horrible degradation! –

CLLR GREEN: Words, words, words! Spiritual corruption, tyranny, degradation, we're not your pupils, ma'am, to be lectured with all this high-sounding gibberish!

CLLR PARKIN: Makes poor old Aggie sound like Mrs Dracula!

CLLR GREEN: What did you *see*? Tell us that in words of one syllable if you can.

JUDITH DRAVE: Lice, filth, hate ... I saw a child who was lovely once, sweet and gentle and truthful, being turned, in that damned house, into a foul-mouthed gutter-snipe, into a snivelling little thief and liar. I could see in her mouth and in her eyes what she has come to be and I damn Mrs Voray!

CLLR GREEN: I protest, Mr Chairman, I protest.

CLLR PARKIN: Hey, steady on Miss, no need to let fly with all them names. She's not a plaster saint – who is?

CLLR TROUNCER: Let the young woman have her say, Mr Chairman.

CLLR MEDLICOTT: But please, the language.

JUDITH DRAVE: What other language should I use? Shall I swaddle everything up nice and cosily so that none of these gentlemen can possibly be offended. Should I find other words for filth, stink, vermin?

CLLR TROUNCER: You say the children are 'ungry, too. Ah don't like that.

JUDITH DRAVE: Yes, they go hungry. They live on bread-and-scrape and weak tea. They never have butter, meat or eggs or –

CLLR PARKIN: 'Ere, that's a whopper, that is. I 'appen to know she buys reg'lar all the meat she's allowed to on six books.

JUDITH DRAVE: But it *never* reaches the children.

CLLR PARKIN: Oh, she wolfs it all down in one go herself does she, like a hippopotamus (*chuckles*).

CLLR GREEN: And as for butter and eggs, I know! I see her grocery list every week! She buys regardless.

CLLR TROUNCER: Ay, regardless of the children perhaps, Councillor Green.

CLLR GREEN: Mr Chairman, would you inform Councillor Trouncer that already one of this young woman's principal accusations has fallen flat. The children do *not* go hungry.

CLLR WORDSWORTH: Because Mrs Voray is known to patronise you and Councillor Parkin! That's not logical.

CLLR GREEN: We're not talking logic Councillor Wordsworth. We're talking –

CLLR WORDSWORTH: I know the words.

JUDITH DRAVE: And you're the men who look after this town. You are the men who guard our health and our morals. *You* look after the children! If (*voice rises*) Mary O'Rane goes to hell then it's *your* fault. It is because of your smugness and blindness, your – your babbling ignorance that a monster like Mrs Voray can batten on children, torture and seduce them! God in heaven, it's happening, under your eyes. Can nothing make you see, can nothing, nothing in God's name *make* you find homes for them, take them away?

CLLR MEDLICOTT: I think, Mr Chairman, we should call in Mrs Voray. There seems to be no point in listening any further to these, to these hysterical insults.

CLLR TROUNCER: Ah'd like to see them kids (*reflectively*).

CHAIRMAN: Send Mrs Voray in.

(*Mrs Voray enters, neatly but rather shabbily dressed, demure and wearing little make-up.*)

CLLR WORDSWORTH: So this is our monster, well I never! (*Mrs Voray looking faded, defenceless, beside the smarter younger woman*)

CHAIRMAN: Won't you sit down Mrs Voray?

MRS VORAY: Thanks very much, but I'd rather stand, if it's all the same to you (*nervously*).

CHAIRMAN: Mrs Voray (*slowly*), extremely grave charges have been made against you.

MRS VORAY: Yes, sir, I know, by this Miss Drave here, she's always going around taking away my character. I don't know why, sir, I've done her no harm.

CLLR TROUNCER: Miss Drave says you keep your evacuees hungry. Is that right?

MRS VORAY: I feed them as well as ever I can. It's a bit of a struggle these days, and you're only allowed seven shillings a week each for them. But we manage somehow. If the worse comes to the worst I can always go short myself ... there, I can truthfully say they all get enough to eat, thank God.

JUDITH DRAVE: So *you* can thank God! Are you going to sit there and listen to this sanctimonious humbug. She's a lying hypocrite! (*turning furiously on the Committee*)

MRS VORAY: Heaven! I don't know what I've done to this young lady to deserve the things she says about me.

CLLR GREEN: I sympathise with you, Mrs Voray ...

CLLR TROUNCER: Miss Drave says that you frequently let out one of the rooms in your house.

MRS VORAY: If there's a word of truth in what she says she should be made to prove it. Where's her proof? *She hasn't got no proof.* All she wants is to take Miss Mary O'Rane away from me. She's got no right to, she's no relation, and there's her own father – Well, I'd just like you to have a look at this, sir. If you please, this is the one. (*gives crumpled letter to Chairman*)

CHAIRMAN: Hm! This, gentlemen, is a letter from Terence O'Rane, the father of the girl in question. He fully approves after a personal inspection of the house ... Send Mr Burrells in. (*Mr Burrells comes in.*)

CHAIRMAN: Mr Burrells, as billeting officer, what is your opinion of Mrs Voray's house?

CLLR GREEN: Go on, Perce, you tell 'em.

MR BURRELLS: Well, Mrs Voray is a woman of character, Mr Chairman. Her way of life may not be everybody else's but I think I can honestly say that – er – considering there's a war on it is my opinion those children are adequately clothed, washed, fed and cared for.

CHAIRMAN: What did you say, Miss Drave?

JUDITH DRAVE: I said another Judas! (*leaves Council Chamber abruptly*)

CHAIRMAN: Well, I think that's all, Mrs Voray. I shall tell the Town Clerk that the complaints passed on to him have no evidence to support them.

MRS VORAY: Thanks very much sir. I knew I could rely on you gentlemen to see that justice was done to me. You've been ever so kind, I'm sure. Good morning. Good morning!

(*Mrs Voray leaves, scene of children in living room follows.*)

NORMA: I'd like plenty of jellied eels all lovely and slimy. Then I'll have peaches and apples and a fruit pie. After that fish and chips. And I'll finish up with a great big jar of ice cream. Plain, strawberry, raspberry, chocolate, and vanilla special with nuts ... and I'd throw the whole down with a pint of wallop!

MARY: Oh you shut your trap!

NORMA: What's the matter ducks, hungry? ...

NORMA: Oh, I wish I was a cannibal. I'd eat old mother Nasty.

MRS VORAY (*entering*):   Oh, would yer? (*in cheery mood after her Council triumph*)

NORMA: And that's the Gawd's truth, dearie.

MRS VORAY: 'Ere, hands off that, young nosey parker! (*takes out new hat with feather*) If I wasn't going out, young Norma, I wouldn't 'arf tan your backside. I'd teach you to keep a civil tongue in your head!

NORMA: Huh! Civil! If I was to tell you what I really think of yer, you'd be burnt to a cinder!

MRS VORAY: Hurry up, young Norma, and just bring my things over here, and do something for a living. Come on! Get a move on! (*to Mary*) You get on with your job!

MARY: The water's cold, can't get the sauce off the plates without hot water.

MRS VORAY: You'll be in hot water, girl, if you don't get the plates clean ... (*tries on her hat*) That alright, Norm?

NORMA: Mm! Just a bit more over the right eye!

MRS VORAY: Oh really, like that?

NORMA: Oh very chick! ...

(*Mrs Voray adjusts her new hat carefully with its splendid feather.*)

NORMA: Oh proper chase-me-Charlie, that fevver!

MRS VORAY: Oh dear, you know me whole future might depend on this 'at.

NORMA: 'Ere, meeting a boyfriend? Making good money ain't 'e?

MRS VORAY: Oh, he's doing alright! ... Norma! Have you seen a packet of fags I left on 'ere at dinner time?

NORMA: No, I ain't seen 'em! You must have left them at the shop.

MRS VORAY: Oh no, I never, I remember as plain as plain leaving them on this dresser.

NORMA: Old Ma Waters was in here at dinner time. You really can't trust some people.

MRS VORAY: I wouldn't trust you neither. I wouldn't put it past you, young Norma ...

NORMA: Ooh listen! It sounds like hail! Now you can't go out in your new 'at.

MRS VORAY: Damn! And I wanted to wear me new 'at tonight, summat special.

NORMA: You better put on your old sailor beware! (*continuing noise of heavy rainfall*)

MRS VORAY: Oh get out of my room! (*in her bedroom, to children*)

MARY: Whenever she looks at my mummy's watch, it makes me feel sick.

NORMA: Mmm, I'd get it back for you, ducks, but she goes to bed with it on. (*Mrs Voray returns with her old hat.*) Oh that's right, I do like you in your old sailor beware!

MRS VORAY: Oh, I want to wear me new hat! I'm damn well fed up with this old thing!

NORMA: Oh no, it gives you a touch of – (*Ronnie has Mrs Voray's lipstick and paints his nose red.*)

GIRLS (*laughing*): Oh, look at our Ron! (*He enjoys their attention.*)

MRS VORAY (*to Ron*):   You rotten devil, take that and that and that! (*slaps Ron*) I'll learn you to use up my lipstick with this blasted war on!

MARY: You leave him alone! (*angrily*)

MRS VORAY: And I don't want no lip from you neither!

MARY: If you hit him again I'll –

MRS VORAY: Just remind me to tan you black and blue in the morning, will yer, I can't stop now. Get off to bed the lot of yer. Don't want sight nor sound of you when I come in. (*leaves*)

NORMA: You want to use tack on her Mary, see, you want to handle 'er with a bit of tack not with a bread knife ... (*Scene changes to pub.*)

(*Scene in pub, crowded bar, piano playing.*)

FREDDIE (*spiv friend*):   I drove the old bus down this country road, see. Me time is nobody's business, miles from anywhere, rain was pouring down. Well I said to this high society bit, I said, you be nice to little Freddie or you'll bloody well walk, I said.

GIRL: Huh! What did she do Freddie? Walk?

FREDDIE: Well she looked at the rain. She looked at her swell evening dress, she looked at the high-heeled shoes, and she looked at me. And *she* didn't walk!

GIRL: Hm! I don't like walking either.

FREDDIE: You're not the walking type. From now on you're riding. In front seat with me.

GIRL: Hah! Hah! What's the back seat for? (*laughter and giggles*)

(*Enter Mrs Voray.*)

BARMAID: A double gin?

MRS VORAY: No, gimme 'alf of bitter.

BARMAID: Paying for it yourself tonight?

GIRL: Ha! Ha! Oh! Give over, Freddie. Give over! That's too far!

FREDDIE: You wait till we get to the Knave of Hearts! I know the guy. We'll have some fun!

MRS VORAY: Hello, Freddie, sorry if I'm late. This awful weather! It is awful, isn't it? Not worth doing yourself up for.

GIRL: Yes, you are late, aren't you!

MRS VORAY: I don't think me and this young lady have ...

FREDDIE: This is a friend of mine. We just met.

GIRL: Mrs Voray – Oh I've seen her before (*dismissively*).

MRS VORAY: Oh 'ave you really? The pleasure was yours I'm sure. Come on Freddie, aren't you going to ask us to 'ave a drink. After all, we did 'ave a date didn't we?

FREDDIE: Did we? I must have been drunk. (*looks her up and down insolently*)

MRS VORAY: 'Ere come off it! You can't expect us to swallow that, making out you forgot! Come on, I can take a joke with the best of 'em!

GIRL: No, you can take the air!

FREDDIE: That's right. Come on ducks! (*goes to leave*)

GIRL: Here you are, Ma, buy yourself a drink. (*tosses her a shilling*) You look as if you need it ...

BARMAID: You haven't touched your bitter Mrs Voray ...

MRS VORAY: I'll have a double! (*Scene closes with singing of 'Run Rabbit Run'.*) Men! (*slurred speech, drunk by now*)

(*Scene returns to living room, where children are playing dressing up.*)

NORMA: Oh, don't we look glamorous eh, like the merry widow!

RONNIE: Well, what about this! (*Ronnie puts on the new hat with the feather.*)

NORMA: Oh, you beat the lot!

MARY: Ron. Look at this 'ouse, and look at the mess too, but she'll notice ... (*In their excitement and play the long feather is broken.*) Oh! Just look what you've done!

RONNIE AND NORMA: We've broke the feather!

MARY (*turning on Norma*):   You did it! You know you did. It weren't Ronnie's fault.

NORMA: It doesn't matter who's done it. Ronnie, me, or the Archbishop of Canterbury! It's broke ain't it!

MARY: Perhaps she'll come in drunk.

NORMA: No, head first, in a wheel barrer! ...

RONNIE (*frightened*):   She'll know I done it! (*near to tears*)

MARY: Don't worry, Ronnie, I'll say I broke the damn feather! (*They try to comfort Ronnie.*) She'd believe you tried on the 'at, but she'd never believe you broke the feather. (*to Norma*) And she'll remember Ronnie painting his nose. She'll put him in the coal hole.

NORMA: But if she does I'll get him out, see!

MARY: Oh, don't you worry Ronnie. I'll get the key and get you out! 'Ere, maybe I could mend it with this? (*Mary struggles to restore feather.*) Oh, if only I could get it stuck in somehow! Then perhaps she wouldn't notice!

NORMA: Perhaps! She got eyes like a hawk.

MARY: Oh blast. Now I've bust it altogether!

(*Children struggle to replace feather on hat. Noises from backyard of returning footsteps.*)

NORMA: Quick! Give me the 'at. I'll hide it. You get to bed!

MRS VORAY (*returning upset and drunk*):   What the hell's this? Why aren't you kids in bed? Go on! Get out of 'ere! He walked out on me! (*in her bedroom, there is heavy rain outside*) All 'cos of the rain! Oh, Oh! (*crying*) 'Cos I wore me old sailor 'at – oh, sailor beware! Damn this 'at! ... I'll wear me new 'at tomorrow night. I'll wear me new 'at tomorrow night! (*shot of children awake, anxiously listening*) Me whole future might depend on that 'at. Makes me look twenty-five! (*In tears, drunk and hysterical, she finds the broken feather.*) The feather's broke! ... (*suddenly sober and speaking with quiet threat*) ... (*in Ronnie's bedroom*) Ronnie! Ronnie! Ronnie! You and me got to 'ave a little talk, *dear* Ronnie. You dressed yourself up tonight, didn't yer! Didn't yer? You went into my room, you dressed yourself up ... You took me new 'at and you went and broke the bleeding feather! (*screaming*) Didn't yer?

MARY: No! He never did! He didn't break your blasted feather! I broke it.

MRS VORAY: You know what I'm going to do with you? Do you know? I'm going to lock you in the coal cellar.

MARY: Stop it! Stop it! You couldn't! You wouldn't dare.

MRS VORAY: And who's going to stop me, eh?

NORMA: Oh, you can't put the kid down there! It's freezing! ...

MRS VORAY (*now furious*):   I'm going to the police station in the morning. I'm not going to have this little swine in this house a minute longer. I've had enough.

MARY: Then Ronnie and me'll go away!

MRS VORAY: Yes, he'll go away. He'll go away alright, when I tell them of the thieving in this house. (*takes Ronnie from bedroom out to backyard and locks him in coal cellar*)

NORMA: Oh, don't worry Mary. I'll get him out somehow! I promise you I will, Mary. Oh, don't cry ducks, I'll get the key and I'll get him out.

MRS VORAY (*locking Ronnie in the coal hole*):   There! That'll learn yer!

(*Later, hearing the children trying to rescue Ronnie from the coal hole in the backyard of the house, Mrs Voray stumbles while walking down the rickety wooden stairway in the pouring rain. The stairs give way in the rainy dark, and she is killed in her fall to the stone flags of the yard.*)

The Beach of Falesá

Dylan Thomas had long been an enthusiastic reader of Robert Louis Stevenson's work and was keen to write a filmscript of his story *The Beach of Falesá*. In his second script based on a literary source, Thomas's version brings a sensuous, poetic power to the tale, particularly in his evocation of the South Seas setting, with its beautiful but mysterious natural world, in contrast to the realism of Stevenson, who knew the place and the people. Thomas brings more drama to his presentation, and a poet's words and imagination convey the opening sequence as the boat bringing Wiltshire comes in sight of the island, the cockerel crowing thrice in warning of the treacherous events ahead. The sentences we read become pictures. Thomas also enjoyed writing the quiet drinking session in the Captain's cabin with its dialogue of the Captain's stories and gossip of Falesá, then Wiltshire's concerns taking over. It is the dangerous but exciting world of seafarers, adventurers and chancers' tales. Atmosphere and setting become crowded with movement and excitement, as when we see boats and their notable passengers, who will contribute to plot and action, whether Wiltshire, Case or the Welsh missionary Jenkins, slowly and dramatically approach. Similarly journeys into the beautiful but mysterious and almost impenetrable interior of the island, with its overgrown paths and dense jungle, are atmospheric, often fearfully so, as in Wiltshire's final journey in vengeful pursuit of Case. In Thomas's language scene, setting and atmosphere become narrative.

The story tells how Wiltshire, setting up as an English trader in the apparent tropical paradise of Falesá, discovers only the dark side, a world of terror and evil set up by his already established rival trader, the sophisticated rogue Case who is willing to murder to keep his power over the frightened and ignorant natives of the island, already in thrall to his black-magic trickery. Case falsely arranges the marriage of Wiltshire and the beautiful Uma, aided by Little Jack – acting as priest – further to isolate Wiltshire as trader through native superstition directed at Uma. Writing to Jan Read, a script editor at Gainsborough, Dylan explains he is simplifying the script by including only one of the previous traders destroyed by Case: 'I've followed the main line of the suggestions ... agreed, and have tried to remember, and interpolate, all the chief points. One thing you'll notice is that I have cut out altogether the *two other traders* and stuck to one alone, calling him by the name of one of the other traders, Johnny Adams. This, I think, simplifies matters. We talk now about only *one* person whom we never see; our plot works back only to the *immediate* predecessor of Wiltshire ... . As you'll see, I've cut all the introduction – by-the-waterfall cock about Uma. I've cut the Long Randall – & burial-alive flash-back. I've cut Namu, the renegade pastor.'[90] Such comments reveal the script writer's duties, regularly sharing consultations with those working full time in film production.

Dylan may have cut out the renegade pastor, but he certainly drew again on his Welsh background to introduce the colourful Welsh missionary Jenkins to this evil South Seas Eden. 'His voice is liltingly Welsh' we learn and with his boast 'I'm the only man in the world who can use the Welsh hwyl in Polynesian dialect' and his dismissal of Case as 'nothing but a sick little moochin picking the wings off bluebottles', he certainly fights the good fight with spirited riposte in his lively dialogue with Case – including with shocked disapproval 'A BA too'. On his moonlit expedition to the island's interior Wiltshire comes upon a 'druidical pile of ancient stones' en route for Case's lair of black-magic props, and also 'a long mound of earth, like a cromlech' – clearly pagan touches. Nature and night animals, particularly birds, are more disturbing than Case's 'ghost train' surreal horrors, and as usual for Dylan Thomas birds are both omens and celebrants of the various times of day and night when they appear. Thomas's wit is also evident in Case's sarcastic conversational comments on religion and belief, and his opening introduction to Wiltshire has a literary quip: 'I myself am a Shropshire Lad.' Dylan's joking reference to himself in a letter to Donald Taylor – 'Why, bless my soul, it is the little Welsher' – is echoed in Little Jack's 'Good day, Mr Wiltshire.' He slurs the words so that it sounds like 'Welsher'. A reviewer found it 'fascinating to see how the personality of Thomas and demands of the film have affected the original tale'.[91]

A picture of Dylan while working on these scripts for Gainsborough is provided by Jan Read.

When he did get down to the script he wrote at great speed .... As a person I found him charming and without side or pretensions. He was unpunctual, it is true, to the extent of turning up for a script meeting a day or two late .... When he did arrive at Lime Grove, it was always in a rumpled blue serge suit, looking like a merchant-seaman on shore leave. There was never much work done on these occasions; instead we inevitably adjourned to the Shepherd's Bush Hotel to down pints of beer and listen to his Welsh stories, which he told beautifully …. Thomas was not the man to bother over much with technical requirements. Most of the points agreed in discussion he would forget in the Soho pubs long before returning to Oxford and work.[92]

It was Read who mapped out changes in construction necessary for filming. But none of the three Gainsborough films was made, as the Rank studio was sold when the film industry went into recession in 1948. Nor is it likely the scripts reached their final revised state for filming. As with *Twenty Years A-Growing*, *The Beach of Falesá* and *Rebecca's Daughters* are edited to make possible the inclusion of all the filmscripts.

THE BEACH OF FALESÁ

It is the hour before tropical dawn, on the hushed, grey, open sea. A boat glides by like a shadow, the moon going down behind her tall sails. The boat sails on, through the very slowly lightening night, through moonlight and music, the soft sea speaking against her sides, and is gone again.

Now, it is nearer dawn, and the moon, still bright, lowering towards the glassy, quivering western rim of the South Sea. To the east, the great sky about-to-dawn is cloudless. And out of darkness, into dying moonlight, into rising dawn the boat glides again.

A bird circles above it and wheels, crying sad and high, then flies away.

The boat is a fore-and-aft schooner, of about a hundred tons. Two dark figures stand on the little deck, looking out into the neither night nor morning. The tall, broad, barehead figure, Wiltshire, his hair tossed in the wind, stands still, upright, tense and quiet. The short figure, the Captain, at the wheel, raises an arm to point.

CAPTAIN: There, over there! D'you see? Behind the break of the reef …

He speaks softly, intimately.
Dawn rises, darkness drains suddenly away from the cloudless sky,

and the cries of birds begin to be heard as from far away and coming nearer, the cries of the wild duck and the man-o'-war hawk, the awakening Pacific sea-fowl. A solitary bird flies towards the line of the island, the lofty, distant, wooded hills and the stretching shore.

CAPTAIN: D'you see? Falesá. That's Falesá, the last village to the east.

The Captain hands a pair of glasses to Wiltshire, who puts them to his eyes.
Through the twin circles of the glasses he sees the surf beating against the high cliffs, the thickly treed valleys, the spurs of mountains, the majestic woodlands, the white flash of streams down the glens, the tumbles of waterfalls, the tall breadfruit trees, the coconut palms, the scattered bamboo houses under the trees, and a few trails of smoke wisping up the sky.

CAPTAIN: D'you see that bit of white there to the eastward? That's your house, Mister.

The circles of the glasses move slowly to pick up a glimpse, between palms and breadfruits, of a white bungalow standing high above the beach.

CAPTAIN: Built of coral. D'you see? Best station in the South Pacific. Strong and pretty and broad in the beam, easy to manage and used to knocking about, just like the women.

Now, as he speaks, the circles of the glasses drop. The island is, suddenly, quite far away again, a mountain line, a reef, a distant scatter of trees, an unidentifiable stretch of surfed beach.
Wiltshire, the glasses dangling in his hand, still stares at the island, and speaks as though to himself: 'I can see the starfish in the water and the parrot fish – red and purple and green.'
The Captain shakes his head slowly.

WILTSHIRE: Can you smell the wild lime? Trees and flowers, hibiscus and pomegranate. (*softly*) I've been down near the line too long – *low* down.

The Captain raises his head to the land wind, sniffs, turns on the deck, and shouts below as loud as a bull with a megaphone and in a voice startlingly unlike the soft, intimate voice he has been using: 'Ngavindi! Ngavindi!'

He speaks over his shoulder, again in his soft voice, to Wiltshire:
'Breakfast, Mr Wiltshire.'

And a cockerel crows. A Kanaka boy appears and takes the wheel.
Great bunches of oranges decorate the stern of the boat; there are
bunches of bananas hung from the topsails and stays. There is a
chicken coop on the lower deck and one cockerel inside it. It crows to
the tropical morning. As Wiltshire and the Captain pass the coop, the
little mild Captain bends for a moment down towards the cockerel,
and, very quickly, makes a slitting movement with his fingers across
his own throat.

CAPTAIN (*to the cockerel*):   Tomorrow, Mister –

In the Captain's cabin, Wiltshire and the Captain sit at a small duty
table laid with glasses and a bottle of gin.

CAPTAIN: Who's going to be mother?

Wiltshire half fills the glasses. He is a broad, dark-haired man in the
middle thirties, stubbled about his broad jaw, shadowed under the
eyes by dissipation or fatigue. He has a reckless twist to his mouth, but
his eyes are contemplative, a man accustomed to some brutality and
much loneliness, to excess and remorse. He looks into his glass,
moving it slowly. A ship's clock ticks on the cabin wall behind him.

The Captain, bald and small and ageless, benignly wrinkled, deeply
tanned and sea-blown, an old salt soak, soft-mannered rogue and prop of
all the Pacific bars, gossip of the islands, raises his glass: 'You've got the
best little trading station I ever seen.' He drinks, 'All shipshape and
Bristol, clean as a skipper's cabin –' He darts a sly look around the cabin.
'Maybe cleaner – snug as a pub in the snow, trim and homey, three rooms
all spit and polish, you could drink off the floor. When Johnny Adams
saw it – Johnny Adams with the club foot, him that was here before you –
he took and shook me by the hand – this one with the mermaid on it.'

He makes the tattooed mermaid on the back of his hand belly-dance
as he speaks: ' "I've dropped into a soft thing here, Conrad," he says.
"So you have," I say, "soft as fevvers." '

The Captain looks at Wiltshire's glass: 'Your breakfast's getting
cold. I only saw him once after that – coughing and weeping, gibbering
when it grew dark, peeping and sneaking and spying through the
window chinks when the night comes on, squealing in his sleep like
pigs. He couldn't get on with the natives or the whites or something. He
carried a gun day and night but he couldn't have shot a whale; his
fingers twitched, like this ...'

He reaches to the bottle, refills the glasses. Wiltshire rises, huge in the little cabin, stares through the portholes at the rapidly nearing island, woods, trees, mountains, beach, the sounding surf, houses, and natives on the beach.

CAPTAIN: Next time we came round, he was gone. Vamoosed. Took a chance passage in a ship from up west. Case saw him off.

As he is speaking, a boat leaves the beach and moves towards the schooner.

CAPTAIN: See a boat coming yet?

Wiltshire nods without turning.

CAPTAIN: *That'll* be Case. *Mister* Case.

The Captain gets up and goes towards the cabin door, followed by Wiltshire. [...]

The boat has drawn up to the schooner's side. The cock crows again. Case climbs aboard. He is a smallish man, strong and wiry. His nose is hawk-hooked, his black beard trimmed. His face is deeply lined, but whether by age or by illness or by a tropical disease of the past it is hard to tell. He carries himself with debonair confidence. He is dressed in perfectly laundered striped pyjamas. He takes off his panama in a salute, first to the Captain and then to Wiltshire. His jet-black hair is oiled flat back and glistening on his narrow head. He smiles and when he speaks, it is in faultless, cultivated English. He speaks not ostentatiously, but almost with wry reluctance, with an amused under-tinge of self-contempt for his poise and mannered diction so incongruous in their settings, so incongruous as held and spoken by a small, beaked, bearded man in pyjamas on board a dirty trader outside a remote South Sea island.

CASE: Good morning, Captain. The compliments of Captain Randall and myself. He is distressed he cannot pay you his own compliments in person.

As he speaks, the Kanakan crew is bringing loads of copra from Case's boat on to the deck of the ship. The Kanakas hurry to and fro, with their burdens across the narrow deck each side of Case, but they in no way disturb his measured, urban eloquence. He turns, smiling to Wiltshire and politely, interrogatively raises his eyebrows.

CAPTAIN: Mr Wiltshire, Mr Case.

Wiltshire holds out his hand. After a barely perceptible pause, Case offers his and they shake.

CASE: A delightful name, Mr Wiltshire. A delightful county. I myself am a Shropshire Lad. As a rival trader, may I be the first to say: Welcome to Falesá! I can recommend the food but not the liquor. The wild pig is delicious. You will like my partner, Captain Randall, too.

CAPTAIN: How much copra you got this time, Mister?

Case glances casually at a sheet of paper in his hand: 'X tons.' Then, with an ironical smile, he addresses himself to Wiltshire: 'Copra, Mr Wiltshire!' He makes a gesture of wry distaste towards the Kanakas unloading the copra. 'To think that both our livelihoods depend upon the indigestible interior of the coconut!' [...]

Case and Wiltshire sit together in the stern of Case's boat. It is loaded with Wiltshire's goods and with cases of gin. The two Kanakan boys are rowing. On the island, Case and Wiltshire see the feathered mountains, and land heaving up in peaks and rising vales, falling in cliffs and buttresses crowned by clouds. Along the beach men and women and children stand waiting for the boat to come in.

The high, gay cries of the children can be heard above explosions of the surf. Case, reclining at ease in the stern, lazily indicates the waiting natives: 'The committee of deception! All in its Sunday best! It's a festival day. There hasn't been another trader on this island since your predecessor – Mr Adams. Look at 'em! Everything that can walk or crawl. Women, children, dogs, lizards, and – girls.'

Case turns his head slightly in Wiltshire's direction and says casually: 'We must get you a wife.'

WILTSHIRE: Yes, let it wait. I'll have a look around. I'm used to being alone. What frightened Johnny Adams off the island?

CASE: Mice. He drank so much native spirit the mice ran over his bedclothes like bison. He used to hear noises up in the bush, terrible strange noises. It was his mice, with bugles. He used to see devils, so they say. Take no notice of the superstitious gossip of the island, Mr Wiltshire. Are you a religious man?

Wiltshire is gazing at the beach. He does not answer, but takes his pipe from his mouth and blows a mouthful of smoke out to sea.

CASE: A pity. They are all Wesleyans here, or Baptists.

WILTSHIRE: And you?

CASE: Ah! *I* was brought up in the Church of England; at school I became a pantheist; at the university I embraced Buddhism, Confucianism, and the daughters of tobacconists; in my early manhood I was a pious Satanist, and celebrated the Black Mass from Tunbridge Wells to Honolulu; now in my wiser years, I have married a Wesleyan Samoan native who secretly worships a shark, and am untroubled by faith or doubt. Shall we go to my house first, Mr Wiltshire?

As he speaks, the boat nears the beach. [...]

In the store or trading-room of Case's bungalow there is a dusty counter, and on it an old pair of scales. Of the ordinary South Sea trading goods there is only a meagre show, and much of that stained, mouldy, neglected: some tinned foods, biscuits, hard bread, cotton stuff. But there is an excellent display of firearms and liquor.

Little Jack leans against the counter smoking a cigar, cleaning a gun, a glass beside him. At a table sit Case and Wiltshire, drinking. A pack of cards is strewn across the table. There are bottles empty and half empty. The table in front of Wiltshire is white with cigar ash. Wiltshire is sitting loosely in his camp chair, his clothes awry, his hair tousled. Case is immaculately sober.

The door between the store-room and the living-room is wide open. Old Captain Randall is still squatted on the floor, his bottle in his hand.

CASE (*affectionately*):   Dear Daddy Randall! Observe, Mr Wiltshire, that fly-blown old grogpot guzzling and sousing there, and reflect!

RANDALL: Leave ... me ... alone.

CASE: Once he strutted and swaggered in all the bars of the South Seas, a bibulous and magniloquent dandy; cut a fine figure at the consulate ball; laid down the law on club verandas; commanded a ship; had a mouse-like adoring wife in Auckland and three fine daughters.

LITTLE JACK: Arabella, Amanda, and Rose.

And Little Jack bursts out laughing in his deep, black voice.

RANDALL: All ... dead ... all ... dead ...

CASE: And three wives in Tahiti. How are the mighty fallen!

WILTSHIRE: What happened to him?

CASE: I think he fell into bad company.

Suddenly from outside the veranda, there is a hubbub of native voices.

CASE: What a pity you do not understand the language! You miss so much! Such an expressive tongue! And the intriguing names! Do you know that in Falesá there is a perfectly harmless old gentleman called 'Drinker of Blood'? And another called 'Not Quite Cooked'? Then there's 'Die out of Doors' and 'Bat's Breath' and 'Father of Cockroaches' and 'Dead Man'.

Suddenly Case pushes aside the empty bottles on the table and says contemptuously: 'Dead men!' [...]

CASE: Oh, there's no harm in the marriage.

LITTLE JACK: I'm the chaplain!

The sudden deep interjection is startling, coming out of the dark corner where the negro stands almost unseen.
In the distance the chanting continues.

CASE: When we met, I said to myself, 'Now here comes a stranger – a delightful stranger – to our little community on this earthly paradise. Let us at once offer him all the hospitality a man well needs: drink and a woman!' The drink is, I assure you, the best available. Why not say the same for the woman?

Wiltshire drinks. Case leans closer, across the table to Wiltshire, his voice lowered: 'Think of the long, hot, loveless nights alone on this little lost island. Alone in your dull, dead room, listening to the silly sea. All alone and nowhere to go in the wide world, no one to care if you sleep or weep or die, no one to care, no one to touch – all the long, hot hours of the night. Uma is beautiful. In your arms she'd be lying still and secret and safe, burning under your mouth.'

Wiltshire drains his glass, staring without seeing, in front of him. Case rises softly, and says in a whisper: 'I'll put up the banns – immediately.'

He goes out on to the veranda, followed by Little Jack grinning. They go down the steps into the chanting evening. [...]

Case is playing his concertina. Captain Randall is playing the fiddle. The tune is a strange yet recognisable version of the Wedding March. They are sitting, playing, at the bottle-laden table.

Wiltshire stands in the middle of the room, a glass in his hand. Near him, holding a book, stands Little Jack. He wears a clergyman's dog-collar of stiff white paper. They are both looking towards the open door leading to the veranda, beyond which can be seen the tropical starred night.

Uma comes in from the veranda, into the lamplit room. She comes in gravely and shy, her eyes looking down. She wears her bridal dress: a kilt of fine tapa, silkenly swathed; a necklace of white flowers; flowers behind her ears; a woven garland on her head; a mantle of tapa tied in a bow on the left shoulder, leaving the right shoulder bare. Her feet are bare, but her ankles wound about with flowers. She crosses, and stands between Wiltshire and Little Jack.

Wiltshire moves a few steps towards her. His eyes are hot and reckless. For the first time she raises her eyes to his. She does not smile. Her eyes are beautiful and trusting.

Case and Randall stop playing. Randall fortifies himself with a swig from a bottle at his side. Little Jack begins the 'wedding ceremony'. Case allows himself, gently, sardonically, to smile.

Shyly, seriously, attentively, Uma listens. Wiltshire looks at her. As the 'ceremony' continues, he glances at Little Jack with an expression of distaste, then looks again at Uma who is confident and tranquil. And Little Jack's voice, black, mellow, deep and unctuous, goes on throughout: 'Dearly beloved ... Those whom God hath joined let no man put asunder ...'

Uma and Wiltshire join hands. The music of fiddle and accordion begins again; this time, gay South Sea music, but with the fiddle apt to shrill and scrape erratically. Little Jack hands a rolled paper with a bow round it to Wiltshire, who puts it in his pocket. Little Jack smiles his great sliced-melon smile.

Case and Randall are still playing. Randall is trying to raise his bottle to his mouth at the same time as he scrapes away on the fiddle. Case is smiling.

Outside Case's bungalow, Wiltshire and Uma walk towards the village, hand in hand. The village is pointed with little fires under the trees. The music of fiddle and accordion dims into the background.

In Cases's bungalow, Little Jack and Randall convivially are passing the gin bottle one to the other, Little Jack rolling his eyes, nudging Randall, making the mock gesture of prayer, then slapping his thigh and doubling up with laughter; Randall tittering and winking. Case still plays on the accordion, not noticing the drunk antics of the two others but gazing fixedly out at the night beyond the veranda, smiling crookedly, thin-lipped, to himself.

Outside Wiltshire's bungalow, Wiltshire and Uma are walking on under the trees towards their house and their marriage night. There is the sounding of the surf and the dim village chanting.

Wiltshire and Uma come into the moonlit bedroom of Wiltshire's bungalow. He strikes a match, lights a lamp. There is a bed in the corner. Uma looks around her calmly. Then she puts out her hand to Wiltshire. He moves towards her, but stops as she says: 'Please!'

He looks at her uncomprehending.

UMA: Please! For me. The little paper he gave. My wedding paper.

WILTSHIRE (*softly*):   No, no.

UMA: Always I want to keep it.

And she smiles, beautifully, trustingly. Slowly he hands her the paper. She holds it to her, standing near the table on which the lamp is shining. She looks up at him: 'Now I am your wife for ever.'

He catches her in his arms. The paper falls on to the table near the lamp. On the lamplit paper in copper-plate writing, are the words:

> This is to certify that Uma, daughter of Faavo of Falesá, is illegally married to Mr Wiltshire, and that Mr Wiltshire can send her packing to hell whenever he pleases.
>
> JOHN BLACKAMOOR
> CHAPLAIN
> [...]

And the voices of the little girls on the beach take up his cry, waving out to sea. Wiltshire, striding along the beach, stops and stares out to sea at the sound of the shrill young voices. There is a long whale-boat, painted white, coming towards the island. Twenty-four paddles are flashing and dipping in the sun. And all the crew are singing. [...]

The white man is getting out of the boat at the edge of the surf. He is dressed in white duck clothes, with helmet, white shirt, and tie. He carries a white sunshade. The children dance about him in delight, but suddenly there are cries from the villagers.

The white man looks up from the children at Wiltshire and Case fighting. Wiltshire knocks Case to the ground. Case rises unsteadily and is floored again. He lies where he falls, in the sand, and Wiltshire stands over him. The white man moves towards them. The villagers make a path for him. He hurries up. As he nears Case and Wiltshire, Case kicks Wiltshire in the side.

STRANGER: Stop!

Wiltshire turns round, his face savage, and confronts the stranger with brutal truculence: 'What do *you* want? D'you want to see me kick him in the fangs?'

But Case has risen and is moving off, his eyes fixed with hatred on Wiltshire. At Wiltshire's words and the tone of his voice, the still crowds gathered behind the stranger begin a suppressed but angry murmur.

STRANGER: Who are you?

WILTSHIRE: I'm Wiltshire. I'm the new trader here. And who the hell are you?

STRANGER: My name is Jenkins. I am a missionary.

His voice is liltingly Welsh. His face is stern.

WILTSHIRE: You look like one. Come on, I've got a job for you.

MISSIONARY: Have you now indeed?

WILTSHIRE: And I want two of your crew as well.

MISSIONARY: Do you now? Would you like my boat too?

WILTSHIRE: I'm not asking any favours. I don't like favours, and I don't like missionaries. This is the sort of job you've got to do whether you like it or not.

MISSIONARY: You don't like missionaries, Mr Wiltshire? And I don't like drunken bullies. It's your kind that's fouling the islands. It's you and the guttersnipes like you that *dare* to sell my people drink and drugs and teach them your own vices. I see the people here know you only too well. They keep away from you. Wise boys!

WILTSHIRE: I'm not drunk, Mr Missionary. And don't you worry about *them*. I'm taboo. I'm the devil.

MISSIONARY: Indeed? I've always wanted to meet you. How is business in Falesá?

WILTSHIRE: I'm not to be made fun of by ...

MISSIONARY (*interrupting*):   Not even by a missionary? Such feeble old fellows we are too, not a spark of fun in us.

WILTSHIRE: I want you to do something for me. I want your help.

MISSIONARY: That's better talk now.

WILTSHIRE: Because you're the only person who can help me. Will you come with me? Please.

MISSIONARY (*dubiously*):   Well I *may* be wrong about you. I'll take a chance.

The missionary turns and calls out in native to his crew. Two of them join him. They are powerful men. They scowl at Wiltshire. The missionary steps up to the side of Wiltshire, and together they walk up the beach. The two native crew walk close and protectively behind.

MISSIONARY: Where are we going?

WILTSHIRE: To my place.

Now the missionary and Wiltshire, closely followed by their guard, are walking up the steps of the veranda of Wiltshire's bungalow and into the trading-room. In passing, Wiltshire quickly, so quickly that it is scarcely possible to see what he is doing, tears a brass ring off the thin blind on the window.

They walk through into the living-room. Uma is there. The missionary takes off his pith helmet. Tufts and little thickets of wiry white hair spring out from the sides of his head, like hair on a clown's head. His white eyebrows are jutting and very thick. Beneath them his eyes are bright and black, missing nothing.

MISSIONARY: Why, Uma, my dear! Well, well!

He addresses Wiltshire: 'We are old friends.' Uma curtsies. The missionary looks from Uma to Wiltshire and then back to Uma.

UMA: *We* are husband and wife.

WILTSHIRE: Uma, give us your marriage certificate.

Uma puts her hand quickly to the breast of her dress.

WILTSHIRE: Come on. You can trust me.

He puts out his hand, and trustingly, but reluctantly, Uma brings out her marriage certificate from the breast of her dress. She hands the paper to him.

Wiltshire turns to the missionary, looking at him squarely: 'I was married to Uma by Little Jack the black man. You know him?'

MISSIONARY: Badly.

WILTSHIRE: This certificate was written by Case. Do you know him too?

MISSIONARY: For my sins. And for his.

WILTSHIRE: Then you can guess what's in it?

MISSIONARY: I can.

WILTSHIRE: And now I've found that Uma is tabooed. Case saw to that because he couldn't have her for himself. And so long as I'm with her I can't trade here and the curse is on me too. All right, I understand that. So this is what I am going to do.

And Wiltshire tears up the marriage certificate and scatters the pieces on the floor.

Uma wails out: 'Ave! Ave!'

She begins to clap her hands and cry with grief. Wiltshire catches hold of her hand.

WILTSHIRE: And this is what I want *you* to do. Marry us properly, with ring and witnesses and everything.

In Wiltshire's open hand is the brass ring he has torn off the window-blind.

In the living-room of Wiltshire's bungalow, Wiltshire and the missionary are sitting at the table, the remains of a meal before them. The native witnesses have gone. Uma brings over to the table a teapot and two cups and saucers which she lays before them. She pours the tea as the missionary speaks: 'Mr Wiltshire, I have to thank you for a very lovely pleasure. I have rarely performed the marriage ceremony with more grateful emotions.'

He takes a sip from his cup, then lifts a bushy, white, inquiring eyebrow at Uma: 'Is this tea?'
Uma, standing near, waiting for appreciation, nods her head.

MISSIONARY (*to Wiltshire*): I shouldn't really be in these parts till the rainy season – it comes down in buckets, worse than Wales. I haven't been home for forty-three years and seven months – but I've been hearing strange stories about Falesá.

He takes another sip, looks at Uma: 'Are you sure this is tea?'
Uma nods again: 'I made it from the packet.'

MISSIONARY: It must be me who tastes of salt, then. It's queer how you hear these rumours flying across from island to island. After a long time you begin to *see* them almost, like puffs of smoke coming over the water. You *feel* there's something strange and wrong somewhere, in the way your boys sing as they row when you're out in the mission boat.

Wiltshire lights a cigar.

MISSIONARY: I heard stories too, mind, about Johnny Adams with the club foot going so sudden, scared off the island, so they said, but I knew there was strangeness blowing before I heard a word. And then, when I stepped off on the beach ...

WILTSHIRE: You were right. There's strange things happening, and I'm not so far off knowing why.

MISSIONARY: Tell me all you know.

Uma raises the teapot and is about to pour.

MISSIONARY: No, no, no more tea!

And the missionary bends forward to listen, his eyes bright under the white eyebushes, looking keenly at Wiltshire and at the glowing end of his long cigar.

Wiltshire puts his fingers to his cigar to take it out of his mouth. The cigar has burnt down to the end.

WILTSHIRE: ... and all the rest, I *guess*.

MISSIONARY: Case is a bad enemy. You were wrong when you said *you* were the devil hereabouts, Mr Wiltshire. He has a very clever representative on the island already.

WILTSHIRE: And he gives himself the devil of a lot of trouble too, just to be the only trader and get all the copra there is.

MISSIONARY (*slowly*):   I wonder if that is all he wants.

The missionary rises from the table. 'Now you leave the taboo to *me*. I'll show these backsliders what for. I'll give them a sermon from First Kings, xix, that'll wither 'em in their pews. I'm the only man in the world who can use the Welsh hwyl in Polynesian dialect. And I'll see Case too.'

He collects his pith helmet and parasol. Uma comes, shyly, into the room. He gives a little bow to her: 'Thank you for your hospitality, Mrs Wiltshire.'

And he shakes Wiltshire's hand and goes out. On the veranda steps he opens his parasol, holding it above him. He hurries off towards the village, a slight, old, indomitable figure.

The missionary is standing outside Case's bungalow. The doors along the veranda are closed.

MISSIONARY (*calling sternly*):   Come out, Mr Case.

And Case's voice answers mockingly from within: 'Come in, Mr Jenkins.'

The missionary goes up the steps. He is about to try to open the door of the trading-store, when the door, as though by itself, swings open. The missionary enters. He walks into the trading-room, stops a little way inside the threshold, his parasol still up. The door closes.

CASE: An open umbrella indoors brings bad luck.

The missionary lowers his umbrella, closes it, his sharp eyes staring under their spiky bushes into the darkness, from which Case's voice comes lightly and banteringly.

CASE: That's better. We are all superstitious here. We never look at the new moon through glass. We never look at the new moon. We believe in omens, auguries, wizards, werewolves. We wave wands and rub rings. We fee faw fum in the night. We say our prayers. We cross our fingers. We touch wood.

Throughout the missionary grips his parasol as though it were a sword of righteousness.

CASE: And here's an old salt we throw over our left shoulder.

Out of the darkness, keeping his back to the wall, Captain Randall sidles into the trading-room, his eyes owl-blinking in the light. He stops, his back to the wall, his eyes on the missionary. Behind the missionary looms Little Jack at the veranda door. The missionary takes no notice of either, but speaks, fearlessly, into the dark.

MISSIONARY: Come out here in the light, where I can see you, Mr Case.

CASE: Come on into the dark, where *I* can see you, Mr Jenkins.

And from the darkness a macaw screams.

CASE (*soothingly*): Pretty Poll! Pretty Poll! His mother was frightened by a missionary.

The missionary moves across to the door leading to the dark: 'Come out here, or by God, I'll come to you.'
He raises his parasol menacingly.
Suddenly there is light in the living-room, bars of muted light across the floor. Case stands now at the open shutters. He wears white trousers, but is bare to the waist. Around his neck are hung native necklaces of sharks' teeth and little bones. His feet are bare. His arms and chest are intricately and hideously tattooed all over, not with sailors' flags and anchors, names, serpents, arrowed hearts, but with tribal signs and caste marks.

CASE: Come to me, if you must.

And the missionary enters the room. He stares at Case, his bright eyes hard and unwavering.

MISSIONARY (*softly*): Very nice, very nice. I should have known.

CASE: You with your sun-brolly and your Bible, your tracts and your gimcrack chapels, spreading your message over the islands like a bucket of whitewash, hymning and ha-ing, what could *you* know?

MISSIONARY: So you have turned savage.

CASE: I was savage from birth.

MISSIONARY: You must have been a very nasty baby.

CASE: I was Caliban's son brought up for the church. I was a child suckled by wolves, brought up to brush my fangs and wash my paws before meals. I was a savage brought up to say 'sir', respect my elders, kowtow before the law, learn to read and write, suffer the classics in a rat-hole for the sons of gentlemen, proceed to hallowed university, take a worthless degree ...

The missionary shakes his head slowly and ruefully as he looks at Case. Case ironically attitudinising, full of disgust and venom there in the fly-loud, fly-blown, bottle-strewn bedded room, his hand at the barbaric ornaments around his neck, the tribal signs, the painted eyes, the exotic tattooing clear on the brown of his arms and chest.

MISSIONARY: A BA too.

CASE: Enter a profession, marry a decent woman, increase the population, achieve prosperity and ulcers, die respected in bed ...

MISSIONARY (*softly*):   I wonder where you *will* die – and instead, you're chief cook and bottle-washer on a tiny South Sea island, trying to teach a handful of natives to be naughty.

CASE: I teach them to be evil.

MISSIONARY: Go on with you, man, I've no patience. Evil is powerful. And you – you are nothing but a sick little moochin picking the wings off bluebottles.

CASE: Oh, my turbulent priest, you are scoffing at me now. You are belittling my bad deeds. I admit quite frankly to you that my opportunities for doing harm here are very small. I could achieve far more were I on the Government of a Great Power. But I do my best.

MISSIONARY: You make up some story or the other about a young girl because you cannot seduce her, and she is tabooed by the village. You pair her off with a newcomer, so that he cannot get any trade. What lies did you tell about the other trader, Adams, to get rid of *him*? How did you frighten *him*?

CASE: Oh, that was simple, even for an amateur diabolist. He has a club foot, you see. I told the chiefs and elders that he wore that ungainly boot because his foot was cloven. After that they would have nothing to do with him. And then he drank till he saw blue devils. And then he ran away. And only *I* was left.

MISSIONARY (*in disgust*):   You're a fraud, Mr Savage Case. Here you are practising your hellish hanky-panky just to keep other traders off Falesá. You profess to love Evil for its own sake – and it's all for profit.

CASE: I want no other trader here because I like the island too much. I want no stranger to share it. This is my island.

Then he speaks with a kind of ironic contempt, satirising his own romanticism: 'I know all the noises and smells of it. I know the beach and the bush and the wild pigs and the duck in the mangroves and the beetles on the vine and the smell of bats in the trees. I know the cries of all the birds in the haunted bush and every chime of the surf; acacias, magnolias, hibiscus, passion flowers, pomegranate; the stars of the night fires outside the houses at deep blue midnight; the drums high away up in the forgotten wood; the death songs; the death dance; the temples and sacred groves, huge terraces of stone all peopled with the dead. I love the ancient fear of Falesá.'

MISSIONARY: And, by God, *I'll* drive it out!

The deep, cracked bell of the Wesleyan Chapel and the high, harsh bell of the Baptist Chapel are ringing. And suddenly both bells stop.

Outside one of the chapels can be heard the voices of the natives singing inside, then the sound of their praying. And then the voice of the missionary is raised in passionate exhortation. His voice is punctuated by the dolorous cries and the pious, fearful interjections of the congregation.

In the chapel, the congregation is sitting on the floor on mats. The women are on one side of the long, low room, the men on the other. In the pulpit at the end of the chapel stands the missionary preaching with great eloquence. Maea is in the audience.

The missionary raises his finger in admonition, storms, warns and wheedles. The congregation responds to his every mood, approving, shuddering, giving little cries or grunts of grief and contrition as he moves them. He speaks loudly the words 'Case', 'Wiltshire', 'Taboo'. Maea, sitting in the front of the chapel as befits a chieftain, nods in solemn approval.

Later the natives come out of the chapel. They are all silent. They are not look into one another's faces. Very slowly, their eyes downcast, they begin in silence to disperse.

The missionary comes out of the chapel. The grieving and humiliated villagers, slowly returning to their homes, to the beach, to the bush, to the green of the village, look away from the missionary in silent guilt and shame.

And then Case, immaculate in white ducks, comes jauntily out of the trees and approaches the missionary. When he is quite near he raises his hand with a dramatic flourish to command attention. The dispersing villagers stop and surround Case and the missionary, still, silent, not understanding them.

CASE: So here is the holy man.

He turns to the villagers and translates his words into native.

CASE: You have been preaching against me, but that was not in your heart.

Again he translates the sense of what he has said.

CASE: You have been preaching for the love of God – but that was not in your heart.

He translates again for the benefit of the uncomprehending crowd whose stillness and silence is now compounded of guilt and shame towards the missionary and fear of Case. The missionary does not speak, holds himself firm and erect, his hands steady on his parasol, his eyes meeting Case's with a fierce disdain.

CASE: Shall I show you what is in your heart?

He turns to the villagers, translates, all with perfect, insolent ease and plausibility. And then, turning again to the missionary, he makes a deft and rapid pass at his breast. Rapidly, professionally, he flashes his hand in the air, opens his hand. In his palm lies a silver dollar. He shows it, flashing it in his hand, before the eyes of the villagers who step back fearfully. A low and terrified murmur spreads through the crowd.

CASE: A silver dollar! Your heart is full of the greed of money.

He translates quickly into native. The word and the news of the miracle ripple through the voices of the crowd, and amazement rolls in their eyes. Case flings the coin to the ground, and those nearest it back quickly away, as though it were a contamination.

CASE: What is your tongue made of?

And again, pattering in native, he makes a deft and rapid pass about the missionary's mouth, flashes his hand in the air, opens his hand. In the palm of his hand moves a live scorpion.

MISSIONARY (*ruefully to himself*): Oh that I had learnt conjuring instead of Hebrew!

Case flings the scorpion to the ground, and the crowd in horror retreat from it. And once more, rattling out in native his prestidigitatorial patter, he conjures from the missionary's head a handful of maggots, which he casts from him contemptuously. And the crowd wails. Some of them run away. Some of them, crying out at the prodigy they have seen, hubbubbing with horror, their guilt and shame towards the missionary vanquished by their fear of Case, cluster around him.

MISSIONARY (*to Case*):   You've won for the moment, with your little parlour tricks. But don't think you'll win for long. I've buried worse scamps than you, Mr Case. I may do you that service yet.

And he goes off, followed by a small band of the faithful. [...]

From above the wide grove in the moonlight, a stream foams out of the descending galleries and gardens of the tremendous, verdurous, impenetrable high interior of the island. It is the grove Wiltshire and the native boys saw when they sat together in a clearing and talked of Tiapolo. Along the narrow winding path through the grove goes the lithe figure of Wiltshire, bearing a lit lantern. The path is that on which they saw, from above, Case walking out of the dense eastward bush.

Wiltshire reaches the end of the path where it threads among ferns and flowers and is lost. His rifle is slung over his shoulder. He hears the distant sounding of the sea. He forces his way through the thick moonlit vegetation at the end of the path.

Once within, the moon is put out, like a candle, by the windy, swarming dark draperies of vine, the arches of interlacing boughs, convolvulus, and giant creeper. All sound is muffled and swaddled. His lantern goes on, like an eye before him.

And then he is out again of the thronged and teeming jungle dark, into moonlight and the far but clear sound of the sea. Before him lies a long mound of stones and great boulders, the beginning of an ancient wall stretching out seemingly endlessly.

There are coco palms, mummy apples, sensitivie and guavas. And all about, the high bush; trees going up like the masts of ships, ropes of liana hanging down, orchids growing in the forks of the trees like fungi.

He goes on, soft-footed, wary now, spying around him. On all sides are to be heard faint and stealthy scurries; the newly unwoken warnings of little, unseen animals; the prying fingering of gusts of wind from the sea, in ferns, leaves, flowers, and shadows. The lantern and the moonlight make the bush all turning shadows that weave to meet him and then spin off, that hover over his head and fly away, huge, birdlike, into deeper inextricable dark. The floor of the bush glimmers with dead wood. The leaves quiver, the great ferns bend and bow, the glimmering deadwood crackles.

And, all at once, he hears a sound of singing on the wind. A high musical ululation that seems to come from many places and many shadows at the same time. The music of the small falling spheres. A wisping and wailing like the tail or wake of a falling rocket. A ghost note rising and swelling and dying away and swelling again. Someone weeping, most beautifully, not of this earth. A harp, glissando'd by drifting leaves and water.

He stops, unslings and cocks his rifle. His eyes range the singing dark, dart this way and that among wavering shadows, weed and creeper, willowing trees, articulate wildness. He takes a few guarded steps forward. Moonlight and lantern-light show the controlled fear on his face, the sweat on his brow. He speaks to himself, softly, to keep his courage up, by challenging the unknown wailing: 'Come on, you beautiful women of Fanga-anaana.'

And the single undulating ghost-note is taken up by a score of others. The bush is highly wild with music. Then the wind blows in a sudden gust, and the leaves before him burst open. He sees a face in the middle branches. Then the leaves close. And out of the closed leaves comes the sound of harping, weeping, and singing. He lays down his gun and lantern, clicks his jack-knife open, sticks it between his teeth, and approaches the tree.

Out of the closed leaves comes the sound of harping, weeping, singing. He climbs the tree, thrusting the vegetation aside. The face grins down at him. He climbs and reaches it. And then he laughs. His laughter, relief from pent-up fear, echoes among the wailing voices, mingles with the singing that comes from the face in the mid-branches. He tears the face down from the branches and, holding it, climbs down on to the glimmering deadwood-littered ground.

The face is a square box, with the face painted on one side. On the other side is printed 'Milady Toilet Soap'. Banjo strings are stretched across the open end of the box. Wiltshire strums his fingers across the strings, then ties the strings of the Aeolian harp on to his belt, picks up gun and lantern, and moves on. As he moves, so, every now and then, a puff of wind plays on the hanging face.

He reaches deep undergrowth. Here he has to force his way through, plying his knife as he goes, slicing the cords of liana, slashing down the great weeds. And still the other harps sing all around him in the trees. He struggles through undergrowth into a clearing.

In the clearing stands a high, druidical pile of ancient stones. And beyond it, a path. The path is very narrow, but well-beaten. He follows it and then stops dead. In front of him is a wall, tumbledown, very old, big-bouldered. The wall faces him, and along the top of it is a line of figures. They are little less than man-size and lurch and bob in the wind. The hidden harps sing as, cautiously, he approaches them. They have hideous carved and painted faces and shudder and twitch as if pulled by strings. Their limbs work with the tugging of the wind. Their eyes and teeth are made of shell. Their straw hair and their tribal garments blow in his face.

Suddenly Wiltshire jerks back with a start. A night bird silently dives down past him and tears at the hair of one of the figures lurching and bobbing there. Then, as Wiltshire moves, the bird flies off with a sharp single shriek. [...]

WILTSHIRE: Go on laughing. Smile at me, Uma. Laugh at me, Case.

His knife is open in his hand. Case fastens his teeth in his forearm, but Wiltshire heeds nothing. He does not attempt to shake off the weasel-like hold of Case's teeth. Wiltshire stabs Case in the body.

WILTSHIRE: For Johnny Adams.

And he stabs him again. 'For Uma!'

Case twitches and lies still. Wiltshire rolls off him. He props himself up and bends over Case. Case's eyes are shut. But he speaks in the ghost of his dry, precise, mocking voice, slowly: 'I did what evil I could. I should have been a politician. There is more scope. Is Uma dead?'

Wiltshire does not answer, stares down at the thin, bitterly twisted dying lips and the shut eyes.

CASE: I wanted to make a clean sweep of you all tonight. It was my birthday. I wanted to kill you and Uma and Little Jack and Daddy Randall. Old friends – all of you. I poisoned Daddy's drink before leaving. I hope he shares the bottle with Little Jack. I think he will. He was always a generous man. Did I tell you it was my birthday today? I keep forgetting. Do you know how old I am?

The thin twisted lips stiffen and then sag. Silence and stillness. Wiltshire stares close at the dead face.

WILTSHIRE: You're very old now.

And a sudden wind sets the harp voices wailing. Wiltshire turns, crawling away.

There is a noise of voices and of feet crushing the underwood. The missionary, followed by Maea, comes through the bush, leading a party of men.

The missionary is leading the men down through the bush above Falesá towards the village. Below can be seen the night fires of Falesá. Beyond them, the sounding sea.

Uma is being carried on a litter of branches. Wiltshire is limping along, supporting himself against one of Maea's braves and Maea himself is bearing sack-wise over his shoulder the dead body of Case.

The party comes out of the bush by Case's bungalow. The bearers carry Uma on towards the village. Maea, followed limpingly by Wiltshire and his supporting native, walks up the veranda steps, Case over his shoulder. He flings the door open.

In the trading-room, where a lit lamp hangs from the roof, Little Jack and Captain Randall sit at the table, their heads sunken. On the table in front of them is a half-empty bottle and two glasses. Also on the table, directly before them, are their two fiddles, the bows by the side. At the top of the table there is one unoccupied chair. And on the table in front of that chair lies Case's concertina.

Maea comes into the room, followed by Wiltshire and his attendant. Maea slumps Case down into the unoccupied chair directly facing the concertina. The three dead men sit before their instruments. Wiltshire stands at the door.

WILTSHIRE (*slowly*):   You wouldn't think they were dead. You'd think they were going to play.

He stares at the three dead men and the fiddles and the concertina.

The missionary, Maea, Wiltshire, and his attendant walk towards Wiltshire's bungalow where Uma is lying in bed in the living-room. The missionary bandages her shoulder. She is smiling. Wiltshire bends down over her.

The stars of the night fires are burning in the village. As though from the inside of Case's bungalow, comes the gay music of fiddles and concertina.

And beyond the bungalow, the gay music continues to the beach of Falesá.

Me and My Bike

'I'm *extremely* keen on the Bike. For me, as a supposedly imaginative writer, it's got wonderful possibilities'[93] was Thomas's response to the projected 'film operetta', and later: 'So glad Sidney was amused by the first chunk of *Me & My Bike*.'[94] Sidney Box has given a vivid memory of Dylan Thomas's excitement when first coming to tell him of what Thomas later called 'a musical comedy film'.[95]

> As always with Dylan, it started with high hopes. His head appeared around my door, like a dissolute cherub's, his eyes shining with excitement. 'I want to write the first original film operetta,' he told me. 'It will be all about a man who loves a bicycle. It's called *Me and My Bike* and it covers the whole span of this man's life. He rides penny-farthings, tandems, tricycles, racing bikes – and when he dies at the end, he rides on his bike up a sunbeam straight to heaven, where he's greeted by a heavenly chorus of bicycle bells.'

This short excerpt from the unfinished first section shows Dylan Thomas's gift for mimicry, parody of other poetic styles, and lighthearted work of fancy. There is charm, too, in the presence of another Dylan Thomas familiar, the fox, who this time joins the chase!

ME AND MY BIKE

We see, in half-darkness, a large country house. We move past the house towards the paddocks, and, as we move, so it grows lighter. We move into the stable-yards, and now it lightens into a cold, grey, winter dawn. And, from the shut stables, we hear a whinnying and neighing of horses and the noise of their hoofs on cobbles. Fred, unseen, is singing –

> I remember, I remember
> The place where I was born
> Over Sir Gregory's stables
> Where the horses neighed at dawn.
>
> My father was head stable man
> And I was stable lad,
> And we'd all be up at the whinny of dawn,
> Me, and the horses, and dad.
>
> And sun or snow or rain or no
> I'd be crawling out of my bed
> And yawning into the Yorkshire dawn
> Whenever the horses said –

Two candles are lit behind the two little curtained windows above the stables. A wooden stair reaches from the rooms above the stables to the yard. Out on to the top of the wooden stairs comes Fred, a boy of about fourteen, pulling on his stable jacket, yawning, rubbing the sleep from his eyes. Still half awake he comes down, steps into the yard, and crosses to a corner where there is a bucket and pump. He pumps water into the bucket, puts it, full, on a bench, plunges his head in and comes out gasping. From the stables we hear a chorus of horses, singing hoarsely in Yorkshire accents –

> Hurry up, hurry up, sleepy head.
> The horses used to say
> Rubbing and tubbing it like a lord
> And taking all the day!
> Hurry up, hurry up, sleepy Fred,
> Jump in your boots and jig!
> If you don't come soon with our oats and bran
> We'll tell Sir Gregory Grig!

Fred scrambles through his washing, runs a horse-comb through his hair, and climbs another flight of wooden steps that leads from the yard to the granary. As he opens the granary door, he looks around him at the park, growing lighter, at the wide frosty paddocks with their gate and water jumps, and at the great manor house, slow wisps of smoke coming out of its chimneys. A cock crows, far away, then its morning warning is taken up here and there from the manor house and the farms beyond. Fred goes into the dark and dusty granary, shoulders a sack and climbs down. [...]

In the manor house, Lady Grig is coming stealthily upstairs, an unlit candle in her hand. She looks cautiously all around her as she reaches the top of the stairs. On tiptoe she moves down the wide dark landing. On the walls are sporting prints, portraits of horses and horsemen, disturbingly alike: against the wall are large glass cases of stuffed foxes. She climbs, stealthily, another flight of stairs. She reaches a smaller landing, stops at a cupboard marked LINEN. Fearfully she opens the door, recoils, fingers to nose. Then, braving herself, she peers in. The deep cupboard is very dark. Nothing can be seen for a moment. Then she sees two eyes low down in the cupboard. With trembling hand, she lights the candle. She reaches the candle into the linen cupboard and looks down. There, in a nest of sheets and pillowcases, lies a fox, suckling its young. Lady Grig lets out a little squeak. And the fox wags its brush. Lady Grig, infinitely cautious, closes the cupboard door. She blows out the candle. Her voice trembles as she exclaims –

'Oh, whatever will Gregory say!'

As she tiptoes away across the landing, all bewilderment and apprehension, she catches the eye of a stuffed fox in a glass case, and winces.

At her boudoir window, Georgina is singing –

> The cold, cold, deep river
> That runs in the dale
> Behind the tall bushes
> Now tells an old tale,
> With a ripple and quiver
> O lover to be,
> The lovely green rushes
> Are singing to me. […]

In the far distance, a young man on a penny-farthing bicycle is riding down the slope of a country lane. He is clad in full bicycling costume of the eighties and rides his fearful machine with an attempt at debonair confidence, whistling the tune of 'Me and my bike' as he wheels down the slope, but wincing as the rubberless wheels bump in each rut […]

They stop suddenly as they see Fred on the penny-farthing wobbling down the drive. Astonished gardeners pop up their heads from bushes and borders as Fred careers down the drive. We follow him on his erratic course. Around the corner of the drive comes, at a spanking pace, Sir Gregory Grig in his gig. Fred, the penny-farthing out of control, goes faster and faster. We see Nell, at the top of the drive, her mouth wide open in horror. We see Augustus and Georgina fluttering with horror on the lawn. One by one the gardeners shut their eyes ... CRASH!

(From Thomas's *Outline of remaining Scenes*)

Scene in the morning room of Sir Gregory Grig's manor.

In this scene, Sir Gregory, in a towering temper, listens to Fred's father making excuses for Fred's unwarrantable behaviour and pleading that it will never happen again. The butler and housekeeper are present to witness the Awful Warning ... Fred hangs his head before Sir Gregory and does not speak. At last Sir Gregory turns to Fred and asks what he has to say.

Fred says: 'But, sir, I don't like horses.'

A silence of numbed astonishment and shock. [...]

Lady Grig, at the top of the stairs, is listening to the hullaballoo from outside. She is in her constant state of harassed bewilderment. Just behind her is the linen cupboard. There comes, from outside, an extra loud cry of 'Tally ho!' from the Dowager Lady Grig; and the linen cupboard door bursts open. Out comes the fox and its young. Down the stairs they run, past Lady Grig, through the hall, over the steps, on to the drive. Fred is now almost at the end of the drive, running all out. Behind him run Sir Gregory, Fred's father, the butler, housekeeper, gardeners, footmen, maids, wizened boy, Georgina, Augustus, and the Dowager Lady Grig, on horseback. Only Nell stands still, watching it all, tears in her eyes. And then the fox and its young, yelping, rush past her. They too join the chase –

Rebecca's Daughters

'Thank you for the copy of the 1st draft of "Rebecca's Daughters". I've now read all the stuff you gave me on the subject but haven't yet started getting down to the writing. I'll be doing this next week,'[96] wrote Dylan Thomas to Jan Read in November 1948. The six months of writing the script kept the usual pattern: in December he writes to Read, 'I am now working *hard* on Rebecca, having somehow managed to tidy out my domestic crisis'[97] and the following February joked to a friend, 'I am working on a film which is trying to kill me.'[98] But the script proved a vividly unfolding story, told in Thomas's strongly cinematic visual and atmospheric prose, of the Rebecca rioters who protested violently against tollgate taxes, Poor Law amendment and consequent poverty and distress. The opening scene of a coach being driven on a wild rainy night through the dark and remote countryside of West Wales is already like seeing the opening of a film. It is of course a part of Wales Dylan Thomas already knew well. What especially fire his imagination are the nightly gatherings of the rioters, mostly peasant farmers with their rough but effective network of information. The darkness initially hiding these raiders is soon bright with the red fires of the burning tollgates. There is Welsh treachery (the blacksmith), English spies, and – hated more than the local aristocracy – English soldiers hounding, albeit incompetently, people of similar impoverished background, in the dramatically presented political struggle. Again the Welsh minister is one of the most vividly drawn figures; an enthusiastic rioter, Mordecai Thomas is comically apt to put himself in danger, despite his 'Rebecca' clothes, with his biblical exhortations. In his sermon in Bethel Chapel, Lord Sarn and his party present, he announces 'the preaching will be in English – there are strangers among us'. He then gives the biblical text for 'Rebecca' and a splendid defence of her cause and the present political conflict. Named Mordecai Thomas, one wonders whether Dylan Thomas was remembering his grandfather's brother, a poet in Welsh who had the bardic name Gwilym Marles, after the stream called Marlais, and of course handed down as Dylan's middle name.

Gwilym Marles was a Unitarian minister and political activist, defending tenants against the local landowners. This preacher-politician was evicted from his chapel. It is likely that Dylan, his great-nephew, knew of his own family's nineteenth-century political radicalism and protest, learned from his father.

The script also has romance in the friendship of Anthony Raine and Rhiannon, warming to love when she discovers he is Rebecca. Enlivening the script, too, are Dylan Thomas's wit and humour. Certainly Sir Henry, with his companion cat 'Rover', as fond of drink as he is, and his witty ripostes – often in Rover's defence, is one of Thomas's congenial comic figures. An exchange with Anthony when they meet in the opening coach drive reveals this deft mingling of politics and comedy.

> 'Every pike-man I've met at every tollgate on this vile road looks like a Welsh stoat that's been crossed with a spaniel – biting and fawning at the same time.'
> Sir Henry strokes his cat with affection.
> 'Not a word against the Welsh, please – Rover comes from Aberystwyth.'

There is, too, an almost Wildean wit in the conversational exchanges between the ladies at the ball.

> 'Ah, the number of times I have lost my heart on a moonlit terrace.'
> 'And,' observes Lady Price-Parry, in a honeyed voice, 'the number of times it has been found and returned to you, my dear.'

And when the ladies are discussing Rebecca's appearance:

> 'I go by my husband's description. After the night he spent in the ditch.'
> 'A very distressing night for Sir Henry.'
> 'Yes, very. And it wasn't even a ditch he knew.'

Sidney Box, the film producer who engaged Thomas for Gainsborough, wrote of his last script that 'It is an original story, written about a period in which he was passionately interested ... . Anyone reading *Rebecca's Daughters* in its present form should be able to imagine the film, as Dylan conceived it, unrolling on the screen before him.'[99] This is so. The film *Rebecca's Daughters* was made in 1992 – forty-two years later. It was Thomas's friend during his film years and his early biographer, Constantine FitzGibbon, who observed that 'he probably put more words on paper in this professional capacity [writer of filmscripts] than in any other'.[100]

REBECCA'S DAUGHTERS

Heavy rain in a wild wind. And winter dusk. Nothing but the torn and blowing sheets of rain, and the wind ripping and wailing.

Then, through the rain and wind, the clopping of horses' hooves and the rattle of wheels, and a closed chaise dashes past us into the wild dusk. Close, we see it as a great rattling blur in the rain and wind; then it is gone.

Now we see it, through the rain, approaching us down a narrow, pooled and rutted country road, bare trees each side of it, tossing in a temper. Blown broken branches scrabble and scrape the woodwork and windows as the chaise lurches on, the horses streaming and breathing out clouds in the dusky gusty cold. Up spurt the waves of mud.

The chaise rounds a corner of the narrow road. And, from the driver's box, lurching and tilting as we go, we see before us another rough stretch of road in the rain. And, some way ahead, a sign-post where the road divides in two directions.

The figure of a man, hat well pulled down and cloak buttoned high, stands beneath the sign-post, a desolate, dripping figure, his cloak swirling about him.

He steps into the middle of the road and holds up his hand.

We see him from the driver's box, looking down along the wet horses' backs. And we see the driver's mittened, soaking hands pull hard on the reins. The chaise draws up.

Of the two dividing roads before us, one is of fairly even surface, the other little more than a bogged and pitted farm-track.

The sign-post arm which points to the rude rough road, says: PEMBROKE.

The cloaked man moves, slushing through pools, to the side window of the chaise, comes close to it, peers through the blurred and streaming glass.

Seen through the glass, Anthony Raine lowers the window. He is a good-looking young man in the scarlet of an Army officer of the period 1843.

Now, from the interior of the chaise, we look past Anthony out of the lowered window to see the face of the cloaked man, Sir Henry Price-Parry, outside.

Sir Henry makes his gruff voice loud to sound above the wind and rain.

'Good evening, sir ...'

'No. An abominable evening, sir. Do not let us misuse words. You are waiting for the mail coach?'

'Waiting for it? Not to misuse a word, sir, I am longing for it. Been here since three o'clock. Soaked to the marrow.'

'You'll be waiting till midnight. We passed it miles back. One wheel half off, two of the horses limping, a lady in hysterics, and the coachman drunk. Where are you going?'

'Pembroke. And me dinner. And a mustard bath.'

'Jump in!'

'Thankee. I'll come in, sir.'

Anthony pushes open the door and, puffing and squelching, Sir Henry enters the coach.

Anthony looks out of the window at the whirling dusk and the two dividing roads. He speaks to Sir Henry over his shoulder as he stares out.

'Quicker to go by the by-road?'

'If your springs'll stand it. It ain't a road by right, it's a lot o' holes strung together by ditches. Save you hours, if you live.'

Anthony calls through the window to the driver.

'Take the road on the left!'

And the driver's voice answers him through wind and rain, as if from a great distance.

'Yes, sir, yes, Mr Anthony. Road on the left.'

The driver is a very small man muffled up in soaking sacks and rugs. Only his eyes and his long cold nose are visible. He whips up the horses.

'Here we go ...'

The chaise lurches violently.

'And we almost gone ...'

From the box, we see the lurching lane. Down we go bumping into a series of holes and pits, and up come spraying waves of mud.

Inside the chaise, Anthony and Sir Henry sit opposite each other.

Anthony huddles deeper into his Army great-coat. He is a young man of quiet, almost mild, demeanour, slow to smile but with a shrewd intelligence and humour deceptively hidden by his air of rather studied nonchalance. His voice is cool.

Sir Henry is a stocky, plump, well-fed gentleman of middling age and rising blood pressure, fond of old port and old jokes. A gruff and canny vulgarian of the 'old school'. He fumbles inside his cloak.

'Got a hip-flask here. If I can find me hip. Haven't felt me *ribs* for years.'

He brings out a silver hip-flask of very generous proportions.

'Ah, here we are. Join me? No? Good health to you, Mister —?'

He ends his toast interrogatively, drinks, sits back, and removes his hat. A river of rain-water runs down over him.

'My name is Raine. Anthony Raine.'

Sir Henry looks up sharply at Anthony.

'Anthony Raine? Thought ye were in India. I knew your father well. Went to his funeral. Missed me breakfast. I'm Price-Parry.'

'Yes. Sir Henry.'

'Heard of me, eh? Don't tell me they know me in *India*. I've never been further than Boulogne myself. Sick four times – once going over, twice there and once coming back. Don't like foreigners. All deaf. Got to shout to make 'em understand.'

The chaise creaks, lurches and hiccups through the mud and rain. [...]

Now outside on the muddy road, the chaise rattles and squelches past the pike-man, alone in the rain, still looking at the palm of his hand.

'Now there's a dishonest gentleman.'

Inside the chaise, Anthony gives Sir Henry a small smile.

'There's a rogue for you! He'd sell his mother for half an ounce of cats-meat.'

Sir Henry looks down at the cat in his lap, and, with a heavy jocoseness, shakes a warning finger at Anthony.

'Ssh! It understands English.'

But Anthony continues in his unruffled, nonchalant way, the rather violent words he uses in marked contrast to the almost priggish calmness of his voice.

'Every pike-man I've met at every tollgate on this vile road looks like a Welsh stoat that's been crossed with a spaniel – biting and fawning at the same time.'

Sir Henry strokes his cat with affection.

'Not a word against the Welsh, please – Rover comes from Aberystwyth.'

'And the number of those legalised highwaymen! These official pick-pockets! There must be more tollgates than liars in the country.'

'You're very peppery tonight, sir. I've always *heard* the Far East was bad for the liver. Mine stopped complaining long ago; it gave up the struggle. Oh, I agree with you, the pike-men are a naughty lot. Always a marvel to me how any toll-money gets into our pockets at all.'

Anthony glances at him politely, not understanding.

'*Our* pockets?'
Sir Henry darts a quick look at him.
'Oh, yes, of course. You've been away.' [...]

The congregation of Bethel Chapel is on its feet, singing a Welsh hymn, as Lord Sarn's party come in. Many surprised, disapproving and enquiring glances are turned in their direction. The hymn finishes, and the congregation sits down. Then Mordecai Thomas, the preacher, mounts into the high pulpit. He is a thin, ardent man of middle age, with fiery deep-set eyes and a shock of wild, black hair. An hour-glass stands on the pulpit before him. He looks down at Lord Sarn and begins. 'To-day, my friends, the preaching will be in English, and for this reason – there are strangers among us. Not strangers to our daily lives, but to this, our humble house. To them we speak a strange and foreign tongue. Therefore will we speak in the tongue which is theirs. And therefore will be bold, as is commanded in the Scriptures, and speak to them what is in our hearts. For who knows but that they have seen the error of their ways and have come among us to worship and repent.'

'Hallelujah,' says Beth Morgan, fervently from her seat in the front row.

All eyes are now on Lord Sarn and his party, sitting awkward and embarrassed among the congregation of small farmers, tradesmen and their wives, in the severe, bare chapel. Children stare wide-eyed at the sight of Marsden in his splendid uniform and Anthony in his host of coats. Anthony and Marsden stare without expression directly before them at the preacher in the pulpit, Rhiannon between them, and sensing their hostility, glances swiftly up at each in turn. Lord Sarn looks cautiously around him at the congregation. A small boy, with a suspicious swelling in the cheek, catches Lord Sarn's eye and hastily gulps. The swelling vanishes. The small boy looks away.

Mordecai Thomas has opened the big Bible. He turns the hour-glass over and begins. 'My text is taken from Genesis, the twenty-fourth chapter and the sixtieth verse. And they blessed Rebecca and said unto her, "Thou art our sister. Be thou the mother of thousands of millions, and let thy seed possess *the gate of those that hate them*." I ask you now – *What* are "the gates"? And *who* are they that keep the gates and that hate Rebecca and her seed? And Rebecca and her seed, who are they among us? It is not revealed to us whether Abraham, Isaac and Jacob paid toll to their enemies at these gates, but it is very sure that the gates were an oppression and an abomination, as are the gates upon the roads of the land wherein we labour. Consider now these gates, and the enemy at the gates and the blessed Rebecca and her seed who shall possess them ...'

The sands are running down in the hour-glass.

Outside the chapel, on the box of the Sarn carriage, the coachman is fast asleep, his head sunk on his chest. He moves uncomfortably in his sleep and snores with his elbow against the woodwork of the box. He mutters in his sleep, crossly, in a drowsy whisper 'Move up! Move up, Mary Ann! Always taking all the covers!'

He elbows his invisible sleeping-partner with so much force he wakes with a sharp groan. He feels his elbow, tenderly. From the chapel comes the droning of the preacher's voice.

The sands are lower in the hour-glass now. But Mordecai Thomas is still speaking ...

'We pay toll at these gates when we travel the roads about our lawful business. And where does the money go? Are the roads kept in repair for those that use them and pay for them out of their poverty? No, they are muckheaps and ruins that wreck our carts and cripple our horses and cattle. Where does the money go that is dragged out from our poverty? It is lost among the riches of the enemy at the gate. Let us now pray for a deliverer that shall be raised up among us, so that the seed of Rebecca, Rebecca's daughters, shall indeed possess the gates of her enemies and *lay them low*!'

He closes the Bible in front of him with a thud. [...]

Along a country road, a man, dressed as farmer, on horseback, gallops past two farmhands in a wagon. As the horseman goes off in the opposite direction he throws a crumpled piece of paper into the back of the wagon. One of the farmhands eagerly scrambles to pick it up and open it. The heads of the farmhands come together over the paper. They whisper, muted but urgent: 'Rebecca!'

In a country lane, a man is cutting the hedges. A horseman trots past him. A crumpled piece of paper falls down from the horseman near the hedger. The hedger picks it up, opens it. Again the whisper, muted but urgent: 'Rebecca!'

In an outhouse, a man is sawing wood. A figure passes quickly by the open window. A crumpled piece of paper falls down by the man. 'Rebecca!'

A cowhouse. In the morning light, we see the milk-pail, the udders of the cow, and the hands of the milker. A crumpled piece of paper is thrown to fall on the milk in the pail. The milker's hand retrieves the paper, opens it. Sound of horses' hooves galloping away. A whisper:

'The daughters of Rebecca!'

A country inn. We see a barrel of beer and the hands of a man drawing a pint mug. The hands put the full mug through the little window of a bar, then move away. On the little bar is left a crumpled piece of paper beside the pint. The first pair of hands picks up the paper and opens it. A whisper:

'They shall possess the gate.'

A sheepdog running in a field. A hand extracts a paper from under the dog's collar. A whisper:

'The gate of them that hate them.'

The farmers are moving to their secret meeting-place. On horseback they come out of their farmyards into country lanes, their lit lanterns swinging.

They ride, in small parties, into deep dark woods, a wild wind blowing.

Alone, they ride between black hedges, their lantern-lights flickering.

Out of the deep dark woods and into open country they ride together through wild wind.

Over street cobbles they come, their horses' hooves covered with sacking.

One rider, on an ancient horse, rides between tall trees, his lantern casting shadows, his umbrella swinging.

Some farmers on foot scramble down hillsides, silent and nimble as goats.

Through hedges and ditches come the young farm labourers on foot, silent and swift.

Over the fields, on a fine black horse a man rides fast, stops, tethers his horse on a tree at the dark fringe of a wood, slips through the wood and is lost.

Horsemen and men on foot, singly and in parties, swiftly, slowly, but always silently, move lanterned through the night.

And by their lantern-light we see that some wear improvised black masks.

The faces of some are almost hidden under black shawls.

And most of them have blackened their faces all over.

And all of them wear skirts.

Some wear their skirts tucked well up above breeches and heavy boots, and wear above them men's dark coats and cloaks.

Others wear their skirts full length.

And some are entirely dressed as women, up to their blackened faces and shawled heads.

And a few have, from somewhere, found old curly white wigs to wear. Black faces and white wigs jog in lantern-light as the horsemen ride on.

And many of them carry shotguns; and some have axes, some spades or pitchforks; and cattle-horns are slung from their shoulders.

We see them on the stormy skyline. All-Halloween riders, and the pitchforks they carry over their shoulders look like the horns and antlers of their familiars.

Now there is moonlight.

And now, silently, they converge from wood, lane, and field, hillside, thicket, ditch and dingle, on the far end of a disused quarry.

They all halt.

And beyond them, below the moonlit quarry fence, a man leaps up on to a great boulder and faces them.

He is black-masked.

He is disguised in traditional Welsh woman's costume, in wide black skirts and shawls. And he wears the tall, black, steeple hat.

Across his shoulder's slung a cow-horn.

The man speaks, and his voice is the voice of Anthony, disguised, though not grotesquely.

'I am Rebecca. Listen to me, my daughters, my beautiful black-faced daughters, my bearded ladies! Never ask who I am. Never tell another who *you* are. Not even your dearest friend. Never speak *his* name or *your* name aloud. There may be those tonight who would sell you to your enemies. You are Rebecca's Daughters! It is the only name your enemies will need to fear. Your enemies are the tollgates and those who put them up and those who grow fat on them. The gates must be destroyed. But there must be no bloodshed. If the pike-men show fight, tie them up and gag them. Do not hurt them. If you have to knock them down before you tie them up, then do it very gently. If you *have* to hurt them, let it be painless. We begin *now*! You know the first gate to destroy. You remember your instructions. Silent then, until you reach the gate. I shall be there with you.'

He leaps from the boulder into darkness.

And the crowd surges into action and begins to move away. Three men on horseback move towards the front of the crowd.

One is Mordecai Thomas, a black shawl concealing most of his face. He carries his old shabby umbrella like a raised sword.

One is Rhodri Huws, with blackened face and bare head.

The other is a farmer, whom we have seen before at Pembroke Market. He speaks excitedly. 'Darro, man, there's a fandango! Rebecca's daughters! There's a boy bach for you! Who was he? Did you know him? Where'd he come from?'

'He's the man for us,' says Rhodri. 'That's all *I* know.'

'A deliverer like unto Ehud and Gideon and Samson,' begins Mordecai, but Rhodri puts a hand across his mouth. 'Hush! you fool!'

The farmer looks heavenward in joyful supplication. 'Oh let there be bang bang tonight and blood all over the shop!'

Rhodri calms him too. 'There'll be no bloodshed, didn't you hear? And don't *you* quote scriptures either. You never know who'll hear you. If you feel a quotation coming on you whistle instead!'

And he rides on, followed by the two others.

We see the road, the gate, and the cottage, quiet and lonely in the moonlight.

And then Rebecca's daughters appear, dismounted, with 'Rebecca' himself at the head.

Silently they advance, led by Anthony in his steeple-hat. But, as they near the tollhouse, suddenly they raise their shotguns and fire into the air, blow on their cow-horns, catcall, whistle and yell. Their lanterns bob and sway.

In the small bedroom of the tollhouse, moonlight slants across the bed in which Jack Wet, the pike-man, and his wife lie asleep.

Quickly they jump awake, sit, night-capped and astounded in bed, as pandemonium sounds below. Jack Wet stretches a shaking hand towards the candle by the bedside.

Outside, the crowd blows, bangs, hoots, howls, hullaballoos.

Anthony, at their head, raises his hand.

At once they are silent. A solitary cow-horn dies on a mooing note.

Anthony steps up to the tollhouse, stands beneath the new lighted window.

And he calls out clearly, 'Jack Wet!' [...]

The crowd takes hold of them [Jack Wet and his wife] without violence.

'Let them see the good work!' shouts Anthony. 'Go to it, Rebecca's Daughters!'

And he turns to the direction of destruction. He gestures one section of the crowd to one end of the gate, another to the other. And these men, the strongest and wildest in appearance, lift the gate bodily from its hinges and carry it off in the direction of the river.

Now the carriers of the gate come down the riverbank, followed by many of the crowd. At a word of command from Anthony, they heave the gate into the river, eagerly helped by all the 'daughters' around them.

One of the 'daughters', Mordecai Thomas with his umbrella, watches the gate strike the water, raises his hand in a kind of benediction and opens his mouth as though to speak some apt scriptural quotation. Then, remembering, he stops, and purses his lips in a whistle instead. He whistles the first bars of a hymn tune.

Now we see, from the top of the riverbank, where Anthony stands near Jack Wet and his wife, the gate floating away down the dark river. One of the 'daughters' whispers to Jack Wet, longingly. 'If orders wasn't orders, you'd be sittin' on that gate, the both of you!'

The current bears the gate away swiftly down river. A single note is blown on a horn. And the 'daughters' who have launched the gate, and their assistants, make their way up the bank again. The gate disappears down the darkness of the river. And the horn is heard again, this time from further away. [...]

Through the window of a country inn, Sir John Watkyn can be seen addressing a group of men. His horse stands tethered outside. Sir John Watkyn sits at a plain wooden table. Opposite him sit Rhodri Huws, William Evan, Dave Button and Mordecai Thomas. Sir John finishes speaking with a sigh. 'So there it is. I've taken up your cause in the House of Commons, done my best to obtain sympathy for it, but the Government is averse from intervening in matters which have a purely local significance.'

Rhodri Huws looks at him with scarce concealed contempt. 'You'd have done better to speak to our Daisy. She do give milk.'

Sir John ignores this and warns seriously: 'I have to tell you – the police are coming from London.'

Rhodri grunts. 'London peelers! We'll make a batch of Welshcakes out of them.'

The landlord puts down a tray of beer mugs on the table. 'Boil 'em up for broth'd be better,' he says.

Mordecai Thomas is staring in front of him like a man possessed. 'And so Rebecca's Daughters must fight alone!'

'They cannot take the law into their own hands,' warns Sir John. Dave Button laughs into his beer. 'Ask the pike-men if they can't!' And William Evans giggles: 'Ask Jack Wet standing in the cold in his nighty.'

Sir John looks up at them sharply. 'I hope, for your own sakes, none of you here belongs to that – rabble.'

His gaze travels past William Evan, Dave Button, Rhodri Huws – all non-committal – and comes to Mordecai Thomas, who rises, like an Old Testament prophet. 'I belong to the company. And I glory in it. I preach the word of God, which is love. I respect the laws of men when they are founded upon the laws of God; but I will not bow down before them when they are founded upon the laws of evil. The evil Rebecca fights against is the evil of selfish gain, and the tyranny of rich over poor. And I will fight with Rebecca and with all who believe in what she believes, for so long as this evil remains and there is love in my heart and strength in my body.'

'Glory be,' adds William Evan, reverently.

Sir John looks down his nose. 'You are a misguided man, Mordecai Thomas.'

'Thank God, I am!'

'Who is this person they call Rebecca?'

The old preacher draws himself up. 'I do not know. But *if* I knew, you could break my bones before I would tell.'

Now, we see William Evan, Dave Button and Rhodri Huws lift up their beermugs. They frame with their lips, silently, the name 'Rebecca'. And they drink. [...]

And Shoni Fawr reads the beginning of the broadsheet ballad, chanting as he reads, while the two police officers look round at all the grinning faces in the bar.

> 'It was on the wild winter nights
>   Of the year eighteen forty three
> When the Daughters of Rebecca
>   Rode out against the enemy.

> 'Rebecca bold was at their head
>   He cared not for soldier or squire
> And his Daughters in dresses and bonnets
>   Were the wonder of all Pembrokeshire.

'They set out on foot and on horseback,
   Black as soot, from village and town,
To spite the proud tyrants and landlords
   And pull the tollgates down.' [...]

Idris Evans is working at the forge. His eyes are intent upon his work
as he speaks. He doesn't look up at the Inspector, who is standing at
his elbow, talking to him. Idris protests: 'I'm not the big mouth round
here. I don't know nothing. I got work to do.'

   'Not so much work as you used to have. Not since the trouble last
year. Somebody told the magistrates, remember?'

   'It wasn't me who told.'

   'Some of your friends think it was, don't they?'

   'I got no friends.'

   'No, not now ...'

   'I'm not a man who wants friends. I go my own way.'

   'So I've heard tell. You're not like the run of them round here, are
you? You're different. I don't know why you stay here, in a hell of a
place like this.'

   'I don't want to stay here. They look at me. But where else can I go?'

   'Now you listen to me, and I might be able to help you. If you were
me, wouldn't you try to catch this Rebecca at one of his meetings when
he tells 'em what gates he's going after? Wouldn't you?'

   'He's got men on the hills, watching. By the time you got there, every
man'd be gone.'

   The Inspector comes closer. 'But suppose some clever fellow I'm
thinking of were dressed up as one of them. He'd hear what they were
up to wouldn't he? And what time of night. And then he'd slip away, in
the dark and let me know, wouldn't *you*?'

   'No,' says Idris loudly. But his eyes are trapped. His 'No' is almost
desperate and broken. 'What about if they caught me?'

   'Catch *you*? Those fools? Beside, we'd look after you – wouldn't
we? There's always jobs waiting for men like you – in better places
than this.'

   'I don't want to do it! I don't want to do anything bad. It's people
always making me. I won't do it! I won't do it!' And tears of misery,
self-pity and self-loathing are in his eyes. But later that night he sits in
the little room behind the smithy, blackening his face with the aid of
candle and burnt cork.

Much later still, in a disused quarry, the masked 'Rebecca' is addressing his followers: 'Daughters of Rebecca!' he cries. 'They have sent the police from London to watch us. There may be spies and informers among us – here, tonight!'

There is an angry murmur from the Daughters.

'Those of you who keep watch, see that no one slips by you, even though he is dressed as one of us! Daughters of Rebecca! We have been *too gentle*. From tonight onwards, every gate must be utterly destroyed. And not the gates alone. Destroy also the tollhouses so that not a stone remains ...'

Axes, pick-axes, crowbars are brandished and the crowd breaks up. Among the 'daughters' is one who looks suspiciously like Idris Evans.

This is the picture of the nights that follow ...

Axes furiously descending on gates. Saws at work on gateposts. Gates blazing on fires. Fragments of gates strewing the road. Torn shreds of gates hanging from their hinges. Terrified pike-men scuttling out of doors in their nightclothes. Furniture being carried out of houses. Slates and masonry descending in clouds of dust. Houses on fire, piles of sawn up gates with notices nailed on offering 'FREE FIREWOOD'. Disguised figures hurrying on horseback by fires and falling roofs. Gagged and pinioned pike-men and their wives. A pike-man's little children clapping their hands with delight as a gate makes a great bonfire. A bound pike-man sitting on rubble under the shadow of a grandfather clock. Police officers furiously arguing – or bewildered. Idris Evans furtively and futilely making excuses for himself.

And this is the sound of the nights that follow ... Anthony's voice calling:

> 'Jack Wet, up you get!
> Tom Brown, you come down!
> Shacki Rees, if you please!
> Dewi Pugh, it's happened to you!'

And Shoni Fawr's voice reciting from the broadsheet ballad:

> And they cried for you, all the poor of the land,
> Who were tied to the tyrant's yoke.
> When Rebecca's Daughters came down on the gates
> And the tollhouses *went up in smoke!* [...]

A hollow in the road, beneath a fence. Behind, lies thick woodland. In the hollow sit the volunteer patrol, which consists of five armed turnpike trustees. They are all in jovial mood. They make a little semi-circle, at one end of which sits Sir Henry's cat. Flasks and sandwiches are produced by all, and also a saucer by Sir Henry, who places it in front of the cat and pours out a measure from his flask. The volunteers drink.

'Confusion to Rebecca!'

'To the volunteers!'

'To the turnpike trusts!'

'To us!'

'To the ladies!' adds Mr Pugh and the cat 'Miaow!'

All settle themselves comfortably.

'What a nice quiet gate to guard!'

'Right on the main coach road.'

'The last one they'd dare attack!'

'Very well chosen indeed!'

They drink again, filled with bonhomie, spirits and security. There is a pause. 'Quite a nip in the air tonight,' observes one of their number, and 'Regular Anthony Raine-y weather!' rejoins Sir Henry.

As the laughter fades, Mr Pugh begins to speak in the voice of one who has all the time in the world on his hands and an improper story to tell. 'It reminds me of a night many years ago, when I was a proper terror! Now what was the girl's name? My, but she was frightened of me! Rosie, was it? Or Rene? No, no – Rachel! Or Ruby. Or ...'

'I hope it wasn't Rebecca!' observes Sir Henry. And almost on the name a pair of hands is thrust through the fence and gags him. Another pair pinions his hand. And suddenly the scene is swarming with masked 'Rebecca's Daughters'. And all the terrified volunteers are disarmed, gagged and bound, and laid out against the bank.

Anthony, dressed as Rebecca, appears on horseback, on the road, surveying the scene. 'Good! Now for the gate and tollhouse.'

The clattering of a horse's hooves is heard in the distance as the men begin to break away. Anthony raises his hand. 'Wait!' And he wheels his horse round to face the approaching horseman. Mordecai Thomas reins up by Rebecca. 'There's a coach on the road!' he whispers.

'I'll come with you,' says Anthony and calls to the 'Daughters'. 'Begin on the gate!'

He and Thomas ride off. The 'Daughters' swarm off in the other direction, leaving the trustees looking up at the stars. One solitary Rebecca-man is left who, after a furtive and hurried look around him, hurries after the rest. He is Idris Evans, the informer. The cat strolls among the bound trustees, lapping up the spirits from their spilt flasks. He rubs himself against Sir Henry's pinioned legs. [...]

Anthony disappears from the window and Dave Button comes to it. He has his hands above his head. 'It's Rebecca, sir, and one of his daughters ...'

'Shouldn't keep his daughter out on a night like this,' Lord Sarn tells him.

'He's got a pistol in my back. He says I'm to drive on till we reach the tollgate. Then you and Miss Rhiannon and Bessy, m'lord, are to get out and see them burn the gate down, m'lord ... I got to do what he says, m'lord.'

'Then don't be a fool! Do it!'

Dave Button, his hands still above his head, disappears from the window. The coach moves on. Rhiannon turns excitedly to Bessy: 'We're going to see them! Rebecca and his Daughters! Oh, Bessy, perhaps I can *talk* to him!'

'How many men will there be, do you think?'

'Oh, lots and lots of them! And they're all daring and fierce with torches and hatchets and everything and all of them with wild black faces and ...'

Lord Sarn's voice breaks in. 'A pleasant evening, I must say. First beetles in the soup and then black men with hatchets!'

Up on the box, Dave Button is grinning with delight, singing a little song to himself, and conducting himself with his whip.

> 'It was on a wild winter's night
> Of the year eighteen forty three
> When the Daughters of Rebecca
> Rode out against the enemy ...'

The coach drives up to the tollgate, which is now in the process of being destroyed. Anthony and Mordecai Thomas ride just behind the coach, one on either side. The coach stops. Anthony waves his pistol at Dave Button who climbs down and opens the coach door. And Rhiannon, followed by Bessy and Lord Sarn come out. There is the noise of sawing and hacking. At a gesture of command from Anthony, some masked and face-blackened Rebecca-ites take charge, without violence, of Lord Sarn and Dave Button and lead them to a point of vantage from which they can see the destruction of the gate in detail.

Lord Sarn is cool as ever. 'If I must watch this entertainment, I demand a chair to sit on,' he says.

One of his captors waves a hand to the Rebecca-ites, who are bringing the furniture out of the tollhouse. 'A chair for his lordship!' And with ironic solemnity two large 'Daughters' bring over to Lord Sarn an old, dilapidated rocking chair. With dignity, Lord Sarn accepts the offering and sits.

Rhiannon and Bessy stand near the coach, watching the destruction. Anthony, disguised, on horseback, is very close to them. Rhiannon looks up earnestly at Anthony who takes no notice of her but looks sternly ahead of him. She whispers his name. 'Rebecca!'

He does not acknowledge her. She tries again. 'Rebecca! I want to tell you that I believe in you. I believe that what you're doing is right. It's the only thing left for the people to do. If no one will listen to them at all, they've got to destroy the gates.'

Bessy who is paying no attention to Rhiannon's words but is excitedly staring at the scene before her, now pulls at Rhiannon's sleeve. 'Oh, Miss, there's a man over there, like a pirate!'

Rhiannon does not need her. She speaks again to 'Rebecca'. 'Rebecca, if I was a man I'd be one of your Daughters. I think you're good, and brave.'

Still 'Rebecca' aloofly and sternly takes no notice of her. [...]

Rebecca, the music begun, is crossing the empty floor to where Rhiannon sits with a young masked partner. She looks up at Rebecca, a little, almost timid, smile dawning on her lips. Her partner leaves with a bow. Wordlessly, she rises and comes close to him, and they begin to dance. The rest of the dancers move on to the floor. We follow Rhiannon and Rebecca dancing. Marsden and partner come into picture, Marsden watching them jealously. But they are oblivious of him. She is looking up at her partner, still with that little smile on her lips. And he looks down, quietly and gravely, at her. We see his hand − the hand that Rhiannon, too, can see, fasten more firmly on hers. At the increase of the pressure on her hand, Rhiannon looks at his. And on one of the fingers of his hand she sees the large and peculiarly shaped signet ring. Her eyes widen. Then she looks up at him again, at the eyes behind the mask and smiles, this time not shyly nor timidly but with full certainty of love.

'I wished you to come Rebecca,' she says softly. 'With all my heart I did.'

Dave Button, shielded by the curtain, is peering in at the dancers.

Rhiannon and Rebecca dance by. He makes little, furtive gestures to attract Rebecca's attention.

'And dancing with *her*!' he whispers to himself. 'Oh, Mafoozulum!'

Rhiannon speaks softly as she dances in Anthony's arms. 'You came to me! You came to me! You mustn't talk, must you? Then I would know who you really are. But I'd never tell! You can speak to me, Rebecca, for ever you can. I'd cross my heart, only you're holding my hand. You can speak to me. But not here. Dance towards the terrace doors.'

And they dance towards the doors that lead out on to the terrace. Quietly, Rebecca opens them and they pass through on to the terrace, which is sheltered from the weather. Rhiannon takes off her mask and looks at Rebecca.

'Now you can speak to me. There's no one to hear you now, only me, and I'm as quiet as ... as quiet as ... Oh, I don't want to say " as quiet as the grave". That sounds sad, and I'm not sad at all. Not now. Take off your mask.'

But Rebecca makes no sound or movement, only looks at her.

'Tell me who you are. You came tonight because we met on the road. Because you saw me once and you wanted to see me again. Didn't you? Didn't you? Tell me that's why you came. I knew it was you. I didn't really need to see that ring on your finger ... Who gave you the ring? Was it somebody you love? Oh, no, it couldn't be. Because you came tonight only to see *me*. Oh, you shouldn't have come! No, no, I don't mean that, but it's *terribly* dangerous for you. But you didn't mind how dangerous it was. You didn't mind, did you? Oh, speak to me, please. I'm saying all the things that I want *you* to say to me. Take off your mask.' [...]

Through Pembroke market square march the new troops. Sullen crowds watch them. There's no sound save for the marching feet of the soldiers on the cobbles and the barked out commands. The crowds remain still and silent. Even the children, who normally at the sight of soldiers would shout and play and mock-march with them, are silent as their elders. In the front fringe of the crowd, Bessy and Sara Jane are standing together. And most of the soldiers passing by have an eye for Bessy at her plump prettiest. One strapping soldier, at the end of the line nearest Bessy, gives her a slow, deliberate and very meaning wink. And Bessy is raising her little mittened hand discreetly and secretly to wave at him when down comes Sara Jane's hand on hers, with a sharp smack which rings out in the silence of the crowd.

Standing close together in the crowd, Rhodri Huws, Shoni Fawr and old William Evan speak softly among themselves. 'Look at 'em! Men just like us — and they come to shoot us down!'

'A shame the hens aren't laying. I could use their eggs.'

'Men like us who never had anything and never will have. Who'll die as poor as they were born. What do they want with Turnpike Trusts? What'll the creepin' lords and squires do for them? They should be fighting with us.'

'We don't want no fighting,' William Evan tells him.

'Talk for yourself, you old bird of peace.'

'Fighting won't get us nowhere.'

'Ach, you old dove!'

'You got to trust Sir John Watkyn,' maintains William, stubbornly.

'You got to trust Rebecca!'

'Leave Sir John to have a go at the Prime Minister. You wait! He'll get him to listen.' [...]

Rhiannon, dressed as Rebecca, and Dave Button, galloping through darkness up to a division of the road. A high wind tossing the black roadside trees. At the division, Dave Button rides one way, Rhiannon the other.

Rhiannon riding through darkness into a farmyard. She pulls up under the farmhouse window, cups her hands, and calls. We cannot hear her voice for the music and the noise of the high wind. The window opens and a man's head appears. Under his thatch of light hair, the man's face is black as coal. Rhiannon, calling her instructions through wind and music, points, her arm outstretched, through the darkness away to the left. The man at the window nods vigorously and closes the window as Rhiannon turns and rides off.

Dave Button riding up to a row of small cottages. Quickly he dismounts, runs to the first cottage, hammers on the door. The door is opened by a man already half-disguised as a Rebecca-ite. We see Dave speak to him urgently, but do not hear his voice for wind and music. Dave mounts again and rides off, and the Rebecca-ite hurries to the next cottage and hammers on the door.

Rhiannon riding out of darkness into another farmyard. A lantern is shining in an outhouse. She rides up to the outhouse and calls. Through the open outhouse door comes a group of three farm labourers, shotguns slung over their shoulders. Again, Rhiannon speaks and beckons her instructions and the men, as she turns and rides off, run across the yard to where their waiting horses are tethered.

Soldiers in rowboats crossing the dark estuary waters towards the four-pointed signal at the top of Rhos Goch guard house.

Rhiannon and Dave Button riding over a dark field towards a wood. Out of the wood comes a group of mounted Rebecca-ites. Rhiannon holds up her hand, and the horsemen stop. Rhiannon, speaking through wind and music, gestures the horsemen to another direction from that which they were taking, and the horsemen, saluting Rhiannon-as-Rebecca, ride off that way.

Soldiers grounding their rowboats on the estuary shore beneath Rhos Goch guard house and scrambling out and up towards the four-pointed signal.

Dave Button and Rhiannon riding on to the top of the quarry. Below them is a group of Rebecca-ites standing by their horses. Rhiannon calls down to them, and signals them to follow her. And the Rebecca-ites jump on their horses and ride towards her. Rhiannon and Dave Button turn and are off.

Rhiannon and Dave Button riding into a valley farm and shouting their instructions to a small group of Rebecca-ites in the yard preparing for the road, muffling their horses' hooves, strapping on saws and pick-axes to their saddles.

Rhiannon and Dave Button at the head of a company of mounted Rebecca-ites riding through darkness towards the Carew tollgate.

At the Rhos Goch tollgate, the soldiers are preparing to meet Rebecca's raid. Under the superintendence of Captain Marsden they conceal themselves in a deep ditch outside of the tollgate, lie down in the ditch with their carbines levelled over the top. Captain Marsden directs other soldiers into the tollgate-house itself, there to wait in concealment at the windows.

Marsden speaks quietly to one of his officers: 'Rebecca – dead or alive. Those are my instructions. But you can forget that last word.'

'I've been thinking, sir – what if Rebecca was Lord Sarn himself.'

'Then we should be saved the trouble of shooting. He's been dead for years.'

Suddenly the officer points excitedly into the dark distance. 'Look, sir!'

In the distance, the bright glow of some great fire is burning the dark sky.

'It's the Carew Gate!' shouts the inspector.

They look at the fire, growing every moment brighter, in silence for a moment. Then Marsden, with barely controlled rage, says 'I wish I had joined the navy. They have a larger vocabulary. You can call the men off.'

And he turns and moves back towards the tollgate.

The soldiers come out of concealment, grumbling among themselves. They sling their carbines back over their shoulders.

'They're not playing fair ...'

'Think I'll join Rebecca ...'

Grumbling, they sit down at the road edge.

'Only shot a rabbit since I been here ...'

'And that was tough as a boot ...'

'One rabbit, and a nasty black crow.'

Grumbling, the soldiers lean against the tollhouse, their rifles against the wall, squat on the road edge, wander about disconsolately.

Suddenly out of the pitch darkness two horses, mounted by Rhiannon and Dave Button, gallop furiously past them, jettisoning a big bundle nearly at Marsden's feet. Then the horsemen are gone, galloping in a flash past the soldiers, caught unawares as they squat or loiter on the roadside. Too late the soldiers retrieve their carbines and fire after the vanished horses.

Marsden and the police inspector bend over the big bundle. It is Idris Evans the blacksmith, trussed and gagged. Pinned to his Rebecca-ite clothing is a note which reads: ONE INFORMER RETURNED WITHOUT THANKS – REBECCA.

Marsden leaves the trussed body and runs towards the tollhouse, where several horses are tethered. Marsden jumps on to one. Rapidly, his officers mount the others. They all gallop off into the darkness after Rhiannon and Dave Button. [...]

A Royal Commission has been appointed to enquire into the – *your* word, Mr Raine – *injustices* of the Tollgate System. [...]

On to a roaring fire are thrown, one by one, the garments of Rebecca's disguise. The flames snatch and devour them.

On to another, greater fire are thrown the sawn and dismembered pieces of a tollgate. Drawing back from the fire, we see the work of destruction is being carried out under the official direction of Sir John Watkyn, the police, and the troops. The flames rise higher.

For a moment, they light up the faces of Anthony and Rhiannon, smiling and close together.

Poetry and the Film: A Symposium

Dylan Thomas contributed to the Cinema 16 Symposium in New York on 28 October 1953, the day after his thirty-ninth birthday and twelve days before his death. He had had, of course, many years of professional film experience. This excerpt selects Dylan Thomas's comments from the transcribed discussion. He contributed directly, vividly, amusingly, with no theory or film jargon. He mocks the more pretentious comments, and his humorous deflation was much enjoyed by the audience. His needling ridicule, sometimes in asides, is very effective, as in his witty 'I haven't a theory to my back.' Clearly he was alert and on good form. Evidently his closest kinship was with his fellow writer Arthur Miller. Miss Deren, also a contributor, speaking of her films, made the point that drama in a film is horizontal, while poetry in a film is vertical. A listening, chain-smoking Dylan comes in at this point.

POETRY AND THE FILM: A SYMPOSIUM

MAAS: Well, Mr Thomas, being a poet, what do you feel about it?

THOMAS: Well, I'm sure that all Maya Deren said was what I would have said, had I thought of it or understood it (*laughter and slight applause*). I was asked, on the side, whether that meant that I thought that the audience didn't understand what Miss Deren was saying. I'm sure they did, and I wish I was down there. But it sounds different from that side, you know. Now I'm all for (I'm in the wrong place tonight) ... I'm all for horizontal and vertical (*laughter*), and all for what we heard about in the avant-garde. The only avant-garde play I saw in New York was in a cellar, or a sewer, or somewhere (*laughter*). I happened to be with Mr Miller over there. We saw this play going on … I'm sure it was fine. And, in the middle, he said, 'Good God, this is avant-garde.' He said, 'In a moment, the hero's going to take his clothes off …'

MAAS: Did he?

THOMAS: He did (*laughter*).

MAAS: All to the good.

THOMAS: But I don't know. I haven't a theory to my back, as they say. But there are, all through films that I've seen all my life … there have always been … bits that have seemed to me … Now, this is a bit of poetry. They might have been in the UFA films or something that I saw as a child. Or somebody coming down some murderous dark, dark, silent street, apart from the piano playing. Or it might have been a little moment when Laurel and Hardy were failing to get a piano up or down a flight of stairs. That always seemed to me the poetry … when those moments came. Well, I have to go a step beyond those UFA films, now, to the non-silent films. In the best of those moments, the words seemed to fit. They were really the right words, even though the right word might only be a grunt. I'm not at all sure that I want such a thing, myself, as a poetic film. I think films fine as they are, if only they were better! And I'm not quite sure that I want a new kind of film at all. While I'm recharging an almost empty mind with an almost empty battery, perhaps Mr Miller would say something (*applause*).

MAAS: Well, I don't think I'll let it go at that, Mr Thomas. Surely you must realise that the film is a popular medium, and you, more than anybody else, have tried to bring poetry to the public from the platform. Don't you think, in the popular art, in the way that the Elizabethan theatre was a popular art, don't you think it would be possible in some way to weld poetry to the film? Do you think that it's just a verbal thing? That it would not be possible in the way that Elizabethan drama somehow welded language to the film?

THOMAS: Well, just as a poem comes out … one image makes another in the ordinary dialectic process (somebody left out the word 'dialectic', well I may as well bring it in, you know). So, as in a poem one image breeds another, I think, in a film, it's really the visual image that breeds another – breeds and breathes it. If it's possible to combine a verbal image to a visual image in this sort of horizontal way, I'd rather see horizontal films, myself. I like stories.

You know, I like to see something going on (*laughter and applause*) [...]

MAAS: Well, doesn't it seem to have something to do with who is going to make this film? Is it going to be the man who has a poetical idea at the beginning, who then decides to work with a film director on this thing? Or is the poet going to work on it himself? Through words or through nothing, but just through a poetical idea, which is both visual and verbal at the same time? If he is going to work with a director, he is going to have to be terribly close to that director. He may as well be the same person. Then you have to have a poet who can also make a film.

THOMAS: Oh, I think that's absolutely true – or you could work very closely with someone who knew film technique to carry it out. But I think the poet should establish a scenario and a commentary that would do that as well. And he may as well star in it as well [...]

DEREN: I wish mainly to say that I'm a little bit flabbergasted at the fact that people who have handled words with such dexterity as Mr Thomas and Mr Miller and Mr Tyler, should have difficulty with such a simple idea as the 'vertical' and the 'horizontal' (*applause*).

THOMAS (*aside*):   Here we go up and down again.

Notes

1. Dylan Thomas, *The Collected Letters*, ed. Paul Ferris (London 1985), pp. 416–17.
2. Theodora FitzGibbon, *With Love* (London 1982), p. 134.
3. Dylan Thomas, *Early Prose Writing*, ed. Walford Davies (London 1971), pp. 142–3.
4. Dylan Thomas, *The Collected Letters*, p. 108.
5. Dylan Thomas, *Collected Poems 1934–53*, ed. Walford Davies and Ralph Maud (London 1988), p. 17.
6. *Ibid.*, p. 34. In the 'Notes' on this poem, p. 196, there is an illustration of this shot from the film.
7. Theodora FitzGibbon, *With Love*, p. 60.
8. *Ibid.*, pp. 57–8.
9. Donald Taylor in conversation with Bill Read. I am here and elsewhere indebted to Bill Read's *The Days of Dylan Thomas* (London 1965) and Constantine FitzGibbon's *The Life of Dylan Thomas* (London 1965), particularly their accounts of Dylan Thomas's work in films. Donald Taylor's answers to Bill Read's questions are in the mss in the Harry Ransom Humanities Research Center, University of Texas at Austin, as is Jan Read's unpublished (4 pp.) essay on Thomas. I am of course also particularly indebted to Paul Ferris's invaluable biography of Dylan Thomas and his *Collected Letters*, together with its authoritative notes.
10. Dylan Thomas, *The Collected Letters*, p. 463.
11. *Ibid.*, pp. 470 and 478.
12. *Ibid.*, p. 493.
13. Caitlin Thomas, *Caitlin*, with George Tremlett (London 1986), p. 79.
14. Andrew Sinclair, *Dylan Thomas* (1975), p. 118. There is an interesting account here of Thomas's work in films.
15. Julian Maclaren-Ross, *Memoirs of the Forties*, (London 1965), p. 132.
16. Nicholas Pronay, '"The Land of Promise": The Projection of Peace Aims in Britain', *Film and Radio Propaganda in World War II* (ed. K.R.M. Short, London 1983), p. 71. I am particularly indebted to this informed and illuminating article in this account of war-time documentaries and their political background. It is a seminal and

revealing essay. Likewise I am indebted to Francis Thorpe and Nicholas
Pronay: British Official Films of the Second World War: A Descriptive
Catalogue (Oxford 1980).

17. *Ibid.*, p. 64.
18. *Ibid.*
19. Giles Goodland, 'Dylan Thomas and Film', *The New Welsh Review* 9
(Summer 1990), p. 20. I am much indebted to this graphic and
illuminating introduction to some of the documentary films.
20. Nicholas Pronay, ' "The Land of Promise": The Projection of Peace
Aims in Britain', *Film and Radio Propaganda in World War II* (ed.
K.R.M. Short), p. 64.
21. Nicholas Pronay, p. 72.
22. J.M. Brinnin, *Dylan Thomas in America*, p. 26.
23. Malcolm Dean, 'Putting Beveridge Back on Track', *Guardian*, 3 October
1992, p. 20.
24. 'Two Views on our Country' (Anonymous), *Documentary News Letter*
(1944, vol. 5, no. 4), p. 46, publication concerned with documentary
films. Quoted in Ralph Maud, *Dylan Thomas in Print* (London 1972),
pp. 139–40.
25. Dylan Thomas, quoted in *A Casebook on Dylan Thomas*, ed. J.M.
Brinnin (New York 1960), p. 196.
26. Dylan Thomas, *Collected Letters*, p. 505.
27. Jack Lindsay, *Meetings with Poets* (London 1968), pp. 24–5.
28. Dylan Thomas, *Collected Letters*, p. 517.
29. Quoted in Gwen Watkins, *Portrait of a Friend* (Llandysul 1983), p. 107.
30. Julian Maclaren-Ross, *Memoirs of the Forties*, pp. 118–20 and
122.
31. *Ibid.*, p. 128.
32. I am indebted for this account to Julian Maclaren-Ross, *Memoirs of the
Forties*, pp. 128–9.
33. *Ibid.*, pp. 129–30.
34. Bonamy Dobrée, *The Spectator*, 10 June 1953, pp. 763–4.
35. Donald Taylor, 'The Story of the Film', *The Doctor and the Devils* (Dent
1953), p. 135.
36. Dylan Thomas, *Collected Letters*, p. 502.
37. *Ibid.*, p. 539.
38. I am indebted for information on this to FitzGibbon's *The Life of Dylan
Thomas*, Paul Ferris's *Dylan Thomas*, contemporary reports in *Welsh
Gazette* quoted in Ralph Maud's *Dylan Thomas in Print*, pp. 72–4.
39. Dylan Thomas, *Collected Letters*, pp. 547 and 549.
40. I am again indebted to Paul Ferris's biography *Dylan Thomas* for this
information (p. 40 fn.).
41. Dylan Thomas, *Collected Letters*, p. 680.
42. *Ibid.*, p. 770.

43. *Ibid.*, p. 681.
44. *Ibid.*, p. 713.
45. *Ibid.*, p. 770.
46. *Ibid.*, p. 792.
47. J.M. Brinnin, 'The Talent of Genius', review of *The Doctor and the Devils*, *New Republic* 130 (25 January 1954), p. 19.
48. Anon. review, *DNL*, p. 71. Quoted in Maud, *Dylan Thomas in Print*, pp. 135–6.
49. *DNL* (vol. 3, no. 6), p. 90, anon. review. Quoted in *Dylan Thomas in Print*, p. 136.
50. *DNL* (vol. 3, no. 7), p. 100. Quoted in *Dylan Thomas in Print*, pp. 136–7.
51. I am indebted for this information to Paul Ferris, *Dylan Thomas* (p. 182, fn.).
52. Dylan Thomas, *The Collected Letters* (ed. Paul Ferris), p. 496.
53. Paul Ferris, *Dylan Thomas*, p. 186.
54. I am indebted for this to an Imperial War Museum Report (no. 99, 25/3/81).
55. See Paul Ferris, *Dylan Thomas*, p. 183.
56. Dylan Thomas, quoted in *A Casebook on Dylan Thomas*, ed. J.M. Brinnin (New York 1960), p. 196.
57. I have here drawn on notes on shots in the film included in the papers with the MOI script, and the Imperial War Museum Report (no. 99).
58. Imperial War Museum Report (no. 99, 25/3/81).
59. Anon. review, *DNL* (vol. 4, no. 3), pp. 145–6. Quoted in *Dylan Thomas in Print*, pp. 137–8.
60. Edgar Anstey, review of 'These Are The Men', *The Spectator*, 9 April 1943, p. 338.
61. Dylan Thomas, *The Collected Letters*, p. 509.
62. *Ibid.*, p. 513.
63. Edgar Anstey, *The Spectator*, 23 June 1944, p. 570.
64. Dylan Thomas, *The Collected Letters*, pp. 521–2.
65. Edgar Anstey, *The Spectator*, 19 June 1945, p. 594.
66. Donald Taylor, *Kine Weekly*, 25 July 1940, p. 21.
67. I have drawn on information in papers included with the MOI script.
68. Jack Lindsay, *Meetings with Poets*, p. 32.
69. Dylan Thomas, *The Collected Letters*, pp. 525–6.
70. *Ibid.*, p. 519.
71. J. Maclaren-Ross, *Memoirs of the Forties*, p. 120.
72. From information included with the MOI script.
73. Dylan Thomas, *The Collected Letters*, pp. 514 and 528.
74. *Ibid.*, p. 134.
75. Thomas Lovell Beddoes, quoted in 'Introduction' to *Selected Poems*, ed. J. Higgens (Manchester 1976), p. 9.

76. Dylan Thomas, *The Collected Letters*, p. 540.
77. Bonamy Dobrée, review of *The Doctor and the Devils*, *The Spectator*, pp. 763–4.
78. Jacob Korg, 'Review', *The Doctor and the Devils*, *The Nation* (New York), 14 November 1953, p. 413.
79. Dylan Thomas, *The Collected Letters*, p. 526.
80. *Ibid.*, pp. 529–30.
81. *Ibid.*, p. 540.
82. Walford Davies, *Dylan Thomas* (Cardiff 1972), p. 50.
83. Dylan Thomas, *The Collected Letters*, p. 540.
84. *Ibid.*, p. 546.
85. *Ibid.*, pp. 660–1.
86. *Ibid.*, p. 774.
87. *Ibid.*, p. 512.
88. Suzanne Roussillat, *Dylan Thomas: The Legend and the Poet* (ed. E.W. Tedlock, London 1960), pp. 7–8.
89. Virginia Graham, *The Spectator*, 29 October 1948, p. 558.
90. Dylan Thomas, *The Collected Letters*, p. 687.
91. Anon. review of *The Beach of Falesá* in *The Times*, 25 June 1964, p. 13.
92. Quoted from Jan Read's unpublished preface for *The Beach of Falesá* in Bill Read's *The Days of Dylan Thomas* (London 1964), pp. 127–8.
93. Dylan Thomas, *The Collected Letters*, p. 680.
94. *Ibid.*, p. 691.
95. 'Foreword' to *Me and My Bike* (London 1965).
96. Dylan Thomas, *The Collected Letters*, p. 691.
97. *Ibid.*, p. 695.
98. *Ibid.*, p. 700.
99. Sidney Box, 'Foreword', *Rebecca's Daughters* (London 1965).
100. Constantine FitzGibbon, *The Life of Dylan Thomas* (London 1965), p. 62.

Bibliography

WORKS BY DYLAN THOMAS

Portrait of the Artist as a Young Dog (London 1940).

The Doctor and the Devils (London 1953).

Under Milk Wood (London 1954).

The Beach of Falesá (London 1964).

Twenty Years A-Growing (London 1964).

Rebecca's Daughters (London 1965).

Me and My Bike (London 1965).

Dylan Thomas: Early Prose Writings, ed. Walford Davies (London 1971).

Dylan Thomas, The Collected Letters, ed. Paul Ferris (London 1985).

Dylan Thomas: Collected Poems 1934–53, ed. Walford Davies and Ralph Maud (London 1988).

Dylan Thomas: The Broadcasts, ed. Ralph Maud (London 1991).

BOOKS ABOUT DYLAN THOMAS (including part material of relevance to his work in films)

Ackerman, John, *A Dylan Thomas Companion* (London 1991).

Brinnin, J.M., *Dylan Thomas in America* (London 1956).

Brinnin, J.M. (ed.), *A Casebook on Dylan Thomas* (New York 1960).

Davies, Walford, *Dylan Thomas* (Cardiff 1972). Revised and enlarged 1990.

Ferris, Paul, *Dylan Thomas* (London 1977).

FitzGibbon, Constantine, *The Life of Dylan Thomas* (London 1965).

FitzGibbon, Theodora, *With Love* (London 1982).

Lindsay, Jack, *Meetings with Poets* (London 1968).

Maclaren-Ross, Julian, *Memoirs of the Forties* (London 1965).

Maud, Ralph, *Dylan Thomas in Print: A Bibliographical History* (London 1972).

Read, Bill, *The Days of Dylan Thomas* (London 1964).

Sinclair, Andrew, *Dylan Thomas* (London 1975).

Tedlock, E.W. (ed.), *Dylan Thomas: The Legend and the Poet* (London 1960).

Thomas, Caitlin, with George Tremlett, *Caitlin* (London 1986).

Watkins, Gwen, *Portrait of a Friend* (Llandysul 1983).

ESSAYS AND OTHER MATERIAL OF PARTICULAR INTEREST

Isabelle Imhof's unpublished thesis 'The Film Scripts of Dylan Thomas' (University of Zurich) provides some useful bibliographical leads and offers some interesting comment on the previously published feature films.

Giles Goodland, *Dylan Thomas and Film*, *The New Welsh Review* **9** (Summer 1990).

Nicholas Pronay, "The Land of Promise": The Projection of Peace Aims in Britain', *Film and Radio Propaganda in World War II* (ed. K.R.M. Short, London 1983).

Francis Thorpe and Nicholas Pronay: *British Official Films of the Second World War: A Descriptive Catalogue* (Oxford 1980).

Documentary News Letter

Monthly Film Bulletin

Editor's Acknowledgements

The Department of Film at the Imperial War Museum, and in particular Jane Fish, and the British Film Institute, including the National Film Archive and the BFI library, and in particular Julie Rigg, have helped me considerably, as has the Public Records Office, Kew. I am indebted to them for access both to Dylan Thomas's films and scripts and related material, and I express my particular thanks. Thanks for their help are also due to the Harry Ransom Humanities Research Center, The University of Texas at Austin; the Lockwood Memorial Library, State University of New York at Buffalo; the Department of Manuscripts of the National Library of Wales, Aberystwyth. I am of course indebted for information from the books and articles cited, but especially to Paul Ferris's indispensable biography *Dylan Thomas* and his magisterial edition of Dylan Thomas's *Collected Letters*. They provide map and compass of the world of Dylan Thomas. Special thanks are also due to Professor Walford Davies who encouraged and supported this work, as in earlier years my *Welsh Dylan* Arts Council Exhibition, and *Dylan Thomas Companion*; to Professor Ralph Maud, for some notes on this topic; and to Hilary Laurie of J.M. Dent, for her patient and valuable assistance, and also to Andrea Henry. A word of thanks, too, to Colin Shewring, Aeronwy Thomas, Barbara Ackerman Jones and Mark Jones, whose technical skills so helped my viewing of Dylan's films; and to Claudine Carter for her enthusiastic typing of the book.

THE GRAHAM GREENE FILM READER

edited by David Parkinson

"MAGNIFICENT ... THE BEST COLLECTION OF FILM CRITICISM ... A SUPERB BOOK! THERE IS RELISH IN HIS PRAISE AND PUNISHMENT IN HIS HOPES AND IN HIS DESPAIR, AND IN HIS LOVE OF THE TECHNICAL LANGUAGE OF THE MOVIES"
 –**PHILIP FRENCH**, TIMES LITERARY SUPPLEMENT

"ONE OF HIS BEST BOOKS...GREENE'S PROSE IS MORE GRACEFUL THAN ANY STAR."
 –**CHRISTOPHER HAWTREE**, EVENING STANDARD

"HIS CRITICAL WRITING ABOUT THE CINEMA IS ALMOST AS IMPORTANT AS HIS CONTRIBUTION TO THE ART OF CINEMA ITSELF."
 –**DILYS POWELL**, THE DAILY TELEGRAPH

"A SUPERB VOLUME! AMONG THE MOST TRENCHANT, WITTY AND MEMORABLE COLLECTIONS OF FILM REVIEWS ONE IS EVER LIKELY TO READ!"
 –**ANTHONY QUINN**, THE SUNDAY TIMES

ISBN: 1–55783–188–2 • cloth • $35.00

WILLIAM GOLDMAN FOUR SCREENPLAYS

William Goldman, master craftsman and two-time Oscar winner continues his irreverent analysis with merciless essays written expressly for this landmark edition of his screen work. Nobody covers the psychic and political terrain behind the Hollywood lot with more cynical wisdom and practical savvy than the much celebrated author of ADVENTURES IN THE SCREEN TRADE.

William Goldman won Academy Awards for BUTCH CASSIDY AND THE SUNDANCE KID and ALL THE PRESIDENT'S MEN

Includes the screenplays:

BUTCH CASSIDY AND THE SUNDANCE KID
THE PRINCESS BRIDE
MARATHON MAN
MISERY

$25.95 • CLOTH
ISBN 1-55783-198-X

APPLAUSE

NEW YORK • LONDON

THE COLLECTED WORKS OF HAROLD CLURMAN

Six Decades of Commentary on Theatre, Dance, Music, Film, Arts, Letters and Politics

edited by Marjorie Loggia and Glenn Young

"...RUSH OUT AND BUY *THE COLLECTED WORKS OF HAROLD CLURMAN*... Editors Marjorie Loggia and Glenn Young have assembled a monumental helping of his work ...THIS IS A BOOK TO LIVE WITH; picking it up at random is like going to the theater with Clurman and then sitting down with him in a good bistro for some exhilarating talk. This is a very big book, but Clurman was a very big figure."
JACK KROLL, NEWSWEEK

"THE BOOK SWEEPS ACROSS THE 20TH CENTURY,** offering a panoply of theater in Clurman's time... **IT RESONATES WITH PASSION."**
MEL GUSSOW, THE NEW YORK TIMES

CLOTH•$49.95
ISBN 1-55783-132-7

APPLAUSE
NEW YORK • LONDON